# A Fiddler's Tale

Adventures are for the adventurous.
Benjamin Disraeli

D'où venons-nous? Que sommes-nous? Où allons-nous?
Paul Gauguin

# A Fiddler's Tale

*How Hollywood and Vivaldi*
*Discovered Me*

## Louis Kaufman

with

## Annette Kaufman

Foreword by Jim Svejda

THE UNIVERSITY OF WISCONSIN PRESS

The University of Wisconsin Press
1930 Monroe Street
Madison, Wisconsin 53711

www.wisc.edu/wisconsinpress/

3 Henrietta Street
London WC2E 8LU, England

1    3    5    4    2

Printed in the United States of America

Library of Congress Cataloging-in-Publication Data
Kaufman, Louis, 1905–
A fiddler's tale: how Hollywood and Vivaldi
discovered me / Louis Kaufman.
p.      cm.
Includes discography (p.    ), bibliographical references (p.    ), and index.
ISBN 0-299-18380-7 (alk. paper)
1. Kaufman, Louis, 1905–  .  2. Violinists—United States—Biography.
I. Title.
ML418 .K28 A3        2003
787.2′092—dc21        2002010217

Love, let us live as we have lived, nor lose
The little names that were the first night's grace,
And never comes the day that sees us old,
What should we know, we two, of ripe old age?
We'll have its richness, and the years forgot.
Decimus Maximus Ausonius (born Bordeaux, 310-395)

# Contents

# Illustrations

## Figures

## Color Plates

*Following page 256*

Lawrence Lebduska, *Portrait of a Collector (Louis Kaufman),*
    1932, oil on canvas
Lawrence Lebduska, *Portrait of Annette,* 1932, oil on canvas
Milton Avery, *Portrait of Chaim Grosz,* oil on canvas
Milton Avery, *Portrait of Louis Kaufman,* 1932, oil on canvas
Milton Avery, *Self-Portrait,* 1949, oil on canvas
Gerda Becker, *Joseph and His Brothers,* 1969, oil on board

# *Foreword*

## Jim Svejda

If one were to judge solely on the basis of how many people actually heard his playing, then Louis Kaufman should be the most famous violinist who ever lived: this for the simple reason that more people have probably heard him play than all those who heard Paganini, Sarasate, Joachim, Kreisler, Heifetz, and Stern *combined*. Any of the millions of people who have seen one of the classic American films of the 1930s, '40s, and '50s— from *Wuthering Heights* and *Modern Times* to *The Magnificent Ambersons* and *For Whom the Bell Tolls*—have heard Louis Kaufman's inimitable artistry. If it weren't for Kaufman, the best-known cue in the history of film music—*Tara's Theme* from *Gone with the Wind*—would not have been heard so expressively, but that's another story and one far better told by the violinist himself.

Although it was a trio of foreign-born composers—Max Steiner, Erich Wolfgang Korngold, and Franz Waxman—who invented the grammar and syntax of film music, it was Louis Kaufman, perhaps more than any other single performer, who gave American film music its voice. In any of more than four hundred films, Kaufman's playing is unmistakable. Although he was a great musical chameleon capable of playing any type of solo in a bewildering variety of musical styles, certain qualities in his playing remained constant: technical brilliance, musical depth, impeccable taste, and that ravishing tone—a round, sinuous, gloriously unaffected tone, as solid and sweet-spirited as the man himself. For over forty years, composers trusted him to bring out the absolute best in their music, and for over forty years he was Hollywood's most sought-after concertmaster because he was incapable of anything less.

Throughout his legendary studio career, Kaufman also devoted copious time and energy to more obviously serious music. He made the first commercial recording of a then little-known collection of violin concertos by Antonio Vivaldi called *The Four Seasons* (a recording which eventually won the coveted *Grand Prix du Disque*) and gave numerous first performances of works by contemporary composers who interested him: Samuel Barber, Aaron Copland, Bohuslav Martinů, Dag Wirén, William Grant Still, Darius Milhaud, Robert Russell Bennett, Henri Sauguet, Lev Knipper, and numerous others who admired his playing and were grateful for his friendship and advocacy.

Yet as remarkable as his playing were his qualities as a man. In a town where the malicious put-down has been elevated to a high art, Louis Kaufman may be the only well-known Hollywood personality about whom *no one* was ever heard to say an unkind word. For the countless colleagues and younger musicians upon whom he lavished his generosity, his implacable loyalty, and—because it was so honest, heartfelt, and carefully considered—his invaluable advice, Kaufman was the most trusted of friends (even for Bernard Herrmann, whom their mutual friend David Raksin once called "a virtuoso of unspecific anger"). And perhaps another reason why no one ever said anything unkind about him was that he never said an unkind thing about anyone else.

I feel genuinely sorry for people who never got to know Kaufman personally. I treasure the memory of the dinners I had with Louis and his charming wife Annette, a superb cook and conversationalist and a brilliantly gifted musician in her own right. These pages not only encompass a fair amount of both Hollywood and modern musical history, but also begin to suggest something of the gentle miracle that was Louis Kaufman.

# *Acknowledgments*

I am deeply grateful to the many people of who have helped me in the production of Louis's memoirs.

I especially wish to thank our mutual friends Lance Bowling and Steven Smith for their infinite help and constant interest in helping me prepare *A Fiddler's Tale* for publication. I am grateful to Carol Solomon who transformed the text to computerese.

I greatly appreciate the valuable advice and supervision of my friends Robert Mandel and Steve Salemson at the University of Wisconsin Press during the preparation of the manuscript. I would also like to thank Susan Brodie for her fine editing of *A Fiddler's Tale*. My thanks to Professor Lawrence Leviton and Margery Morgan-Lowens, who read and approved the manuscript. I particularly wish express my appreciation to Susan Goldberg Kent and her husband, Rolly Kent, for their constant encouragement of my efforts to tell Louis's story.

Annette Kaufman
Los Angeles, April 2003

# A Fiddler's Tale

# Bucharest to Portland and Back

Love was an irresistible force in Romania. It catapulted my father and mother out of that Latinized Balkan country, abandoning their families and his military duties, to the haven of the United States. Thus I was born in Portland, Oregon on a Sunday morning, 10 May 1905, covered by a "caul," which according to a Romanian legend indicated that I would have a special life. As far as I know, there were no musicians in the immediate Kaufman or Adler families.

The family chronicle before my arrival on the scene was worthy of an old-fashioned movie scenario. My father, Isaac Kaufman, one of six brothers, was born 27 March 1881 in Buzău, a provincial village and later a full-fledged bustling city not far from the Ploesti oil fields. He was medium tall, handsome, and blonde with blue eyes and a rakish mustache. His temperament was assertive, gregarious, and generous, with natural good humor and quick temper—all sprinkled with hard-headed common sense. He had received a good education in a Catholic school in Buzău that accepted a small quota of Jewish students. He gathered more than a smattering of general education and many languages, including Greek, Latin, French, and German. At home his family spoke Romanian and Yiddish.

My mother, Paulina Adler, was the oldest of nine children in Bucharest. When she was quite young, her father died suddenly of a massive heart attack, induced by shock. He had returned from a buying trip to Paris and discovered his shop and home burned to the ground. His wife, Sarah, was so badly burned that she had been placed in a type of glass coffin (an ingenious treatment to protect the burned tissue from infection) in the house of a Catholic neighbor.

Immediately the Adler children were fatherless as well as homeless.

Louis's father, Isaac Kaufman, in Romania, 1902.

Paulina, who could sew beautifully, obtained work as a seamstress in an elegant shop that made clothes for the royal family, and she assumed the care of her mother. The rest of the children were farmed out to relatives and eventually made their way to the United States, where they kept the Adler name.

One summer day in 1902, during a brief holiday in the country at the home of relatives, the Abramovitches, Paulina met my father, a young

Louis's mother, Paulina Adler—the photograph that provided a first-class ticket to the United States, 1901.

soldier in the Romanian Army. He had hoped to study art in Paris, but the Russian-dominated Romanian conscript machine made that impossible. He was already engaged (by his parents) to marry a young lady he did not love (his family heartily approved of her large dowry). He had been told by his parents to pay his respects to the influential Abramovitch family whenever he was near their home during summer maneuvers. Love's uncontrollable power in Romania was proverbial. In the 1920s, Prince Carol began a lifetime obsession with Jewish Madame Magda Lupescu; apropos, England's Queen Mary reportedly told King Edward, when informed he wished to marry Mrs. Simpson, "After all, Edward, *we* are not Romanians."

Paulina and Isaac fell in love at first sight. Because of Isaac's engagement, the young lovers had no possible chance to marry in Romania. Isaac's thoughts turned to possible escape from compulsory twenty-year service in the army, and dreams of freedom abroad with the opportunity to marry the love of his life. I well understood his thoughts and behavior from photographs of my mother taken at that time. She may have been of Sephardic origin, with coal-black hair, beautiful white skin, and dainty features—a pretty girl all around. Many years later, I had the gifted Czech artist Lawrence Lebduska paint a portrait of her in Romanian peasant costume, and it is an extraordinary likeness. Mother's physical presence did not belie her inner nature—a personification of goodness and completely unselfish love and devotion to our family.

By chance, two of Paulina's brothers had immigrated to the United States to avoid military service and settled in Pittsburgh, Pennsylvania. They had a photograph of their oldest sister in their home. A young Romanian friend fell in love with the portrait and offered to pay for Paulina's trip to the United States if she would marry him. Thinking this a great opportunity for their dowerless sister, they agreed, but only wrote to Paulina that they were sending her a first-class ticket to the new world, presuming they could persuade her to marry their generous friend after her arrival.

This providential letter offered my parents a way out of their hopeless dilemma; Isaac could desert the army, his family, and his fiancée. Paulina's first-class ticket could be exchanged for three steerage tickets, for the happy couple and her mother as chaperon, until their marriage could take place under a *chuppah* (canopy), in New York. The army's maneuvers made escape easier. However, at the last moment, Papa confided the plans to his brother, Osias, who was in the same regiment. Osias immediately informed their parents, who, outraged by Isaac's irresponsible disobedience, promptly reported his imminent desertion to the army. Papa was quickly placed in an improvised guardhouse. He found a way to inform Paulina, who proved very resourceful. She hired a haywagon and driver, bribed the sole guard watching Isaac, prepared herself and her mother for the journey, and obtained clothes for Isaac from her brothers. When night fell and a prearranged signal sounded, she and her mother were waiting in a haywagon across the river from the army encampment. Isaac easily escaped and began swimming across the river, when an unexpected changing of the guard took place. Finding the cell empty, the replacement guard noticed Papa swimming and fired at him. Papa was a strong swimmer and dove underwater, making the crossing unscathed. Under the cover of darkness, he clambered up the bank and was hidden in the hay. They raced to the border and a new life. Passports were not necessary for crossing borders before the First World War, so they encountered no obstacles.

The three Romanians made the steerage crossing to New York and were met after clearing Ellis Island immigration formalities by one of Paulina's brothers. I can well imagine his astonishment to find his sister and mother accompanied by her happy prospective bridegroom. This affair was eventually settled amicably. Her brothers repaid the disappointed Romanian suitor in Pittsburgh and the newlyweds repaid their passage money to the Adler brothers. My father had to make his way as an apprentice hatmaker, at the prevailing wage of three dollars per week, until he acquired knowledge of this métier.

Baron Moritz von Hirsch (1831–1896) had organized a fund in London to help persecuted Jews leave Russia, Poland, Romania, and other troubled areas, and later established a $2.5 million fund in the New World to aid newly arriving immigrants leave the overcrowded New York tenements for other parts of the United States. As there was a nucleus of Romanian Jews in Portland, Oregon, my parents decided to take advantage of this opportunity to join some relatives and fellow countrymen on the Pacific Northwest Coast.

Romania is a wooded and beautiful country, and Portland, surrounded by forests, mountains, and parks, reminded them of home. They arrived in Portland in 1903, and Isaac immediately applied for United States citizenship. His older brother Avram and his wife, Rebecca, welcomed them. It was not long before he established his own hat store in Portland that eventually grew into a chain of four stores boasting the proud slogan, "THE BEST $2 HAT ON EARTH." He purchased Stetson seconds and refinished them with mother's help, adding hat bands and other details to hide small flaws. It was his boast that he could converse with customers in his hat shop in any language, including Turkish.

He was a most devoted father. He loved to have his four sons around (I was the eldest) when he played golf, swam, took steam baths (we were paid a nickel if we could remain in the steam for five minutes), danced, or played cards. We enjoyed the sports but found the evening activities boring, as we were usually tired and sleepy.

Papa Kaufman (left) at his hat store in Portland, Oregon. Louis Kaufman is on the counter at right, and two employees are in the background.

In 1910, when I was five years old, Papa decided it was time to return to Romania to prove to his parents the wisdom of his choice of wife and introduce his two blonde sons (Ernest arrived when I was three). Once there, he decided to stay in Bucharest for an extended period. He opened a *Bazaar American* with a local partner, which flourished for two years. We lived in luxury, in a large flat with our own horse and carriage. I have vivid memories of that sojourn, riding in a carriage the immense length of the Calle Victoria, and sitting in outdoor cafes on warm evenings. Every table had a large glass container filled with delicious green walnuts in water.

An unpleasant memory is that of street hawkers who sold scurrilous leaflets featuring caricatures of evil serpents with ugly human heads and so-called Jewish features with huge hooked-noses and no chins, calling out "Jidani pacatosi" (cursed Jews). A more pleasant experience was the mysterious taste of Romanian chocolate pastries, called *prajituri*, perfumed by a special taste I never forgot. Years later when my wife, Annette, and I visited Romania, we tasted some in a tearoom and I said, "This is it!" and explained why American chocolate pastries were so different. (These were spiked with rum.)

Rather like Marcel Proust, whose *Remembrance of Things Past* recounts how a wealth of recollections sprang to his mind when tasting a madeleine, I find food memories stir my reminiscences. Our favorite Romanian foods included broiled *mititei* (also termed *carnots*), small beef hamburger with lots of garlic; *patlagele,* an eggplant hors-d'oeuvre; the *graschitsa,* broiled sweetbreads; broiled steaks served on a wooden plank; Greek olives with *icre* (sturgeon caviar); and the delicious *mămăliga,* cornmeal almost identical to Italian polenta, usually served with a sharp white cheese, *brinza,* similar to feta. There were also excellent *tocanas,* stews made with either carp or beef as a base with potatoes, peppers, cauliflower, string beans, and tomatoes, and *givetch* (sauerkraut).

I attended school in Bucharest and caught the usual childhood diseases. When I succumbed to scarlet fever, I was taken to a gypsy healer who had a great local reputation. She placed a sheet over my head and dripped melted lead over it, which proved useless. I was placed in a hospital and eventually recovered. There I had my first taste of yogurt, which became a lifelong enthusiasm.

An attractive young neighbor, a violinist, noticed my obvious interest in her playing and began to teach me a little about the violin. Destiny took over again. My father's partner in *Bazaar American,* seeing how prosperously affairs were going, ran away with the entire proceeds of the establishment and was never found. This left Papa in a bad financial state, so the family decided to return to Portland.

Papa's brother Herman was to be married in Buzău so we attended the festivities before our departure. In Romanian villages, a wedding was a five-day continual celebration. I vividly recall the singing and violin playing of Romanian Gypsies, the *hora* dances, and copious eating and drinking. The peasants were given wine, which was poured into their large felt hats, so they had to drink it quickly. They soon became quarrelsome. The virtuoso Romanian folk dancing, panpipe players, and exciting Gypsy fiddling fascinated me. This intoxicating spirit is graphically captured in George Enescu's *Romanian Rhapsodies.*

Our family's good luck was fantastic. Papa bought passage for the maiden voyage of the *Titanic* in 1912, but through an error between Bucharest's booking office and Bremen our steerage reservations were not honored when we arrived. After Papa's stormy scene with the agent, we were shunted to a third-class cabin on the next ship, the S.S. *Kaiser Wilhelm der Grosse,* for a very rough but safe passage to New York. I was seasick most of the journey. I still heartily dislike sea voyages and have never been a good sailor. Mama was also seasick and left the boat without her corset, where she had sewn all the family money. Papa dashed back to the

Louis Kaufman—the best dressed little boy in Bucharest, with Papa Isaac and Mama Paulina, 1910.

cabin to retrieve the garment and a small medal Mama greatly prized, which Queen Marie had presented to me for being the best dressed little boy in a Bucharest children's show.

Once more starting from scratch in Portland, Papa opened a hat store and we lived in the poorer section of South Portland, on the top floor of a two-story duplex with an outside sleeping porch. In warm weather Papa arranged for us to sleep outside, which he considered healthier. He soon bought a troublesome automobile, a Case Six, and became a road hazard, as he drove extremely slowly. On weekends we made excursions along the spectacular Columbia River Highway for picnics of cold roast chicken and salads, with watermelon cooled under Multnomah Falls for dessert.

Occasionally in summer, we took a whole day to drive to nearby Seaside. Papa insisted on stopping en route for a generous picnic lunch followed by an hour's nap by the roadside. Sometimes he rented a house in Seaside for a month. We children had great fun on the beach, swimming and searching for large meaty razor clams, which we enjoyed digging out of the sand with little shovels and pails. Mother prepared them deliciously with her Romanian touch.

I became a young gourmet at Multnomah County Fair. I entered a pie-eating contest in which prizes were awarded to lads who consumed the greatest number of fruit pies in the shortest time. While other youngsters stuffed their mouths with pies, I slowly ate only one delicious berry pie, which I did not finish until the contest was over, much to my family's amusement!

I have always been fascinated by circuses since my father took me to see my first one when I was eight years old. This early experience made a lasting impression. As we entered the circus grounds, a barker was touting his cure-all remedy with, "Will someone in the crowd come up and try this lotion?" I noticed a young man walking up to the podium. Then Papa and I entered the tent and enjoyed the various animal acts, the human jugglers, horseback riders, and acrobats.

When the show was over, as we were leaving I observed the same barker, who was at the same part of his spiel asking for a volunteer, then saw the same man step out of the crowd. I shouted, "Look, Papa, that fellow is a crook!" To my surprise my father hit me, the first and last time he ever punished me, saying, "Louis, I want you to remember that you have done something bad. Never stop a man from making a living. He probably has a little boy like you and has to provide food for him and his mother." This rather relaxed moral precept grew in my adult mind into a conviction that speaking badly about a musical performance of a colleague or an artist should be avoided, and, thanks to Papa, I always concentrated on the achievements of fellow students or professional soloists and disregarded any slight flaws.

Portland is bisected by the wide Willamette River, a shipping artery spanned by several steel bridges. On clear days one can see the nearby beautiful snow-capped Mount Hood. Portland's gentle rainy climate produced beautiful gardens, green parks, and colorful flowers. The annual Rose Festival featured a magical enchanting parade, honoring a "Rose Queen" that all Portland acclaimed. It may have been suggested by Pasadena's Tournament of Roses Parade, but it was much less commercial.

Golf courses were lined with trees bearing plums, nectarines, cherries, quinces, and apricots. One course recently established near our home offered special "dollar" coupons entitling one to play without time limits. When Papa played golf (only counting good strokes), we retrieved his lost golf balls. Midway on the course, he would nap under a shady tree while we climbed the trees to pick the luscious fruit that we stuffed into his golf bag. Those evenings we enjoyed fresh fruit for dessert. The remaining fruit Mother turned into tasty compotes, tarts, and jams. After these excursions Papa would say, "What an improvement from our mercantile existence in Bucharest! Where else could one take a few hours off from the store, play golf, engage in healthy sports, enjoy the fine climate, and enjoy such delicious fruit?" And he would end up with, "Truly this is God's country and no mistake about that."

# 2

# I Become a Violinist

A journey of a thousand miles begins with one step.

Ancient Chinese proverb

On my daily walk to public school, I passed the home of a violin teacher named Albert Kreitz. Hearing sounds of a violin again, I thought that it would be a marvelous accomplishment if I could learn to play tunes like "Yankee Doodle" on this enchanting instrument. I pestered my father constantly until he bought me a small violin and took me to Mr. Kreitz for lessons. After six months of study and playing only by ear (I didn't learn to read music until some time later), my progress impressed my family and their friends.

One day I noticed at the neighborhood movie house an announcement of an amateur talent contest after the western film. I reported, "Papa here's a chance for me, the first prize is three dollars, the second is two dollars, and the third is one dollar. I might be able to play and win." My father had great confidence in my judgment. He and mother even consulted my opinion on various family matters. He replied, "Sure, go ahead, Lou-ius." (Papa could never decide whether my name was pronounced the American way of "Lewis" or the French way of "Louis.") I announced this coming event to my first-grade classmates and friends, who loyally planted themselves in the front rows at the Friday night amateur contest.

After several turns by undistinguished singers, jugglers, and animal acts, I bravely went on stage with my violin and music stand. I placed on the stand the music, which I could not read, and began to play the current piece I was studying, a potpourri of tunes from Verdi's opera *Il Trovatore*, arranged by Jean-Baptiste Singelée. As I started sawing away, I beat time with my foot, as my teacher had suggested. This spirited "Miserere" greatly pleased my young friends and amused the adult audience, who gave me enthusiastic applause. They were laughing hilariously after the first minute, considering this a type of comedy act. I carried off first prize, and from then on my father was convinced that I was destined for the violin. He encouraged my studies and lessons, with the result that I began to play in local concerts when I was eight or nine years old. My mother made velvet black pants and white satin blouses with a flowing black silk tie for me to wear on these occasions, and always bought me patent leather pumps, a few sizes too small, since she considered large feet the sign of a peasant. This resulted in my feet aching, and I was acutely uncomfortable when performing.

Due to my small stature, I was placed in the second violin section of the school orchestra. The teacher soon noticed I constantly played first violin parts (I couldn't read the second violin part), so I was elevated to the first violins. Papa began to buy recordings of Enrico Caruso, Mischa Elman, Alma Gluck, Fritz Kreisler, Efrem Zimbalist, and Maud Powell, and I was taken to innumerable concerts as a youngster. We sat in the balcony and I probably slept through many recitals, but a great deal of what I heard made indelible impressions on my developing ideas of what a violin sound should be. Papa loved classical music and I later discovered he admired Beethoven's music more than that of any composer. My love of music thus began in my early childhood.

Soon Papa started to ask any celebrity who performed in Portland to come and hear me play. Some agreed to listen, and the general reply was that I had "some talent" but should be sent to New York, where there were fine teachers. I was probably eight years old when I first encountered Philip Pelz, a tall, flamboyant Russian of Jewish origin. As far as I could tell, he was practically illiterate in every language, but his fantastic gifts made him an unforgettable personality. Although the trumpet was his favorite instrument, he could play violin, viola, cello, and possibly the whole woodwind family. His repertoire, however, was extremely limited. I was never sure he could actually read music but that did not deter him from conducting orchestras and bands with considerable flair and effectiveness. I saw him in action several times, when grandiose movie houses used to maintain quite large orchestras. He inaugurated in Portland special Sunday morning concerts with middlebrow musical fare that pleased customers until the early afternoon cinema got under way. It was quite a sight to see Philip Pelz in a dazzling white uniform with a row of medals across his ample chest, giving energetic guidance to his colleagues, with

Louis at age seven, Portland, Oregon, 1912.

an occasional beat that might have felled an ox. The audience was impressed with the primal force of his attractive personality. He was even engaged as head bandmaster in San Francisco for the 1915 World's Fair.

As to the medals, which he claimed were conducting awards from the Czar of Russia and other royal families of Europe, skeptics claimed that those glittering honors came from pawn shops. I confess I belonged to the group that did not mind this innocent fraud. He had an earthy sense of humor; Papa found his company enchanting as a poker-playing partner, a colorful musician, and inspired inventor of high jinks. He seemed to possess an irresistible attraction for many women.

Before one Christmas school holiday, Pelz proposed to my father that I join him and his current "wife" in a musical act. Although I had begun to play here and there in Portland and seemed to have made a favorable impression, I had never traveled away from my family. Pelz's idea was to visit smaller towns in Oregon and Washington to perform in movie houses.

Off we went. I particularly remember the name of one town, Walla Walla. It was very much like all the towns we visited, a main street with one or two movie palaces. Snow on the ground didn't stop our venturesome leader with his clanking old Ford from carrying out his plan. He would size up the theater and boldly approach the owner or manager to convince him to engage us as a special attraction. He stressed that he was an international star as trumpeter to the Czar (with medals), assisted by his wife, a soprano of Metropolitan Opera capabilities, and a boy prodigy of "great renown."

He was reasonably successful in promoting our act, which featured his repertoire. His wife, accompanying herself on the piano, sang Carrie Jacobs Bond's "A Perfect Day," with Pelz tootling an obbligato on trumpet; then he played "Carnaval de Venise" with virtuoso variations, followed by my solo, possibly a Hungarian dance of Brahms. We usually lasted only one performance per cinema, as audiences made it obvious they preferred the western film. As Pelz demanded a large percentage of the box office, usually fifty percent, it quickly dawned on the manager or owner that we weren't much of a local attraction. We decamped with as much of the take as Pelz could wangle in a hurry. This resulted in our playing in an inordinate number of towns before the vacation ended. One evening, I felt a splinter in a finger of my left hand, which I showed him. I said, "Look, Mr. Pelz, I can't play this evening." He calmly replied, "That's all right, Louis, play without that finger." So I did. I sent home one hundred dollars each week. This tour was a prelude to a much longer tour when I was ten.

Mademoiselle Rozika (née Rheingold), a very pretty brunette in her early twenties, aspired to become a classical dancer. Completely devoted to her art, she had a dance studio for children. She wished to tour, and hearing of my "success" with Pelz, thought it would add interest to have me play short solo pieces while she changed costumes. She persuaded my parents to let me audition with her in Seattle, where she had a personal introduction to Alexander Pantages, who directed a considerable vaudeville circuit stretching from the West Coast to Denver and Salt Lake City as well as cities on the Pacific Coast down to San Diego. This experience could well have destroyed any serious future for me as violinist.

Rozika's act consisted of various national dances, including a "Dying Swan" à la Anna Pavlova, in tutu, and ended with a Hungarian *czardas* performed in national costume complete with boots. Our audition seemed to please Pantages, as he immediately accepted us for a two-week trial engagement. We evidently made a good impression, for that tour was extended to six months and covered his entire circuit. I have sometimes wondered why we were kept on this tour for such a long time.

For the last number of our act I played a Brahms Hungarian Dance and attempted to lead the pit orchestra by waving my violin up and down in a tempo that suited Rozika. Occasionally the orchestra took a slower tempo, ignoring me and the floundering dancer, whose leaps and jumps required a minimum speed to execute. If the music was too slow, Rozika lost her balance and angrily walked off stage, leaving me to finish the number in solitary grandeur. Perhaps audiences presumed this was part of the act.

We were surrounded by the unusually friendly camaraderie of the Royal Gascoynes, who had a singing, juggling, and tumbling act. The family was led by a jolly brawny Irishman, with his pretty wife and their brood of enthusiastic youngsters. The slam-bang climax of the show was a group of singers and chorus girls led by an unusually handsome young tenor, in the popular style, who was pursued by all the girls.

Early in our tour, Rozika attracted a young businessman in the audience, who dropped out of his ordinary life to follow us from town to town like a young puppy. Rozika did not disdain his attentions, and he showered her with flowers, chocolates, and elaborate dinners. When she went out with him she bought me magazines and assorted goodies to compensate for my being alone in my hotel room, which I rather enjoyed. It gave me a chance to practice.

One evening Rozika came to ask for my youthful advice. "What shall I do? He's from a good family, has a prosperous jewelry store, and is very nice. He wants to marry me, but I don't love him." "Don't be silly, Rozika, marry him. If you don't love him now, you will in time." But she was waiting for a "grand amour" and refused the ardent swain, saying her career

Louis at age ten, on a vaudeville tour with Mademoiselle Rozika.

was her life. Poor Rozika never found her ideal love and eventually developed a mental illness that led to an early death. This sad example troubled me, and later I asked my father, "How do you know when it is the 'real thing' and you are truly in love?" He replied, "Don't worry Louius, you will know immediately. If you have to think it over a long time—forget it."

Our tour gave me my first glimpse of the Pacific Coast cities Seattle, San Francisco, Los Angeles, San Diego, and others on the way. I vividly remember Salt Lake City and Denver, where we visited the Garden of the Gods and Pike's Peak. Rozika's unflagging maternal care and general solicitude for my well being saw to it that I was seldom left alone to get into mischief.

However, Los Angeles produced the strongest impact on me. I met my uncle Osias "Jack" Kaufman, who kindly became our guide. The city was brilliant with sunshine, waving palm trees, and clear air (alas, now only a fond memory). We rode in a red streetcar to Venice at the beach, where I swam and marveled at the smooth sandy strand. I devoured unforgettable ice cream cones. It was not surprising that the general ambiance of Los Angeles seemed by far the most attractive of all the towns we visited. I secretly decided that this was the place where I would live when I became an adult.

The touring life was pleasant, with very little effort on my part. We performed twice a day, a matinee and evening show, seven days a week, with the traditional holidays free. It was a six-month absence from school, although I read omnivorously in my free hours. All our expenses were paid and we lived in deluxe hotels, eating whatever we chose. This was an unusual chance to savor new cities and foods on a large scale.

I had learned a few publicity tricks from Pelz, so whenever Rozika and I arrived in a new town, we visited the local newspaper and proclaimed I was ready for a violinistic "duel" with anyone of any age. This resulted in press coverage with pictures of us both. No one ever took up this challenge, which was most fortunate; for if any trial of skill had occurred with a repertoire beyond Massenet's "Méditation" from *Thaïs* and my Brahms Hungarian Dance, I would have had a most humiliating experience. It was certainly sobering for me a few years later, when I reached New York and heard younger violinists of great ability. However, I was able to regularly send home $150 per week, which was of considerable help to my family.

The less favorable factors were that I missed regular schooling and violin studies for half a year. I am thankful my parents removed me from this vaudeville career and placed me again in normal family life and studies, even though Rozika and I had been offered an extension of our tour. It may also have been due to public school authorities making inquiries about my absence from school. I had become rather roly-poly due to unsupervised eating and had gained about twenty pounds, which took some time to lose.

I had also become very self-reliant, as well as accustomed to playing for large audiences, which proved an asset in my later barnstorming years. When I lived in New York after my bar mitzvah, the prospect of being away from home and family presented no real or imaginary terrors. I was used to taking care of myself. Of course, New York was not yet the mugger's paradise that it became starting in the 1960s.

I always remembered the overwhelming kindness and concern the vaudevillians shared for their companions of the road. A colleague in need could have the shirts off their backs. I did not encounter this type of warmth in any other realm of the musical world.

My father, with burning ambition for my violin studies, was somewhat dissatisfied with the limited qualities of my violin instruction, which he mysteriously gauged. The idea occurred to him, and obsessed him for many years, that I could garner violin playing "secrets" beyond the scope of any individual teacher if I studied with many. From Russian immigrants Papa heard rumors that a pathetic one-eyed Jewish klezmer musician, named "Professor Matelsky," was an exponent of the famed Russian school. Papa found it attractive that he would share violin expertise with me or mow a lawn for the sum of fifty cents. This may have been due to a scarcity of pupils. After two lessons, I announced with finality, "Papa, have him mow the lawn." Poor Matelsky drifted out of our life and resurfaced years later.

After a few years of serious study with Franz Kneisel in New York, while I was on a summer's holiday in Portland, I again encountered this "mini-gifted" man. Philip Pelz graciously invited my family to attend an auspicious premiere of a new great act he had conceived. This inventive trumpeter of brilliant virtuosity was still occasionally touring in vaudeville with varying ensembles. His *new* approach was to offer movie houses a small, less costly act.

Knowing Pelz's limitless imagination and bravado, we were curious to attend this show at the Blue Mouse, a local theater. We settled in close to the stage, and the curtain rose on an astounding spectacle, which the program listed as *A Night in Istanbul.* The scene, bathed in a rosy glow, revealed Pelz in his resplendent white uniform, garnished with the usual assortment of medals on his increasingly ample chest, his handsome blond head uncovered, his trumpet in hand. Close by was his current "flame," a somewhat overripe peroxide blond costumed in Turkish pantaloons, wearing slippers with turned-up toes, seated facing an upright piano. Professor Matelsky was seated on the stage floor in front of the piano, also wearing pantaloons and turned-up oriental slippers and an eyepatch.

He was holding his violin between his legs like a cello, ready to manipulate his bow horizontally, Turkish style.

They sailed into Pelz's piece de resistance, the inevitable "Carnaval de Venise," with variations brilliantly tootled by Pelz & Co., and a good-natured tittering began in the theater. The second number, a vocal solo, brought the audience to a crescendo of uncontrollable laughter. It was the soprano's rendition of her own tour de force, a ditty with the refrain, "Mexico, my dearest Mexico," sung to her own accompaniment, with the energetic aid of Pelz and Matelsky. This spectacle completely devastated the audience; they reacted with hysterical laughter, catcalls, and denigrating expressions more suitable to a disappointing athletic event. The curtain descended quickly to quell an incipient riot. We made a hasty exit to avoid a postmortem meeting with Pelz.

In retrospect I believe that Pelz's bizarre attempt was ahead of its time. Although he did not realize its mad humor, this type of surrealist diversion would be very popular after the Marx Brothers' zany antics opened the way for the looniness of many contemporary film and television comedians.

Back in Portland, Papa discovered Frank Eichenlaub as my next teacher and he became a delightful friend. I sometimes stayed at the Eichenlaubs' home for the weekend and enjoyed both my violin lessons and the delicious meals his wife prepared. One special treat was chicken fricassee with dumplings, an interesting change from the Romanian Jewish cuisine of my home.

I was unhappy when Papa took me away, still searching for better instruction. This time he found a legitimate professor, Henry Bettman, who had studied with Henri Petri, a student of Joseph Joachim in Europe (and also for a season with Eugène Ysaÿe, the monumental Belgian violinist). Bettman gave me basically correct disciplines, insisting that I play scale studies and work on fundamental problems of violin and bow technique. I finally learned how to read music!

David Tamkin, who eventually studied composition and wrote the great opera *The Dybbuk*, was also a Bettman pupil at that time, and we became friends for life. Marcus Rothcowitz, who later as Mark Rothko attained world fame for his Abstract Expressionist paintings, was my classmate at Shattuck public school, as was the later distinguished federal judge Gus J. Solomon, for whom the Federal Court House in Portland was named in 1989.

Papa frequently took me and Mother to concerts, so I heard the dazzlingly beautiful sound of Mischa Elman, the magical tone and charm of Fritz Kreisler, the dashing and awe-inspiring performances of Jascha

Heifetz, the impressive musicality of Efrem Zimbalist, and the extraordinary vitality of Maud Powell, the most celebrated woman violinist of her time. Maud Powell visited Portland a few times and at one of her last recitals was accompanied by a talented young pianist, Arthur Loesser, who later recalled Papa bringing me in tow to play for them. Arthur and I struck up a lifelong friendship, ended only by his untimely death. His witty and informative book *Men, Women and Pianos* will ensure that his remarkable erudition is long remembered. Some of his poetic playing has been preserved on two International Piano Archive records issued by the University of Maryland. (His brother Frank created many successful musical comedies, including *Guys and Dolls, How to Succeed in Business without Really Trying,* and *The Most Happy Fella.*)

Maud Powell advised Papa to send me to New York as soon as possible. Efrem Zimbalist commented, "A talented boy, but he needs better violin schooling—send him to Franz Kneisel in New York." Kneisel was brought to the United States in 1885 at nineteen by Wilhelm Gericke, conductor of the Boston Symphony, to be his concertmaster. In 1903 he founded the Kneisel Quartet, the first important string quartet in America, and became head of the violin department at New York's Institute of Musical Art, which was later absorbed by the Juilliard School.

My parents celebrated my thirteenth birthday with a grand bar mitzvah party, since I was the oldest son. The guests included all our relatives and numerous Jewish friends, members of local organizations, the Shriners of the Masonic Order, the Rotarians, Order of the Moose, and B'nai B'rith, all of which Father had joined enthusiastically to help him in business. We had moved to a larger house in a better neighborhood. A huge crowd filled our home, and what an honor it was to our family when the mayor of Portland, George Baker, arrived! I attended the local *cheder* (Hebrew elementary school) to learn enough Hebrew for my brief speech at the synagogue, declaring myself "a man" with all the inclusive obligations and duties pertaining to that state.

Mother prepared a huge Romanian feast, which kept her occupied for days. After dinner, I played a few violin pieces, Pelz trotted out his trumpet to regale the guests by playing his variations on "Carnaval de Venise"—and another of his blond lady friends sang "A Perfect Day." The children went to bed and the remaining adults settled down to an after-dinner game of poker.

Pelz had bad luck, so the evening closed with him owing Papa fifty dollars, which he paid with much protest. Feeling ill-treated, he then sued Papa for nonpayment of fifty dollars for professional services at my bar mitzvah. The trial took place several weeks after my departure for

New York, and I learned the details in a letter from my father. In the courtroom, Pelz insisted he had been engaged professionally to entertain the guests. The judge inquired, "Were you not also a guest who had been invited to partake of the dinner?" Pelz replied, "What dinner? I had nothing to eat that night!" This was too outrageous for Mother's wounded culinary pride. She rose up from the observers' section and shouted, "Pelz, you're a damned liar! We had gefilte fish, *patlagele,* roast chicken, stuffed cabbage, *mămăliga,* compote, strudel, and assorted cookies!" The judge stopped her, saying she was out of order, and let Pelz continue. He joked, "The only chickens I saw there were walking on two pretty legs."

After this testimony, the judge declared in favor of plaintiff Pelz and ordered Papa to pay him fifty dollars for his services. As they walked out of the courtroom, side by side, Papa quietly said, "Pelz, you won't see a nickel. I'll take it to the Supreme Court if necessary." Pelz threw his arm around Papa's shoulder, declaring, "Don't be foolish, Isaac, I don't want your money. I just wanted to show you what schlemiels these *Amerikaners* are. You can tell them anything and they will believe it. When will we play again?" Eventually the affair was mutually forgiven.

Shortly after, a black man entered Papa's store, holding a pawn ticket, saying, "Mr. Kaufman, I heard your son plays violin. I have a fine fiddle but need money badly, so I had to pawn it. If you give me ten dollars, you can have it."

Papa decided to visit the nearby pawn shop with this man, when Pelz appeared, asked what was going on, and decided to join them. At the pawn shop, Pelz waxed enthusiastically about the rather battered instrument, exclaiming, "It's probably a Stradivarius. If you don't buy it, Isaac, I certainly will." Knowing well Pelz's tricks, Papa said he'd think it over. Later at his store, he spoke kindly to the black man, asking, "Tell me the truth, where did you get that violin? I'll give you any hat in my store that you want." The grateful man replied, "I never saw that fiddle in my life. The other man gave me two dollars to tell you that story." I proceeded to New York with an old Tyrolean violin in mediocre condition that Pelz, now a violin dealer, had sold to Papa as a "great bargain."

# 3

# New York and Kneisel

In early fall of 1918, Father and I set off on the long cross-country train journey to New York, sitting up five days and nights on coach seats. We made our way to the Bronx, where we stayed with Papa's Romanian cousins, the Boyumescus. The husband, wife, and her aged mother were happy to welcome a young, ambitious student and were not bothered by my practicing during the day. I had a small private room, and these kindly relatives shared their uninteresting and colorless meals with me—a far cry from Mother's delicious cuisine.

I played an audition for the imposing Dr. Franz Kneisel. He was tall and portly, with black hair and eyes and a ferocious black mustache. His class was full, so for the first six months I was to study with Hugo Kortschak until Kneisel could find a place for me. This period was slightly shortened after I played Aleksander Zarzycki's Mazurka in a school recital that Kneisel happened to attend. My interpretation was strongly influenced by the verve with which Maud Powell had played this piece in Portland, still a vivid memory.

The Boyumescus lived a long subway ride from the Institute of Musical Art, and I wasted much time commuting to and from Manhattan. My busy schedule included two violin lessons a week, composition and harmony classes, secondary piano lessons, and orchestral practice, plus my general high school studies in the Bronx.

I attended Morris High School and was soon noticed by a group of young violin students (from the pressure of holding the violin, I had a tell-tale red mark on the left side of my neck). Twenty years later a fellow student, Sydney Beck (who became the music librarian of the New York Public Library and a distinguished musicologist), told Annette and me that I had dramatically changed all their lives. The violin students had

Dr. Franz Kneisel, with whom Louis studied for eight years. (Photograph from The Kneisel Hall Archives at The Juilliard School)

invited me to hear them play at one of their homes. I was appalled at what I heard, for they all studied with a local charlatan, who, to impress their parents, had them attempting to play concertos far beyond their capabilities by composers such as Mendelssohn, Tchaikovsky, and Paganini. In turn, I played a Viotti concerto honestly, with all the notes in tune and correct tempi, and then proceeded to lecture them. I told them they were being "conned" by a faker and no one could guess what notes they were playing, nor even what music; it all sounded garbled to my intolerant young ears. They accepted my frank counsel and departed en masse from their so-called teacher and followed me to the Institute. They studied with other professors there and eventually took their places in the New York Philharmonic, the Philadelphia Orchestra, the Boston Symphony, and, later, the NBC Symphony under Toscanini.

My first year in New York was marred by illness; a small pimple on the left side of my face rapidly developed into erysipelas (a streptococcal infection of the skin), which spread over both sides of my face. I was miserable, with constant burning and itching. The Boyumescus found a doctor who instantly diagnosed the malady, which can cause blindness and even death. I was bedridden for a month and in constant pain. Imagine my surprise one day when, after a knock on the door, Dr. Franz Kneisel entered! His portly figure had climbed the six flights of stairs to the Boyumescus' flat to see how the "stocky lad from Portland" was getting on. He spoke kindly and cheered me by saying he hoped to see me back in class soon.

I practiced as much as I could, for I was well aware of my shortcomings and was inspired to work harder when I listened to more advanced students who were younger than me. Kneisel permitted his students to listen in at other students' lessons, but I was the only one who systematically attended colleagues' lessons to hear unfamiliar repertoire; I wanted to make the most of my ability and Papa's hard-earned money. I learned from their achievements as well as their errors.

It is difficult for young people today to imagine how limited the opportunities were to hear classical violin music at that time. Public concerts, musical radio programs, and violin recitals were few and far between. Few violin works had been recorded intact, as the duration of the old 78-rpm records was about four minutes per side. Listening to my colleagues' lessons gave me extra exposure to the violin repertoire.

Kneisel asked at one lesson how many hours I devoted to practice. I explained that as my attendance at Morris High School and homework took up much of each day, I could only manage two hours on weekdays. He exploded, "You *cannot* remain in my class with such little work. You *must* do at least six hours daily to achieve the necessary progress." "Dr. Kneisel," I weakly protested, "the Institute requires that I graduate from high school to obtain an Artist's Diploma." "That's true," he grudgingly admitted. "Well, I'll arrange that with Dr. Damrosch, so it will not be necessary for you to waste so much time in general studies. You must get a private tutor to compensate." Someone recommended a young Jesuit priest for his comprehensive knowledge. However, my general studies with him became swamped by theological debates. After a few such discussions, I dismissed him and read more vigorously: history, novels, and general literature about music and the arts, which were and still are my primary interests. I decided to cut down my commute by renting a room from a reliable family in an apartment near the Institute. I ate in automats and cafeterias.

I had a naturally friendly attitude to life and people due to my loving family, vaudeville colleagues, and friends, so Kneisel's ogre-like behavior did not faze me. I felt his outbursts of temper much less keenly than other students, who often wilted under his cutting remarks. I have always wondered why teachers who obviously know infinitely more than their pupils speak so sarcastically and unpleasantly to students who lack stylistic or instrumental skills. I think one should be kind and helpful to young people who hope to acquire mastery of the violin.

Kneisel had at first presumed I was German and often spoke to me during my lessons in German. I was too awed by him to say I did not understand what he said, so I often gave the impression of being stupid. When he yelled *"Fest!"*(meaning to play with firm fingers), I would scamper on the fingerboard, thinking his broken English meant "fast." This caused him to shout *"Dummkopf!"* which I understood. Once, hearing him shout Romanian oaths, I laughed, since I knew the meaning of those terms and thought they were funny. He thus discovered I was Romanian.

The first grueling year was difficult for me; Kneisel would periodically threaten, "I'll have to send you back to Portland," so I philosophically presumed my studies were to end at the close of the school term. However, I worked harder than ever to learn as much as possible in the allotted time. In any event, I never had two bad lessons in a row; the next was always better, as I learned at someone else's lesson what Kneisel wanted.

My first bitterly cold New York winter offered a new problem—icy fingers. My colleagues and I soon found the Institute's warm basement an ideal place to warm up both fingers and instruments before braving Kneisel's sarcastic wit. I arrived a half-hour early to be sure I could play with some semblance of agility. A great proportion of his most gifted students were Jewish, such as Jacques Gordon, Sascha Jacobsen, William Kroll, Joseph and Lillian Fuchs, and Mike Gusikoff, and he seemed to be often irritated by what he considered to be excessive Jewish emotionalism. This never bothered me, although he often called me *der kleiner Rabbiner* (the little rabbi) when he thought I had overstepped the bounds of correct taste. Even as I respectfully adhered to his basic musical tenets, I insisted on performing in my own way, as I had been so strongly influenced by the playing of Mischa Elman, Jascha Heifetz, and Fritz Kreisler.

About a year after I entered Kneisel's class, I began to choose violin literature that interested me, submitting my choices for his approval, and he in turn suggested unfamiliar works that he considered necessary for my progress. One day he said, "There's a very nice piece by Henri Vieux-temps, a Rondino, which you ought to study. Get a copy and bring it next week."

I immediately bought a copy at a music store near the Institute and took it home. I couldn't make heads or tails out of it. It seemed to be no more than a bunch of scales. I realized I had to get some idea of the piece, which I hadn't heard in class, to avoid being torn apart at my lesson. Kneisel was a very exacting teacher. On many occasions, a pupil could hardly play two consecutive bars without being stopped for corrections about lapses in style, intonation, or rhythmic inaccuracies. Some students could not survive such harsh analysis and fled to seek gentler lessons with Auer, Flesch, or Ševčík. Kneisel never permitted us to turn a page of the music we were playing, for he expected us to know what followed. My lesson to play the Rondino was strikingly different.

I returned to the music store and asked if they had a recording of the Rondino. It happened they did. I asked if I might hear it (years ago one was allowed to listen to records before purchase). The salesman handed me a disc recorded by the legendary Eugène Ysaÿe. I took the record into a listening booth and was overwhelmed by the elegance, artistry, dash, and verve of his interpretation. I handed back the record, mumbling, "Sorry, I didn't like it," as I could not afford to buy it. I rushed home to attempt to profit by this revelation.

At my next lesson, for the first time Kneisel let me play the entire piece without a single interruption, politely turning pages for me, as he continued to puff on his inevitable cigar. When I finished, very surprised by this unusual experience, his only comment: "That's a marvelous record of Ysaÿe—bring something else next week." He must have been very amused by my sponge-like absorption of Ysaÿe's refined style, certainly a great distance from my usual provincial approach.

My father arrived in New York, and to my delighted surprise, Kneisel told him I had made remarkable progress and would be a fine violinist! He firmly stated, "Louis should continue his studies by going with me and my class to Blue Hill, Maine, where I have a two-month summer school. A summer holiday in Portland would be too long a time away from violin studies." Father agreed, so I had the chance to extend my progress in the summer of 1919, with only violin lessons and practice. Since my Tyrolean fiddle had irregular dimensions, Kneisel insisted I should have a standard-sized violin. I found a Heberlein violin (a German factory fiddle) for sixty-five dollars at Wurlitzer's, which served me for several years.

All students benefited from this fantastic, constructive experience in Blue Hill. I took a train to Portland, Maine, then an overnight boat to Bar Harbor, where I boarded a bus to Blue Hill. The Institute's secretary gave me the address of a family who not only provided some of us with a room to sleep and practice in, but also fed us excellent New England cuisine. We enjoyed delicious soups, Boston baked beans, fresh corn, fruit pies, and ice cream with walnuts from their orchards. We swam in the cold bracing water of the bay and cleaned up once or twice a week in the "old swimming hole" creek. By mutual agreement, boys and girls had their own appointed days.

The tuition costs were very modest. We had violin lessons twice a week with Dr. Kneisel, and he donated his time for nightly chamber music. From 8 P.M. to 10 P.M. every evening in Kneisel Hall, students played string quartets with two or more on a part. We would work through almost all the Haydn, Mozart, Beethoven, Schumann, Schubert, and other repertoires. There was no end to the work we accomplished.

One summer, I met Nicolas Moldavan, recently arrived from Russia via the Orient, who became a close friend. Kneisel urged him to give up the violin and devote himself to the viola. He became an eminent violist and member of the Elman Quartet, then the great Flonzaley Quartet and Coolidge Quartet, and subsequently he joined the NBC Symphony, ending his career under Arturo Toscanini's masterly direction. Leo Godowsky, son of famed pianist Leopold Godowsky, also took private lessons with Kneisel and joined our chamber music sessions, but even then he was intensely interested in photography. He and David Mannes (whose conductor father, Leopold, founded the Mannes School of Music in New York) later worked together and invented the color processes of photography, which they sold to the Kodak Company and became millionaires. Leo later married George Gershwin's sister, Francis.

Kneisel's friends offered a cash prize for the most diligent student each summer. I was determined to win it. I shared a room with a young Hungarian student, Milton Feher. I devised a scheme worthy of Pelz to ensure that our house should never be silent. We would never practice at the same time—we would alternate and thus impress Kneisel, who passed our house each day en route to Kneisel Hall. The plot succeeded. At summer's end I carried off the one-hundred-dollar first prize, and Milton received second prize of fifty dollars.

Several of Kneisel's friends visited Blue Hill, including Felix Kahn, a financier who adored the violin and had an outstanding collection of fine instruments, including the famed Sancey Stradivarius. He explained to all who were interested how necessary it was to preserve these fine violins and keep them in clean and perfect playing condition. Other visitors were Mischa Elman, Fritz and Harriet Kreisler, Jascha Heifetz, Dr. Frederick Bierhof (a prominent urologist who was a close friend of Bruno Walter and many other musicians), conductor John Barbirolli, pianist Josef Casimir Hofmann, and members of the London String Quartet. Dr. Bierhof's remarkable wife, Hannah, became a dear and close friend to me (and later to Annette).

Since I was so young, I was relegated to playing second violin parts, which I found dull, so I asked Kneisel if I might play the musically more interesting viola parts. He was pleased, as violists were scarce in Blue Hill. I quickly learned how to play a sort of "instant viola." I asked a fellow student, Bernard Ocko, "How do you read the viola clef?" He replied, "Just the same as the violin clef, but play everything a third lower." This trick worked and I had an easy method to read viola parts if they were not too complicated. I was sometimes confused by accidentals (sharps and flats), until I began to read the clef and knew definitely what the notes were, as well as the true sonority of the instrument.

Being able to play viola led to my being invited to many interesting chamber music parties in New York. I had the privilege to fill in at quartet sessions with violinists Mischa Elman, Efrem Zimbalist, Jascha Heifetz, Fritz Kreisler, Carl Flesch, Bronislaw Huberman, and Paul Kochanski; cellists such as Pablo Casals, Gregor Piatigorsky, and Felix Salmond; and pianists Josef Hofmann, Mischa Levitzki, Nadia Reisenberg, Frank Sheridan, and many others. This was a great opportunity for me to absorb at first hand the special interpretative gifts of these preeminent artists while in my teens. I was taking the place of older musicians as a sort of pinch-hitter for the regulars, who were vastly more skillful and experienced than I was. I took it for granted that I could fit in, not fully realizing what a wonderful experience it was to be so closely associated with artists of great stature. I greatly benefited from hearing their remarkable artistry at close range. This deep immersion into supercharged musical activity with New York's musical elite propelled me into a new world whose horizons have never ceased to expand.

Chamber music with the Elman family took place at Papa Elman's large apartment on Riverside Drive, with Mischa's three sisters, Minna, Liza, and Esther (all pianists), his parents, and friends all enjoying the marathon proceedings and delicious Russian food. Mischa's tone was velvety and opulent; one never heard rosin on his bow or any extraneous sound. He loved to have his colleagues play as beautifully as possible, always encouraging us to "sing out" when we had a solo phrase. It was impossible to perform casually when his imperious eye urged you to give more.

Kneisel was not the most gifted violinist—there were others with finer tonal quality and flashier technique—but as a constructive teacher and musician, his influence was unique. Franz Kneisel's lessons were seared into the memory of all his pupils. Although a great musician, he was a most complex and difficult personality, extremely harsh, intolerant, and demanding. All my colleagues agreed they had never met anyone of his stature in their musical lives. I never met another teacher or colleague remotely in his category, both for his subtle concept of style and the solid musicianship and vitality of his interpretations. He premiered the Brahms and Paganini concertos in America when he was concertmaster of the Boston Symphony. He was a close friend of Brahms and spent summer holidays with him at Bad Ischl, Austria.

His Kneisel Quartet was the first outstanding string quartet to tour widely in America and was unchallenged in its preeminence. They premiered all the chamber works of Brahms and Dvořák in America, as well as the Debussy quartet, although it took Kneisel many years to persuade his colleagues to perform that French masterpiece. They also premiered Arnold Schoenberg's *Verklärte Nacht* string sextet and works of Charles Martin Loeffler, who sat on the first stand with Kneisel when he was concertmaster in Boston. They premiered many contemporary composers. Chamber music was his battlefield.

Kneisel was mainly concerned with transmitting the inner spirit and nobility of the music of Haydn, Mozart, Beethoven, Schubert, and Brahms. His devotion to the inspired, pure discourse of four stringed instruments opened our young minds to transcendental vistas of human emotions. Dr. Abram Chasins described for me his impressions of Kneisel's quartet, which he had heard many times in New York (I never heard them, since the quartet had disbanded before my arrival). His recollections were of "amazingly matched sonorities, very lively performances, with a probity of highest musical conceptions." He concluded, "It was always like an inspired lesson." Catching Kneisel in an expansive mood, I asked if recordings existed of his celebrated quartet. He replied, "We made some tests, but I was very disappointed in the results. We did not wish to be judged by what those primitive and distorted machines produced."

We fortunate students benefited from his dedication to passing on his love and mastery of this remarkable literature, as well as his unstinting gift of his time. Each Sunday morning at his home in the West Eighties of Manhattan, there were obligatory chamber music classes, where we students were expected to play every part. The violin class, almost every day of the week, was with Kneisel, whom fellow students dubbed "the old man." There were always school concerts to prepare, ranging from eighteenth-, nineteenth-, and twentieth-century composers—solo works, chamber works, and small orchestral compositions. When we played sonatas or suites, we violin students were somewhat miffed that Dr. Kneisel was as interested in what our accompanists played as the violin part. He would coach pianists with as much detail as he devoted to us.

Our favorite piano collaborators were Carroll Hollister, who later became the permanent pianist for the popular tenor John Charles Thomas, and the pianist André Kostelanetz, who had recently arrived from Russia. André had a most sympathetic touch and seemed to know the entire violin repertoire. Before long he was busy conducting and coaching choruses, then made the leap into conducting orchestras for the emerging radio broadcasting and recording industries with outstanding success.

Kneisel's devotion to music and teaching was not appreciated by all of his students. Some could not recognize the opportunities he gave us. Everyone could benefit, if they adhered to his routine for violin mastery. One could then take his or her place in solo literature, orchestral, chamber music, or even commercial work. Kneisel often said that one could be the best violinist imaginable, but would not succeed if he or she did not get along with their colleagues.

For those with fortitude to stay the course, there were many rewards. Kneisel often told us his aim was to create constructive musicians, not merely violinists, who could play some of the flashy repertoire then in vogue with good tonal quality. His idea was to develop practical musicians. Those who had more interesting personalities and violinistic gifts could reach for higher echelons. Very few Kneisel pupils who stuck it out were ever completely lost as adults. They managed to take their places in the musical life of their time. One of his maxims was, "If you are Hungarian, try to avoid Gypsy-like exaggerations. No matter what your background ethnically, it will come through. A Frenchman will sound French, or an Italian person Italian, whether he realizes it or not."

The Institute often provided concert tickets, and school patrons invited students to attend recitals or operas. I took advantage of these benefits, for Kneisel's lessons included reporting to him on New York's violin performances, especially those of great virtuosi. He insisted that we attend all of Kreisler's recitals (Kneisel had been a student in Professor Jakob Gruen's class in Vienna concurrently with Kreisler). Only illness was an accepted excuse. I found it a welcome duty. On hearing the first phrases of a Kreisler program, my analytical faculties would melt away under this Orpheus's spell. His magnetic charm—the incredible tonal beauty that directly transmitted human sentiment—bewitched me, and I was in a sort of mystical nirvana. I could not associate what I studied in class with the compelling rhythmic vitality and radiant sound this supreme artist displayed. Kneisel demanded a thorough analysis of this musical Apollo, who inspired his and my generation. There were postmortems on recitals of Jacques Thibaud, Mischa Elman, Paul Kochanski, Jascha Heifetz, Carl Flesch, Franz von Vecsey, and innumerable others. These discussions were to discover how much we had been able to absorb or understand of each performer's talents and musicianship.

He also instructed the class in deportment, stressing the need to be polite, neat, and tidy in dress, and to have good manners. Sometimes he spoke kindly—just as often harshly. One leavetaking before a holiday gave me a dramatic lesson. I proffered my hand to shake his and he called out for the other students to come back, pointing out what a shocking gaffe I had committed. *"Never"* he roared, "does a younger person offer his hand to an older person. You must wait until his hand is offered to you!" (For many years, I mentally calculated whether an acquaintance was older than I was, before shaking hands.) He gave us practical and wise suggestions for our adult lives, saying, "What you do as a violinist is only part of what you will achieve in your careers. If people do not like you, you will fail no matter how well you play."

Kneisel stressed the importance of matching tonal expressiveness to the musical content, remarking, "Some phrases are intense, of love and exaltation, and some are prosaic, the equivalent of 'pass the bread and butter.'" After a few years of fundamental studies, covering innumerable etudes, sonatas, and early violin concertos, I began to delve into virtuoso literature. I had studied a Vieuxtemps concerto, and then Kneisel suggested that I try his seldom-played Third. I inquired at my usual secondhand music shop for this work, and discovered it priced at two dollars! I was on a tight budget—one dollar or less for concertos—so I asked if they had another Vieuxtemps in that range. The salesman found a slightly battered copy of the First Concerto for one dollar, which seemed a good switch to me. This proved to be almost my undoing. I had no idea it was a fiendishly difficult work, bristling with high-velocity staccato passages at break-neck speeds and consequently avoided by most violinists.

I began struggling with this violinistic monster, and although I had a reasonably good command of bowing at slow or normal tempi, I simply could not manage to speed up my staccato. Kneisel became impatient after a few weeks of hard work without progress. He declared that I would have to stick to this work until I acquired the necessary velocity. His own method for this tricky bowing was based on the classic small wrist motion usually adequate for normal tempi but impossible for a very fast staccato.

After some weeks of hopeless struggle, I still could not energize my bow arm to the required speed, a controlled rapid "stuttering." I visualized the rest of my season's study going down the drain in this unequal contest. Fortunately, I observed Bernard Ocko display, at his lesson, an exceptionally rapid staccato. I told him of my problem and he provided the solution. Earlier he had studied with a Russian violinist who had shown him the physical process involved, which consisted of tightening the muscle of the upper right arm and using this forceful propulsion on the bow! From then on it was only a matter of coordinating the velocity of the bow arm with the fingers of the left hand. It approximated a sort of controlled spastic fit of the bow arm. Evidently this was a Russian tradition passed on by Henri Wieniawski, the great Polish virtuoso, who used this device effectively in some of his brilliant etudes and his diabolically difficult F-sharp Minor Concerto.

Following Ocko's advice, I tensed my forearm biceps by scratching as loudly as possible on one note. When I could feel tremors start, I attempted to correlate this controlled fit with the left hand. To my surprise, after a few hours each day of this painful process, I could feel this impulse but then had some trouble coordinating both hands in very fast passages. Occasionally someone would knock on my door to inquire if anything was wrong with me that I should be making such an awful racket.

The fateful morning of my next lesson dawned and I walked to the Institute with some anxiety and foreboding. On entering the classroom, I saw a tall, elegant visitor with a mustache and goatee. Kneisel presented me to his colleague and friend from Boston, the violinist and composer Charles Martin Loeffler. The portrait of this courtly gentleman by John Singer Sargent hangs in the Isabella Stewart Gardner Museum in Boston. He was born in Alsace and lived for a period in Imperial Russia, for his father served in the French diplomatic service. In 1895, Mr. and Mrs. Jack Gardner purchased a Stradivarius violin in Paris, which Mrs. Gardner presented to Loeffler in 1918.

When my turn to perform arrived, I was asked to play my accursed Vieuxtemps concerto. Luckily, to my surprise, it went off well with all the rapid passages in tempo. Kneisel listened quietly, turning pages but making no comment, which was highly unusual. Mr. Loeffler seemed pleased by my efforts and spoke kindly and encouragingly to me. Kneisel turned to him with, "You see, Loeffler, they all get a fine staccato with my method."

In the mid 1930s, the great Jascha Heifetz confirmed the traditional Russian solution of staccato velocity. He invited me to play chamber music at his summer home in Balboa, California. Seeing his arrangement of Dinicu's "Hora Staccato" on the piano stand, I asked if he would explain to Annette and me the rapidity and perfection of his bowing in this piece that always dazzled audiences. He answered that he had to get into training weeks ahead of his tours, like an athlete. It involved strengthening the right forearm muscles systematically, until the controlled tremor permitted the required speed.

I had obtained a worn copy of the Joachim-Moser edition of Johann Sebastian Bach's collection of solo violin partitas and sonatas. These editors wisely printed their own phrasing suggestions on one line and on a line below printed Bach's urtext. This gave me the idea to use their device when I edited some Telemann sonatinas and sonatas.

At one lesson, I played the last movement of the G Minor Partita, where Joachim indicated practical patterns over the urtext, which had indicated separate notes. I followed a few bars of the Bach line. Suddenly Kneisel roared, "Kaufman, how dare you think *you* know better than Joachim!" In retrospect, I think we were both right, for the eighteenth-century composers left much to the interpreter's discretion. Kneisel rarely played at lessons but one morning, he picked up his violin to play an entire grave movement of Bach's D Minor Partita. With hardly perceptible vibrato, he played with a most subtle rubato and delicate tonal gradations that made an indelible impression on me. In a flash I realized what infinite possibilities there were in this inspired music. This deepened my sense of loss at not having heard his quartet in its heyday.

At a subsequent lesson, hearing me struggle with a difficult Paganini etude, Kneisel asked, "Does your hand feel strained, Kaufman?" I responded that it did, and he quickly said, "Stop Paganini! Be careful! *Never* strain your hand. Take something else." Then, in an expansive mood, he continued, "When I was a young student in Vienna, I encountered an old gentleman who clearly remembered hearing Paganini in concert. He vividly recalled the audience being deeply touched by the lyric expressive quality of Paganini's tone. People were weeping with the emotions he aroused, not merely dazzled by his amazing pyrotechnics." I queried, "What violinist's tone do you think the most beautiful you have ever heard, Dr. Kneisel?" To my surprise he answered, "Pablo de Sarasate's — he sang like a nightingale."

I have since thought that Paganini not only invented technical feats that profoundly influenced Schumann, Chopin, Brahms, Liszt, and Rachmaninoff, but he also may have introduced the singing, modern use of vibrato that became the norm for later virtuosi such as Wieniawski, Vieuxtemps, and Ysaÿe. This was confirmed years later, when I read Sara Chapman Bull's memoirs of her late husband, Ole Bull, the celebrated

Norwegian violinist, who had often attended Paganini's concerts in Italy. He expressed great admiration for the "bel canto" singing of Paganini's tone as well as for his dazzling technical displays.

Ernesto Camillo Sivori, Paganini's only pupil, recounted to the Scottish violin collector David Laurie one of his master's tricks of showmanship. When Paganini played the "Moses Fantasy on the G String" based on Rossini's opera, *Mosè in Egitto* (a fiendishly difficult piece), he used a three-quarter-sized Amati violin, putting the low G string in the middle of the violin (displacing the D string), which made the performance child's play. Sivori boasted to Laurie: "I play the piece on a full-sized Jean-Baptiste Vuillaume, a copy of Paganini's Guarnerius del Gésu [bequeathed to him by the master], with the strings in normal position!"

It was difficult to attract a public for violin concerts during Paganini's life (as it is now). On one of his typical programs in England (which I later saw in Hill's historic London shop), he included tenor and soprano soloists accompanied by a small orchestra. Paganini announced he would perform a newly composed viola sonata for the event, then end the evening with violin fireworks, imitating on his great violin barnyard animals such as cows, pigs, and roosters!

Kneisel urged his students to listen to opera singers as models to emulate in shaping a melody. Thanks to the Institute's patrons, students were occasionally offered opera tickets. Thus I heard Enrico Caruso, Fyodor Chaliapin, Lauritz Melchior, Geraldine Farrar, and other luminaries. Caruso's velvety rich tenor and his unique expressiveness were unforgettable. The early primitive recordings could not dampen the power and eloquence of this king of vocal art. These recordings, currently being re-released, are still unique in vocal splendor.

I first heard Mussorgsky's *Boris Godunov* with Chaliapin as Tsar Boris. He seemed eight feet tall through the force of his personality, which filled the stage, and his noble bass voice reached the highest rafters.

Thus I became aware that the human voice, with its infinite expressivities and color, rising to the limits of emotional intensity, is the true royalty of our musical art. The closer string instruments approach this ultimate truth, the nearer they are to the fusion of wood, glue, and strings into pure human utterance. This may not be adequately achieved with outmoded methods of position changes or mere convenience of fingering. Absurd ideas abound that, since eighteenth-century musicians may have performed inexpressively and awkwardly, we should follow this arbitrary, unnatural, and retrograde idea. Performance cannot be frozen in amber, unchanging, instead of attempting a closer approach to the warmth of an inspired singer. The human emotions great composers wished to express have been revealed in an intuitive way by such tonal geniuses as Elman, Kreisler, and Heifetz.

Once front-row tickets placed me in back of mercurial Artur Bodanzky, conducting a memorable *Siegfried*, with Melchior superbly singing the role of Wagner's young hero. During an orchestral passage, when a horn player made a false entrance, Bodanzky burst out in a whisper that reached the front rows, "What the hell is wrong with you?" The Metropolitan orchestra and chorus at that time frequently lacked precision.

Geraldine Farrar was a lovely vision; her soprano voice had endearing charm. I did not agree with some critics who had reservations about her technique. She once observed, "At least when I am old, the critics can't say that I've lost my voice. They seem to think I've never had one!" I also was privileged to hear Emma Calvé and Mary Garden, who had arresting personalities; they were sopranos of distinction and ultimate refinement of the vocal art. My love for opera has continued throughout my life.

Richard (Dick) Rodgers, who later achieved international fame for composing innovative musical comedies with lyricists Lorenz Hart and Oscar Hammerstein II, was my fellow student at the Institute in Percy Goetschius's composition and counterpoint classes. We both attended Henry Krehbiel's poetic lectures on the lives and works of Mozart, Beethoven, Schubert, and others. Dick wrote entertaining music for the school's annual musicals; he displayed an extraordinary gift for using available talents and an unerring instinct for pleasing the crowd. I enjoyed his musical *Say It with Jazz,* a witty spoof based on Rimsky-Korsakov's *The Golden Cockerel.* For the *Baton,* our school newspaper, he conceived a satiric *Diary of a Prodigy,* which ran serially for several months. Dick may well have been the author of a popular Institute jingle, "Rootie Toot Toot! Rootie Toot Toot! We are the boys from the Institute! We don't play rough! We don't play tough! But our class won the Bible."

Sometimes, in a mellow mood, Kneisel would speak to the class about his conversations with Johannes Brahms. We presumed that his ideas of tempo and important details of interpretation of Brahms's chamber works, string quartets, piano quartets, and piano trios were sanctioned by the composer. One day he analyzed the first movement of Brahms's second symphony, pointing out wonderfully organized relationships of themes and their development. I ventured to ask, "Dr. Kneisel, is it possible to plan in advance all these complicated series of interlocking relationships?" He answered, "That's a good question, Kaufman. You know I asked Brahms that same question. Brahms replied, 'No, certainly not consciously. The thematic and rhythmic materials seem to develop a life of their own, like a plant or a tree, that develops branches and fruits.

Sometimes, after a work is completed, I am surprised at all the relationships that have developed.'"

Kneisel added, "Brahms, like Beethoven, took morning walks in the woods surrounding the village of Bad Ischl before starting to compose. Nature was an inexhaustible inspiration to Brahms. The village children soon learned of Brahms's daily constitutional, as he always carried small candies in his pockets and would dole them out as favors. When Brahms was complimented on one of his beautiful melodies, he replied that almost anyone could write a melody, but this was not important, for only after a theme was developed did it become the personal expression of its composer."

Kneisel analyzed the subtle give and take of rubato very clearly, sometimes measuring on a musical chart the way of staying within the phrase, taking some liberty without destroying the fundamental beat. He stressed that the exact Spanish triplet as used in habaneras must be in absolutely strict tempo; it was sacred. This gave a subtle freedom to Spanish and French music in Spanish style. Of course, French and Spanish composers know this, but not many others are aware of this important tradition.

Kneisel once remarked, "I consider pupils similar to raw material akin to marble, which must be carved and developed before they can become artists or professionally capable. Since superior or even unflawed marble is difficult to find, I, like a sculptor, cannot achieve good results with poor material."

Some weeks later, I dared to take on Paganini's "Di tanti palpiti," a violinist's nightmare. I managed to traverse most of its technical passages, except for a noted series of double harmonics, equivalent to walking on a tightrope.

I still played the sixty-five-dollar Heberlein. Although its measurements were correct, its tone was inflexible and harsh. With this coarse quality, it was impossible to play single harmonics clearly, let alone double ones. As I played this section, Kneisel stopped me, saying sardonically, "That's enough." He urged me to obtain an Italian violin with some quality and tonal flexibility, sagely adding, "It will be more difficult for you to play an Italian violin later if you continue with your worthless fiddle."

A Sunday morning series of public concerts was inaugurated at the huge Capital Theater on Broadway, with a large orchestra directed by Hugo Riesenfeld. He occasionally invited Institute pupils to perform concertos. When I was asked to play, I suggested a double concerto of Charles Dancla, with Milton Feher as second violin. Feher had a modest Italian violin of the Ruggeri school, loaned by his violinist father. Some of the class came to hear us. After the performance, I asked what they thought of the balance. They replied, "Your fiddle doesn't carry. All we heard was the lower part in thirds and sixths. You were barely audible." I demanded, "You *really* couldn't hear me?" They chorused, "*No*—we couldn't!"

This disappointing experience made me anxious to have a better violin. I haunted Wurlitzer's, the main violin establishment in New York, and became friendly with Rembert Wurlitzer, who permitted me to try out all sorts of fine Italian violins. After learning about various luthiers (violin makers) and playing on various fiddles at the studios of many New York dealers, I finally selected an eighteenth-century Nicolas Gagliano, in pristine condition, from Wurlitzer's collection. Kneisel approved of it.

I had informally organized a string quartet of colleagues, as Dr. and Mrs. Bierhof had invited us to dinner at their large apartment to play for them and their guests. It was an opportunity to try out a program scheduled for the Institute. After dinner we began to perform. The doorbell rang and unexpectedly Mischa Elman walked in. We immediately asked him to play but he had not brought his violin, he had only thought to visit his friends. I thought this was an excellent chance to hear him play the Gagliano before deciding to purchase it. This was the first violin of fine quality I had found in my price range. Its remarkably fine condition and intact orange-amber varnish were infinitely more attractive than my factory fiddle. I handed the Gagliano to Elman, urging him to play first violin, then commandeered the second fiddler's violin and played his part. What a revelation! With a strange violin and bow, Elman played with the most ravishingly beautiful, rich tone. I was convinced the Neapolitan Gagliano was one of the greatest violins, equal to any Cremona master, even Stradivarius or Guarnerius.

The next morning, I rushed to Wurlitzer's to buy that violin. However, things do not always work out as one would wish. I struggled with the "obstinate beauty" for three years, and it almost drove me out of my mind. Its tone was hard and glassy, brilliant on the higher strings but lacking richness on the lower register. Every time I put a little pressure on the strings with my bow, the tone would break, reminding me of Kneisel's frequent admonition, in fractured English, "As more you press, as less comes out."

Bernice, an Institute piano student whom I knew slightly, asked me to play sonatas with her one afternoon in a nearby flat where she and her sister shared a small room. After a brief session, I invited both girls to see an early movie. I left my Gagliano in its case on top of her upright piano. When we returned, my violin was gone—nowhere to be found! The landlady was summoned. She was certain no one had entered the flat during our absence. I phoned the police, highly indignant about the robbery of my first good Italian instrument. I told the officer, "The violin is insured. It came from Wurlitzer's, who have complete information about it." The theft was reported in the New York press.

After two desolate days, Bernice called and said excitedly, "Louis, your violin is here—come right over!" I ran to her flat. There was my Gagliano, in its case, contents intact! The police had been notified, so an officer was already there. Bernice was explaining, "Our landlady found it a few minutes ago on the fire escape outside our window." The policeman suggested that the thief tried to pawn it or sell it but then discovered it was "hot" and decided to return it. I surmised the landlady was the culprit and demanded, "Can I prosecute the thief?" The officer wisely replied, "Listen, kid, you got your fiddle back. *Forget it!*" But I never did. I constantly made sure I had my violin (or any instrument I was responsible for) with me. I never left an instrument in any doubtful place.

My purchase of the Gagliano was not altogether foolish. It taught me an important lesson. I realized that even celebrated instruments of impeccable lineage do not have an "ideal sound," that great artists can make almost any instrument "speak," and that one had to learn to distinguish between the quality of concert artists and instruments they played. This realization helped me choose my next violin, which once belonged to Efrem Zimbalist—a Giovanni Baptista Guadagnini of 1771, made in Turin. I continued to visit Wurlitzer's regularly. Rembert allowed me to play on any of the great violins and bows in their collection in the Forty-second Street shop. Occasionally he would call me to demonstrate tonal qualities of their finest violins for prospective clients. He allowed me to trade in the Gagliano at its full value. With additional funds from teaching and small jobs and my father's generous graduation gift, I was able to purchase the Guadagnini.

# 4

# More Kneisel — Auer — Graduation — Chamber Music

After a chamber music session in 1922, a guest approached and offered me a contract to perform piano trios nightly at a hotel he managed in Miami, Florida. I would play in the dining room for winter season guests. His offer included round-trip fare from New York plus room and board for a weekly fee of $150. At age seventeen, I found this a very attractive offer. The next day I signed the contract, for I keenly felt an obligation to reduce Father's expenditures for my studies and living in New York.

At my next lesson, I informed Dr. Kneisel of my imminent departure to Florida for two months, and was overwhelmed by his wrathful outburst. "Kaufman! I thought you had *some* intelligence — but I see you are a real *dummkopf*! If you *dare* abandon your studies, you'll be absolutely finished forever and never achieve anything worthwhile on the violin. I've seen this too often. Talented young people abandon their studies too soon. They sink into *mediocrity!* You'll be on the beach, become a loafer, meet girls. You'll stop practicing seriously and it will be the end of you!"

"Dr. Kneisel," I timidly offered, "What can I do? I've already signed the contract." Mollified by my rapid capitulation, he calmly continued, "Have the man call me. I'll explain that I am your guardian and you are under age and have no right to sign anything or make such important decisions without *my permission*. You have only a few more precious years to work untroubled by problems and complications of adult life. These arrive soon enough, Kaufman. Prize every hour in which you can make significant progress. You will have your whole life to earn money."

This revealed Kneisel's true concern—that each pupil achieve as much as his or her individual talents allowed. Only later did I fully appreciate how he saved me from such a grave error in judgment.

Still anxious to earn money, I answered a *New York Times* ad for a violinist to play weekends at a Brooklyn movie house. I arrived early for the audition; a long line of applicants followed me. As a sight-reading test the manager presented music I already knew and the job was mine; he dismissed the other fiddlers. The pianist in the pit liked classical music, and after the first night of playing the boring cue sheets that accompanied the film, he said, "Why don't you bring some good music to play tomorrow?" So during the matinee we played concertos and sonatas to the accompanying clamor of yelling and Cracker-Jack–eating youngsters, who were excited by the chases and shooting in the western film. The manager, angered by our playing classical music during these frenetic scenes, fired me on the spot!

During the Christmas holiday, Daniel Saidenberg, the cellist and conductor (later a modern art dealer), called to ask if I would like a vacation with pay in Baltimore. He was hired to accompany a Spanish dancing team, "Carlos and Sedana." Carlos, a handsome, muscular Spaniard, and Sedana, a shapely American blond, wanted a "classy" combo to play on stage as they glided and stomped their way through tangos and fandangos. Someone had told the blond that a double bass would dress up the ensemble, and Danny proposed me as double bass player. When I arrived at rehearsal carrying a viola, she looked at Danny with disappointment and said, "Isn't a double bass bigger?" Danny nonchalantly replied, "As you can see, he's small, so he has to play a small one!" Sedana believed Danny's explanation. I played viola, faking double bass parts, and we had a jolly and profitable Christmas recess as I succumbed to the gracious historic charm of Lord Baltimore's city.

Kneisel offered me chances to teach. One pupil was the ungifted and uninterested grandson of Harry and Louisine Havemeyer, who had a most impressive residence at One East Sixty-sixth Street. The Kneisel Quartet had been a favorite group for their Sunday musicales, traveling from Boston to play the one-and-a-half-hour programs for the Havemeyers' distinguished guests, mostly painters, sculptors, and architects. The walls of their residence displayed masterpieces by El Greco, Manet, Courbet, Goya, Pissarro, and Degas, most bought on the advice of Mrs. Havemeyer's friend Mary Cassatt. Seeing these wonderful paintings undoubtedly sparked my lifelong interest in visual arts.

The Havemeyers' grandson played a Gemünder violin (Gemünder was an American luthier who studied in France with Jean-Baptiste

Vuillaume). He showed me the great King Joseph Guarnerius, which was owned by his grandparents. He kept this lovely violin in a little case under his bed. Although the five-dollar fee was useful, after a few weeks I decided his complete disinterest made it a hopeless struggle and dismissed him.

A more enjoyable source of income was playing chamber music with Kneisel's rich amateur-musician friends, who provided excellent dinners and paid me five dollars for playing with them. Irving K. Hall, an importer of teas and spices, had a rare passion for chamber music and a son whom he hoped to interest in violin playing. He had the genial idea of arranging chamber music on Sunday afternoons at his brownstone house in the Seventies. A light meal was served in late afternoon, followed by our evening performances. The circumstances were interesting: he engaged Felix Salmond, a distinguished English cellist, to be our coach and play with us. Bernard Ocko was violinist, Frank Sheridan, an American artist, was pianist, and I was violist. These programs encompassed most of the masterworks of the piano quartet repertoire and were sheer enjoyment, for we had one or two rehearsals before each event. With these colleagues I learned the extent and richness of that remarkable literature, for we performed most of the piano quartets by Brahms, Beethoven, Schumann, Dvořák, Fauré, and other distinguished composers.

At the elegant Warburg home on Fifth Avenue (now the site of the Jewish Museum), surrounded by old master paintings, including some remarkable Dutch masters and Rembrandts, I played the inspired Schubert two-cello quintet with cellists Felix Salmond and Gerald Warburg. After this experience, I could appreciate the emotional effect that Schubert's supreme lyricism had on the elderly Henry Krehbiel, the dignified music critic of the *New York Herald Tribune,* who occasionally lectured at the Institute. Whenever he spoke about Schubert, he would be so overcome by the pathos of Schubert's brief life that tears would well in his eyes, causing him to cover them with a large handkerchief. He would slowly walk off the platform, unable to continue.

About 1925, I began playing first violin in quartets with my colleagues. The Institute occasionally recommended advanced students for local concerts, and proposed my quartet for a program at the Ethical Culture Society. Their concerts took place in a fairly large hall on New York's Lower East Side, and were almost exclusively patronized by Jewish immigrants. Tickets were priced at twenty-five cents and attracted a large, receptive audience. Our program comprised a Mozart string quartet and the Schubert two-cello quintet. We invited a few friends and colleagues to attend. It was exhilarating to play for such an emotionally charged group. In the first rows sat aged Jewish men with flowing beards and traditional sidelocks under their brimmed black hats, which they wore throughout the evening. The wonderfully expressive adagio of the Schubert evidently touched a sympathetic chord in these patriarchs. Some were openly weeping. Their final applause for our program was heartwarming.

Backstage, as we placed our instruments in their cases amid the crush of well-wishers, one aggressive old gentleman, who considered himself "official critic" of such programs, elbowed his way through the crowd and exclaimed loudly, "I can only give you 65 percent!" Puzzled, I replied, "Thank you very much," and turned to continue obligatory handshaking and conversations with friends. He was not to be put off, again pushing his way to confront me, shaking his finger, "Only 65 percent." As we edged away from him, we heard his repeated "Only 65 percent." In retrospect, it is possible that he was very disappointed by our youthful efforts. We certainly had enthusiasm but were definitely not as polished an ensemble as the professional quartets that were occasionally heard on this series.

I had the privilege of studying with Franz Kneisel until two weeks before he died of cancer on 26 March 1926 — altogether a period of eight years. My father had often suggested that I secretly study with other New York teachers. He was still obsessed by the idea that there were secrets that I could only learn by studying with many other teachers. I deeply appreciated how valuable Kneisel's teaching was for me and remained faithful to his musical precepts.

For my last lesson I went to his home, for he was too ill to teach at the Institute. It was an extraordinarily long session, devoted to another Vieuxtemps concerto, that never seemed to end. He kept on speaking about style, rubato, and general effectiveness in performance.

I always had an independent point of view, which possibly annoyed this towering musician, but I always tried to please him. One day he dryly remarked, "I know you play this way, Kaufman, to please me, but as soon as you are by yourself, you'll play it the way *you* want!" I certainly had a taste of what appeals to audiences and my natural bent was to play in a manner I considered expressive and effective. Kneisel usually considered this personal showmanship rather too emotional.

In any event, this long final session left me physically exhausted. I had been steadily playing over two hours. As I thanked him, saying "Goodbye, Dr. Kneisel," I suddenly noticed he looked very worn and tired. Later, I thought he might have surmised this was to be our last meeting.

It was a great sorrow to the entire musical community when Kneisel died. We pupils were especially shocked. The funeral service at the Institute recital hall is a poignant memory. There were many ceremonial speeches, but my most vivid recollection of that very sad day was the image of Fritz Kreisler, playing the adagio of Bach's E Major Concerto with tears falling down his cheeks, to an organ accompaniment of Gaston Dethier. Kneisel's own description of this heavenly music was unforgettable: "It is the discourse of a consoling angel to a grieving mortal." I felt particularly bereaved at the loss of my mentor, as only two months remained before my graduation.

The Institute gave me opportunity to study the last few months with aged Professor Leopold Auer, who temporarily joined the faculty to replace Kneisel. Although he had been a most accomplished violinist and inspired teacher, he was well into his eighties and could no longer demonstrate what he wanted on the violin.

For my first lesson, I played the first movement of the Brahms concerto and was astonished that he let me play it through without saying a word. What a contrast to Kneisel's microscopic analysis. He commented, "That's quite good Kaufman, but there are a few passages where I don't hear all the notes. You might try it again and see if you can play them cleaner. Either you have to play them slower—or play them better. Also, you take a few too many liberties. When you play with an orchestra, you'll find it's not practical to use so much rubato with conductors. You have to play more precisely in time for the sake of ensemble." This was very good advice, which I later appreciated more fully. He continued, "At the end of the cadenza, when the orchestra reenters, you can make a slight glissando to a harmonic on the A string. It's a pretty and graceful effect." It surprised me that he would want me to disregard the original Brahms phrasing. The original phrasing of composers was sacred to Kneisel and he drummed this into his pupils. I said, "Thank you very much, Professor Auer," and departed. I spent the week diligently following his advice to clean up dubious passages and straighten out excessive rubato.

The second lesson was rougher. He stopped me here and there with good suggestions on violinistic and interpretative details. Finally I arrived at the end of the cadenza and played the original phrasing instead of his suggested glissando, which involved breaking up Brahms's original phrasing. Again Professor Auer stopped me, obviously not sure whether he had mentioned this detail of violinistic skill, saying, "I want to show you something effective here." He picked up his violin and illustrated the glissando to a harmonic, as best he could, continuing, "Try it once more. I think you can play it cleaner and more precisely." Again I expressed my thanks.

The third lesson was truly rough. I later learned from one of his former students that this was a good sign of his growing interest. He stopped me frequently with detailed criticism, and again I arrived at the fatal cadenza. This time he remembered clearly that he had told me about the glissando effect. I held firmly to the original phrasing and he stopped me with words I never forgot: "Tell me, Kaufman, are you stubborn or are you stupid?" I returned my violin to its case and politely replied, "Thank you very much, Professor," and left the room—never to return. I have deeply regretted that my lessons with him ended so abruptly and impolitely on my part. The heedless bent of youth is not an adequate excuse for the loss; I undoubtedly suffered by not benefiting from this noted master's long experience and wisdom. However, at this time the pressure of preparing concerts with the Musical Art Quartet, my struggle to prepare for graduation from the Institute of Musical Art (which included playing a solo violin recital), plus the problem of finding an apartment for my family (as Father had decided to bring Mother and my two brothers to New York to attend my graduation) effectively stopped any further lessons with Professor Auer. I did not have time to adequately prepare additional repertoire for this historic master. Alas, that at twenty-one I was so set as a musician that I would not accept, even temporarily, a violinistic glissando!

I rented an eight-room apartment on Riverside Drive for $250 per month for my family's two-month sojourn. It was completely furnished and offered linens, beautiful dishes, utensils, and cutlery. Papa grumbled a bit, for it seemed rather expensive by Portland standards. My family arrived and quickly settled in; I was very pleased to be *en famille* with Mother's delicious cooking and affectionate care. Father loved to entertain, and Mother had the ability to prepare tasty meals for any number of guests. We entertained relatives, friends, and my colleagues with copious meals of Romanian Jewish cuisine plus chamber music. Gus Solomon was studying law at Columbia University and we saw each other frequently. Even Philip Pelz surfaced and enlivened dinners with racy tales of his continuing colorful adventures. I practiced diligently for my graduation recital, a crucial test. My program included the first solo Bach Sonata in G Minor, the Paganini Concerto in D, and several shorter virtuoso pieces.

At this decisive event, I felt uneasy when I saw that Professor Auer was on the board of judges. He might well have remembered my tactless and ungracious behavior that ended my studies with him. The other judges were Dr. Walter Damrosch, the Institute's founder, and Felix Salmond. By chance, my parents sat in the auditorium directly behind Professor Auer and the jury and overheard some of their remarks during my recital.

Customarily, judges asked contestants to sight-read. Sometimes this would be a not too difficult movement of a standard string quartet, or a modern solo work that could be sticky. One never knew in advance. I recalled when Kneisel was judging Babushkin, a pupil of the distinguished violinist Edouard Dethier. Kneisel asked the lad to play the final allegro of Beethoven's Opus 18 C Minor Quartet. Although the young man played a fine recital in every respect, he played the allegro (a fast movement) slowly and deliberately to be sure he was playing the right notes. Kneisel rejected him on the spot! He stated indignantly, "*No one* has a *right* to an Artist's Diploma who is ignorant of the *correct* tempo for such a standard work." This destroyed poor Babushkin's hopes for a musical career and he returned to Florida for nondescript work.

After my program Damrosch asked Auer, "Would you like Mr. Kaufman to sight-read some music?" Auer replied, "No, it's not necessary in his case." I was generously let off the hook! My parents became very excited and pleased when the time for grading arrived. Damrosch queried, "Professor Auer, what do you think we should give him, 90 or 100?" Auer enthusiastically exclaimed, "I give the young man 150!"

This thrilled my parents and they hurried to tell me about this remark, and when they returned to Portland, they informed everyone they knew. So I graduated cum laude and received the Artist's Diploma, the highest award of the Institute.

At the end of the term, a gala concert was given at Aeolian Hall (now demolished). I was excused from my regular duties as concertmaster of the Institute Orchestra, a post I had held for two years, to perform the first movement of the Brahms concerto. To honor my late master, I played the Kneisel cadenza. After the intermission, and after all the year's selected soloists had performed, Damrosch asked the audience of students, families, and friends, "Who do you think has won the Loeb $1,000 prize?" The audience roared back, "Louis Kaufman!"

# 5

# The Musical Art Quartet
# Is Launched

## *I Become an Art Collector*

He who really does what he should will obtain what he wants.

Bhagavad Gita

In 1926, at the age of twenty-one, I was formally invited to join the Musical Art Quartet as violist. We had been playing informally for about a year. Sascha Jacobsen, a Kneisel student, was first violinist, and Marie Roemaet-Rosanoff, a Casals student, was our cellist. We tried out various second violinists and finally settled on Paul Bernard, a pupil of Paul Stassevitch.

Sascha Jacobsen was already a fine violinist when he arrived from Russia to study with Kneisel. He was an amiable and pleasant companion, very witty and sophisticated. He owned a lovely Stradivarius violin, which he played with rare artistry. Sascha considered it very vulgar and unnecessary to give signals for starting movements or to move the body unduly in performance. We had to listen very carefully and sense what he might do. It was a splendid postgraduate course in musicianship and artistry for me.

We had informal rehearsals and very enjoyable quartet parties at the home of Efrem Zimbalist and his wife, the celebrated Romanian singer Alma Gluck, and also at the Warburgs' mansion. Mrs. Zimbalist particularly liked our musical approach and us personally; she gathered their many wealthy friends to contribute to our financial support and help us establish a reputation.

The Musical Art Quartet, *from left:* Paul Bernard, second violin; Sascha Jacobsen, first violin; Marie Roemaet-Rosanoff, cello; Louis Kaufman, viola.

The Zimbalists arranged the financial backing for our quartet on a permanent basis. We each received $5,000 per year for rehearsing and shared equally whatever came in from concerts. After my parents returned to Portland, I joined the Musical Art Quartet in New Hartford, Connecticut, for summer rehearsals. We worked through a great deal of quartet literature and had delightful beach parties and excursions in the bucolic countryside.

The Zimbalists lived on nearby Fishers Island, in a spacious summer home, where we enjoyed musical parties. I recall one day when we played chamber music with Efrem Zimbalist and colleagues until we were all exhausted. The party ended with a fabulous clam bake, my first taste of this New England treat. A large barrel had been filled to the brim with lobsters, chickens, clams, and corn on the cob, all layered with seaweed, placed on a bed of hot rocks at the bottom of a pit, and buried in the sand to cook all day. After performing we ravenously devoured this regional specialty, picnicking in the dusk.

The Zimbalists noticed that my small viola was not of particularly good quality and thought I should have a better instrument. They generously loaned me a Lorenzo Storioni viola, of small dimensions but with unusually fine tonal quality. It was not tiring to play this instrument. I used this viola until I resigned from the Quartet.

Before embarking on our first series of three concerts at Aeolian Hall in New York, we were invited to play a program of Haydn and Debussy quartets at the elegant home of Dr. Walter Damrosch, the pioneer conductor of the New York Symphony Society. He had invited a memorable audience: Efrem and Alma Zimbalist, Maestro Arturo Toscanini, Pablo Casals, musician and writer Samuel Chotzinoff and his wife, Ambassador and Madame John Work Garrett, Frank Crowninshield (editor of *Vanity Fair*), and many other luminaries. After our performance of the Debussy, we were delighted when Maestro Toscanini complimented our quartet! Then Pablo Casals spontaneously decided to join us as first cellist, so the soirée concluded dramatically and poetically with the Schubert two-cello quintet. It was extraordinary that Casals sat in, but we did not have the slightest difficulty in achieving an unusually good ensemble, for his tempi were so naturally right. Damrosch gave each member of our quartet an autographed photograph of himself as a souvenir of this musicale.

One of our first quartet engagements, at Carnegie Hall on 10 April 1927, had unusual significance. It was devoted to the American premiere of George Antheil's music. His premiere audition in Paris was both a critical and popular success, and both Aaron Copland and Virgil Thomson acclaimed his talents. This concert was devoted to his string quartet, *A Jazz Symphony,* and *Ballet Mécanique.* It was paid for by the noted book publisher, Donald Friede, who admired Antheil and was a patron of avantgarde events. (Coincidentally, Friede occupied a box with his mother and cousin Belle, who later married my friend Nicolas Moldavan.)

During the rehearsal of Antheil's quartet we would become hopelessly lost, due to the complexity of the score. It was not the only time we encountered overly complicated musical writing concealing a paucity of musical content. We devised signals where we could indicate spots to reassemble in case we got lost. Antheil, who resembled a sawed-off prizefighter, attended a dress rehearsal at Marie Roemaet-Rosanoff's flat. He listened to our performance with tears in his eyes and warmly shook our hands, asserting he had never heard his music played so meaningfully.

There was much publicity and interest in Antheil, and the concert sold out. But the string quartet, which went off not too badly, earned only tepid applause. *A Jazz Symphony* was met with mild approval mixed with scattered booing. The *Ballet Mécanique* was the piece de resistance of the program, with full percussion, xylophones, and ten pianists, among them the composer and Aaron Copland, who pounded rhythmically using only forearms and elbows. Airplane propellers, amplified typewriters, and assorted "bangers" created such a noisy clamor that the audience grew more and more restive. When the airplane propellers and typewriters reached their climax, the crowd reacted with loud catcalls, booing, and shouts of extreme disfavor!

One gentleman in a front box held up his cane, with a large white handkerchief attached, and waved it vigorously. A shower of programs folded into paper airplanes floated down from the balcony. The time was not right for this sort of event, and this concert proved to be the *coup de grâce* for Antheil's reputation. Later he composed more traditional scores and wrote some interesting music for the film industry, as well as articles for newspapers on such diverse subjects as military affairs and advice for the lovelorn.

In New Hartford I had visited an exhibition of local painters with Paul Rosenbloom, a local friend. A small canvas of the Brooklyn Bridge appealed to me. It was painted by Mary Kumpf and priced at twenty-five dollars, including the frame. I thought it would be very attractive in my one-room apartment and bought it. I was told that I could pick it up at the close of the exhibit, which coincided with my return to New York.

The Hartford painter Aaron Berkman, while visiting me in New York, was dismayed at the mediocrity of my Brooklyn Bridge painting. He convinced me it was commonplace and worthless. I began to dislike it, so I put it up at auction and recovered my twenty-five dollars. Berkman told me, "If you want to see some *real* painting, I'll take you to see Milton Avery. We young painters admire him." I became fascinated by Avery's works, rich in tonality and texture. He and his wife, Sally Michel, were interesting and charming people. It was highly entertaining to visit their tiny one-room loft studio in the Lincoln Office tenement, where the Lincoln Center now stands. I soon asked if I might buy a still life of a large bottle and fruit, rich in color and impasto and reminiscent of Ernest Lawson and Cézanne. I asked what he wanted for it. Milton replied, "Well, would twenty-five dollars be all right?" I said, "Sure." Sally later told me I bought the first oil painting Avery had ever sold. These were lean years for Milton, and Sally supported him with the very stylish drawings she made for the magazine section of the *New York Times*. Avery's only other collector was a Catholic priest, Father Kelly, who lived in a poor parish in Hartford. When his superior heard of his art collection, he informed Father Kelly that his personal indulgence was not in keeping with his calling and ordered him to sell his collection of watercolors and give the funds to the needy. I visited Milton and Sally as frequently as possible and learned a great deal from their artistic insights. Milton was a great observer and his brief comments were enough to put me on the right artistic track.

I began to haunt art galleries on Fifty-seventh Street and to visit the Metropolitan Museum of Art and the Museum of Modern Art. I read Bernard Berenson's books on Italian masters, and books about modern art by Roger Fry, Clive Bell, Reginald Wilenski, and Dr. Albert C. Barnes. I became immersed in the world of contemporary art as well as old masters. Some art dealers like Manfred Schwartz (also a painter) and J. B. Neumann became my friends. Neumann's wide interests covered old masters, German expressionists, Coptic weavings, and modern Americans. It was he who at that time exhibited Max Weber and his pupil Marcus Rothcowitz, whom he advised to shorten his name to Mark Rothko. Some striking small paintings by David Burliuk caught my eye. One rather small surrealist portrait of a sailor's head had fish for eyes, a bottle for a nose, and a small boat for his mouth. When I asked the price, Neumann asked, "What do you do?" I replied, "I'm a violinist." Neumann kindly suggested, "Why don't you buy it directly from Burliuk? Obviously you haven't much money, and he is very poor—that way you'll both benefit. Here is his address."

I thanked Neumann and set off for a cold-water flat on Eighth Street near Broadway, where I introduced myself to tall, imposing Burliuk. The self-proclaimed "Father of Russian Futurism" wore highly decorative waistcoats, a single long pendant in one ear, and a tall silk top hat with a long formal afternoon coat for going out. Red-headed Madame Marussia Burliuk, with her long pointed nose and large expressive blue-green eyes, gave the impression that she lived in another world.

Burliuk had discovered and encouraged the ill-fated Russian futurist poet Vladimir Mayakovsky. Later he had lived next door to Wassily Kandinsky in Munich and joined the *Blaue Reiter* group. In Russia he belonged to a futurist group, *Bubovy Valet* (Jack of Diamonds Society). I bought the canvas exhibited by Neumann and another painting of a Russian sailor with a balalaika, and I continued to buy paintings from him for many years. Among his other early collectors were Dr. Christian Brinton and Katherine Dreier's *Société Anonyme*, and later collectors included Harry Abrams and Joseph Hirschhorn.

Isamu Noguchi, the eminent Japanese American sculptor, fascinated by Marussia's splendid head, made a plaster portrait of her in 1933. When I saw it in the great disorder of Burliuk's small flat, I asked Burliuk, "Do you think that fragile plaster head might be damaged? Would Noguchi

mind if I paid for casting two bronzes—one for you and one for me?"
Burliuk nodded in approval. "I'll ask him." Noguchi liked the idea and
had the bronzes cast. He also made a beautiful stand of lignum vitae
wood for my casting and gave it a handsome light green patination. This
striking image is one of his most outstanding portraits. We still have this
remarkable work, which retains its pristine power. When the Russian
French painter Kostia Terechkovitch and his wife visited our home in
Los Angeles many years later, as they entered the dining room and saw
the Noguchi, he exclaimed "Voilà Marussia!"—for he had known the
Burliuks in Russia and Germany.

# 6

# The Musical Art Quartet

Our first series of three concerts in Town Hall went off very well with fine reviews. Among the many personal and musical dividends of chamber music playing are treasured memories which are outside the usual experiences of touring—the rounds of travel, hotels, rehearsals, and concerts in colleges or concert halls. We had many pleasant encounters with interesting audiences and agreeable companions. I had the opportunity to play in and visit many great mansions in New York furnished with handsome European and American antiques and filled with splendid old master paintings and sculptures.

Vivid memories remain of the special occasions we participated in at the Bohemian Society. One outstanding event was our world premiere of Efrem Zimbalist's string quartet. Even more memorable was the program to honor Fritz Kreisler's fiftieth birthday. Many famous musicians came to this celebration. There were many tributes and speeches by Dr. Walter Damrosch, Harold Bauer (president of the Bohemian Society), and others. It was a most distinguished gathering attended by leading violinists, cellists, pianists, conductors, and New York's musical elite. Each member of our quartet received the three-volume set of Thayer's *The Life of Ludwig van Beethoven* as a memento of our performance. Jascha Heifetz, the only great violinist absent, was touring in Japan and sent a congratulatory cable.

During a wonderful dinner with many champagne toasts, Harold Bauer announced that the Warburgs had loaned their quartet of Stradivarius instruments for the evening and that everyone wanted to hear Kreisler play (this had all been arranged beforehand, but we had no opportunity to rehearse with Kreisler). He graciously consented to perform with our quartet and made a most charming speech in his soft Viennese accent: "I am most grateful for this magnificent tribute and I will play only one movement as first violin, and as I look over this distinguished audience, I will only perform on the condition that some of my colleagues will also play in the Schubert quartet." So with general applause Kreisler moved to the first stand, Sascha Jacobsen went to the second stand, Marie Roemaet-Rosanoff went to the cello stand, and I followed with the viola to the small podium. Kreisler shook hands with each of us before we began playing and thanked us for performing with him!

The first movement of the Schubert A Minor Quartet was unforgettable for everyone. Kreisler unlocked the case of the Warburg Stradivarius and just barely tuned it before commencing to play in an angelic manner, with such an incredible tonal beauty and depth of expression, conveyed with such simplicity, that we practically held our breath to listen to him. When the movement ended, Kreisler again shook hands with us and thanked us for playing with him, replacing the Stradivarius in its case.

Now there was a great to-do! People shouted all sorts of suggestions. Leopold Auer was there, so an outcry arose that he should play next in this Schubert quartet. He graciously consented, came to the podium, and began plucking the strings of the Titian Strad. He realized when he glanced at the music that he didn't have his glasses and couldn't see without them. William Kroll, a fine violinist who had studied with Kneisel, was close by and asked, "Professor Auer, would you like to try my glasses?" Auer put on the proffered *brillen* and announced *"Das ist besser,"* and then, sliding them halfway down his nose, added, *"Das ist sehr gut."* Kreisler said, "Professor, may I assist you as second violin?" Auer was obviously pleased, so Kreisler sat at the second stand and played on the "Spanish" Strad. Marie and I stayed the course. The aged professor manfully struggled with the first few lines and then without any indication skipped about half a page that he couldn't see. Kreisler gave us a broad wink and we all jumped with him, as it was obvious where Auer was playing. He was slightly flustered but a good sport, so it turned out well. We ended the shortest Schubert andante ever played to a lot of applause.

Cries arose for Mischa Elman, who always enjoyed playing and said, "Certainly." He walked to the podium and tried the Stradivarius with a dazzling display of pyrotechnics. As he sat down to play, Willie Kroll walked over to me and asked, "Louis, would you like to change places with me? I'd like to play viola." I was eager to listen and thought it a good idea. He took over the viola and Mischa requested that Eddy Bachman join him; then he summoned Horace Britt, an excellent French cellist, who regularly played in his quartet.

The Minuetto (third movement) gathers warmth as it rises to an emotional crescendo. Mischa became so engrossed in projecting the maximum expression that his bow got caught in the strings. This rarely happens, but with a strange violin and bow and the excitement, he could not disentangle the bow for a few bars. It all ended well, for he infused the movement with his exceptionally beautiful tone and poetic concepts.

A clamor arose to hear Carl Flesch play the last movement. Sascha returned to play second, William Kroll continued as viola, and Marie went to the cello stand. This was less fortunate, for Carl Flesch, though a great musician, was not born with the intuitive facility that many fiddlers have. I greatly respected him after hearing his debut recital at Town Hall. It was an admirable exhibition of formalized perfection from the first to the last note, played in fine taste. Nevertheless, everything he did had to be worked out and analyzed. Flesch always had to warm up his fingers, and on this occasion that was not possible. He tuned his strings and started in cold, but it was not his night. His performance was heavy and lacked Schubertian charm. Nonetheless, the evening was exhilarating and the audience was extremely happy to have shared Kreisler's engaging personality and heavenly sound. His remarkable modesty and simplicity of manner remains a precious memory.

Another unforgettable evening, at the Bierhofs' apartment, had Kreisler as first violin, Sascha as second, Felix Salmond as cellist, and myself as violist. George Gershwin was a guest. He loved chamber music as well as orchestral and opera performances. After we played Mozart and Schubert quartets, everyone urged George to play. He often "took over" at chamber music parties. Whenever George started playing his own arrangements of his enchanting tunes, no one could stop him until he was exhausted, but everyone was delighted to listen for as long as he wanted to play. He had invented a musical language uniquely his own, quite different from that of most jazz pianists. It was a great loss that these impromptu flights of his creative imagination were never written down. The piano rolls he made completely lacked the inspired freshness of his spontaneous improvisations. He croaked the witty lyrics of his brother Ira in a most engaging manner. Kreisler was as enthralled as the rest of us.

This evening George stopped, after completely captivating us for about an hour, and asked, "Mr. Kreisler, would you play for us? Something from *Apple Blossoms*?" This Kreisler operetta, a current Broadway success composed in the Viennese Lehár tradition, had beautiful melodies, colorful orchestration, and the charm and grace that personified Kreisler. Kreisler sat down at the piano and played with the same tonal beauty and seductive appeal that he brought to the violin. George was as fascinated as the rest of our group. At these chamber music evenings George was always unpretentious, affable, and friendly. His modesty was inversely proportionate to his major contribution to American musical comedies and his astonishing success in the symphonic and operatic world.

In 1927, the Walter W. Naumburg Award competition for piano and violin was announced. The prizewinners were to receive a debut recital at New York's Town Hall. I decided to try for it. The jury included Felix Salmond and Madame Leah Luboshutz, a violin professor at the Curtis Institute. The Naumburg Foundation did not announce the winners, and the *New York Times* morning edition did not mention them either, so I called the Foundation and asked the secretary, "Could you please tell me who won the Naumburg awards? This is Louis Kaufman." She replied, "Oh! Didn't they tell you? You won for violin and Adele Marcus won for piano."

My violin debut under such distinguished sponsorship attracted almost a full Town Hall on 29 October 1928. There was terrific competition that evening, for the Metropolitan Opera opened their season, and the pianist Rudolph Ganz was playing at Carnegie Hall. My program included Handel's Sonata in D, Lalo's *Symphonie Espagnole,* Chausson's *Poème,* and smaller works, ending with Paganini's "La Clochette." My reviews were gratifying.

*New York Sun* 30 October 1928: "Mr. Kaufman acquitted himself with much credit—with generally fine tone, clarity of outline, and good style. The Chausson *Poème* gave the young player opportunity to display his never-failing accuracy of pitch and a commendable sense of poetic coloring. An audience of good size gave the young artist the warm approval he deserved."

My old grade-school friend, the painter Marcus Rothcowitz (Mark Rothko), shared a flat with a pianist from Portland, Gordon Soulé. I had studied piano with Gordon's aunt, Marie Soulé, as a lad in Portland, and Gordon and I became friends. Gordon had recently become the director of Artists and Repertory for the Edison Company, and he asked me to make a recording. He approached me with, "Louis, would you like to earn twenty-five dollars?" A recording session was scheduled and I made simple arrangements of two popular songs that Gordon had suggested, "Ramona" and "House on the Hill." A colleague, Louis Spielman, made his own piano accompaniment. Edison supervised the recording session. It was not easy to play in his studio. Thomas Edison was deaf and judged sound by a needle indicator. When I played, normal vibrato caused the

Louis wins the Walter W. Naumburg Award for violin, 1927.

needle to shake, and Edison thought this showed an uncertain bow arm. So he fired both Gordon and me. However, I received the promised fee, the record was commercially released, and I entered recording history. Gordon became A & R director for Gennett Records and engaged me to form a trio to accompany an (unmemorable) Irish tenor.

Another interesting concert was the quartet's engagement to play at the Curtis Institute of Music in Philadelphia. We were all delighted to perform the Brahms F Minor Piano Quintet with the celebrated Polish pianist, Josef Casimir Hofmann, Dean of the Institute. Our rehearsals were in his beautiful home in nearby Merion, near the famous Barnes Foundation collection of major art works by Paul Cézanne, Pierre Auguste Renoir, Henri Matisse, and others.

During rehearsals, I was very impressed with Hofmann's complete mastery of every detail and the great clarity and vitality of his playing. There was no hint of the awesome *"terribilità"* of the virtuoso pianist that can easily override a symphony, but he had unusual sensitivity for the delicate balance of our quartet. The youthful singing quality of his playing inspired us. I glanced at his piano score—it was so marked up with indications for fingerings and dynamics that one could hardly see the original printing. When I expressed my enthusiasm for his inspired freshness of approach, he replied "Young man, only after I have studied a work inside and outside and become honestly weary with it, can I begin to express some freedom and liberty in performance." In later years Annette and I never missed a Hofmann recital (or any performance of Sergey Rachmaninoff or Vladimir Horowitz).

I was very interested in hearing new instrumental music. I attended some of the historic Copland-Sessions concerts, as well as the premiere of George Gershwin as pianist in *Rhapsody in Blue,* with the Paul Whiteman Orchestra, at the Aeolian Hall on 12 February 1924. Another unforgettable concert of the New York Symphony Society was the premiere of Gershwin's *An American in Paris,* conducted by Dr. Walter Damrosch at Carnegie Hall, 13 December 1928. Gershwin's compositions brought engaging vitality and originality to the concert world.

Mr. and Mrs. Charles Mitchell, friends of the Zimbalists and Garretts, were among our quartet's first sponsors. In 1929, Mrs. Mitchell invited us to play concerts for a week at their baronial mansion in Southampton on Long Island. In addition to our fee, we were handsomely provided with room and board. We played nightly programs for their guests. Occasionally Mrs. Mitchell, who had studied piano with Ernest Schelling, joined us in playing a piano quartet or quintet. Mr. Mitchell, an important financier, did not care for chamber music and preferred to sit on a back terrace and chat with his cronies during our performances.

At the end of this pleasant interlude, Mrs. Mitchell expressed her tremendous pleasure with our music-making, saying, "I would like to reciprocate by giving you some financial advice. As you know, Charlie is chairman of the board of Anaconda Copper and City National Bank and other companies. He said to tell you to buy Anaconda now, at $149 per share. Beg, borrow if necessary, for it will double or triple in value very soon."

Returning to New York in early fall, I called a stockbroker. He advised me to buy on 5 percent margin, so I might control a larger amount of shares with my $2,000 in savings. I followed this expert advice. I called my father in Portland, who had been urging me to ask the wealthy patrons of the quartet what investment advice they might have. He, in turn, advised relatives and friends of this great opportunity.

Within a week my stockbroker called with news that Anaconda and the market had fallen drastically, and that I must put in another $2,000 or be wiped out. There was no possibility of further investment. I quickly learned this financial Moloch was not for me. Anaconda fell within a few months to seven dollars per share. I resolved to buy art rather than stock certificates in the future.

Years later in Europe, people often asked me, "Is it true that some Americans killed themselves after the stock market crashed in 1929?" I had to answer yes. After World War II, when people learned how precious life and freedom were and how little possessions mattered, it seemed inconceivable to them that those Americans had so little appreciation of the true values of existence.

I acquired the habit of visiting the Averys frequently to see what Milton would be turning out next. In spite of poverty, he painted with an inspired fury that quickly consolidated his position as a chef d'école. Sally prepared laundry boards covered with dish toweling as a surface for his paintings, as regular canvas was too costly. This laconic and subtle artist became a strong influence on such "advanced" American artists as Mark Rothko, whom I first took to the Avery studio, Adolph Gottlieb, George Constant, John Graham, and many others. These evening visits were engrossing for I was irresistibly drawn to the sober, rich poetry of Avery's canvases.

It seems improbable now, but hardly anyone I cajoled into visiting the Averys (with possible purchase in mind) would buy his work. Exceptions included my dentist, Dr. Abelson, who bought a landscape, and Terese Schwarz, a friend from one of the quartet's concerts in Europe, who sat for a stunning portrait, which she acquired. When I took Adelyn Breeskin of the Baltimore Museum to the Avery studio, she fell in love with Avery's work. She later arranged an Avery touring show under the auspices of the Ford Foundation and an Avery retrospective at the Baltimore

Museum of Art. Annette and I were pleased to loan Avery's portrait of Louis Michel Eilshemius for the exhibit.

When French dealers Durand-Ruel and Rosenberg settled in New York, they were delighted by his painterly qualities. A half-century of world turmoil and innumerable artistic developments have only confirmed the fundamental validity of Avery's artistic vision. His grand concept of space and personal use of color are now regarded as some of the best contemporary work in Europe and America.

# 7

# In Baltimore and Capri with the Musical Art Quartet

The roaring, roistering English colony of Maryland, so-called because the inhabitants . . . were prone to make merry and get fuddled with mint juleps.

Washington Irving, *A History of New York*, 1809

In 1930 Felix Warburg loaned us his remarkable Stradivarius Quartet for an indefinite period. What an opportunity for us to play and study these superb instruments. I was privileged to play the "Lord MacDonald" viola, reputed as the most perfect of the nine Stradivarius violas that make up this incredible master's oeuvre. It had a heavenly contralto sound, not the baritone sonority of the Brescian luthier Gasparo da Salo, preferred by most violists.

Ambassador John Work Garrett and his wife, Alice, engaged us for six weeks to stay in a spacious cottage on the grounds of Evergreen House, their home in Baltimore, and perform string quartets. Evergreen House was filled with souvenirs of the Garrett family and beautiful paintings by Giovanni Battista Tiepolo and Canaletto. They also had fine twentieth-century paintings by Picasso, Bonnard, Utrillo, and Modigliani. The Ambassador had a splendid collection of Persian miniatures of the sixteenth and seventeenth centuries. His important library contained, among other rare editions, a Gutenberg Bible and a first folio of Shakespeare. They later bequeathed their estate and library to Johns Hopkins University. On one library wall, Miguel Covarrubias, the distinguished Mexican writer and artist, painted a small mural depicting a

On the grounds of Evergreen House, the Garretts' Baltimore estate. *From left:* Louis Kaufman, Sascha Jacobsen, Efrem Zimbalist, Marie Roemaet-Rosanoff, Samuel Chotzinoff, and Paul Bernard.

Brazilian scene, with tropical foliage, exotic birds, and animals. This "memory-scape" recalled the Ambassador's official years of service there.

Alice Garrett was a serious student of classic dance. She was a patroness of the Spanish artist Ignacio Zuloaga, studied painting with him, and worked diligently. Zuloaga made an excellent portrait of her in Spanish costume à la Velázquez and a dignified portrait of the Ambassador in modern dress. Both of the Garretts valued participation in the arts, fine achievement, and music.

We played two string quartets of Romantic and modern repertoire six times each week in their private small theater, decorated by the Russian artist Léon Bakst, who created scenery for Diaghilev's Ballets Russes. Bakst, a close friend of the Garretts, designed Madame Garrett's clothes for official affairs. These private musicales occasionally were preceded by ceremonial dinners attended by interesting personalities: diplomats, senators, congressmen, singers Alma Gluck and Lucrezia Bori, violinist-composer Efrem Zimbalist, pianist-critic Samuel Chotzinoff, and *Baltimore Sun* editor Hamilton Owens (who persuaded Penguin Books to move to America from England) with his wife, Olga. Art world guests often included Douglas and Winnie Gordon, collectors of eighteenth-century French drawings; MacGill James, later director of the National Gallery of Art in Washington, D.C.; Mrs. Adelyn Breeskin, later director of the Baltimore Museum (who wrote a fine book about Mary Cassatt); John Erskine, novelist; Miguel Covarrubias; and the John Nicholas Browns from Providence, whose family established Brown University in Rhode Island (their son John Carter became director of the National Gallery of Art in the 1980s).

Usually before evening performances, after dining in our cottage on excellent Southern cuisine, Sascha and Paul puffed on their pipes and Sascha suggested, "Why don't you try it, Louis? It's very relaxing." My father never smoked and it had never tempted me. I bought a corncob pipe and some tobacco, tried it for three evenings, became nauseated, found it very disagreeable, and decided smoking was not for me. Later I learned even hardened smokers are wary of the astringent combination of corncobs and tobacco.

Being in Baltimore under such distinguished patronage gave us "open sesame" to the homes of many of the Garretts' friends. We were frequently invited to preconcert parties where they served mint juleps. A dinner at the home of MacGill James introduced our gregarious quartet to the julep's insidious effects. We each drank one, and our host pressed us to have another. We accepted, having no idea of its potency. We all became drunk and hardly remembered playing that evening's program. We had the hazy impression we were playing very well. Everything was bathed in a rosy glow.

Early the next morning Madame Garrett came to our cottage, indignantly demanding, "What on earth happened to all of you last night?" Sascha asked, "What do you mean?" She continued, "I have never heard you play so badly. What was the matter?" Marie said, "We don't know, we tried our best." Madame Garrett was very fond of me and said accusingly, "Even Louis sounded dreadful!" Then she added suspiciously, "Where did you go for dinner? What did you do before the concert?" On learning we had dined at the Jameses' home and had two mint juleps each, she decided we could attend parties, but she would call each host to state we must be limited to *one* of those drinks. We willingly accepted this restriction, and our concerts returned to professional standards.

During our sojourn at Evergreen House, Efrem (Zimmie) and Alma Zimbalist were also houseguests. They were always gracious and charming, and Alma was delightfully vivacious. They rarely spoke of their successful careers, unless to account amusing experiences.

In conversation with our quartet, Zimmie remarked that many talented students enjoyed playing fast and carelessly for the sheer pleasure of scampering on the fingerboard, with the result that they "practiced" without progress. Famous for the extraordinary fleetness and suppleness of his left-hand technique, he stressed that technical details should be practiced in slow motion at one-tenth the normal tempo, so players could hear their exact intonation and analyze any technical inaccuracies. As I walked on the grounds of the estate, I would hear Zimmie practicing in this slow careful way. He then would speed up and play the phrases at faster-than-normal tempi to prove his control!

Our after-concert parties usually ended with high jinks and we were not the better for them. One night, I performed a burlesque dance with a white sheet draped over my head, while accompanying myself playing Saint-Saëns's *The Dying Swan* on the viola. I ended up lying on my back with my legs in the air, while I played a "dying tremolo" as I "expired." MacGill James grabbed my legs and dragged me over the polished floor to great applause, which ended the festivities. This was such a success that I was urged to repeat it at a subsequent party. Then, like most capers, it would not bear further repetition—and entered into the legend of the Musical Art Quartet.

When John Work Garrett was appointed American Ambassador to Italy, Madame Garrett offered to take our quartet with them to Capri for six weeks in the spring, after our New York season closed. They provided us with first-class passage on the Cosulich Italian Line. Marie's cellist husband, Lieff, accompanied us at his own expense. We crossed the Atlantic in unaccustomed luxury. I was impressed with everything, including the elegant hors d'oeuvres of Caspian caviar on tiny blini (thin Russian pancakes).

In Naples, we transferred to a small launch bound for Capri, dazzled by the sun and view of the large harbor and hilly city, with imposing Mount Vesuvius facing us. As there were no landing facilities on the island, we reached the Marina Grande in small rowboats. We engaged two horse-drawn carriages to transport us and our luggage. Then we set off to find the villa on the Marina Piccola, with its own rocky beach, which the Garretts had rented for us (complete with housekeeper and cook) from an Italian count, who undoubtedly overcharged them for the miserable repasts we were served. We were tortured by mosquitos, which were not deterred by white netting that covered our beds. However, the beach was excellent and the salt water seemed to soothe the bites. I swam three or four times daily.

For their residence, the Garretts had rented the world-famous home of Dr. Axel Munthe, mainly constructed by his own hands. This successful physician chose the highest precipice in Anacapri for his dwelling, on the site of one of Emperor Tiberius's villas. He named it San Michele after the patron saint of the local parish. Italian princes and millionaires were his patients, and he used their fees to care for and feed poor people living in Roman slums. His successful book *The Story of San Michele* was translated into twenty-seven languages. It was written at the suggestion of one of his visitors, Henry James.

The house was small, with few rooms and little furniture, but there was a Dürer etching and a Greek bas-relief on the whitewashed walls. Munthe built loggias, terraces, and pergolas around it, so he could watch the clouds, Mount Vesuvius, the sun and sea. The stately cypress trees he planted formed a pathway to the chapel, where we played for the Garretts late each afternoon. These concerts were solely for their own pleasure, and they seemed enchanted to hear string quartets in such an idyllic place.

Every afternoon shortly before four o'clock, the Garretts would send their car and chauffeur to bring us and our instruments up to the chapel. Immediately after our concert, the chauffeur, Ernesto, would appear to take us to our unappetizing supper at our villa. However, we never complained, as Marie's husband thought it might offend the rascally count and make him anti-Semitic!

Only one visitor joined us that spring for a concert, which ended with an unforgettable conversation. The guest was Dr. Axel Munthe himself, a most charming old gentleman, tall, thin, and slightly deaf. We

The Musical Art Quartet en route to Naples, 1930.

played a short program of Mozart and a Beethoven Opus 18 string quartet. Dr. Munthe listened patiently and offered us polite compliments at the end of our program. I sensed he did not particularly care for this type of music.

As we left the little chapel, we had to walk single-file along the narrow tree-lined footpath which led to Dr. Munthe's villa. Our quartet proceeded like little quail, trailing the Ambassador, Madame Garrett, and Dr. Munthe. We were all greatly amused by their ensuing conversation. Due to Dr. Munthe's deafness, Madame Garrett was compelled to speak rather loudly: "Dr. Munthe, we had the most dreadful experience last night. I can't begin to tell you how distressing it was. About three o'clock in the morning, we were awakened by a fusillade of shots, which frightened us out of our wits. We didn't know what had happened. We rushed to the front of the villa, wondering what this commotion was all about and whether we were in a war with some *banditti!*"

Dr. Munthe replied, "Madame Garrett, have you studied the mosaic stone floor that we installed in the little chapel? You know, it was dug up in the vicinity and I think dates back to the time of Tiberius. It is very rare. We had to remove it, stone by stone, and then reconstruct it here." Madame Garrett continued, "After we ran on the porch, the shots were flying all around us and I shouted, as loudly as I could, "*Non fare la caccia qui!*' [don't hunt here], and still bullets kept coming towards us. I thought the Ambassador's life was in mortal danger!" Dr. Munthe continued unruffled, "But you know, Madame Garrett, perhaps the most interesting object of all is the Eros, the small bronze at the entrance. It is one of the rare Greek works that was discovered along the seacoast. I was extremely happy to have found it and to be able to place it in that niche." Madame Garrett persisted, "My shouts seemed to have a calming effect. They finally stopped the shooting, but we were terribly frightened. It was a horrible experience. We could have been wounded or killed! How do you control these outrageous poachers that insist on entering the grounds and shooting recklessly?" Dr. Munthe commented, "I'd also like to call your attention to the marble Greek column which forms part of the chapel's portico. I take great pride in it, you know, because we had to roll it up here in a most primitive way to install it without any damage." By this time, we had arrived at the villa, and the quartet departed with Ernesto, leaving the Garretts and Dr. Munthe to continue their conversation of non sequiturs. This surreal conversation gave us a nonsensical slogan for the rest of the season, *Non fare la caccia qui!*

It is very easy to join in the Italian way of life. We practiced daily in view of the sea, swam, played a concert every afternoon, and were surrounded by beautiful vistas as we journeyed to and from the Munthe villa. We often joined the evening *passeggiata* (promenade) to the main piazza, where we would look into the fashionable cafe, with its accordion player and violinist who performed for tango dancers and tipplers.

Paul and I were interested in the Blue Grotto, a famous tourist attraction. One day we engaged a rower to take us there. This natural deep grotto, cut into high rocks on the seashore, was near two huge rocks called I Faraglioni. Our guide brought along a good-sized flask of Chianti to temper his boredom during this frequent pilgrimage. After entering the grotto, we decided to swim in its crystalline waters. This was a mystical experience. With the afternoon sun's reflections, the deep cavern began to glow with a magical cerulean blue that painter Fra Angelico might have envied. To see our limbs gliding in this mysterious element had a strange aesthetic dimension. It seemed a sort of aqueous music, if such a transmutation is possible. When we had fully savored this extraordinary experience, we clambered back into the rowboat, to return to our villa.

Meanwhile, our guide, fortified by the Chianti, was in a jolly mood. As he began rowing, he started to sing, not badly, and soon was so inspired that he abandoned the oars and stood up to dance, to our consternation. We immediately yelled, "Sit down!" and grabbed the oars to row ourselves back as dusk approached, with his accompanying serenade. The unforgettable ambiance of the Blue Grotto vibrated in my senses for a long time.

Soon after, I decided to train for a long swim to I Faraglioni, the famed Capri landmark, about two miles from our villa. Each day, I would swim a little further towards it. Finally, I was ready for this feat and asked Paul to follow me in a *sandolino* (a narrow boat, easy to handle, with a doubled-paddled oar, rather like an Alaskan kayak). I intended to swim to Faraglioni and back, not realizing how far it was. I swam at a leisurely pace and finally reached my goal, but then Paul shouted, "For God's sake get in the boat! We've got to hurry back—we'll miss our concert!" He had a watch, and aware of the late hour, pulled me into the *sandolino,* saying, "You've broken all records for slowness." If I had continued plodding along, we would have returned at sunset!

Shortly before our departure, Alice Garrett suggested that we play a benefit concert for the local hospital. Dr. Munthe may have proposed the idea. We spent six enjoyable weeks, isolated from natives and tourists on our own rocky beach. We deeply appreciated the Garretts' giving us luxurious passage to Naples and back to New York, as well as a private villa, housekeeper, and cook, however incompetent. We were delighted to join in such a worthy effort by performing for the local Capri crowd, and looked forward with pleasure to playing for a large audience in the grand ballroom of the Grand Hotel Quisisana, the finest hotel in Capri.

Before the program, we were served a superb dinner in the imposing dining salon, and regretted we had to be prudent and dine lightly, for we had to play well that evening. We ruefully agreed that although Madame

Garrett generously wanted us to have the rest and quiet of a private dwelling and cook, we would have been much more comfortable at the Quisisana—and it might well have been less costly for the Garretts! The concert was a huge success in raising a large sum for the Capri Hospital, and a musical triumph for *Ambasciatore e Ambasciatrice* Garrett and *Il Quartetto Americano*. We only regretted that we met some interesting and charming people just as we were leaving this enchanting island.

# 8

# Paris!

What a large amount of adventures may be grasped within this little
span of life, by him who interests his heart in everything, and who, having eyes to see what time and chance are perpetually holding out to him
as he journeyeth on his way.

Laurence Sterne, *A Sentimental Journey through France and Italy*
*by Mr. Yorick, 1768*

While packing to go home, I suddenly realized we were close to
France. What a great opportunity! Instead of using the expensive boat fare to return to New York in luxury, Paul and I
could take a train to Paris, live there a month, and return via an inexpensive boat without any additional expense. Paul liked the notion, and we
immediately asked Madame Garrett's permission. She graciously agreed,
saying "What a capital idea!" and on the spot wrote two checks, handing
them to us with heartiest good wishes.

We thanked the Garretts and made our farewells to Sascha and his
wife, Kitty, and the Rosanoffs as they left on their sybaritic sailing. Paul
and I set off from Naples with second-class railway tickets. We shunned
expensive sleeping cars and meals on trains and slept in modest hotels
near the station, only traveling during the day. We bought inexpensive
box lunches in stations, with roast chicken, pasta, a small flask of wine,
cheese, roll, and an apple or orange.

Arriving in Paris, we parted ways; Paul went to stay with friends in the
outskirts, where he could play tennis and enjoy country life. I settled in a
comfortable room at the small Hôtel de Chevreuse, in the Eighth arron-
dissement near the Avenue de Wagram, with a demi-pension serving delicious *cuisine bourgeois*. Then I started off to see the treasures of the

Musée du Louvre, the Musée du Jeu de Paume, and art galleries on the Right and Left Banks of the Seine.

My first visit to Paris was exhilarating. The patina of history and the beauty of art infused the city with sheer elegance. The handsome public buildings, palaces, the magnificent cathedrals, the beautiful parks, and spacious tree-lined boulevards of the City of Light had irresistible appeal. It is quite impossible for me to list the myriad charms of Paris and the glories of nearby Versailles and Fontainebleau, which I hastened to visit. I was deeply impressed by the former grandeur of France.

In the summer of 1930, Paris was without industrial smog and the automobiles, trucks, and buses that clog the streets now; the atmosphere was ideal. I walked on uncrowded boulevards and side streets, browsed in galleries and bookshops. I strolled along the quais on the Seine, looking at and buying books, bric-a-brac, and prints. Paris was vitally important as a contemporary center for the creation of music, art, literature, and drama. I visited Zborowski's gallery on Rue de Seine, on the site of the printer that had produced Balzac's books. Zborowski "discovered" such gifted painters as Modigliani, Utrillo, Soutine, Pinkus Kremegne, and Henri Hayden, among others. There I also met the fascinating Russian artist who adopted the name John Graham. This dark-haired, slightly bald painter, née Dombrowski, appeared taller thanks to the erect carriage he had acquired as a cavalry officer. We visited galleries together and had spirited discussions about American art. We browsed through the Marché aux Puces (flea market) looking for Chinese nineteenth-century paintings on glass, which interested John. I bought a few small Peruvian bronzes, which turned out to be early Chimu works.

Graham considered Stuart Davis the greatest American painter alive. I agreed that Davis was a fine artist but countered by telling him of the great qualities of Milton Avery. Graham had never heard of him. We made a date to visit the Avery studio when we returned to New York.

At Galerie Zak I met the charming widow of the gifted Polish Jewish painter Eugène Zak, and bought two Othon Friesz paintings. Stanley Zborowski, brother of the dealer (who later inherited the gallery) took me to Friesz's atelier on rue Notre-Dame-des-Champs. I was impressed by Friesz and also met France's Minister of Education, M. Édouard Herriot. I reflected on the fact that the United States did not have such a ministry in our President's cabinet. Such a national official in America might have avoided educational inequalities, which historically have caused so much strife. Stanley also guided me to Giorgio de Chirico's atelier. At this period Chirico had abandoned his early surrealist manner and was searching for an expression closer to "old masters."

Graham introduced me to the Russian painter Jean Pougny. I was fascinated by the sensitive poetry and subtle color of his paintings. Pougny had been a futurist and friend of David Burliuk in Russia and Berlin. His father had been an amateur cellist and bequeathed Pougny a Stradivarius violin and cello. After Pougny and his wife, Sonya, left the Soviet Union, he sold the instruments to Hill's in London, which gave Pougny funds to survive the desperate days before he found collectors and a gallery.

Arriving in Paris, he discovered the paintings of Pierre Bonnard and Édouard Vuillard, which he adored. At the Marché aux Puces he searched for worthless old paintings, which he bought for a few francs and used as canvas to paint on. This gave his works a richer patination.

Pougny loved classical music and violin music in particular. They invited me for a Russian dinner at their small atelier on the rue Vércingétorix (demolished to make way for the huge Cité Montparnasse complex). Pougny asked if I would bring my violin and play for them after dinner. Sonya prepared Ukrainian borscht (with beef, cabbage, beets, and tomatoes) accompanied by *piroshki* (tiny meat-filled rolls). We had varied Russian *zakuski* (hors d'oeuvres), served with vodka. She must have spent the entire day preparing this excellent dinner.

That evening I bought two of Pougny's views of Paris: one of the Porte de Vincennes and the other of a busy little street near his studio. Afterwards Pougny asked me to play something. After drinking vodka, what to play? I began with some movements of Bach partitas and sonatas and then played Paganini caprices until I was exhausted. I wanted to leave at midnight, but Pougny, enchanted by the music, hated to see me go. He impulsively offered, "Just one more request—if you'll play the Bach chaconne, I'll give you any one of my gouaches or watercolors that you choose." With this irresistible incentive, I played the fourteen-minute chaconne as well as I could and as my reward selected a gouache dated 1919, a semi-cubist body of a cellist holding a cello. It later gave me much pleasure as a souvenir of my youth in Montparnasse.

Sonya Pougny supplemented their income in the 1930s by acting as dealer for their artist friends. I bought two Konstantin Terechkovitch paintings from her; an early André Lanskoy interior, which depicted Fernand Léger; portraits of Jean and Sonya Pougny; Lanskoy's self-portrait; and Terechkovitch, Guillaume Apollinaire, and Marie Laurencin seated around a table bearing a small Christmas tree. Graham invited me to join him at Oskar Kokoschka's atelier, where we both were surprised at not seeing *any* of his paintings. Kokoschka complained to us that no one paid any attention to him in Paris, but there was much acclaim for frivolous work. He only displayed a few artifacts from a recent visit to North Africa, and seemed to be very interested in archaeology. He showed us a few pencil sketches of North African scenes.

Graham and I visited the Galérie Ascher on the rue de Seine, which became my favorite haunt. Ascher had African, Egyptian, early Greek, and pre-Columbian art from Mexico and Peru, all selected with discrimination. I purchased some elegant African masks and figurines, a remarkable horn carved from an ivory elephant tusk, and an exquisitely carved Baoulé head.

I also picked up a first edition of James Joyce's masterpiece *Ulysses*. On returning to New York, I learned our customs considered Joyce's book scandalous and had barred it from entry into our country. I was informed I would not be permitted to bring in any of my recent acquisitions if I refused to sign a document authorizing customs to destroy the book, which they had seized from my luggage. I reluctantly signed the paper in order to retrieve my paintings and sculptures.

I visited the Averys as soon as possible. Milton decided I looked "older and dissipated" and made a portrait of me in a white shirt with reddish suspenders, a departure from his more sober palette. Graham had accompanied me and announced with typical Russian exuberance, "Milton is the greatest American painter," and for a time he actually adopted Milton's imagery and color, before going on to a Picasso influence. I bought a Graham portrait of Eleanore, his actress wife, which Annette and I donated to the National Gallery of American Art in Washington, D.C., in the 1980s.

Graham invited me to join him in a visit to Arshile Gorky's small Greenwich Village studio on lower Broadway. We entered a cluttered room filled with paintings of various sizes, many obviously works in progress. While Graham and Gorky were talking, I saw a large upright canvas on a stretcher, face down. Curious to see what the surface displayed, I couldn't resist turning it around. Instantly, Gorky yelled: "You stupid foolish man! You've ruined my composition! I am painting that side as a background for a still life! GET OUT!" To my great disappointment, this ended our visit. I had hoped to buy a canvas . . . .

The quartet's routine rehearsals and periodic concerts in Town Hall, with brief out-of-town tours, had become less appealing. I was offered the post of principal violist in the New York Philharmonic Orchestra, then conducted by Willem Mengelberg, but I refused, as I did not wish to continue my life as a violist. I continued to practice violin daily and stashed the viola under my bed when I returned from quartet rehearsals, forgetting it until the next event.

# Italian Concerts

*Encore Paris*

In spring 1931, Ambassador and Madame Garrett engaged our quartet for a tour of major Italian cities to benefit the National Committee of Mothers and Children for Prevention of Childhood Tuberculosis. The Garretts provided all our transportation and expenses so that all concert receipts would go directly to this worthy cause. The Italian announcements were impressive: *"Concerto beneficio offerta dalla L.L.E.E. ambasciatore e l'ambasciatrice d'America."* What a regal example of the Garretts' customary generosity!

Our tour began after another luxurious Atlantic crossing on the Italian Line to Genoa, where we were met by Ernesto, the Garretts' chauffeur, and proceeded to Rome in their spacious Lincoln limousine. We were elegantly housed in the Rospigliosi palace (the American Embassy residence) for one week. The palace contains Guido Reni's celebrated painting *Aurora.* Our quartet played two concerts in the grand ballroom of the palace for small, distinguished audiences. Between rehearsals and concerts, I managed to visit the Borghese Gallery, Roman Forum, and Sistine Chapel in Vatican City.

One afternoon Madame Garrett invited me to accompany her to an exhibit of contemporary Italian painters, where she acquired two large handsome paintings by Felice Casorati. I bought two small canvases by Massimo Campigli—three disembodied heads (like Coptic portraits), and a portrait of his Romanian sister-in-law. Both Madame Garrett's and my purchases were exhibited at the Embassy before our concerts.

Our next official concert in Rome at the Doria Pamphili palace, sponsored by Prince Doria, attracted a most distinguished audience. We were very impressed to meet the celebrated composer Ottorino Respighi and his very attractive Mexican wife, also a composer. Maestro Respighi was most complimentary about our quartet's performances.

For our tour, the Garretts' oversized limo carried us and all our luggage comfortably through the beautiful Italian countryside. In his smart uniform and cap, Ernesto resembled a general in a De Sica film. The effect of our quartet arriving in such an elegant limo, with Ernesto at the wheel, soon proved disadvantageous. Seeing us descend from the limo with Ernesto's aid, concierges charged us exorbitant rates.

We devised a stratagem. I was appointed negotiator. Ernesto would park the limo around a corner, out of sight. Then I would enter the hotel lobby without a jacket, hat, or tie, and request modest accommodations for traveling musicians, three rooms (one with two beds) with meals. (Paul and I shared quarters.) The tactic worked! We obtained customary tourist rates. Without exception, when the limo rolled up to unload my colleagues, instruments, and baggage with Ernesto's supervision, the concierge would clutch his head with both hands, sighing *"Mama mia!"* or *"Maledizione!"* over the lost chance to raise the rates!

Our Naples concert gave me a brief glimpse of Pompeii and some idea of life in ancient Roman times. Our concerts in Milan were in the famed Teatro alla Scala. At Parma, we performed in the Ridotto del Teatro Regio, receiving headlines in the newspaper, *"Ovazione e applauso prolungato."* Before leaving the city we all visited Niccolò Paganini's tomb. In Florence we performed in the imposing *grande sala* of the majestic Palazzo Vecchio. Our "Musical Art Quartetto Americano" received commemorative medals from Naples, Milan, and Parma that were presented to each member. In Venice we played in the elegant eighteenth-century Teatro la Fenice. Our concerts were all gratifying artistic and financial successes.

In Turin our concert was in the Conservatorio Giuseppe Verdi. After the program, the Principessa Yolanda (née Maria José) invited us to perform piano quartets in her private apartment in the Royal Palazzo. Her mother was Belgium's Queen Elisabeth, who had founded the International Music Competition of Belgium to honor her violin teacher Eugène Ysaÿe. The Principessa was an accomplished pianist who had studied seriously with excellent professors. She performed Mozart and Brahms piano quartets with us, and she was very musical. Then she invited Sascha and Marie to join her in a Beethoven piano trio. The small audience included her husband, Prince Umberto, other members of the royal family, and a few intimate friends.

After this tour, my colleagues sailed to New York from Genoa. Once again I used my passage fare to return to Paris via train, for I had friends among artists and art dealers awaiting me. I settled again comfortably at the Hôtel de Chevreuse.

The year 1931 brought a vast colonial exposition, which I found enchanting. I visited the site several times to admire the gigantic replica of Angkor Wat, an immense architectural and sculptural creation of the ancient Khmers. I was fascinated by the sinuous, lithe young temple dancers in exotic and costly costumes whose formalized movements were accompanied by the magical, gently percussive sounds of a large gamelan orchestra.

Entering through a golden door, visitors came upon an *ile de bonheur* (Isle of Happiness) where delicious refreshments were served; ices and champagnes added to the festivity. This stunning introduction to the art and music of Southeast Asia—a region then named Indochina—led to my visiting the Musée Guimet, a treasure house of Khmer and Asiatic arts. The exposition also had an extensive African Pavilion where I bought more small statues, wooden masks, and fetishes for my growing collection.

I chanced to meet Mischa Elman on the Champs-Elysées and he generously invited me to join him in an unforgettable Russian lunch at the Moscow Café, then one of the best in Paris. Mischa was always forthright in saying exactly what he thought. Carl Flesch had asked him, in his professorial manner, *"Was ist ein Ton?"* (What is a tone?), and Mischa quipped (in German) "What you do not have, Professor!" Mischa discussed the vast difference between notoriety, which is fleeting, and fame, which has longer duration. He resented that mediocre efforts in music and the arts often received undue acclaim.

I visited the Paris atelier of Massimo Campigli and his Romanian wife. They had heard of my purchase of his paintings in Rome and were most cordial. He discussed in a most innovative way the subtle style and elegance of Etruscan and Roman art.

I bought a small Rouault landscape from poet–art dealer Van Leer on the rue de Seine. It was not signed, so I left it with the gallery to be sent to me, after Rouault signed it on his return to Paris from a summer holiday. I visited museums and galleries and bought a Souverbie painting from Galérie Bernheim-Jeune.

I thought that flying to London would be a good way to avoid seasickness on the rough Channel. Fortified by a glass of cognac, I made my first flight in a twin-engine airplane without a pressurized cabin or other comforts of present-day air travel.

London was impressive. The grandeur of Regent Street, the great

Victoria and Albert Museum, treasures of the National Gallery, the English painters Turner and Constable, and early English masters at the Tate Gallery fascinated me. I paid my first visit to the historic violin establishment of W. E. Hill & Sons on New Bond Street, which had been in the same site since the time of Stradivari. I attended a performance of Lehár's charming Viennese operetta *The Land of Smiles* and heard the Austrian tenor Richard Tauber sing. The enthusiastic English audience demanded he repeat one of their favorite arias at least ten times!

Returning to New York from Southampton on the *Arnold Bernstein* steamship gave me an opportunity to consider what my future life might be. I wondered whether I would ever fulfill my childhood dream of living in sunny Los Angeles. In New York, the Musical Art Quartet resumed rehearsals, two to five times a week. A brief fall tour in the Midwest gave us the honor of inaugurating a huge new auditorium at Northwestern University in Evanston, Illinois. This hall featured an enormous pipe organ and special lighting effects. We traversed the immense stage to seat ourselves to play a Joseph Haydn quartet of delicate texture. We felt like four acoustical fleas as we tried to project this chamber music into the vast space.

Could the affable stage manager have been influenced by the advanced ideas of composer Alexander Scriabin, who fused sound with corresponding colors, lights, and even odors to accompany his symphonic works? For as we embarked on the first movement, we were surprised by a gradual dimming of the stage lights to match every soft nuance, and a corresponding brightening when we played louder animated passages. In spite of our frantic signals to the stage manager, this ebbing and rising of light continued. Consequently, we dared not play most of Haydn's quartet less than forte, whether or not it made musical sense. We managed to complete the work in spite of patches of Stygian gloom on stage. We retired to the wings to explain to the busy majordomo that it was really necessary for us to see our music! He assured us that all the lighting would be consistent.

We returned on stage to perform a Beethoven Opus 18 Quartet and encountered another trial: the stage lights began to range from tender pinks to light blues and yellows (which nevertheless permitted us to read the music). At intermission, Sascha asked the stage manager to refrain from color-enhanced interpretations of our performances. The manager apologetically explained, "Folks are proud of this new hall. I only wanted to show them lighting possibilities." He cheerfully added, "Would you like to hear our great new organ? I'm sure folks would enjoy it." I wasn't sure the small group of about four hundred chamber music devotees lost in the great hall would agree. However, Sascha, with his lively sense of humor, said, "Why not?" The stage manager was pleased and offered, "You can choose any disc you'd like to hear." Sasha replied, "Play John Philip Sousa's 'The Stars and Stripes Forever.'" A roaring sonority issued from that impressive organ that literally shook the walls and perhaps impressed the audience with this excursion into a boundless sonic future. Then we took our places on stage to conclude our program with Claude Debussy's sensuous impressionistic quartet, returning to the chamber music scale of sound!

On our trip back to New York we consoled ourselves with thoughts that the audience had at least experienced some optimum possibilities of light and sound facilities in the new auditorium. None of us could possibly imagine the sonic disaster that would arrive during the next forty years of our century, when electrified rock music would blast its raucous and deafening influence worldwide.

In Utica, New York, Professor Percy Saunders, a chemistry teacher, warmly welcomed our quartet before a Hamilton College concert. He came backstage to inform us he did not wish to hear the scheduled Grieg quartet, and he handed us parts for the Opus 18 Beethoven Quartet. Sascha decided to humor Professor Saunders, so we performed the unscheduled Beethoven.

After the concert, our quartet dined at a nearby Greek cafe, to while away time before boarding a late train to Manhattan. A group from the Utica audience recognized us, came to our table with compliments, and also expressed disappointment that we had not played the Grieg quartet. Sascha offered, "We'll play it for you here."

We took our instruments out of their cases and sailed into the melodious Grieg, creating an unusual effect, as the tiled floors and walls augmented the natural resonance. Besides sharing a tasty repast, other appreciative diners and waiters joined the Utica concert contingent in sending us off to the depot with loud applause and cheers!

# 10

# "The Real Thing"

## Romance and Annette

The Heart has its reasons which Reason knoweth not.

Blaise Pascal

In spring 1932, it occurred to me that I had reached the age of twenty-six and become set in a life pattern. I did not wish to continue without true motivation for my career. I loved the violin and its great literature, while the viola repertoire was quite limited. I definitely did not want to continue my musical life in New York playing viola, either in chamber music or as a soloist. Sigrid Onegin, a splendid Swedish singer, asked me to accompany her in Brahms's "Four Songs for Contralto, Viola and Piano" at her Town Hall recital, which I enjoyed. She was a subtle musician with a beautiful rich voice.

My life seemed controlled by a powerful force that inexorably led me in directions that gave meaning to my unfolding chronicle. At decisive moments, that mysterious force called my "karma," in combination with the enchantment of music, always brought unexpected opportunities. My entire life resembles an American success story in reverse, for the impelling influences of music and art always prevailed over the seductive sirens of material gains.

Whenever I vacationed in Portland, my parents presented me to young ladies of their Romanian Jewish community, whom I invariably found boring or unattractive. One summer they related a strange tale: a wealthy South American couple visited Portland to ask my parents to accept their daughter as my wife. Papa replied from his own romantic experience that they could not speak for me in such a personal matter. I cannot recall ever meeting that young lady or her parents.

Julius Weitzner, an art dealer friend, specialized in old masters. As a youth he studied violin (his father was an orchestral violinist). Julius married lively, vivacious Ruth Klug, an excellent pianist. I occasionally joined them to play chamber music and met their friends and families, including his cousin Marcy Holstein. Later they moved to London, where Julius made some extraordinary discoveries of "lost" or "misattributed" masterworks and garnered world attention. He always tried to interest me in his field, saying, "Why do you buy that modern junk?" This would be more applicable to much art that was highly touted in the 1980s and 1990s.

In April 1932, I invited Marcy Holstein to a soirée in my one-room flat. Most of my lady friends were indisposed, so I asked, "Marcy, could you bring along a nice girl?" She brought Annette Leibole, an attractive auburn-haired young pianist, who had attended one of the Musical Art Quartet concerts. My parties were innocent affairs. I served Fig Newton cookies and ginger ale (this was during Prohibition) and played movements of Bach's solo partitas. Then we discussed music and art, for I had paintings of Avery, Burliuk, Pougny, John Graham, Terechkovitch, and Lebduska on my walls.

People began leaving about 11 P.M. Marcy called for a taxi, and I turned to Annette and asked, "Where do you live?" She replied, "I share an apartment with a pianist friend, Luba Shapiro, on West Seventy-sixth Street." My flat was at Eighty-sixth Street and Riverside Drive. I asked, "May I walk home with you?" She seemed pleased at the prospect. On the way, Annette told me she studied with Ignace Hilsberg at the Institute of Musical Art during the afternoons, and three evenings a week was completing a two-year high school term (in one year) at Rhodes School on 125th Street. She had not wanted to attend my party, as she had gone directly to Rhodes from the Institute, with no time for supper. Marcy called just as she had entered her apartment. Luba had urged, "Do go, he's lots of fun, you'll have a wonderful time." The die was cast!

Fascinated by Annette's personality and maturity, I asked, "Would you like to go rowing in Central Park tomorrow afternoon?" I loved the quiet charm of the Park and often went rowing alone. Annette replied, "What a lovely idea." We made a date for 2 P.M. Saturday. When I arrived, Luba opened the door and said, "Annette, who is this man?" We discovered she had spent an entertaining evening with my Hartford friend, Paul Rosenbloom, who occasionally used other people's names as a prank. Paul had told her he was Louis Kaufman.

We walked to Central Park, and while I rowed, we discovered we shared many interests. We have continued talking enthusiastically to each other about music, art, opera, drama, history, literature, and poetry ever since. After leaving the park we ate at a nearby Chinese restaurant. I invited Annette to join me in visiting Mrs. Florence Schwarz and her two daughters, Terese and Louise, whom I had met in Paris and Rome. I was interested to see what impression she would make. When we walked back to her flat, I asked if she would join me for dinner the next evening after her Institute lessons; we discovered we liked the same foods.

After that next dinner, we visited the Averys' one-room apartment on Seventy-second Street. Annette fell in love with Milton's work and with his wife, Sally. That evening I bought my first large Avery—a portrait of Sally in a white slip, leaning on a dark table that held a white bowl containing fruits. Annette thought it was a masterpiece. (In 1977, we gave this painting to the National Gallery of American Art in Washington, D.C.)

I spent every free moment with Annette. We shared daily lunches or dinners, depending on our schedules for work and study. We ate in Italian, Greek, Hungarian, Romanian, Chinese, Russian, French, German, and good American coffee shops and automats. We walked miles visiting art galleries and museums on weekends. She never was tired or bored, as my other friends often were. She wore sensible shoes and was accustomed to walking. The breadth of her reading constantly surprised me, for Annette was as avid a reader as myself.

By the third day after our first encounter, I decided this was the ideal girl for me and asked her to marry me. Without hesitation, Annette said, "Yes." We both realized she was only seventeen and wanted to complete her studies. I needed time to earn enough money to leave the quartet. I also thought we should not make any announcement until I could obtain her parents' consent. I was certain I could begin a new life as a violinist with Annette and live in Los Angeles, which I had considered my future paradise ever since the vaudeville tour with Rozika. "Annette," I cautiously began, "would you consider living in Los Angeles?" She responded, "Of course, we'll live wherever you like, even the North Pole, if you'd be happy there. I'd like to be your accompanist. I don't want you to travel all over without me." This seemed too good to be true!

Annette's mother's family came from Lithuania and Poland, her father's family from Kiev, Russia. Her parents met and married in Chicago, where Annette was born. They soon divorced; Annette and her mother joined her uncles and aunts in Bismarck, North Dakota. Annette studied piano first in Bismarck, then in Seattle, where she first heard a live symphony, and also in Philadelphia and finally New York. We each had been born on Sunday morning, and we each grew up in ethnically diverse neighborhoods. An unexpected blind date began our mutual adventures.

Annette Leibole (Kaufman) in her engagement photograph, New York City, 1932.

We were inseparable for the remaining four weeks of my rehearsals and concerts with the quartet.

I often took part in chamber music evenings with Mischa Elman at the apartment of his parents and sisters. Annette accompanied me to a long afternoon of playing string quartets with Mischa and his regular quartet members, Eddy Bachman, second violin, and Horace Britt, cello. I played viola. Nicholas Moldavan and his delightful fiancée, Belle Friede, were among the guests, and I introduced my fiancée, Annette, to them. We were served a delicious Russian dinner, and then Mischa decided to play for the assembled guests the program for his approaching Carnegie Hall recital, accompanied by his new Estonian pianist, Vladimir Padwa. Around midnight Annette whispered, "I would like to leave now, I have early classes tomorrow!" I murmured, "Impossible! We must stay until he's played the entire program and encores." So we departed at 2 A.M. the next morning, exhilarated by Mischa's expressive and poetic performances.

Another lengthy afternoon-evening chamber music party with members of our quartet was at Jascha Heifetz's spacious Park Avenue apartment. Heifetz and his wife, Florence Vidor, a former movie star, greeted us warmly. While waiting for other guests to arrive, Jascha, Sascha, Annette, and I were standing near a radio, which was broadcasting a great Fritz Kreisler recording. Jascha commented, "Every time I hear that man play, I feel like breaking my violin." Sascha agreed that he felt the same way. We all laughed at such a preposterous idea. Among the guests were Rudy and Pauline Polk (her brother married a sister of Heifetz); Ruth Posselt, a fine violinist, and her husband, Richard Burgin, concertmaster of the Boston Symphony Orchestra; Gregor Piatigorsky; Nadia Reisenberg, a remarkably fine pianist; the playwright Samuel N. Behrman, married to another Heifetz sister; plus a sizable group of music-loving friends.

We began with a Haydn Quartet. It was always elating to perform with Heifetz, his lordly virtuoso approach was infallible. In sight-reading a new work he was unusually surefooted, and like a cat he always landed on the right note at the right time! This supreme violinist sometimes took tempos that were not easy to keep up with, but they were always musically right.

We were about to play Schubert's inspired two-cello quintet. Annette and I were highly amused when Marie Roemaet-Rosanoff sat down at the first cello stand, remarking to Piatigorsky, "I don't know the second part." With typical Russian directness, he playfully pushed her off the chair and seated himself before the first stand, saying firmly, "Neither do I!" He played the first part, Marie played second cello, Jascha and Sascha, classmates from their Saint Petersburg days, played violin, and I played viola, in what turned out to be an unusually fine performance. Then Nadia Reisenberg joined Jascha, Piatigorsky, and myself in an exciting rendition of Brahms's G Minor Piano Quartet. Heifetz was a modest and generous host. At intermission, a copious Russian buffet was presided over by Florence, whom Jascha addressed affectionately (in Italian) as *Firenze*. The entire afternoon and evening was enlivened by his affability and amusing anecdotes. He enjoyed imitating a struggling student playing difficult virtuoso passages to the mirth of the appreciative guests.

Rudy Polk, who had studied with Carl Flesch in Germany, often hosted chamber music at his beautiful apartment. When Flesch visited New York, I joined him in quartets at Rudy's. His performances were always musically correct, but somewhat lacking in the tonal warmth of the New York Russian school.

Shortly after another quartet soirée at the apartment of pianist Harry Kaufman and his wife, Lillian, the time arrived for my long-planned summer holiday with my parents in Portland. They were quite dismayed when I announced, "I've just met the girl I am going to marry." They asked, "What's your hurry? You are very young. Don't be in such a rush! Who are her parents?" I rarely contested their opinions, but this time I quietly replied, "I don't know and I don't care. Annette is the girl for me!" That closed the discussion!

During that summer of 1932 I worked steadily on violin repertoire and played two sonata recitals at Reed College with an excellent local pianist, Ruth Bradley Keiser. Annette remained in hot, steamy New York until the Institute's summer school closed. She successfully passed her school tests and received a diploma. She returned to North Dakota to visit her mother and stepfather, Frank Leibole. While there she continued her French studies with Mademoiselle Cécile Champeau. We wrote to each other daily about what we read, heard, and did.

In autumn 1932, we resumed our life and rehearsals together and moved into the Park Crescent Apartment Hotel on Eighty-ninth Street and Riverside Drive, living on different floors. I continued rehearsals and concerts with the Musical Art Quartet. Each year, for the previous four years, we had presented four programs at Town Hall. I persuaded Annette to study with James Friskin (a graduate of London's Royal College of Music) at the Institute.

I knew most of Mozart's chamber and orchestral music, but Annette introduced me to his operas, which she had attended with Luba. We first heard Ezio Pinza in *Don Giovanni* with Elizabeth Rethberg as Donna Anna. Warning Annette to expect some static interludes, I invited her to *Parsifal*. Artur Bodanzky's dynamic, expressive conducting, with Lauritz Melchior as Parsifal and Kerstin Thorberg as Kundry, was overwhelming. We both were totally absorbed by the music and became confirmed Wagnerites.

That winter we attended wonderful performances of *Die Meistersinger von Nürnberg* and the glowing, flaming, passionate *Tristan und Isolde* with Melchior and Flagstad at the height of their powers. Years later, Annette and I attended three complete *Ring* cycles in Seattle, two conducted masterfully by Henry Holt and the unforgettable third led by our French friend Manuel Rosenthal. We were enchanted with Lotte Lehmann as the Marschallin and Jarmila Novotná as Octavian in Richard Strauss's *Der Rosenkavalier*. We have never missed a performance of this opera when it was playing where we chanced to be.

We visited art galleries, the Whitney Museum (then in Greenwich Village), the New School for Social Research (to see new Orozco and Thomas Hart Benton frescos), the Hispanic Society of America, and the American Museum of Natural History, and every Sunday we visited the Metropolitan Museum of Art. Often the Schwarzes invited us to dinner. I bought a carved wood portrait by Chaim Gross of his young wife, Renée, at Manfred Schwartz's Eighth Street gallery, where Annette and I were delighted to meet the young Gross couple. Later we learned it was Gross's first sale of his work in a gallery. I loaned two Terechkovitch paintings to the first New York exhibition of his work at Schwartz's gallery that spring.

We spent two or three evenings a week at the Averys' flat. He created work at a furious pace, sometimes two or three paintings each day. I had introduced Mark Rothko to the Averys and he was frequently at their studio with other Avery fans—the painters George Constant, Wallace Putnam, and Adolph Gottlieb. Mark's somber palette lightened quickly under Milton's influence. I commissioned Milton to make two portraits of Annette: one in a white dress and one in a green velvet dress with lace-trimmed sleeves. Milton made striking portraits of Eilshemius, Chaim Gross, Marsden Hartley, and a Japanese artist, Thomas Nagai, which we acquired over a span of many years.

We frequently visited J. B. Neumann's gallery and were impressed with his eclectic taste and lively conversation.

We visited Steiglitz's gallery to admire Georgia O'Keeffe's paintings and John Marin's watercolors, and Weyhe's Lexington Avenue bookstore gallery, where we acquired rare books over a period of many years. We had long conversations with Stephen Bourgeois at his Fifty-seventh Street gallery, debating his theory that artists could endure neglect, poverty, and failure while producing great works, but that too much success often ruined artists' lives and creativity. Annette and I disagreed for we knew that Rubens, Van Dyck, and Raphael were successful during their lifetime, and that many other great artists died prematurely from neglect, such as van Gogh and Modigliani.

Bourgeois was attracted to naive art, so I showed him some Lebduska paintings. As a result, one evening Lebduska appeared at my flat, saying, "Mr. Kaufman, Stephen Bourgeois will give me an exhibition at his gallery, but wants me to paint a few larger works. I don't have enough money to buy paints and canvas." I asked, "How much do you need?" He answered, "One hundred dollars." I gave him that sum and he left happily.

In Milton Avery's studio in New York City, Milton painted Annette's portrait, while Louis played his violin, 1944.

About two o'clock in the morning, I was awakened from a deep sleep by a jangling telephone and Mrs. Lebduska's tearful voice: "Mr. Kaufman, what did you do to my husband?" I responded, "What do you mean? He came to see me and asked for a hundred dollars to buy paints and canvas for a show at the Bourgeois Gallery. I gave him the money." Evidently he had visited a speakeasy to celebrate the good news—or someone had given him a Mickey Finn and poured him into a cab that delivered him to

Annette with the completed Avery portrait, 1944.

his home in Brooklyn, without money to pay the fare. This was my first inkling that he was an alcoholic.

Two weeks later, while I was on tour, Annette received a call from a hysterical Mrs. Lebduska. "I don't know what to do. I'm going to have a baby. Since we couldn't pay for the last baby, the hospital won't accept me." Annette reassured her, "Don't worry Mrs. Lebduska, I'll get back to you quickly." She telephoned my friend Dr. Morris Krosnick (father of the cellist Joel Krosnick) and explained the situation. Dr. Krosnick called back in a few minutes, "Annette, I have five doctors lined up in all parts of

Brooklyn. Have her call me so I can give her precise directions." Annette reported this good news, and was surprised by, "Oh! I'm busy ironing now and can't go tonight." Suspiciously Annette asked, "Mrs. Lebduska, when do you expect the baby?" She drawled, "Oh, in about eight months!"

Lebduska began decorating a speakeasy, Nino's on Forty-sixth Street. On each floor, he painted the four walls with scenes remembered from his Bohemian childhood. He lovingly depicted country fairs, horses running in the fields, women picking berries in the summer, and peasants working at various farm tasks. The entire brownstone house had been converted by Lebduska's genius into a magical world of orderliness, peace, and contentment. What a tragic artistic loss that undoubtedly these splendid works have been destroyed, without any photographic record of their existence!

A few weeks later Durand-Ruel's Fifty-seventh Street gallery mounted an important exhibit of modern French floral still lifes. Thinking Lebduska would enjoy it, I invited him to join us. He did not say one word about the chefs-d'oeuvre of Manet, Monet, van Gogh, Cézanne, Fantin-Latour, Rousseau, Derain, and Renoir that were so handsomely hung and lighted. As we walked out into Fifty-seventh Street, I asked, "Didn't you enjoy the show?" He replied, "Mr. Kaufman, they were all cheap flowers — daisies, sunflowers, pansies, asters. I'll paint you some *real* flowers."

The next week, he arrived one morning at my hotel with a large painting, which I immediately bought. It depicted a bouquet of long-stemmed roses laid on a large table, and under the table was a long box (to show they were purchased and expensive). In the box he had painted a little white card, inscribed "To my dearest friend."

Lebduska wanted to paint my portrait. Since I lacked time to pose, I gave him a photograph. He painted into the background some of his paintings I owned and the Chaim Gross sculpture that Lebduska had observed on his visits. This painting has been reproduced in the Herbert Hemphill and Julia Weissman book, *Twentieth Century American Folk Art and Artists,* and the *World Encyclopedia of Naive Art.* Dr. Sherman Lee, former director of the Cleveland Museum of Art, admired this portrait, as did our friend Gilles Artur, director of the Musée Gauguin in Tahiti, when they visited our home. I commissioned Lebduska to paint Annette's portrait, again providing him with a photograph. He was inspired to paint Annette's head as a framed, colored photograph placed on a desk, in an interior with an open window through which one could see the Bavarian castle of King Ludwig II in a fanciful landscape.

A few weeks later, Lebduska complained to me that Nino had refused to pay him for the murals of the speakeasy or the supplies that he had so freely used. Wishing to help, I consulted Victor Gettner, a young lawyer friend of the Schwarz family, who generously offered to attempt to collect payment for Lebduska's services and supplies without fee. Later Victor informed me that the case was lost. Lebduska had told a completely different story in court. This mystified me. Years later, I surmised that the underworld characters who owned the place had threatened Lebduska's family, so he had been too terrified to tell the truth at his trial.

Annette's parents, concerned about her absorption into my life, decided to visit New York to investigate the circle of artists their eighteen-year-old daughter had entered. The evening they arrived, we took them to Jules and Ruth Weitzner's spacious flat to hear me play first violin in string and piano quartets. They greatly enjoyed the music and my friends. While we shared a delicious buffet, Arthur Langley, the evening's violist and an amateur financier, informed us that the United States was in a severe economic crisis and the nation's banks might soon close.

In a taxi returning to the Leiboles' hotel, I asked Annette's father and mother for their permission to eventually marry Annette, and they consented to our engagement. Dinner at the Averys the next evening gave them the chance to know more about me. They admired Milton's paintings and were fascinated by his quiet charm, Sally's bubbling enthusiasm, and their new baby, March. They bought a small painting and a watercolor. Milton, always pleased to have a new model, made a remarkably handsome portrait of Annette's mother, which she bought.

Deciding to heed Langley's advice, they returned to Bismarck sooner than planned to cope with bank problems and their business. The nation's banks did close a few days later. I took care of Annette's expenses until they reopened. I removed some paintings by Avery, Burliuk, and Lebduska from storage to decorate Annette's room, which delighted her.

Burliuk, in dire straits, visited me one morning to sell some of his small works. He observed the large Avery portrait of Sally and announced, "Avery is an aristocrat of color as Modigliani is of line." He remained a faithful admirer of Milton's work, writing about Avery in his occasionally printed arts journal, *Color and Rhyme*.

Ominous news of terrible events in Germany was reported in the press that spring. Leopold Godowsky, the celebrated pianist-composer, arrived from Europe and informed waiting reporters, "Germany has returned to the Dark Ages of the Inquisition." A few weeks later, Fritz and Harriet Kreisler arrived at New York Harbor. Harriet announced, "Everything is normal in Germany." One reporter inquired, "Isn't your husband Jewish, Mrs. Kreisler?" She protested, "He hasn't one drop of Jewish blood in his body." Harriet's brusque personality had not endeared her to many New Yorkers, so Godowsky's quip, "Who could believe poor Fritz is so dangerously anemic?" was widely circulated in musical circles.

My last New York appearance as violist with the Musical Art Quartet (the final concert of our series at Town Hall) on 16 March 1933 garnered fine praise. The *New York World-Telegram* of 17 March said, "The Musical Art Quartet, well established among the premier chamber music organizations of the day, played its program with quite remarkable finish, aplomb and sincerity. Although comparatively young in years, this Quartet has acquired a balance and rapport among its members that older organizations might well envy. The high water mark of last night's concert was achieved in the Brahms quartet in B flat, Opus 67. The sensuousness, warmth and tenderness of this music were revealed in all its nuances. Particularly eloquent was the playing of the third movement. It glowed with a joyous, wistful voice that only Brahms seems capable of invoking."

Francis D. Perkins's review in the *New York Herald Tribune* noted: "Mr. Kaufman merited praise for the quality of tone manifested in the third movement in which the viola often plays virtually a solo role."

Mischa Elman's gifted sister Liza invited me to join her in a sonata recital. The *New York Times* carried a small notice: "Liza Elman, pianist, and Louis Kaufman, violinist, will be heard Friday evening at Bronx House in sonatas of Mozart, Beethoven and Strauss." This was the first time Annette had heard me play violin in a concert hall and she became insistent: "Louis, you must leave the quartet and go on your own as soon as possible." I played an audition for Willem van Hoogstraten, conductor of the Portland (Oregon) Symphony, and he engaged me to play the Bruch G Minor Concerto in autumn 1933! Annette and I celebrated this bright omen with a joyful Romanian dinner at the Moscowitz and Lupowitz Romanian Restaurant in lower Manhattan.

Suddenly I realized this auspicious Portland concert made it imperative to marry Annette as soon as possible, to achieve my lifelong dream of living in Los Angeles. Before proceeding west, I could leave the quartet and take her to France for further piano studies, providing opportunities to widen her cultural horizons. Then I could resume my violin career, and we could begin our ideal life in enticing Los Angeles. Sascha commented gravely (since Annette is two inches taller than me), "If you marry Annette, you will develop an inferiority complex, and become very unhappy. Think it over carefully, Louis." I refrained from replying that his wife, Kitty, was taller than he was and that had not proved harmful.

We telephoned Annette's parents in North Dakota, urgently requesting permission to marry immediately; to our delight, they consented.

Annette's father offered, "We will send you the money a wedding would cost and that will provide for her Paris studies and some of your sightseeing and expenses." Annette's parents always understood and encouraged us to fulfill our musical aims. In retrospect, I was certainly without brilliant prospects. I would be leaving the quartet's financial security for an uncertain future after our European honeymoon.

I was to leave New York late Sunday evening, 16 April, for a three-week quartet tour which would close our current season. That determined our wedding day, for our boat would depart the morning of the quartet's return. Annette joined me at City Hall to apply for a marriage license. Florence Schwarz arranged for our marriage in Rabbi Enelow's study at Temple Emmanuel on Fifth Avenue. The evening before the wedding, the Schwarzes arranged a dinner party for us with a small group of friends, including their postman, Arnold Friedman, an extraordinary painter. Although he did not know us, he brought a wedding gift of a small landscape painting, which we still cherish. Flo and her daughters, Terese and Louise, were our only witnesses on the bright Easter Sunday afternoon of 16 April 1933. They met us at the synagogue, and presented us to Rabbi Enelow. He spoke eloquently and poetically about the universe and creation, and about our great Hebrew heritage, which we should cherish throughout our lives together in loving kindness. He concluded, "You may kiss the bride, you are now married." We were greatly impressed with the simple ceremony, which joined our happy destinies together for over sixty years.

After the brief ceremony, we five piled into a taxi to the Schwarzes' Central Park West apartment, and cheerfully dined on leftovers from the prewedding gala. Then Annette and I returned to our hotel rooms. I picked up the viola and valise, embraced Annette, and dashed off to join the quartet at Penn Station. Annette spent the evening addressing and mailing off our wedding announcements. The morning of my return, I found Annette ready to set off immediately. She had packed both our trunks and returned the art, music, and books to storage. I had left Zimbalist's Storioni viola with Paul Bernard. I quickly dashed off a letter of resignation to the quartet so they could find a replacement violist during the long summer. We taxied to the Embarkation Wharf, where dear Hannah Bierhof had impulsively come to see us off with her blessings and a charming gift. We arrived in the nick of time; as we entered our small stateroom on the S.S. *Westernland,* the ship's engines started and we were sailing toward *la belle France!*

# 11

# Together in Europe—
# Our Honeymoon

The eight-day voyage to France was an enjoyable preamble to our future life. Sitting on deck chairs, covered with blankets, we discussed the important problems of what we might do in unknown California, where we did not know anyone. We were used to living alone and accustomed to undisturbed practicing and reading, but we talked about what it would be like to share our lives at close quarters. We firmly intended to spend the rest of our lives together, and were optimistically confident we would fulfill the modest aims we shared. We also spent long hours reading and discussing the art and history of places we intended to visit.

Our financial future was extremely vague. I had withdrawn most of my meager savings, plus recent quartet fees. Other assets included $375 Annette had received for selling her grand piano, and we had the generous wedding funds from her loving parents which paid for our trip and her Paris studies.

The boat docked at Le Havre early on a gray morning. We were fascinated by the pearly sky, lush green countryside, and sober gray buildings facing us. The soft quality of the light resembled impressionist paintings of Boudin, Monet, and Pissarro. After clearing customs, we walked to a nearby cafe to await the Paris boat-train. When the waiter brought us coffee, I asked, "Are there any interesting sights to visit here?" His smiling reply was, "You young people shouldn't bother with that. We've a warm room and comfortable bed upstairs!"

In Paris, we taxied to the Majestic Hotel on the Right Bank (during World War II it became Gestapo headquarters). Our first morning, we were awakened by an early call from the concierge, "Mr. Kaufman, a bicycle has arrived for your son." Sleepily, I explained, "I do not have a son and have not purchased a bicycle!" This is one of the amusing mix-ups we have had with my name. The Majestic being too costly, we set off to look for more modest lodgings. The same morning we found the comfortable, inexpensive Hôtel des Acacias just off Avenue Wagram on the little rue des Acacias. We could afford two small rooms at opposite ends of a long hall on the second floor. I rented a small upright piano for Annette's front room, which permitted us to practice at the same time. The concierge and staff never believed we were married. To Annette's annoyance, they invariably greeted her, *"Mademoiselle, votre ami est sorti"* (Miss, your friend has gone out). This elicited an indignant, *"Ce monsieur est mon mari!"* (That gentleman is my husband!).

I called Maurice Eisenberg, an excellent cellist and assistant to Pablo Casals, to ask him to suggest a piano teacher for Annette. He recommended Madame Jeanne Blancard, assistant to Alfred Cortot at the École Normale de Musique and a most accomplished pianist. Madame Blancard suggested two lessons each week at her nearby apartment. We both worked diligently in the morning so as not to disturb other tenants. We met for late luncheons followed by afternoon sightseeing. I enjoyed showing Annette the wonders of the Louvre, the Jeu de Paume's impressionist masterpieces, medieval treasures at the Musée Cluny, and fabulous Cambodian sculptures at the Musée Guimet. We visited Notre Dame Cathedral and the Sainte-Chapelle with its magical stained glass windows. On a few days we visited contemporary art galleries on the Right and Left Banks of the Seine. Sundays were devoted to the Louvre or excursions to Versailles or Fontainebleau.

I called the Pougnys and invited Jean and Sonya to the Moscow Cafe for an excellent Russian lunch. Sonya pleased me by saying, "Annette is the perfect Mrs. Kaufman." Later we all visited an exposition of Jean's work at the Galérie Jeanne Boucher in Montparnasse.

One afternoon at the American Express office we unexpectedly met pianist Theodore Saidenberg, the younger brother of Daniel, my cellist friend. We joined forces for the day, and embarked on the Seine boat to visit Saint-Germain-en-Laye. Teddy was en route to Russia the next day to marry an American, Eleanor Levin, who worked in a Moscow cinema factory. (Her brother, Herman, later produced the successful musical *My Fair Lady*.) They had met a year earlier during Teddy's world tour accompanying violinist Efrem Zimbalist. Teddy and Eleanor discovered they had lived in Philadelphia within two blocks of each other and had never met! Their karma was as unlikely as ours!

Teddy mentioned that he had spoken with the famous art collector, Dr. Albert C. Barnes, at a Montparnasse cafe the previous night. We greatly wished to see that fabulous and unapproachable collection of Renoirs, Cézannes, and Matisses; but the irascible Dr. Barnes refused admission to collectors and all museum directors! I persuaded Teddy to return to Montparnasse, hoping to meet the legendary doctor. No such luck!

We enjoyed dining with Teddy and wished him happiness for his marriage and a safe journey. Teddy, learning we planned to live in Los Angeles, suggested we look up Alfred Newman, a pianist-conductor who was working there, and gave me the Los Angeles address of Emmanuel Bay, Heifetz's accompanist.

Annette and I visited the Zborowski Galérie, now owned by Leopold's younger brother Stanley, who was away visiting Los Angeles. His wife, Madeleine, permitted me to exchange my Modigliani watercolor-touched drawing for paintings by "lesser-known artists"—Henri Hayden, Pinchus Kremegne, and Konstantin Terechkovitch. I was distressed that Rouault had entirely repainted the small landscape I had left with Van Leer two years earlier to be signed. He kindly permitted me to exchange it for a Derain portrait of a young woman.

While standing in line at the box office of the Paris Opera, I noticed tickets were available for two tiny four-person loges above the top uppermost balcony, at one-fourth of the price of a cinema ticket. The Garnier's acoustics are extraordinarily fine and vision was quite good—we only lost the very extreme right or left sides of the stage, depending on which loge we had. Thus we heard splendid performances of Wagner's *Tristan und Isolde, Götterdämmerung* (in French, *Le Crépuscule des Dieux*), Mussorgsky's *Boris Godunov*, Henri Rabaud's delightful *Mârouf, savetier du Caire* (Marouf, shoemaker of Cairo), and Gounod's *Faust*. The singers were universally excellent, and the sets and costumes handsome, fulfilling the visions of the librettist and composer. No one then could have dreamed of the bizarre and disastrous productions that would be inflicted by *les enfants terribles*, producers and directors at the end of the century.

We frequently visited a large record shop on Boulévard des Italiens where, for a tiny sum, we could listen with individual headphones in a private booth to masterly performances by Jacques Thibaud, Pablo Casals, Fritz Kreisler, and the Capet String Quartet. We saw a Spanish film of *Don Quixote*, featuring the legendary Fyodor Chaliapin, at a nearby avenue des Ternes cinema. The aged basso retained his magic in spite of primitive film sound, and we were impressed by his remarkable portrayal of the tragic knight-errant.

Stanley Zborowski returned to Paris and we joined him at some

Louis in Paris on his honeymoon, April 1933. Photograph by Annette Kaufman.

Annette on honeymoon, in front of the Paris Opera, April 1933. Photograph by Louis Kaufman.

afternoon art auctions. At one, I purchased a Modigliani painting of a Polish boy. Stanley, convinced that I had an unusual eye for quality, urged me to join him as partner in their gallery. Annette and I attended an auction at the Hôtel Drouot of the famed Vautheret collection, which contained some of the largest and most handsome paintings of Cézanne and Renoir. Chester Dale and other important American and German collectors purchased many canvases. None of these masterpieces sold for more than $5,000 in June 1933.

Reading the *Paris Herald Tribune*, I noticed Ambassador and Madame Garrett had arrived at the Hôtel Georges V. When I telephoned the hotel, Madame Garrett invited us for afternoon tea in their suite. There we met some charming visitors from Baltimore, who were as surprised as the Garretts were to learn that I had resigned from the Musical Art Quartet to pursue a violinist's career. Madame Garrett, curious to hear me, asked if I would play a few days later, at the Left Bank apartment of her friend, the Countess de Béhague. Annette was tied down preparing two weekly lessons, so I invited Madame Blancard to play sonatas of Mozart and César Franck for this morning musicale. Annette offered to turn pages for her.

The Countess's sunny Left Bank apartment contained fine modern paintings, two handsome screens decorated by Pierre Bonnard, and a splendid large painting by Francesco Guardi, *View of the Giudecca and Zattere, Venice.*

The audience consisted only of Madame Garrett, the Countess, and Mrs. Mary Rogers (whose daughter, Millicent, later settled in Taos, New Mexico, where her two sons founded the Millicent Rogers Museum in her memory). They seemed delighted with the program we played and Madame Garrett cheered me with, "Louis, you'll knock the spots off most violinists!"

A few days later she phoned and said, "Louis, would you and Loretta [for some reason, she always called Annette "Loretta"] care to join me in visiting Zuloaga's atelier?" This seemed a fascinating opportunity. As we looked about his vast imposing studio, we shared the idea that these elegant works were too steeped in Velazquez's style and eighteenth-century Spanish traditions. (He had recently painted Madame Garrett as a Spanish *Maja.*) Zuloaga, who sensed our reactions, observed, "Art cannot be created out of a vacuum—out of nothing! All artists need parents. Nature gives us our being and parentage, which is sometimes most unfortunate. Only artists have the unique privilege to choose their ancestors, and they may select the best lineage possible!"

Madame Garrett and Mrs. Rogers invited us to perform at an after-dinner soirée. To our surprise, when we entered the brightly lit Grand Salon we recognized the newly-wed Princess Mdivani, née Barbara

Hutton, the Woolworth heiress, and her husband among a large group of guests. We played a brief program, which seemed to please. As we departed we received warm praise from Madame Garrett and an envelope. Opening it in the hotel lobby, I read, "Dear Louis and Loretta, Best wishes for your marriage. I give nothing for second marriages or divorces! Love! Alice Garrett." A good-sized check was enclosed! The next day a wedding gift arrived from Mrs. Mary Rogers, a large silver eighteenth-century French wine cooler, which we still cherish. Exhilarated about playing our first concert together, we walked the whole length of the Champs-Elysées from the Rue de la Paix to the Place de l'Étoile and down Avenue Wagram to "our" Rue des Acacias, stopping off near the Madeleine for a celebration *coupe Jacques* (ice cream with brandied fruits) at Chez Wéber.

Due to intensive practicing, a large painful cyst developed under the left side of my jaw. The swelling and pain persisted for two days, so I called the American Hospital in Neuilly. They recommended a Dr. Boucher (French for butcher). After examination, Dr. Boucher assured me, "This type of cyst is quite common. Many violinists and even non-performers develop them." He proposed excision the next morning, in his office. Hospitalization was not necessary; the procedure would only take one half-hour.

At nine the next morning, I entered Dr. Boucher's office, which had fine École de Paris paintings on the walls. After an hour in the waiting room, Annette became worried. The surgery lasted one and one-half hours. The delay was due to much scar tissue from two previous clumsy New York operations necessitated by years of constant pressure and irritation caused by poorly designed chin rests. I emerged with my head and neck swathed in white gauze bandages, barely able to speak. Annette helped me into a taxi. We rode back to our hotel in a sudden downpour of rain with lightning and thunder that matched our emotions.

Annette put me to bed and I managed to recount my ordeal. During surgery Dr. Boucher said the scar tissue and cyst were close to my jugular vein. Since space for growth was restricted, the cyst had sent out branches that he had to remove. While closing the incision, he realized the local anesthesia had worn off and said, "If you can endure the pain, I'd rather not give you more anesthesia. It might make you nauseated and cause complications." I murmured, "Go ahead," so I felt most of the stitching.

The storm continued as Annette spoke seriously about this occupational hazard. "You don't have to play violin if it will threaten your life. Zborowski admires your artistic judgment and you could join him as an art dealer." I answered, "Let's wait for Dr. Boucher's opinion." Annette gave me a couple of aspirin for the pain and left me to sleep through the afternoon and night.

The next two days we walked about our *quartier* and ate in local bistros where everyone asked, "What happened to you? Do you have a toothache?" On the third day Dr. Boucher removed the bandages and told us good news: the removed tissue was benign! He placed a small patch over the new little scar, which was much less noticeable than the large red scar I had under the left side of my jaw since my student days.

Dr. Boucher warned, "Don't play violin for at least six weeks or the wound will not heal well." Annette asked, "Will it harm Louis to continue playing?" Dr. Boucher replied, "Don't worry about not being able to perform. If you stop playing for any reason, you'll have a large depression in your neck, I removed so much tissue." I was delighted, for the only career that interested me since childhood was to be a violinist.

The next afternoon, walking down the Champs-Elysées, I noticed a poster announcing a 70 percent reduction on Italian railroads for round-trip visitors to Milan, Venice, Florence, and Rome during July and August. This would be an ideal way to spend my enforced rest, and an unexpected chance to guide Annette through the wonderful country and art works I had seen. On previous Italian trips, constantly occupied with rehearsals and concerts, I had had only scant time to study interesting sites. Now I could visit museums, churches, and palaces with Annette for as long as museum hours permitted. We bought second-class tickets for the tour, wrote our parents about this unforeseen opportunity, stored our trunks at Hôtel des Acacias and my violin at a nearby bank, and explained Annette's absence for the next three weeks to Madame Blancard.

We departed on this exciting adventure in late July. We traveled by day and descended to hotels near stations for overnight rests. We decided to take sightseeing bus tours on arrival in each city, then we could return to observe in depth whatever attracted us.

In Milan, we had a small room at the imposing Principe di Savoia, where the quartet had stayed (I learned that grand hotels had less costly rooms available, so we could enjoy their ambiance at modest prices). We spent long hours at the Brera Gallery and intimate Poldi Pezzoli palace, impressed by the Lombard school and Raphaels, Mantegnas, and Crivellis. The Ambrosiana Gallery permitted us to study masterpieces of Leonardo da Vinci and his pupils Bernardo Luini and Ambrogio de Prédis, and Raphael cartoons for tapestries. We made a pilgrimage to the monastery containing Leonardo da Vinci's *Last Supper* and admired the Palazzo Sforza with its fascinating collections. The great Duomo, Europe's first Gothic cathedral, overwhelmed us. We admired the generations of artists who had embellished its vast spaces since the twelfth century. Guides pointed out Leonardo's invention to reach the highest spires—a sort of basket elevator with pulleys!

We reached Venice at sunset and descended into a gondola, amazed by the magical experience of floating past islands of elegant palaces with oriental ogive (pointed-arch) windows and extraordinary churches. Our hotel room at Albergo Monaco e Grand Canale overlooked the Grand Canal and faced the imposing Church of Santa Maria della Salute, and we enjoyed delicious Venetian specialties served at our hotel. We walked miles visiting masterpieces of Venetian painting and glorious frescoes in the Doges' Palace and the Accademia. What magical colorists Titian, Giorgione, the Bellinis, Tiepolo, Guardi, and Canaletto were!

Alessandro Longhi's interior scenes of eighteenth-century salons and musical activities and Giovanni Domenico Tiepolo's lively commedia dell'arte panoramas fascinated us. We traveled in *vaporetti* (water taxis) to view the Tintorettos at Scuola Grande di San Rocco and nearby Santa Maria Gloriosa dei Frari, with masterly Bellinis and Titian's superb altarpiece, *The Assumption of the Virgin*. We strolled through the palace of Ca' d'Oro, an architectural gem, without guards or any other visitors.

Bernard Berenson's scholarly books on Italian art were invaluable guides for us. How we regretted returning to the normal world of roads and traffic!

Our comfortable hotel in Florence provided us with a room overlooking the Arno near the Ponte Vecchio. During five enchanted days we absorbed the unique artistic treasures of the Uffizi and Pitti palaces, the Duomo and Baptistery with Lorenzo Ghiberti's fabled bronze doors, and remarkable mosaics of its cupola. The Uffizi's immense collections of tapestries, fabulous drawings, and world-famous paintings of Botticelli, Ghirlandaio, Fra Fillipo Lippi, Michelangelo, Leonardo da Vinci, Fra Angelico, and Piero della Francesca made indelible impressions. The collection of artists' self-portraits became the source of my personal interest in acquiring self-portraits of artists I collected. We admired Michelangelo's statues in the Medici chapel and his gigantic impressive *David*, the great sculptures of Donatello, Bartoldi, and Verrocchio, and the ceramic marvels of the Della Robbias in the Bargello Museum. We stopped to rest before enjoying dinners of delicious Florentine specialties. Then to bed, resting our eyes (and feet) before setting out early to stroll along the shops within the Ponte Vecchio, admiring antique and traditional workmanship in modern jewelry, bibelots, books, silk ties, leather gloves, and wallets. Passing a shop near our hotel, we decided to buy a beautiful linen tablecloth for Annette's parents. As it was wrapped, I had a complicated discussion with the saleslady about receipts for export and American customs. When we returned to our room I checked the *lire* in my wallet to be sure I had enough to pay our hotel before going to Rome. Seeing I had too many, I told Annette, "We didn't pay for the tablecloth!" We ran back to the store, which was about to close, to pay the saleslady. She had found they were short, but had not connected it with us! Our *lire* balanced their accounts, and they thanked us effusively. We enjoyed our farewell dinner even more, for I knew the saleslady might have had to pay the difference from her meager salary.

We both always appreciated this opportunity to study the extraordinary Florentine architecture, the writers Dante and Boccaccio, and supreme artists. We also admired the remarkable Medici family that had for generations encouraged and supported architects, painters, sculptors, philosophers, scholars, musicians, and scientists. A later Medici ordered a matched set of instruments (two violins, a viola, and a cello) from Antonio Stradivari! They created great libraries, gardens, fountains, sculptures, and monuments which embellished Florence and became royal patrons of the Italian Renaissance.

Rome was crowded as always by tourists and pilgrims, but we managed to find a modest hotel. Most museums in Rome closed at midday, so we started off very early to visit the fabulous Vatican collections, Michelangelo's frescoes in the Sistine Chapel, and Raphael's incredible *stanze* and *logge*. The treasures inside and the beauty of Saint Peter's Cathedral with Bernini's imposing colonnades and fountains made indelible impressions. The Roman Forum and Coliseum vividly evoked the glory that was Rome. I have always been fascinated by Rome's history and architecture—aqueducts, coliseums, triumphal arches—and it was especially enjoyable to have Annette's unflagging enthusiasm for whatever I suggested visiting. The elegant Borghese Gallery, in a superb palazzo surrounded by handsome gardens, contained impressive Roman mosaics, outstanding Bernini sculptures, and masterpieces of Raphael, Titian, and Caravaggio. I was captivated by Canova's seductive marble statue of Napoleon's sister Pauline Bonaparte.

The oppressive Roman heat induced our indulging in the Italian *dolce far niente* (sweet idleness) by taking siestas in our darkened room, after intensive morning sightseeing and hearty luncheons. Rising in late afternoon we would sip *cafe granita* (iced coffee) at a sidewalk cafe watching the crowds stroll by and admiring the reflections of the setting sun on beautiful fountains.

Knowing our rail tickets had to be validated at the Quirinale to ensure the 70 percent reduced fare, we walked into the imposing palace. To my surprise, the immense rooms displayed mainly items and photographs celebrating Mussolini's regime—views of Il Duce from childhood on, vaunting his triumphs. This was most boring! I said to Annette, "Let's leave." We turned back, walking towards the entrance—but a few armed guards shouted, *"Avanti!"* (proceed), gesturing with their bayonets that we MUST continue through the exhibition. The required stamp could only be obtained in the last exit room! During our return train trip to Paris, we wondered what sort of regime existed in Italy. Madame Garrett had warned our quartet to never mention Mussolini's name, only to refer to "Mr. Smith" if we wished to comment on any condition we observed. Back in Paris, at a *quai* bookstall, I picked up an Italian expatriate's book explaining fascism and providing insight into the festering political conditions occurring in Germany.

Annette resumed weekly lessons with Madame Blancard. At her final session, Madame Blancard, with typical French thrift, counseled, "Madame Kaufman, you have enough technique and should not pay for lessons. Your husband is a superb musician, just study with him!" I invited her and her teenaged son to join us for a farewell celebration at a Romanian restaurant on the Champs-Elysées that featured a Gypsy orchestra led by a Romanian fiddler, with cimbalom (a type of Hungarian hammered dulcimer) and an exciting panpipe soloist.

It was a jolly affair. The Blancards enjoyed the exotic cuisine. As we departed, Madame Blancard sincerely said, "It has been a great pleasure for me to know you both. I've never encountered such serious Americans as you, who visit museums and attend operas and concerts. The ones I've met only cared for night clubs, horse races, shopping, and frivolous pursuits." We assured her we were not unique; we knew others with the same interests. Annette and I expressed our deepest gratitude for her musical assistance. We hoped we would meet again soon.

On a dreary rainy day, we cheerfully set off from Paris on the Calais boat-train, in happy anticipation of our new life in California. We endured a stormy, rough Channel crossing to England and arrived rather late at London's huge Regent Palace Hotel, comfortable and inexpensive, in Piccadilly Circus. We entered one of the dining rooms for a light bite and ordered poached eggs on toast and tea. The formal waiter replied, "Our chef would not serve that for dinner, sir, you must have them with white sauce." We immediately sensed a more rigidly traditional life and behavior in London. English cooking was decidedly less colorful than *la cuisine française* we had been enjoying. Fortunately, I discovered excellent European cafes nearby in Soho.

The London National Gallery, British Museum, Victoria and Albert

Museum, and Tate Gallery attested to the impeccable taste and discernment of generations of English collectors. The impressive scholarship of their curators and staffs provided exact titles of works, places of origin, and dates of artists' lives, infinitely more informative and helpful than scanty data given in France and Italy at that time. We greatly admired masterpieces of the splendid artists Turner, Constable, Blake, and the Pre-Raphaelites, who fascinated me. At that time they were considered unfashionable, but I thought they were extraordinarily gifted draftsmen and colorists. Now, a half-century later, the art world realizes their true merits.

We visited Hill's historic violin shop on New Bond Street (it was moved to the countryside in the 1980s). I purchased a fine Hill Pernambuco bow with a tortoise-shell frog from Alfred Hill, a courtly white-haired gentleman who greeted us most cordially. Taken by Annette's interest as well as my own, he showed us part of their large collection of excellent French bows. He explained that eighteenth-century French ladies desired deep purple dresses, so the silk-making center Lyon imported from Brazil huge amounts of Pernambuco wood, which produced the magical color. In nearby Mirecourt, *archetiers* (bow-makers) discovered that the remarkable flexibility of this wood was ideal for bows. They chopped logs with axes, using only the central part, making merely ten or twelve bows per tree. The nineteenth-century *archetiers* used mechanical saws, cutting against the grain, and produced two hundred bows per log, increasing yield but compromising the playing qualities of the more modern bows.

On our last night we attended a West End play and were highly impressed by British actors. Early next morning, a gray rainy day, we left London via train to Southampton to board the Red Star Line S.S. *Westernland,* for our return to New York. This was one of its last passenger voyages, for the steamship company owned by Arnold Bernstein was appropriated by the Nazi regime.

After a rather rough Atlantic crossing, the ship docked in New York, and we were delighted to see the Statue of Liberty. We cleared customs, ordered our recent acquisitions sent to my storage facility, and then taxied to a midtown hotel. When we reached our room, I discovered I had only five dollars left in my wallet!

During two hectic days in New York, we dined with Florence, Terese, and Louise Schwarz to recount our experiences in Europe and deliver a charming Parisian street-scene painting by Elisée Maclet, as they had asked me to buy a painting for them. I ordered our trunks, art objects, music, and books sent to a Los Angeles warehouse and withdrew all my modest bank savings. Finally we were en route via train to Portland for my first solo appearance with the Portland Symphony and the gratification of introducing my bride to my parents!

In transit, we enjoyed a month in North Dakota with Annette's parents, relatives, and many friends. We both practiced assiduously for approaching concerts. We soon learned that Bismarck's only public-school music teacher had lost her post due to the city lacking funds to pay her salary. These were the dreary depression years. I immediately offered to play a benefit concert at the Bismarck Auditorium to raise the necessary funds. With assistance of the Thursday Musical Club and Professional Women's Club, who sold tickets, the two newspapers, and radio station KFYR, we had a sold-out hall! The *Bismarck Tribune* headline: "Large Audience Delighted with Kaufman Concert," adding, "One of the finest presentations in the history of the Capitol City." The funds raised assured music instruction for the entire year. Elated by the auspicious results of this event, we continued on to Portland and whatever the future might hold for us in California!

# 12

# Hometown Triumph and California Here We Come!

It was very gratifying that my parents, although disappointed that I avoided a big wedding in Portland, were delighted with my bride. My father was greatly upset to learn we planned to live in Los Angeles. He always assumed I would settle in Portland when I married. Since I usually avoided contesting his opinions, only Annette constantly defended my decision when future plans were discussed. Papa sadly commented, "Annette has not married the family, she's just right for Louis. She's just as crazy as he is." However, they were mollified by the universal praise that followed my homecoming performance, which vindicated their long years of support for my studies:

*Portland Oregonian* (by Hilmar Grondahl) 22 November 1933

Louis Kaufman Wins Symphony Audience

Portland proudly proclaimed one of her own last night when Louis Kaufman, native-born violinist, made his orchestral debut with the Symphony. . . . The subject he chose for his homecoming appearance was Max Bruch's violin concerto in G minor. From the intensity of the applause, which the thousands seated in the large hall sent forth, it was apparent that musical Portland was both proud and pleased by his return and success.

The concerto lies comfortably within the abilities of the soloist. It accommodates his vibrant tone. It responds to the free play of his effortless technique. Its rhythmic diversities are splendidly within his control. The composition displayed its beauties so eloquently through his interpretation that the audience was delighted.

*Portland News Telegram* (by Emil Enna) 22 November 1933

### Soloist Winner Kaufman Feature of Brilliant Symphony Concert

The brilliant performance of the orchestra was surpassed by the brilliancy of the soloist, Louis Kaufman, one of Portland's own musicians who recently returned. He played the magnificent Bruch G minor concerto and proved to be a most satisfying artist. He is a violinist of dynamic ability and a poet of interpretation. He is bountifully endowed with every technical gift but overshadowing all is his exquisite musical fineness. A veritable ovation was tendered at the conclusion.

This laudatory review was crowned by a brief tribute from the *Portland Journal*'s editorial section:

23 November 1933

### His Hometown Triumph

Portland is discovering some of its own talent that has already won recognition elsewhere. Monday night at the Auditorium as soloist of the Portland Symphony, Louis Kaufman heard his hometown applaud him as he has been applauded in the East and in Europe for several seasons. His violin sang eloquently in response to the talented and intensively trained touch as it has many times before, but behind it all seemed a more intimate touch born of the occasion. Kaufman was playing for his parents, his friends and his fellow citizens. . . . The idea is excellent.

Mischa Elman arrived to play a beautiful recital in Portland, which we greatly enjoyed. After the program, he invited us to join him at a nearby cafe. Surprised by my decision to settle in Los Angeles, he observed, "Louis, you have a fine reputation in New York and you belong there. Your nature is too gentle for Los Angeles, where I've been told that musicians are apt to be jealous and cruel to confreres." I quietly replied, "I'd like to try it." Mischa kindly added, "Well, I'll give you names of people who may be helpful in San Francisco and Los Angeles. Abrasha Koodlach, a fine violin and bow repairman in Los Angeles, takes care of my violins and bows." We appreciated this helpful and friendly counsel.

Two weeks later, on 3 December, I played, with Annette's assistance, a benefit concert for the Library Fund of the Portland Symphony. To publicize the event, we played for local radio KOIN. Again we garnered praise for a filled-to-capacity Lincoln High School Auditorium performance. The *Portland Journal* headline:

Kaufman Plays First Concert for Portland Audience

Louis Kaufman, violinist, with his wife, Annette, at the piano played the difficult Ernst concerto, a Handel sonata, and a Gusikoff-Machan concerto that Efrem Zimbalist introduced in New York two years ago. The audience liked it and said so with volleys of applause. Mrs. Kaufman proved an excellent pianist.

Station manager Chuck Myers and his wife became our friends. Chuck thoughtfully offered to give me letters of introduction to some colleagues in San Francisco and Los Angeles. Chuck's letters proved most effective.

Ruth Bradley Keiser joined me at Reed College, playing three evenings of violin and piano sonatas, including all three of Brahms, two of Beethoven, and one each of Mozart, César Franck, Grieg, and Richard Strauss. These programs were for a small chamber music series and attracted devoted audiences.

Mother prepared a delicious farewell dinner party for our family, relatives, and friends, and the mood was rather melancholy for they all shared misgivings that Annette and I were leaving their comfortable family nest for a precarious future.

My family's fates and activities took completely different paths from my life. My three younger brothers unfortunately were destined to precede me in passing away. Brother Ernest, whom I remember as a nervous, irritable child, died in his early teens from a streptococcus infection after clumsy adenoid surgery in Portland. Harry, easygoing child number three, after vigorously resisting higher education, served in World War II as a private, ending his military service as a guard at the Nuremberg Trials. He subsequently took over the Kaufman Hat Store until stricken by Alzheimer's disease, dying in his early eighties. Sidney, a charming youngster, served in World War II in the U.S. Navy in Latin American communications and died in his mid-fifties from cancer. My cheerful, gregarious father, Isaac, died prematurely at fifty-six from uremic poisoning, and my dear mother, Paulina, died in her seventies.

Arriving in San Francisco in mid-December 1933, we were captivated by its beautiful site and the impressive Palace of the Legion of Honor Museum, with a splendid collection of French eighteenth-century paintings and furniture, in a lovely park with a superb view of the bay. The cool misty weather was much like that of Portland. We soon found a clean, modest hotel on unfashionable Ellis Street. At this time of economic depression we shared a twin bedroom with private bath for five dollars per week!

I called one of Mischa's friends to convey his greetings and heard an unpleasant female voice: "What do you want?" I replied, "Nothing," and hung up the phone. Deciding to forget personal calls and armed with Chuck Myers's helpful letter, we entered the imposing NBC building. I handed the document to a haughty, fashionably coifed receptionist and received an appointment for the next day to meet Captain Dobbsie's private secretary. His radio program included a good-sized orchestra conducted by Meredith Willson. I was informed that an audition was required for soloists.

The next afternoon when I was auditioning, with Annette at the piano, my childhood friend, David Tamkin, a violist in the orchestra, passed the studio, glanced in and saw me, and invited us for dinner at his flat where we met his wife, Peggy. That evening the Tamkins introduced us to many musicians of the orchestra. Peggy's hospitable and delicious dinners were special occasions.

We encountered Nathan Abas, a colleague from Kneisel's class, who had arrived to be San Francisco Symphony's concertmaster. He soon left that post and formed his Abas String Quartet. We shared an excellent Italian lunch at a picturesque old cafe, The Fly Trap, said to be a favorite of Fritz Kreisler, and we soon became habitués.

My audition passed muster and I was offered a future appearance on Captain Dobbsie's Del Monte Products program. Early the next week, a call came from the Captain's secretary: "Mr. Kaufman, we want you to play two pieces in three minutes!" I turned to Annette. "They can't be serious, they've changed their minds. I'll have to see the Captain and tell him it doesn't pay to have me, as I'd have to ask a fee of fifty dollars." Annette nodded, "They'll never pay you that much. Ask for one hundred dollars. It will sound more impressive."

The next afternoon, I entered Captain Dobbsie's inner sanctum, beginning, "Captain, I appreciate the chance to perform on your show, but it doesn't seem feasible for you to have me play for only three minutes, as I couldn't play for less than one hundred dollars." Dobbsie replied, "My boy, we only have the *best* artists on my show; we wouldn't have you if you played for less." After that surprise, David Tamkin made orchestral accompaniments for my two solos, half of Schubert's *Ave Maria* and half of Cecil Burleigh's *Moto Perpetuo,* which totaled exactly three minutes! Annette hastily sent off news of this broadcast to our families and friends, for it was on the national NBC coast-to-coast network.

David had begun to spend most of his free time composing an opera, *The Dybbuk.* The libretto by his younger brother Alex was based on S. Ansky's celebrated play. In New York, Annette and I had attended a remarkable production of that *Dybbuk* by the Habima Theatre from Russia, with sets and costumes by Marc Chagall. We shared David's enthusiasm for Ansky's chef-d'oeuvre.

One evening after a pleasant Tamkin dinner, which included Meredith and Renée Willson, we began sharing musical memories. Meredith at that time was working on a musical comedy, *The Music Man.* Meredith reminisced about his early days in New York as star pupil of celebrated French flutist Georges Barrère. Meredith played second flute to him in the New York Philharmonic under Arturo Toscanini. Barrère had prepared a long page of obligatory phrases that all his students had to play daily, in addition to solo repertoire and regular etudes. Before long they could play this complicated potpourri by heart.

During intermission at a Philharmonic concert, Bruno Zirato, the manager, informed Meredith that Barrère, suddenly taken ill, had departed and that he would have to play first flute in the concluding Ravel *Daphnis et Chloë* suite, which he did not know! He had only practiced the second part, and he had no time to even look at the unknown part. Panic-stricken, he took his place in the orchestra with his heart pounding. He began to play the unfamiliar solos when he suddenly realized that these notes were part of his daily Barrère routine, which he could play in his sleep! At ease, he could watch Toscanini's indications. From then on, whenever he encountered the Maestro, Toscanini greeted him cordially. Meredith added, "What a wise old boy Barrère was to have prepared his pupils for practically every solo in the whole orchestra literature!"

Willson continued, "Louis, would you play with me next Sunday? I have a Standard Hour evening program of symphonic music, just for the Pacific Coast. I can't offer a fee like Captain Dobbsie, but you could play an *entire* movement of a concerto and I could pay thirty-five dollars." I eagerly accepted and we scheduled the first movement of Mendelssohn's violin concerto for the following Sunday.

Annette and I were engaged to play two radio recitals over the Don Lee CBS station. For the second broadcast on 31 December, at 5 P.M., we performed the Gusikoff-Machan jazz concerto before joining the Tamkins and their friends to celebrate a most auspicious reinauguration of my solo violin career—and to hail 1934!

A friendly manager, Miss Alice Seckels, urged me to remain in San Francisco to form a Kaufman String Quartet. Annette suggested, "Perhaps we should stay here, Louis; everyone has been so helpful." However, my heart was set on Los Angeles, so we proceeded southward.

# 13

# The Goal

## *Los Angeles*

It is a part of probability that many improbable things will happen.
Aristotle, *Poetics*

We arrived at the Los Angeles railroad station, a Spanish-style building surrounded by palm trees and flowering plants, on a bright sunny morning in January 1934. What a dramatic change from the gray December skies of Portland and San Francisco! I was ready to fulfill my childhood dream of living in a house surrounded by flowers and fruit trees near the Pacific Ocean. This obsession had endured for almost eighteen years, and I returned with my ideal wife at the mature age of twenty-seven. I had always believed life was to be lived and enjoyed as a couple. Fortunately, Annette shared this conviction. I had no doubts I had made the right decision!

First we stayed at the Hotel Monarch at Fourth and Olive, where I paid five dollars per week for our twin bedroom and bath. Our first evening stroll on deserted Los Angeles streets made us wonder where the restaurants and theaters were. We soon learned that Los Angeles was made up of several spread-out communities linked by bus lines. For our separate work we needed a house. We didn't like any of the unattractive bungalows shown by rental agents, but we boarded a Wilshire bus to look again at one less-objectionable dwelling. Descending by error at Western Avenue and walking about the area where I thought the house might be, I noticed a sign, "For Rent," in the large window of a handsome two-story house at the corner of Ingraham Street. A next-door neighbor, the agent, ran out to show us the pleasing, sunny interior. It had a living room with an adequate grand piano, dining room, kitchen, small bedroom, and bath on the first floor. Upstairs there were two large sunny bedrooms that shared a bathroom (two other bedrooms and a bath were reserved for the owners, who were schoolteachers). It was completely—and nicely—furnished, and the rent and utilities, including telephone, came to only thirty-five dollars per month! I paid the first month's rent and we quickly settled in. Our music, trunks, and paintings were sent from New York and were delivered from the local Lyons Storage. We again had Avery, Terechkovitch, Burliuk, Pougny, and Lebduska paintings on our walls. Our landlords approved of our unusual decor and did not mind our practicing!

Nearby Westlake Park had a small lake among palm trees, with canoes for rent. So on a few Sunday afternoons, I rowed Annette around the lake. We both enjoyed these quiet interludes. Later, the park was renamed MacArthur, and Wilshire Boulevard was regraded to bisect the lake into two small ponds, which unfortunately ended boating.

We presented Chuck Myers's letter to the NBC radio station KFI, heard from western states to Chicago, and were immediately engaged by program manager Jose Rodriguez to play a fifteen-minute recital each week from 10:15 to 10:30 P.M. He sent out press releases and had Don Willson announce our programs. Don later achieved national fame as the announcer for the Jack Benny program. We thought the slot was too late for most listeners, presuming many people turned off their radios when the news ended.

When I visited Abrasha Koodlach's violin shop on Broadway to buy strings, this cheerful Russian Jewish craftsman was very enthusiastic about our radio programs. We were pleased someone had heard us. He urged me to join the musicians' union, saying I would not be permitted to play chamber music with local musicians if I were not a member. Following his advice, we both joined Local 47, American Federation of Musicians. We were very surprised to learn there were two organizations, one for white musicians, the other for darker-hued members! We helped to end this unnatural situation, and Local 47 eventually became a fully integrated union.

We were remarkably happy in sunny Los Angeles, with no problems in paying our rent and household expenses. Besides our radio fees, I soon had a few pupils and was engaged for concerts at modest fees in outlying communities such as Santa Barbara, Riverside, and San Bernardino. After a few pleasant weeks of performing and teaching, I realized one must have an automobile to live and work in such a sprawling city. I bought a secondhand Model A Ford, a canvas-topped two-seater road-ster, with the condition that the salesman must teach me how to drive. He agreed, and I handed over $275 in total payment.

He drove me to the busy corner of Wilshire and Western Boulevards, a block from our rented house, and got out and moved to the passenger seat to let me drive. Then he said, "This is the gear shift. This way is first gear, that way is second, and the other way is reverse. Now drive." I was in a cold sweat but managed for a few blocks. The salesman changed places with me again, then deposited me and the Ford in front of our house, say-ing, "You're okay," and departed. I realized I must practice, so I got up each morning very early to drive over deserted streets. Then I applied for a driver's license and passed! Fortunately the examiner did not ask me to back up, for I was not sure how to do that. Abrasha Koodlach's son, Benny, who studied viola with me, offered to help and gave me some les-sons, after which I became comfortable behind the wheel. What a boon it was when Annette and I shopped for groceries to place the packages in the buggy and drive home! We kept this jalopy for over a year; it served us well.

One morning I received a call from Mickey Whalen, MGM's musical contractor, asking, "Are you Kaufman, the violinist?" "Yes." He contin-ued, "Our studio's making a film, *The Merry Widow*. Mr. Ernst Lubitsch, the director, tried out all the violinists at MGM and didn't like anyone. Last night he heard you over KFI and decided that you are what he wants for solos." I instantly replied, "Thanks, Mr. Whalen, and thank Mr. Lu-bitsch, but I do not want to play for films. I came to Los Angeles to play concerts and teach. I've heard you work very long hours. Frankly I don't think I would fit in."

Whalen, presuming I was wily—hinting for more money—added, "Mr. Kaufman, we'll pay you double union scale." I didn't know what sin-gle scale was. "Why not try it? If you don't like the work, you don't have to return, and if we don't like you, we won't ask you back." I turned to An-nette and asked, "What do you think?" She replied, "Why not try it? If you're not happy, you don't have to continue." That seemed logical, so I agreed to be at MGM's Culver City studio at ten o'clock the next morn-ing. The die was cast for the next fourteen years!

# 14

# Hollywood

## *The Golden Years*

Following Mickey Whalen's directions to Culver City, I entered the gate of MGM's vast premises about 9:45 the next morning. The guard indicated the music building. When I walked into the spacious recording studio, the orchestra was already seated. I introduced myself to the composer and conductor, Herbert Stothart. It was most interesting to rehearse and record under the baton of this polite, efficient gentleman. There was much special work in his score, based on Franz Lehár's lilting music, with violin solos gliding in and out. The musical demands were modest. I quickly decided to play the solos freely, with certain elements of Kreisler's ingratiating style for popular tunes. This seemed to please Stothart and Lubitsch, who looked in occasionally to hear what was going on.

We worked from 10 A.M. to 12 P.M. and from 1 to 6 P.M.; then after a two hour dinner break, from 8 P.M. to 2 A.M., with periodic rests to hear playbacks. I ate in the studio commissary with Tullio Carminati, an Italian actor I had met in Rome. I could not call Annette until 9 P.M.; earlier there had always been a long queue waiting for the set's sole telephone available to musicians. When the phone was free, I dashed over to call her. At that moment, Annette had taken a walk around the block after waiting inside all day to hear from me. No response!

After the long session ended, Whalen asked if I would continue for the rest of the week. I agreed. As a colleague and I placed our violins in the cases, I asked, "How much did we earn today?" He replied, "union scale, $137.50." For me, $275! This seemed a very substantial sum at this time of economic depression. At the end of the week, I received a check for about fifteen hundred dollars!

Mr. Stothart requested me for his next score for *Mutiny on the Bounty*, starring Charles Laughton as Captain Bligh. I accepted, and then terminated our NBC broadcasts. However, that first night, driving home through deserted streets, I considered the infinite possibilities offered by this unexpected windfall. Annette, deeply concerned at not hearing from me all day, was waiting anxiously. I recounted the long day's experiences, concluding, "Willy-nilly, dear, I *have* to do this work, we have no choice. This can be our El Dorado, the means to have our own home, and we can continue to do whatever we wish musically."

Word traveled fast in the film-music industry that I was capable, adaptable, and dependable. For about fourteen years, I recorded film scores for Max Steiner, Alfred Newman, Franz Waxman, Bernard Herrmann, Erich Wolfgang Korngold, Victor Young, Roy Webb, Hugo Friedhofer, and others. With this work I juggled yearly solo recitals in Los Angeles and Pacific Coast cities, and from 1938 on annual recitals at New York's Town Hall. Annette and I prepared new concert programs each year, which we played in transcontinental tours during March and April, the studio's quiet time.

Max Steiner, a most charming and witty Viennese composer-conductor, had arrived in Hollywood in 1929, after success in English theaters, often under pseudonyms. He requested me for one of his first RKO scores, *The Life of Vergie Minters*, then for his compelling, Oscar-winning score for John Ford's masterpiece, *The Informer*.

Max, an extraordinarily gifted composer, created film music which intertwined thematic cues for actors, their moods and motivation, in rather Wagnerian fashion, manipulating his beautiful Lehár-inspired melodies to great effect. I always enjoyed working with him. He was invariably polite and good-natured, exceedingly meticulous, and knew exactly what orchestral color fitted each scene. Time pressures did not permit him to orchestrate, so he carefully prepared notes for orchestrators. If they did not achieve the effects that Max envisioned, he would call out corrections on the recording stage, such as "Woodwinds play at bar B to D, horns tacet." Or "Flutes play that phrase instead of oboes." Orchestrators and copyists on the set hurriedly copied out parts for waiting players.

Among the Steiner scores I played were *The Gay Divorcee* and *Shall We Dance* with Fred Astaire, *I Dream Too Much* (featuring operatic solos by soprano Lily Pons), and a daring score for *She*, from H. Rider Haggard's fantastic novel about an Egyptian princess, eternally young for centuries, discovered by a young archeologist. Max's exotic, inventive music enhanced that sci-fi "hocus-pocus." I played solos in Max's scores for *The Treasure of the Sierra Madre* and his Oscar-winning *Since You Went Away.*

Another unforgettable Steiner score I played at RKO, the first version of *Of Human Bondage,* dramatically demonstrated how skillfully Max saved that film: RKO had previewed the film, starring British actor Leslie Howard and a young Bette Davis, without a musical score; technicians fitted it with prerecorded sound tracks. A complete disaster! Each time Miss Davis raged at lame Mr. Howard, the audience roared with laughter. It was impossible to sympathize with the actors' plight, and the audience left with a total misunderstanding of Maugham's tale. The producers, foreseeing box office disaster, called Max, who composed a remarkable, psychologically poignant score that placed audiences in an emotional vise. The film won outstanding success, stardom for Miss Davis, and artistic recognition for Mr. Howard and Mr. Maugham.

Other outstanding Steiner scores I played included Selznick's *A Star Is Born* (with Fredric March and Janet Gaynor*), The Charge of the Light Brigade, Now, Voyager, Casablanca, The Life of Emile Zola,* and *Intermezzo* (which introduced Ingrid Bergman to Hollywood, with Leslie Howard as the concert violinist). I was concertmaster and soloist for the entire score, while Toscha Seidel was engaged to record the theme used for the main and end titles. Miss Bergman was shown listening to that theme in an emotionally charged scene. What a challenge for me to try to match Toscha's unusually beautiful sound! Max's great musical gifts made all these films unforgettable. I still remember many of his inspired themes. He had a delicious sense of humor, once commenting on the behavior of some Hollywood character, "He is every other inch a gentleman."

One Sunday morning, Max called unexpectedly. "Louis, are you free today?" "Yes, Max." "Come right over with your violin. I have some themes to submit to Selznick for *Gone with the Wind.* He wants to hear them. It's not very interesting with just piano." Annette and I drove to Max's home, where he had set up a small recording machine. Max and I tried out and played over the themes for Scarlett, Rhett, Melanie, Tara, etc. Selznick enthusiastically approved these samples. I recorded this poignant score with Max and consider it a historical achievement in film music. Even today, excerpts of Max's compelling score are widely recorded.

When Max's father, Gabor, arrived from Vienna, we were occasionally invited to dinner. Gabor's modest manners hid some distinguished accomplishments. He had been a Viennese theater impresario and conductor (many of Johann Strauss's works were premiered in his theaters), and had also constructed the huge Ferris wheel in the Prater. The Austrian

Emperor Franz Joseph, the Czar of Russia, and regents of Europe and Asia had bestowed on him jewel-encrusted decorations, which the Nazis had confiscated at his departure. In 1989 a Viennese street was named after Gabor Steiner.

Prohibition had recently ended, and we once again could enjoy alcoholic beverages. Gabor considered American beer rather sharp, which surprised Max and Louise. I agreed the European beers were milder, which pleased Gabor. Over our refreshments we enjoyed listening to his fascinating memories of important Viennese personalities and events.

One evening he related, "Men wore celluloid collars and cuffs in those days. One night after Strauss returned home from conducting in my theater, a great musical idea came to him. Afraid to lose this tune, he scribbled it on his cuffs before falling into bed. Awakening early the next morning, he had forgotten the theme, but remembered writing something on his cuffs. He looked for his shirt, but it was gone! He called his housekeeper, who had just returned from delivering soiled clothing to the laundress a few doors away. In his nightshirt, Strauss frantically dashed into the street and retrieved his shirt and cuffs—just before the notes of 'The Blue Danube Waltz' were washed off!"

When Gabor passed away in 1944, Max called to tell me the sad news and asked me to play "The Blue Danube Waltz" for his funeral. We drove to Forest Lawn in Glendale, noticing en route a sign that proclaimed, "Forest Lawn, Where You Sleep With The Best People."

Arriving early, we waited for the previous occupants to depart before entering the chapel. I walked into an adjoining cubbyhole on the right side, handed my music to a seated staff organist, and said, "We must play this softly, very slow." A small open window, covered by a dark blue velvet curtain, permitted me to peek into the empty chapel. I asked Annette to go out to judge the balance. She quickly walked into the chapel, mounted the small podium, and turned to discover she was imprisoned behind Papa Steiner's coffin, which had shot out silently behind her! The coffin filled the width of the podium, so she had to squeeze down underneath it to crawl out on her hands and knees. She had been startled to see Gabor's beautified features so unexpectedly but reported that the violin and organ balance was excellent! The dignified service proceeded to the strains of muted violin and organ performing the beloved Viennese waltz, so close to Gabor Steiner's heart.

Max's personal life encompassed the sorrow of three failed marriages and the suicide of his adored son Ronald in Honolulu, after an AWOL escapade. But Hollywood brought him substantial rewards, earned by harried, intense, concentrated effort. Max's musical achievements influenced a whole generation of composers and orchestrators. His scores still attract worldwide attention—never competing with dialogue or motivation, but always underlining actions, moods, and inner emotions of characters. Max's musical work remains a precious legacy of his unique personality.

Charlie Dunworth, Alfred Newman's efficient, affable English contractor (a friend from Newman's Broadway years) called me to record a sprinkling of solos for *The Goldwyn Follies*, with George Gershwin's music. George was often on the set. George Balanchine prepared a ballet sequence using Gershwin's *American in Paris*. Goldwyn abruptly dismissed both ballet and music! Vernon Duke then composed two ballet sequences for *The Goldwyn Follies* featuring Norwegian ballerina Vera Zorina. This score with its many violin solos favorably impressed Balanchine, who praised my playing to Goldwyn, who immediately called Alfred Newman with instructions to engage me! The film was not the success Goldwyn anticipated, ending his brief interest in musical films. However, it is still seen occasionally on late-night TV.

George complained frequently of headaches. His family and friends considered this hypochondria. While playing his Concerto in F with the Los Angeles Philharmonic in February 1937, he lost control of his fingers and blacked out for a few seconds. Doctors saw no problem. In July, he entered a hospital for tests. George died on 11 July 1937 during brain surgery. What a sad fate to be cut off so young.

Merle Armitage, impresario for George's two February Philharmonic concerts, related that George had mentioned composing a string quartet mentally; its themes haunted him, but his hectic career prevented him from writing it down. I often regretted that my reticence in his presence prevented me from suggesting that he compose a violin concerto. Nor did Heifetz, who was close to him, encourage George to write in that form. What a great loss to the concert and chamber music world!

Gershwin's amalgam of Broadway's vernacular breeziness was uniquely combined with growing mastery of orchestration and classical forms. His saucy, sparkling musical comedies and innumerable catchy songs are part of his remarkable legacy. His popular opera *Porgy and Bess* has survived all sorts of productions (we attended many) to enthusiastic world acclaim. This opera, *Rhapsody in Blue, An American in Paris,* Piano Concerto in F, and *Cuban Overture* constitute important American musical landmarks of the twentieth century.

George greatly aided Arnold Schoenberg, Ernst Toch, and other refugee composers to become members of the American Society of

Composers, Authors, and Publishers (ASCAP). He assembled a fine collection of Ecole de Paris paintings, assisted by the knowledge of his cousin Henry Botkin, an artist, whom I had met in Paris art galleries in the 1930s. George had an unusual flair for painting and created excellent portraits of Schoenberg, Botkin, and himself.

Alfred Newman came to California from New England. He was an excellent conductor and accomplished pianist. Alfred conducted Gershwin musicals on Broadway while in his teens. Fritz Reiner thought that young Alfred might achieve a career as a symphony conductor. Alfred was the sole support of his mother, two sisters, and three brothers (Papa Newman had abandoned the family). He was always interested in the finest possible performance of his scores and his orchestra and music were of virtuoso quality.

Among many of his scores I played in were *Dodsworth* (for one scene I performed Debussy's "La fille aux cheveux de lin" as a violin solo with staff pianist Urban Thielmann; visually the music floated across a lake) and *Wuthering Heights*. Alfred was so pleased with my solos for that score, virtually a nonstop series of solos, with occasional obbligatos by cellist Nicolas Lhevienne, that he expressed his appreciation by paying us triple scale. I also played orchestral solos for *They Shall Have Music*, which featured Jascha Heifetz playing a concert to benefit a neighborhood music school, and for *The Rains Came* and *Stella Dallas*.

*We Live Again*, a version of Tolstoy's *Resurrection*, directed by Rouben Mamoulian, was an epic Goldwyn chose to launch the ill-fated Russian actress Anna Sten, hoping she would become another Garbo. The film's climax was a Russian Easter service composed by Newman for orchestra, chorus, and solo soprano, sung by an enormous Russian coloratura, Nina Koshetz. (Mamoulian told me that Koshetz, who was thin and glamorous in Russia, attracted Sergey Rachmaninoff, who occasionally played her piano accompaniments.) It was tonally overwhelming—Madame Koshetz's beautiful soprano soaring over a splendid chorus and orchestral performance under Newman's masterly baton. Ecstatic praise from Mamoulian immediately brought Goldwyn to the set.

Due to the sound engineer's inattention (his wife was in labor and he called the hospital at every break), the Easter service emerged in reverse from the loudspeakers. The entire orchestra, Newman, and Madame Koshetz, realizing the engineer's error, remained frozen in silence as Goldwyn enthusiastically declared, "It's the greatest thing I've ever heard!" But even the glorious recording (played in proper sequence) could not save that film and star from disaster! Alfred, who always spoke in the English manner of Ronald Colman, stated, "We can dress up a corpse but we can't make it live!"

Among other Newman scores I played were *The Little Foxes* (Alfred conducted Meredith Willson's score), *These Three* (based on Lillian Hellman's play *The Children's Hour*), *Captain from Castile, Dark Victory, Foreign Correspondent, Blood and Sand,* and *The Greatest Story Ever Told.* I also played in Alfred's scores for *Young Mr. Lincoln* and *Gentleman's Agreement.*

For *The Hunchback of Notre Dame* Alfred had the collaboration of Robert Russell Bennett and Ernst Toch. Toch composed a vivid contrapuntal sequence underlining Charles Laughton's (the hunchback) vertiginous climb to the great cathedral's tower. Newman, delighted with this exciting sequence, achieved an impressive performance, stressing Laughton's extreme anxiety and fear. At a preview, Laughton, outraged that his groans and grunts for this scene were obscured, demanded the music be eliminated. Later when Annette and I saw the film, we were dismayed that the silent climb, except for Laughton's groans, was so completely ineffective without the music.

When Arnold Schoenberg arrived in Hollywood, Newman briefly studied composition with him. It became fashionable to study with this great master. For a limited period, he had such unlikely pupils as orchestrator Edward Powell, composer David Raksin (I played in Raksin's score for *Laura*), and acid-tongued pianist Oscar Levant. The Schoenbergs lived in our area. He taught composition at nearby UCLA, and Annette and I often encountered them while shopping for groceries or at our bank, and we would briefly discuss his music.

Alfred asked me to organize a string group to perform Schoenberg's sextet *Verklärte Nacht* when the Schoenbergs attended our next chamber music soirée at Newman's Beverly Hills home. We worked assiduously to prepare the work as we assumed it would please the composer. To my surprise, when we finished, Schoenberg approached me and said, "Let yourself go. Be more *free*, Kaufman, play it *more* romantically!"

I played for Newman's scores for Charles Chaplin's *Modern Times*, his French satire, *Monsieur Verdoux*, and *The Great Dictator*. Chaplin supervised every detail of his masterpieces, creating little tunes and perfect themes for his films, as well as simulated languages for French or Italian. In *Modern Times*, Newman usually agreed with Chaplin's suggestions; however, for one sequence where Chaplin described to the girl, Paulette Goddard, what their future dream house would be, he wanted the music "Mickey Moused" for laughs.

Alfred insisted this would destroy the mood of the dream and convinced Chaplin to accept a lyric passage. Alfred placed me with muted violin very close to a microphone, separated from the orchestra by a large screen for greater clarity, which permitted the muted violin to soar over the orchestral texture. He used this device for many solo passages in this score. Chaplin, who knew how to play violin backwards, fingering with the right hand, was delighted with the results. I greatly enjoyed my rare encounters with that unique film genius.

A tempestuous stormy night in March 1936, after my solo recital at the Wilshire Ebell Theatre, was the final straw for my Model A canvas-topped Ford. As I drove home with my violin case and music safely held on Annette's lap, wind drove pelting rain onto the car floor, sloshing over our feet and ankles and drenching us. Once in our garage, we opened the car doors and water gushed out, resembling a Keystone Cop film! The next day we bought a new Ford hard top-sedan, with radio and heater, for $750.

The telephone was ringing as we entered our home, dripping wet. The caller was Joseph Achron, a gifted Russian violinist-composer, an Auer student who had won Saint Petersburg Conservatory's coveted gold medal and played for films. His high-pitched voice said authoritatively, "Louis, it appears you have some talent." This was high praise from Joseph. I had played Ernest's fiendishly difficult F-sharp Minor Concerto to prove I could meet this challenge.

Achron had composed a lively *Stempenyu Suite* for violin and piano, based on Jewish folk songs and dances, which I frequently played in concerts. Achron had a most generous nature. He left Russia via Constantinople, and legend grew that he gave free lessons in violin and composition all the way to Hollywood. He had the respect of Schoenberg, Klemperer, and David Tamkin, who orchestrated his *Children's Suite*. His compositions included chamber music, a piano concerto, and two violin concertos; one was written for Heifetz, who refused to play it. Klemperer asked Joseph to perform it with the Los Angeles Philharmonic. Annette and I attended the concert. Joseph's dry tonal quality did not match his facile technical prowess. Due to extreme nervousness, Joseph forgot a section and left the stage to return with music to complete his concerto.

Achron died in 1943 at age sixty, of uremia. The mourners at his funeral included Tamkin, Heifetz, and many other musicians, including ourselves. One of his pupils played Achron's hauntingly expressive *Stimmung* ("mood") for violin and piano. Its depth of sentiment obsessed Annette and me; we played it often and I recorded it. Bernard Herrmann fell under its spell and made an orchestral accompaniment, which I broadcast later with him for CBS in New York. The death of Achron's wife followed soon after. She had entrusted Achron's original manuscripts to a negligent neighbor whose inattention led to the destruction of his chamber works.

During my long career, I observed African American jazz or swing musicians greatly expanding the technical and tonal possibilities for their instruments, which gradually influenced European- and American-trained woodwind and horn players of great orchestras. Benny Goodman, clarinetist and early crossover artist from swing to classical music, arrived at 20th Century-Fox in January 1944 for the film *Sweet and Low-Down*. I rehearsed and recorded two movements of Mozart's Clarinet Quintet with Goodman, John Pennington on second violin (he was first violin of the London String Quartet before coming to Hollywood), Paul Robyn on viola (previously with the Gordon Quartet and then the Hollywood String Quartet), and Kurt Reher on cello (first solo cellist of the Los Angeles Philharmonic). Goodman was amiably pleasant with our quartet. His beautiful tone, impeccable intonation, sensitivity, and rhythmic verve made this a memorable experience.

MGM unexpectedly called me to record virtuoso passages from Tchaikovsky's violin concerto for *Three Hearts for Julia*, a film featuring Ann Sothern as a concert violinist, undecided as to which of three admirers she prefers. With click-tracks (a device used to achieve exact timing for film music), I recorded some virtuoso sections. Seeing the film playback with music, I pointed out to the director, "She doesn't move her fingers, her left hand clutches the violin neck like a baseball bat." The actress had only been coached to move the bow up and down! His reply was, "Don't worry about that, Louis, no one notices such details!" I also recorded with click-tracks for Disney's *Snow White and the Seven Dwarfs*, *Cinderella*, and *Pinocchio*. I recall Pinocchio sliding down into the whale to the sound of a glissando on my E string!

Alfred Newman produced, at his own expense, the first recording of the four Schoenberg String Quartets, which the Kolisch Quartet had previously performed in four concerts that Annette and I attended at UCLA's Royce Hall. (Rudolph Kolisch, first violinist, who played lefthanded, was Mrs. Schoenberg's brother.) This limited edition, made at United Artist's sound stage under the composer's supervision, was Alfred's personal homage to his celebrated mentor, who had long wished to have these quartets recorded. The four-volume set is now a prized collector's item.

Newman loved chamber music. I often arranged quartet evenings at his Beverly Hills home. He joined my California String Quartet in playing a Mozart Piano Quartet at his home. Later he performed with us Dohnányi's Piano Quintet at a Pro Musica Los Angeles concert on 24 February 1935. We repeated this successful concert program in Long Beach.

When occasional scoring sessions continued until dawn, Alfred provided the orchestra with midnight sandwiches and coffee from the Brown Derby, now disappeared. A Hungarian music-loving headwaiter served the grateful players. After an inspiring Mischa Elman recital, Annette and I invited Mischa for lunch the next day at the Brown Derby, which was next to his hotel. The headwaiter, recognizing me from midnight studio encounters, approached our table. Knowing he was a violin buff, I presented him to Mischa, who ordered Crab Louis. The beaming headwaiter offered, "That's interesting, Mr. Elman, Albert Spalding always orders Crab Louis whenever he comes here." Mischa dryly remarked, "I'm pleased to hear we have something in common." Albert Spalding, of the wealthy sporting goods family, was the leading American violinist of his time. He gave the premiere performance of the "unplayable" Samuel Barber violin concerto; many years later I made the premiere recording of this work for Concert Hall in Switzerland.

Alfred was attracted by the paintings on our walls. Los Angeles art galleries rarely exhibited New York artists during those years. I wrote to Milton Avery, Lawrence Lebduska, and David Burliuk, asking them to send a few works on consignment hoping I might find a few new collectors for them in Los Angeles. This was greatly appreciated by the artists during these years of the Great Depression. Thus Alfred Newman and Richard Day, the art director at United Artists, bought some Averys, Burliuks, and Lebduskas. Their checks were made directly to the artists and I paid shipping costs as my contribution.

The history of my California String Quartet was short-lived but colorful! Cellist Nicolas (Kolya) Lhevienne, son of a Jewish Russian language professor in Paris, read of oil discoveries in Baku, immediately moved there with his family, bought land, and became a millionaire! Kolya, a rare talent with a ravishing cello tone, studied with Julius Klengel in Berlin, arriving with precious Oriental rugs as gifts for his teacher. Impoverished by the 1917 revolution, Kolya escaped hunger by joining a small group accompanying legendary ballerina Anna Pavlova to the United States. He had the appearance and manners of a grand lord.

Violist Herman Kolodkin, the tall, impressive former first violist of the Detroit Symphony, was carried off to Hollywood by an imperious wealthy widow he had married. She often distracted him, commenting, "Herman, don't use the pinkie finger. It doesn't look good." Finally, bored by being left alone while he worked, she proffered, "If you'll take a voyage with me, I'll give you $25,000." Irresistible bait—Herman vanished!

Slim, elegant Michel Perrière, a violist from Nice, son of a croupier in Monte Carlo, replaced him. Michel, one of our first friends when Annette and I played at KFI, taught her to prepare niçoise recipes. Michel later became a fine conductor leading orchestras nationwide in performances of his friend Meredith Willson's musicals, *The Music Man* and *The Unsinkable Molly Brown*. Later he conducted the San Bernardino Symphony and I enjoyed being his soloist, playing the Beethoven concertos and the Saint-Saëns Third Concerto, and Mozart's *Symphonie Concertante* for violin and viola with conductor Michel as violist.

Second violinists were plentiful and talented. George Beresowsky, whose name was soon shortened to Berres, was one of the most reliable. He later became a conductor of local groups.

It was not easy to keep a string quartet working seriously, for the seduction of Hollywood recordings played havoc with rehearsals and concerts. When some of Kolya's Russian colleagues visited Hollywood, he arranged a chamber music evening with Vladimir Bakaleinikov (violist-conductor in Pittsburgh) and his brother, cellist Constantin Bakaleinikov (later a capable conductor for RKO films). Toscha Seidel approached me, demanding, "Louis! How can *you*, a serious musician, work in Hollywood films?" I quietly replied, "No one ever asked me to play badly, Toscha, and the checks are always good."

A number of New York colleagues resented what they considered my betrayal of serious music. Their supercilious view of my activities lasted for many years. What a far cry from the 1990s, when opera stars and concert performers proudly crossed over from classical music to pop tunes! Both Dr. Otto Klemperer and later Dr. Alfred Wallenstein, when they conducted the Los Angeles Philharmonic, asked me to be their concertmaster, which I respectfully declined. I did not know the vast orchestral literature and preferred to devote my studies to more contemporary violin solo works and chamber music literature.

My quartet often performed at chamber music soirées in Alfred Newman's beautiful Beverly Hills home, remodeled by Lloyd Wright, son of Frank Lloyd Wright. Lloyd was the exact image of his father. He was fascinated by acoustics, played cello, and designed the original and successful shell for the Hollywood Bowl. Among the usual listeners were

Lloyd and his actress-wife, Helen, orchestrator Edward Powell, Herbert Spencer (who hailed from Chile) and his wife, Diana, Cyril Mockridge (who accompanied the enchanting soprano Dame Maggie Teyte), Myrna Loy and her film-producer husband, Arthur Hornblow Jr., Richard Day (Goldwyn's set designer with a strong penchant for English Chippendale interiors), and actors Ralph Bellamy and Charlie Butterworth. During the filming of *Wuthering Heights,* Laurence Olivier and Vivien Leigh attended and seemed to greatly enjoy the music. Dorothy Parker and her young husband, Alan Campbell, attended one evening (during the filming of *The Little Foxes*) but both obviously preferred Alfred's well-stocked bar, where they remained all evening. Playwright Sidney Kingsley and Harry Kurnitz (a Philadelphia violinist turned screenwriter) adored chamber music and were highly appreciative listeners. Goddard Lieberson and his wife, Vera Zorina, attended during the *Goldwyn Follies.* Boston's Moses Smith, who wrote an unauthorized biography about composer Sergei Koussevitzky (which we enjoyed reading), also attended and became a friend.

As a result of our friendship with Lloyd Wright and with the unexpected boon of Hollywood recordings, in 1935 Annette and I decided to build our own home. Lloyd volunteered to find a suitable lot. He selected a hilly corner at the confluence of three streets in West Los Angeles near UCLA. His plans fit a two-story house into this space in a style we both admired: the Monterey houses of Northern California. I persuaded Lloyd to use this New England style with its slightly pitched roof and balconies. He constructed a practical, attractive home for our art collection, music, and books that proved ideal for work and pleasure. Annette's parents, always supportive of our projects, loaned us additional funds, which we repaid within one year.

We furnished our home with inexpensive English and American antiques. Film studios rented period furniture from antique shops. Dealers calculated they were well paid by rentals and sold used items at modest prices. One afternoon, I purchased an 1830 Empire New York mahogany-backed, seven-foot-long sofa from a dealer who needed space for a new shipment. He offered, "Louis, if you'll take that large piece out of here today, you can have it for $125." It had been handsomely recovered in blue brocade by a film studio. Lloyd had suggested blue carpet for the living room and entry. I called a van and the sofa was immediately installed in our home, where it remains today!

Lloyd had worked for a brief time with his father in Japan during construction of the Imperial Hotel. He admired the spartan decor of Japanese interiors, with a single *takemono* (scroll) on a wall that might change

Louis and Annette rehearsing in their West Los Angeles home, 1936.

with the seasons. Dismayed by what he considered clutter in our home, he complained, "Kaufman's house is an international junk shop." He never included our home among his architectural achievements, but its clean lines have always pleased us and our friends. One afternoon, the doorbell rang. I opened the door and was surprised to see actor Melvyn Douglas, who said, "Please excuse me, but I have often driven by this house. I admire it and wonder if I might see the interior." I was pleased to show him the rooms.

After Ambassador Garrett's death in 1942, Madame Garrett visited Los Angeles and called me. Annette and I entertained her at an Italian cafe, Lucey's, in Hollywood, later driving her to our home. With her usual exuberance she exclaimed, "Louis, you have a regular Palazzo Pitti!" She was enthusiastic about our collection and evidently reported favorably about us to Ambassador and Mrs. Robert Woods Bliss when she visited them in Santa Barbara. Subsequently, the Blisses came to visit us and borrowed some pre-Columbian sculptures for an exhibit they were arranging for Santa Barbara's museum. Mrs. Bliss much preferred Byzantine art and told us she found some pre-Columbian works rather barbaric. However, their great Dumbarton Oaks Museum in Washington, D.C., has important pre-Columbian sculptures as well as Byzantine masterpieces.

Lloyd, one of the first to laud Palm Springs's charm as a small Indian community, never dreamt it would rapidly transform into a spa city attracting international commercial development. The exclusive Racquet Club was headed by the actor Ralph Bellamy, who greatly enjoyed Alfred's musical soirées. Ralph graciously invited Al, my quartet, and all our wives for a pleasant weekend at the Racquet Club to enjoy their large swimming pool and tennis courts. After a refreshing swim and excellent dinner, the ensemble played Mozart and Debussy quartets, which the club members enthusiastically applauded.

Annette and I were awakened from a deep sleep in our elegant quarters by a furious sand storm. I found it difficult to breathe, closed the windows, and suggested, "Let's leave immediately." We left a thank-you note for Bellamy explaining our abrupt departure, and fled home. The windshield of my car was so scarred and pitted by driven sand that it had to be replaced. I learned we were not suited to desert living!

When Jascha and Florence Heifetz decided to build a home in Balboa, California, and were looking for an architect, they inspected our house. They liked its large windows, glass doors, and built-in spaces for art, music, and books. They engaged Lloyd to construct a handsome, spacious house on an impressive Balboa Island site facing the Pacific Ocean. I frequently drove there for chamber music afternoons with Heifetz, Rudy Polk, Sascha Jacobsen (he and Kitty had bought a home nearby), Emanuel Feuermann, and others. At one session, Heifetz's nine-year-old daughter Josepha sat next to Annette, making grown-up conversation, remarking, "Your husband is a violinist, isn't he?" Annette nodded, "Yes." Josepha continued, "My mother's husband also plays violin!"

One Sunday Heifetz called to ask me to play viola. I had a small French viola I had purchased for chamber music; it had very old strings. As we played quartets, my strings kept breaking. Feuermann jokingly asked, "Mr. Kaufman, is this why they pay you so highly in Hollywood films?" This great cellist then played second violin, holding the violin between his legs like a cello! What a superb artist he was! What a tremendous loss for the musical world that he died so young (the result of complications from a minor operation).

Actor Basil Rathbone's memoirs recount his and his wife's delight in attending Jascha's chamber music parties (with delicious suppers) and my participation in these events in the semitropical ambiance of Heifetz's living room facing the ocean. Many years later, after Jascha and Florence were divorced, the house was sold, and, as became customary in California, the new owners, not appreciating the beauty of Wright's elegant simplicity, tore it down and built another California "marzipan-style" dwelling!

Our long friendship with Alfred Newman endured through his three marriages. His last and most felicitous companion, Martha, was mother of their five children: Lucy Lee; Alfred Jr., gifted for finance; David and Thomas, who both became film composer-conductors; and Maria, a professional violinist and composer. Alfred's premature death from overwork, cigarettes, and drink ended an epoch. A private family service prevented Newman's many Hollywood colleagues and friends, including us, from paying last respects to this valued colleague of the "Golden Years." Robert Russell Bennett wrote to me on 28 March 1970, "I hear our friend Alfred cashed in. This is news none of us can take lightly. He was a remarkable man."

I first met Victor Young, an excellent Polish violinist-conductor, at Columbia Studios in the 1930s when he directed an aria from *La Bohème* with soprano Grace Moore. Thoughtfully, Victor called Moore aside to indicate where she was singing a few wrong notes. Furious, she had him dismissed pronto, and replaced by Victor Baravalle. Her unprofessional attitude surprised me. I thought she should have been grateful for such helpful advice. She also had a gifted young tenor singing Rodolfo removed from the film, fearing he would take attention away from her singing. She had become a *monstre sacré* (a contemptuous French term for self-centered, aging performers). In contrast, Victor was polite, friendly, and pleasant to work with.

At Paramount, I played in several of his well-written scores, including *For Whom the Bell Tolls* where he evoked the Spanish idioms of Granados and de Falla. This was among the first film music to be issued on commercial records by the enterprising Decca Record Company. I appreciated Victor listing my name on the record label. I played for his last score, *Around the World in 80 Days*, and joined his colleagues in mourning his sudden death only a few days after that exhausting recording. A truly grandiose "swan song."

Among other Paramount film scores I played in were *Holiday Inn*, which featured the beguiling "White Christmas," and under Robert Emmet Dolan's musical direction for *Going My Way*, which featured Bing Crosby as a helpful Catholic priest in a poor neighborhood.

The considerable strains of Hollywood recording took a great toll on Hollywood composers and players. Due to union penalties for orchestral sessions continuing after midnight, conductors would ask me to record intimate solos after dismissing the large orchestra at midnight. This intense solo effort for the microphone after a long day's work as concertmaster often resulted in my left hand and arm muscles being extremely tense and tired. Annette suggested that instead of driving home to West Los Angeles in the wee hours and rising exhausted for the next day's recordings that I remain in Hollywood, take a steam bath at a Swedish sauna near the studios, have a relaxing massage, then sleep there before returning to an early morning session. This proved a lifesaver on those occasions when I had several consecutive days of recording. Other times Annette occasionally traveled to Hollywood via bus to join me at dinner breaks and then accompanied me back to the studio to await the session's end, so we could drive home together.

We led healthy lives in Southern California. Every free day Annette and I took long walks at nearby beaches or swam in the unpolluted Pacific Ocean. We browsed in bookstores and visited Earl Stendahl's art gallery, where we bought pre-Columbian sculptures and some paintings. We traveled to nearby museums — San Marino had the splendid Huntington Library, Art Collections and Botanical Gardens, with exotic plants and flowers. The San Diego Museum was fascinating for the old masters purchased by the Putnam sisters: splendid works by Bernardino Luini, Francisco Goya, and Andrea del Castagno, a great Zurbarán, and impressive Byzantine icons.

We often drove to Santa Barbara, a charming city with Spanish-style architecture, where Wright Ludington had an extraordinarily fine collection of modern French paintings and Greek sculptures, which he eventually gave to Santa Barbara's art museum.

We made hurried trips to San Francisco to enjoy special exhibits from New York, and became friends of Dr. Grace McCann Morley, who headed the San Francisco Museum of Modern Art. Years later, we visited her in Paris when she worked at UNESCO. As a result of her fine work there, Indira Gandhi invited Grace to be director of the art museum in New Delhi, where she continues to dwell. We also enjoyed visits with Dr. Walter Heil, director of the de Young Museum, who acquired some great old masters for that important collection.

We fortunately became friends of the elder Mr. Gump (founder of the famous store), who, in spite of blindness, knew every object in their fascinating shop. We also met his son Richard, and Mr. Rosenblatt, who headed their Oriental department. Over several years we acquired many important Indian, Khmer, and Thai sculptures from them. Gump's granted me museum status, which meant special attention and reduced prices for important Southeast Asian masterpieces.

Franz Waxman arrived from Germany's Universum Film AG films, after being brutally attacked by Nazi thugs. Waxman fled Berlin in 1933, with his wife, Alice. After a brief Paris sojourn, they reached Los Angeles in 1935, where they made a large contribution to the city's musical life. Franz saved his father and mother from the Holocaust, bringing them to Hollywood, somewhat reluctantly on their part, as they so loved their fatherland.

I played in Franz's first American score, *Bride of Frankenstein*, a seminal work which influenced many later horror-film composers. There were many solos in his MGM score for *Boom Town*. Other effective Waxman scores I played in were *Suspicion, Rebecca,* and *Magnificent Obsession,* where he introduced the theremin to film music, which added an ominous intensity to the plot. Clara Rockmore, who had been a colleague of mine in Kneisel's class, became devoted to popularizing this eerie-sounding instrument.

For *Sayonara,* Franz wanted an exotic sonority for the Japanese American love story. I suggested a muted viola, and then recorded solos on my small French viola, which provided the desired color. In Franz's score for *To Have and Have Not,* the film that introduced Lauren Bacall (supposed to be a singer—a Hollywood convention of that period, everybody sang), I softly played a "sweetener track" close to her ear to keep her on pitch. I frequently recorded such inaudible "sweeteners" at Fox for Sonja Henie's singing during her film career. Her skating expertise was not matched by a tonal sense. However, she had a great eye for painting and collected a splendid group of French modern masterpieces, now the core collection of a museum in her native Norway.

Annette and I spent many pleasant evenings with Franz and Alice at their Hollywood hillside home or ours. Sometimes we played music together, discussing art, music, composers, and conductors. A mutual pleasure was listening to Toscanini's and Koussevitzky's symphonic programs, broadcast nationally each week. Koussevitzky's innovative programs introduced works of Sibelius, Britten, Martinů, Bartók, Copland, Roussel, etc. Toscanini's performances of traditional symphonic and operatic great works were infinitely superior to what was generally heard in America and Europe. We still remember his thrilling performance of Verdi's *Requiem,* then rarely heard.

We admired Franz's unflagging devotion to classic music. He founded (and partly funded) the Los Angeles Music Festival, which presented unusual modern and classical repertoire at UCLA's Royce Hall for many years. He was the only conductor to program major Stravinsky works during that composer's residence in Beverly Hills, while the Los Angeles

Philharmonic virtually ignored his compositions. I vividly remember Franz's eloquent and stirring performance of Stravinsky's *Oedipus Rex*.

In spring 1952, Franz invited me to play and conduct baroque concerti of Bach, Bonporti, Telemann, and Vivaldi with a chamber orchestra, which received gratifying praise from the audience and press.

Franz had most unusual courage and integrity in his personal and musical life. He composed excellent concert music and used a baton expertly. His masterly orchestrations were influenced by Mahler, then unfamiliar to most musicians. He was invariably pleasant and polite to musicians and colleagues, and his scores were always interesting to play. Our friendship continued in Europe and America (he conducted in the Soviet Union and Israel), until the premature death of Alice from cancer, followed a few years later by Franz, who succumbed to the same malady. Their son John is devoted to furthering his father's significant contribution to the film and concert world.

I first encountered Robert Russell Bennett, a remarkable composer-conductor, at Universal Studios in 1935, while recording Jerome Kern's *Show Boat*. Bennett's orchestration indicated a solo passage for two violins, which didn't match. Russell, extremely observant, said, "Play both parts, Louis." I answered, "You'll be sorry!" He smiled, "I don't think so." I recorded the phrase in double stops in one take. That evening, I reported to Annette, "I've met the most gifted and charming man today, Robert Russell Bennett." She replied, "Don't you remember? He composed a fine *Abraham Lincoln* symphony and an opera, *Maria Malibran*." Her memory always impresses me!

A week later, I happened to sit next to Russell at Roy and Jeanie Webb's dinner party for Russell and Louise Bennett, Cyril Mockridge, Annette, and me. I had often played in Webb's scores including *Becky Sharp*, *Abe Lincoln in Illinois*, and *Joan of Paris* at RKO. I urged Russell to compose some violin pieces in the popular idiom.

Two days later, a Sunday morning, he called. "Louis, come over and get your piece." "What piece?" He responded, "What was all that campaign you gave me the other evening about a new piece for fiddlers?" "We'll be right over!"

Picking up my violin case, I immediately drove Annette to Bennett's Beverly Hills home. Russell sat down at his grand piano, handed me violin parts, and we sailed into his *Hexapoda* or *Five Studies in Jitteroptera*. The movements, *Gut Bucket Gus*, *Jim Jives*, *Betty and Harold Close Their Eyes*, *Jane Shakes Her Hair*, and *Till Dawn Sunday*, were breezy, brilliant, and poetic! I offered, "Russell, I'll play this at my next Town Hall recital in April. Could you play it in New York with me?" "Definitely. I'll be in

New York for rehearsals and the opening of *Oklahoma*." (Russell was the orchestrator for Gershwin, Jerome Kern, and Richard Rodgers-Oscar Hammerstein II musicals.)

*Hexapoda* was a great hit with the audience. Russell and I had to repeat two pieces, and New York's press gave us unstinting praise. Russell towered over me by almost a foot. Due to complicated cross-rhythms in *Jim Jives*, I unconsciously tapped my right foot slightly to keep in place, which gave a rather jazz-combo effect. Russell received an SOS telegram from Boston's *Oklahoma* tryout just before we went on stage. He left that night after the performance for Boston to rework some routines and orchestrations before the Broadway opening night made musical comedy history. Shortly after *Oklahoma*'s successful premiere, Russell recorded *Hexapoda* with me for Columbia Records. (*Ed. note:* That historic record was rereleased in 1991 on CD by Bay Cities and reissued by Cambria Records.)

The following summer, Heifetz called me from Balboa to request some chamber music, adding, "Bring along that *Hexapoda* piece, Louis. I'd like to hear it." After a long afternoon of playing quartets, Annette and I played Bennett's pieces for Jascha and his friends' enthusiastic approval. We were delighted when Jascha declared, "I'll play it." I immediately sent off this good news to Russell. The Bennett piece met with great success in Jascha's recital and he had to repeat it, as marked on the program. Jascha later recorded *Hexapoda* with pianist Emmanuel Bay for Decca Records. Russell had thought of writing a violin concerto for Fritz Kreisler but always lacked time for its composition. I suggested he write a fiddle concerto for me. He became interested and promised he would compose one at the first opportunity.

Russell and his wife, Louise, pulled up stakes, sold their Beverly Hills home, and moved back to a New York apartment for a weekly radio program with orchestra for WOR Mutual Broadcasting's network. He composed delightful half-hour opera programs based on popular American tunes: *Oh! Susanna, The Man on the Flying Trapeze, Jeannie with the Light Brown Hair,* and *Take Me Out to the Ball Game* (Russell was a baseball fan). These enchanted us when we heard the broadcasts in Hollywood. Nadia Boulanger, a distinguished French Russian teacher and mentor to many distinguished American composers, who was spending the war years in New York, was equally enthusiastic about these fascinating programs. The routine of writing a work of his own choice each week led Russell seriously to consider writing my violin concerto.

Russell was a splendid conductor, always polite and pleasant to musicians. I have stressed composers' and conductors' behavior to orchestras, for I noticed untalented, incompetent conductors (hired via nepotism) were often rude, loudly berating musicians to conceal their own lack of knowledge and skill. My Hollywood colleagues were astonished when I refused to play for such types! Russell heard of my abrupt departure from Fox in the 1940s due to the atrocious behavior and language of an incapable relative working there, and he sent me a note:

> Dear Louis,
> Lack of time makes it difficult to write letters of any length, but I owe you thanks for many interesting notes and clippings. I was glad to hear you left FOX since the reasons were so clear. I'm always glad to see a friend with the same idea I have, which is a quotation from a very fine businessman, Max Dreyfus, "THERE ARE SOME KINDS OF MONEY THAT YOU DON'T WANT."
> We look forward to your recital in March. Josef Coleman (WOR's concertmaster) and I have a plot to turn out a concerto within a few weeks, but whether it will be worthy of your steel or not remains to be seen. Also remains to be seen whether lack of time makes us call the whole thing off, but I hope not.
> Yours ever, Russell

On Friday, 6 December 1941, another bulletin from Russell:

> Dear Louis,
> The concerto well played by Joe Coleman last night although an air raid test broke into it at one point, spoiling the recording. I'll be happy to have you play it and will send you the violin part soon. The piano accompaniment will be a problem because there isn't any. I had to make a cut in the Andante for time, but believe it should not be made for concert or recital. If I can possibly do the piano arrangement, I'll do it within the next two weeks.
> A Happy or Courageous New Year to you both, Russell

On 14 July 1944, another report:

> Dear Louis,
> I am rewriting the entire VIOLIN CONCERTO. The only radical change being practically a new finale. The first movement has mostly changes in orchestration, and a different beginning for the cadenza. The second movement has a change in the middle. The Scherzo is intact, and God help you in the Finale! Sorry you have had a cold. Take good care of yourself and may we meet again soon. I'll send the new CONCERTO in a few days.
> All send love to you both,
> Russell

An 8 August 1944 letter had news of the changes:

Dear Louis,
I am enclosing a hastily copied solo violin part of the CONCERTO in its new and I hope permanent form. Passages that are changes from the old way, aside from a few minor changes in orchestration, have a red line under them in this solo part. I have rearranged the orchestration for four horns, third trombone, and tuba, and made a complete new copy of the entire score. I don't know how soon I can get a piano arrangement in shape because the hectic season is now on, but I wanted to send you the violin part to show you just where I had double crossed you.
Love to both of you,
Russell

Russell played his Concerto in A with me at my New York Town Hall recital in March, which made a good impression. Irving Kolodin wrote in his review of 26 March 1942: "The Bennett concerto has the air of musical breeding native to his talent—a score whose distinctions would undoubtedly multiply, given proper orchestral background." Charles Mills in *Modern Music* for 19 February 1942 mentioned my broadcast with Russell on his WOR *Notebook* program: "A surprisingly nice work. This is undoubtedly his best piece."

Leon Barzin, a gifted Belgian conductor, engaged me to perform the Bennett concerto with his National Orchestral Association orchestra at Carnegie Hall in February 1944, which brought a note from Russell:

Dear Louis,
Looking forward to seeing you before long. I made the changes in the orchestration of the concerto according to the way we played it at Town Hall. The cuts we made for the piano performance should be restored for orchestra unless they don't do it well. After some study, I decided that the Scherzo is largely effective for its unexpected shortness. However, the whole piece will get a good going over sometime before I die. Barzin is very sound in tempo and understanding as to balance and dynamics. I look forward to your performance with him. I've had a very hard year of work just past, and certainly hope for more time for serious study this year. *Carmen Jones* is a big hit, so the year 1943–1944 was not a total loss artistically. Let us know when you are to be with us.
A very prosperous New Year to you both. Love from us all,
Russell

On 14 February 1944 Carnegie Hall was packed to the rafters for Barzin's program, which featured my performance of Russell's concerto.

Robert Russell Bennett and Louis at Bennett's New York apartment.

We all gathered fine praise from the audience and press. Louis Biancolli in the *New York World Telegram* headlined: "Bennett Concerto Jazz-Tinged," concluding, "Mr. Bennett can no more avoid syncopation than Bach could avoid fugues. But he knows how to dress it up for a Carnegie airing and bring it in classic line with fine grasp of technique."

Leon and his wife invited Russell, Louise, Annette, and me to their Central Park West flat for a private celebration after this auspicious event. Russell was a charming, modest man and delightful conversationalist, which made our visits with him memorable. But he could be caustic when he encountered arrogance. He once remarked to an overbearing producer who pompously informed him about a musical matter, "I know you want it to smell bad, just tell me what flavor."

During one New York visit I performed the last movement of the Tchaikovsky violin concerto, with Russell conducting the WOR symphony. At the rehearsal, I said, "Russell, let's not play it too fast." After the performance, which seemed very comfortable to me, Russell said, "Louis, you played much faster than at the rehearsal." I replied "Really? I thought we played it slower." Russell smiled, "It's what the French call *le trac*—due to the adrenaline of the performance, one's idea of tempo changes. Each minute seems like five, so you think you are playing slower!"

Russell later composed a lyrical, colorful *Song Sonata* in five movements for violin and piano, which Annette and I played frequently in concerts. Heifetz later added it to his repertoire. I recorded it with Theodore Saidenberg, and it was released on CD by Cambria Records.

Our devoted friendship with Russell endured until his death in New York in 1981. We always visited with the Bennetts whenever we were in the New York area, even if only for a few days. Nicolas Slonimsky's tribute, "success haunted him," only refers to Russell's Broadway musicals and his music for the NBC series, *Victory at Sea,* composed with Richard Rodgers. This greatly gifted, attractive gentleman also made important contributions to concert music.

Dr. Miklós Rózsa, a Hungarian composer-conductor, contributed much distinguished music to films with his fine melodic gifts, masterly orchestrations, and dynamic conducting. He wrote major symphonic works and chamber music during his Hollywood residence, composing a brilliant, romantic violin concerto, premiered by Jascha Heifetz, and an equally effective viola concerto premiered by Pinchas Zukerman in Pittsburgh, with André Previn conducting. We attended several of his concerts when he conducted local orchestras. Annette and I became close friends of Miklós and Margaret, his English wife, for we shared interests in painting and sculpture as well as musical ideas. Miklós assembled an impressive collection of old master paintings and Roman and Etruscan sculptures. We occasionally dined together and met in Rome and Prague while touring. I played in some of his scores, including *Ben Hur, The Lost Weekend,* and *Double Indemnity.*

Mehli Mehta, father of Zubin, conducted a performance of Rózsa's Concerto for Violin and Cello. I played with Hungarian cellist Gabor Rejto and the Los Angeles American Youth Symphony. I performed the Brahms concerto under Mehta's direction and also the Los Angeles premiere of Ernest Bloch's concerto with Mehta and his extraordinary youth orchestra. Thus I can attest to his genius in imparting, style, tradition, and vitality to countless young musicians, who have gone on to posts in major symphonies.

A letter from Miklós Rózsa from Salita, S. Agostino, Santa Margherita, Italy dated 27 July 1982 is worth quoting:

Dear Annette and Louis,

It was really heartwarming to read the wonderful review, *The Kaufman Legacy.* True enough, there were (and are) very few concert violinists who play and record the music of their contemporaries, instead of the thousand times heard and recorded well-known works. But it needed courage, guts, and faith in the new composers and Louis had them—bless him.

A whole generation of his contemporaries owes a debt to him. Fortunately he chose sane composers and Schoenberg's miserable concerto remained a closed book for him. Louis Krasner had his fun with this one and now that Stravinsky and Bartok became classics, who plays Schoenberg, apart from a few fanatics—no one. I hope it will stay this way.

Visiting Ricordi's New York shop in 1942, Annette and I found Aaron Copland's *Ukulele Serenade* in a violin folder. It looked very interesting. Deciding to play it, I wrote to Copland, who replied on 8 December 1942:

Dear Mr. Kaufman,

I was glad to get your letter and to know of your plans in regard to *Ukulele Serenade.* Although the piece was composed as long ago as 1926, it has never caught on, that is, with violinists. Therefore, I was particularly pleased to hear you thought it an addition to the repertoire. I myself don't know of any performance in Los Angeles or Boston. Naturally there is no way of my being absolutely certain that no such performance took place, without my knowledge. Of course, I'd be glad to go over it with you in the spring. Looking forward to meeting you personally.

I am, sincerely yours,

Aaron Copland

Aaron was pleased that Annette and I performed it on concert tours. It made a great hit at my 16 March 1943 Town Hall recital. Virgil Thomson wrote in the *New York Herald Tribune:* "Its hard-as-nails brilliance shone like steel. Both piece and performance were a pleasure."

When Aaron visited Hollywood to compose and conduct his score for *The Red Pony,* I seized the opportunity as concertmaster to ask him to arrange the "Hoedown" from his ballet *Rodeo* for violin and piano. Aaron protested, "I arranged it for orchestra from a fiddle tune—why restore it?" I persisted, "What you did with it is terrific! Let us fiddlers have it in your version."

On 14 June 1945, he wrote:

Dear Louis,

Thanks for your letter. As it turned out, I went to the wilds of New Jersey instead of Paris. It was bad for my impresario career, but excellent for my composing! I'm beautifully settled in a cottage with a cook and a baby grand piano and hope to do lots of work. Sometime during the summer, I want to get around to doing the "Hoedown" arrangement for you. I feel a little worried without you nearby for advice; but if it is no good, we can always start all over again. Have just finished reading *The Fervent Years* by my friend Harold Clurman. I think you'd be interested in it—hope you will read it.

My best to Annette.

Yours, Aaron

Another note, 19 October 1945 from Copland:

Dear Louis,

Forgive the slow answer to your nice note. I was off to Boston and New York hearing performances of *Appalachian Spring*. I'll make the arrangement of the "Hoedown" from *Rodeo* and mail it off on November 1 at the latest. You can depend on it. Excuse the haste—but I imagine this is mostly what you want to know.

Regards,

Aaron

A few weeks later the manuscript arrived. I wrote Aaron to tell him what a great piece it was and he suggested I edit the violin part. Annette and I played it in many concerts and later recorded it and *Ukulele Serenade* for Vox on a 78-rpm disc that is like a cat with nine lives. Concert Hall bought it; it was reissued by Canadian Masters of the Bow series, reissued in 1991 by Bay Cities, and later reissued by Cambria. It is gratifying that my pioneer recordings are considered worth "new life" as recording systems have rapidly changed.

After Aaron returned to Hollywood, I played in his remarkable, Oscar-winning score for *The Heiress,* which starred Olivia de Havilland and Montgomery Clift. Aaron composed a Sonata for Violin and Piano in memory of a colleague who was killed in World War II, which he performed with me at New York's Town Hall. It garnered impressive praise for us both. Aaron was very pleased, for his previous performance of the sonata had been devastatingly panned!

Hugo Friedhofer, a native Californian with a vandyke beard (unusual then!), created fine orchestrations for many Hollywood films. He greatly profited from his association with such masters as Korngold and Waxman. He composed scores of high quality, sometimes as ghostwriter. I was concertmaster for his scores for *The Adventures of Marco Polo, The Best*

*Years of Our Lives,* and, later, *Boy on a Dolphin.* He was extremely courteous and polite, and truly interested in music—rare in Hollywood, where people in the trade almost never attended concerts. Annette and I often met him at chamber music and orchestral concerts.

Rudolph Polk arrived in Beverly Hills as Heifetz's personal manager, soon becoming an agent for performers and composers who surfaced in sunny California. The amiable Rudy and his wife, Pauline (a gifted painter), bought a Beverly Hills home and resumed pleasant dinners and chamber music afternoons or evenings as they had done in New York. Annette and I were invited frequently, and I played second violin to Jascha Heifetz, with William Primrose or Virginia Majewski as violist, and cellist Lauri Kennedy (first cellist of the Los Angeles Philharmonic).

In one memorable session we played the Brahms G Minor Piano Quartet with Vladimir Horowitz, Virginia Majewski, and Lauri Kennedy. Heifetz, who had already played Mozart and Beethoven quartets, graciously said, "I'd like to rest. You play it, Louis." Horowitz performed with grandiose panache. When we reached the finale's frenetic climax, Horowitz winked at us and improvised a dazzling cadenza in Hungarian-style, instead of playing Brahms's own cadenza (printed in minuscule, near-illegible notes). Exhilarated by his virtuosity, we joined in with gusto for the thrilling coda. The small audience was delighted by the compelling élan of his pianism.

Rudy told us of Darryl Zanuck's ignorance of the violin world. He had tried to persuade Zanuck to feature Heifetz in a film. Zanuck pointed to a copy of *Life* magazine on his desk, with a cover photo of Yehudi Menuhin, remarking, "If your man is so good, why isn't his picture there?" I reassured Rudy that Zanuck relied on the musical advice of his masseur, former wrestler Fidel La Barba, who only knew two pop tunes: the theme for the radio show *Calling All Cars* and "Dinah." If a composer's theme strayed too far from either of these models it was often rejected. However, when Alfred Newman, whom Zanuck greatly admired and trusted, arrived at Fox, La Barba's vox populi status abruptly ended.

Rudy brought composer Mario Castelnuovo-Tedesco, his wife, Clara, and their son, Lorenzo, unexpectedly to our home one evening. They were recent refugees from Florence, Italy, and we shared a great appreciation of Italian painting, sculpture, and architecture and of Shakespeare. Mario, Clara, and Lorenzo all had exquisite manners and a gentle affability. Mario taught composition to such gifted musicians as pianist Leonard Pennario, pianist-conductor André Previn, Jerry Goldsmith, and concentration-camp survivor Leon Levitch.

Mario also made orchestrations for films, sometimes as a ghostwriter. Toscanini and Heifetz featured his symphonic and violin compositions. Mario particularly admired Annette's playing of my accompaniments.

In 1958, Mario won a Milanese competition for an opera to be produced at La Scala with his opera *The Merchant of Venice*. Mario told us that after the premiere at the Florence's Maggio Musicale, a young twelve-tone composer was ecstatic about his opera. Surprised, Mario replied, "I am perplexed that you who are so committed to that school like my music." The young man replied, "Oh Maestro, I can't write a melody!"

Annette and I attended the American premiere of *The Merchant of Venice* by the Pacific Coast Opera Company at the Shrine Auditorium, with singers Nell Rankin, Chester Ludgin, Richard Torigi, and Brian Turner, with Dick Marzello conducting. We also attended and enjoyed many local concerts of Mario's music. My quartet organized a concert of his music at Barnsdall Park including his String Quartet, Opus 203, which the Castelnuovo family attended. I believe his lyrical genius will be appreciated more as the musical world realizes the poverty of inspiration in electronic sound.

Several German Jewish refugees, firmly convinced of their superior culture, informed us that the German translation of Shakespeare's immortal masterpieces improved the original! Some immigrant composers and writers had difficulty adjusting to our different world.

Rudy told me that he introduced Ernst Toch, a distinguished Viennese composer, to film director Josef von Sternberg. The director, attempting to impress both visitors, walked to a piano in his office and loudly struck middle C and announced, "THIS is the note I want featured in the score." Toch turned abruptly and walked out of the room, and Rudy heard him mutter, "I can't work for such an idiot."

Other composers handled such uninformed encounters with greater tact. Alexandre Tansman, a distinguished Polish composer who also wrote film scores in France, told me that when he arrived in Hollywood, and was presented to an RKO executive, he was greeted with, "Mr. Tansman, we're making a French film, it takes place in Paris, and we have French actors Charles Boyer and Michele Morgan, so you must write absolutely French music, as French as Tchaikovsky!" Without hesitation, Alexandre replied, "Naturally," and scored the film. Tansman and his wife, an excellent pianist, played several of his violin and piano works for Annette and me and gave us manuscripts of these scores.

Rudy Polk coproduced with Sam Jaffe a series of half-hour films featuring Jascha Heifetz, Artur Rubinstein, Gregor Piatigorsky, Jan

Pearce, Marian Anderson, and the Coolidge String Quartet. The first set, personal accounts of Heifetz's and Rubinstein's life at home, contained musical performances. Annette and I were invited to a preview and thought they were very interesting. These charming musical interviews might have found a worldwide audience on public television, but they were fifty years ahead of their time. Rudy and Sam failed to find adequate distribution, and only a few colleges and schools here and in Canada subscribed. The resulting financial disaster caused cancellation of the second series. Most of the performers accepted cancellation without fuss, but Heifetz, upset by what he considered Rudy's irresponsible behavior, placed a legal attachment on the Polk residence for nonfulfillment of contract. The regrettable affair ruptured the Polks' friendship with Heifetz. Tragically, the well-meaning Rudy died from a massive heart attack shortly afterwards.

Ernst Toch arrived from Austria with his wife, Lilly, and their daughter, Franzi. They purchased a home in Santa Monica and converted a large wooden packing box, which had transported Ernst's grand piano from Europe, into a beach house. They found a deserted spot for it on the beach, where we occasionally joined them for a swim and a picnic lunch (later the beach house was swept out to sea by a winter storm). We became friends and visited each other's homes for dinners and musical soirées, enlivened by Toch's musical and Jewish jokes. Toch was an excellent pianist and I often took part in performing his chamber music. Annette and I attended a performance of his delightful opera, *The Princess and the Pea,* at a Los Angeles New Music Festival.

In 1938, Toch composed *Cantata of the Bitter Herbs,* Opus 65, in memory of his mother, at the suggestion of Rabbi Jacob Sonderling of Fairfax Temple in Hollywood. The Fox orchestra offered their services for this work written for orchestra, chorus, and soloists. I took part as concertmaster, and little eight-year-old Franzi sang in the chorus at a Passover Celebration concert.

Elizabeth Sprague Coolidge, indefatigable champion of chamber music ensembles and composition, commissioned Toch to write a piano quintet (Opus 64). Alfred Leonard, owner of the Gateway to Music record shop and host of a popular radio program about music, arranged for Toch and my Kaufman Quartet to perform this newly composed quintet in a public concert and to record it for Columbia Records. They engaged Nicolas Slonimsky to write the program notes. Alfred and Toch supervised the recording of Toch's *Spitzweg Serenade* for two violins and viola (myself and Grissha Monasevitch on violins and Raymond

Louis on Santa Monica Beach, with Franzi Toch and Ernst Toch taking their picture. Photograph by Lilly Toch.

Menhennick on viola) for Vox Records. Alfred, an enterprising refugee and a prominent local personality, later founded the Music Guild, which still exists, to present distinguished chamber music ensembles. I premiered Toch's Second Sonata for violin and piano with Toch's accompaniment at a Los Angeles recital and the same spring at New York's Town Hall with pianist Vladimir Padwa.

Years later, in 1958, violinist Joseph Stepansky, violist Louis Kievman, and cellist George Neikrug and I recorded Toch's String Quartet, Opus 18, in D-flat Major, composed in 1909 when the composer was twenty-one, which received the Mozart Prize, thus deciding his fate as composer (rather than a doctor as his father wished). With the same group, sans cello, I again recorded the *Spitzweg Serenade* for Contemporary Records, a company formed by blacklisted Hollywood writer Lester Koenig to record definitive versions of the works of contemporary composers. I found it extremely helpful that Toch supervised these recordings.

Working under the baton of Erich Wolfgang Korngold, a splendid composer, conductor, and virtuoso pianist of winning modesty, fascinated me. He arrived in Hollywood in 1934, accompanied by his wife, Luzi, and two sons, Ernest and George, exact images of their father. By good fortune the Korngolds had escaped the horrors of the German takeover of their

Austrian homeland. The close-knit family eventually occupied three adjoining homes in North Hollywood.

Max Reinhardt, engaged to mount and direct Shakespeare's *A Midsummer Night's Dream* at the Hollywood Bowl, transformed the hillside into a wondrous fairyland. He invited Korngold to compose a score for his production.

Warner Brothers seized the opportunity to have this world-famous composer write scores for their Burbank studio productions. His extraordinary melodic gifts and masterly orchestrations enhanced Warner's historic and daring adventure films.

Working with Korngold was pleasant. His Viennese tact and charm made him a devoted friend of everyone he encountered. He was exceptionally modest, and his bons mots became legendary. When someone at the Hollywood Bowl complained that airplanes flew over the site during the softest music, he quipped, "All the pilots have scores." My favorite was, "Even a *great* performance can't spoil a fine composition."

I played his scores for *Juarez* and all the swashbuckling films of Errol Flynn: *Captain Blood, The Sea Hawk, The Adventures of Robin Hood, Anthony Adverse,* and *The Private Lives of Elizabeth and Essex,* among others. He was invariably polite and good-natured at recording sessions, although meticulous in achieving precisely what he wanted. He was unfailingly cheerful, and always inquired after our morning break, "How was the lunch, boys?" (there were also women players in Warner's orchestra).

Korngold, Steiner, Waxman, Rózsa, and Herrmann all shared a comprehensive knowledge of music and orchestration, which their scores reflected. Many of today's musicians and composers lack understanding of the orchestra's capabilities, which accounts for the monotony of their sonority. Korngold, sitting at the piano, could approximate the range and color of an entire orchestral score and with a few gestures achieve exactly the performance he envisioned.

The Nazi political and cultural blight, which forced Franz Werfel, Thomas Mann, Arnold Schoenberg, Ernst Toch, Bruno Walter, Darius Milhaud, Otto Klemperer, Lion Feuchtwanger, and many others into the New World, cruelly cut Korngold off from the European opera houses that competed for his premieres. His opera *Die tote Stadt* was simultaneously premiered on the same night by opera houses in Hamburg, Cologne, and Vienna with great success.

Unfortunately, American critics were merciless in their contempt for composers, conductors, and performers who had "sold out" to Hollywood. This caused Korngold much sorrow. When Heifetz premiered the Korngold violin concerto in Dallas, it received great acclaim from the public and press, with the sole exception of one New York critic who couldn't resist a cheap-shot headline, dubbing the work, "more Korn than gold," which was widely repeated. This lyric concerto will long outlast many arid twelve-tone concertos now praised by self-styled "Beckmessers." Time alone will sort out the music and art worthy of enduring admiration.

My final recording under Korngold's direction was his score for the unfortunate Warner Brothers remake of Somerset Maugham's *Of Human Bondage*. I remarked to Annette, "This is where we came in; it's time to leave."

There were other compelling reasons. I had tempting opportunities to record classical music in Europe, thanks to the success of my recording of Aram Khachaturian's violin concerto. Two of my subsequent recordings, Vivaldi's *Four Seasons* (for Concert Hall), and Smetana's Trio with pianist Rudolph Firkusny and cellist Willem van den Berg (for Vox), were listed by the *New York Times* among their Best Recordings of 1948. Then Editions Amphion released my *Quatre Saisons* in Paris. Thanks to Vivaldi scholar Marc Pincherle's enthusiasm for this recording and his membership in the Académie Charles Cros, the recording was awarded the French 1950 Grand Prix du Disque. Annette and I decided to leave Hollywood as soon as possible.

One fortunate result of my playing and recording Smetana's Trio with Rudolph Firkusny was his suggestion that I visit Bohuslav Martinů on my next New York visit and obtain a copy of his recently composed *Concerto da Camera* for violin, piano, and string orchestra, which Rudy considered a masterpiece.

Martinů and his French wife were childless and loved Firkusny as a son. When I visited Martinů, the composer welcomed me warmly and gave me a manuscript copy of the unpublished concerto. At our hotel I immediately began to study it and discovered some triple stops that were not possible for one violinist to play. However, by rearranging a few notes in these chords any professional soloist could play them. I knew Martinů had been a professional violinist in a Paris symphony and it seemed arrogant for me to tell him how to write for violin. I discussed this with Annette, who urged me to speak frankly to Martinů, who might not be aware of this problem. We visited Martinů, and I said, "I think it is a great work and I'd very much like to play it, but I've found it almost impossible to play these chords as written. Would it be possible for you to rearrange the notes so you'd keep the harmony you want?" To my surprise, Martinů was delighted, and replied, "Kaufman, two violinists have told me the work was unplayable but didn't explain their problem. So I

Louis with Bohuslav Martinů at Martinů's flat in New York City, 1949.

never knew *why!* Of course your suggestion is excellent, I'll change those chords. You know, I'm so used to writing divisi parts for orchestral violinists, I sometimes am unaware that one fiddler cannot play all the notes in a chord that I've envisaged."

Edouard Nies-Berger, also a great admirer of Martinů's music, had formed a chamber orchestra and he invited me to premiere this dramatic work under his baton in 1950 at Town Hall. It received such warm praise from the press and audience that Capitol Records decided to have me record it later in Paris. Martinů could not attend the premiere as he and his wife had returned to Paris. Firkusny sent us the following letter on 15 January 1949:

> Dear Annette and Louis:
> Thank you for your wonderful letter. I was very pleased that our Smetana Trio was listed among the year's best—and I certainly hope that this was only a beginning of our further cooperation. I'm happy that everything worked out well. I won't be here unfortunately when you play it—but I will be thinking of you and hope to see you both very soon.
> Yours very sincerely,
> Firkusny

# 15

# Another Aspect of Hollywood—
# Art and Music

## *William Grant Still—Darius Milhaud*

We often visited Earl Stendahl's art gallery on Wilshire Boulevard and entered the world of art we had enjoyed in Paris and New York. Earl had great vitality and boundless enthusiasm for the arts. His adventurous spirit led him to world explorations, and he enlivened Los Angeles by arranging stimulating exhibits. He showed Galka Scheyer's collection of the *Blaue Reiter* painters Klee, Kandinsky, Feininger, and Jawlensky; and Picasso's comprehensive paintings and studies for his great mural *Guernica*. He introduced pre-Columbian masterpieces to Los Angeles and Europe. His son Alfred, a pilot in the Pacific theater during World War II, enlarged the family's scope with the arts of India and Cambodia. We spent many fascinating hours with the Stendahls at their gallery and home. His wife, Enid, was an excellent chef and we enjoyed gastronomic dinners at their Hollywood home, and later with them at restaurants in New York, Mexico City, and Paris. Years later, when Galka Scheyer died, Earl was responsible for keeping her collection intact and making it part of the Norton Simon Museum of Art in Pasadena. When he heard from Mexican artist Miguel Covarrubias that a fine Alaskan museum was absolutely without funds and its important artworks would be sold off, Earl flew there and bought the entire Rasmussen collection. He refused all offers to sell it piecemeal and accepted a very low price so our friend, Robert Tyler Davis, of the Portland (Oregon) Art Museum, could acquire it. After Davis's departure the Portland Art Museum unfortunately did sell off part of the collection.

Earl introduced us to their neighbors Walter and Louise Arensberg. Their home was furnished with beautiful antiques, including some Queen Anne chairs from Mrs. Arensberg's family. They welcomed artists, collectors, art world professionals, and writers, who were invariably served cold pineapple juice and thin slices of pound cake. Although they were forty years our senior, we considered them more youthful in spirit and enthusiasm than most of our colleagues. They listened to what their visitors had to say. This led to stimulating discussions about art, artists, music, drama, photography, archeology, et cetera whenever we spent an evening in the midst of their oasis of enchanting contemporary and ancient art.

Some people reported having difficulties with them, but since we were musicians and never contested their opinions we only had most agreeable visits with them. Their collection comprised sculptures of Constantin Brancusi; almost all the notable works of Marcel Duchamp, including three versions of *Nude Descending a Staircase,* one of his glass paintings, and some "ready-mades" (ordinary objects with incongruous titles, signed); three small important Cézannes; a large Douanier Rousseau *Jungle Scene;* several Paul Klee paintings; a Calder mobile sculpture; assorted cubist paintings of Picasso and Braque; an early Matisse (a stunning female portrait); an important large cubist Chagall; a great Juan Gris Parisian landscape; Dali's *Premonition of Civil War;* and early works of Jacques Villon, Renoir, Jawlensky, Fernand Léger, Metzinger, and Picabia. Their collection of pre-Columbian art grew each year and comprised outstanding stone and pottery sculptures.

They gave us Jean Charlot's book, *Art from the Mayans to Disney* (Sheed & Ward, 1939). Charlot considered Louis Eilshemius "the greatest American painter of his generation," a view shared by Marcel Duchamp! Charlot, a remarkable painter and muralist, worked in Mexico at the time José Clemente Orozco created great murals. We acquired some of Charlot's etchings and paintings from Stendhal.

Besides their passionate obsession with art, Walter was involved in research to prove that England's Lord Chancellor Francis Bacon had written the poems, comedies, and tragedies attributed to William Shakespeare. Annette and I were also intrigued by this subject and thought Christopher Marlowe might also have been the author or worked closely with Bacon.

We met many interesting artists, museum directors, scholars, and writers at these Arensberg open house soirées: New York collectors Sidney and Harriet Janis (who came to see our collection and borrowed two Lebduskas for a national exhibit they organized to publicize their book,

*They Taught Themselves,* about primitive American painters), Bernard and Becky Reis from New York (who assembled an important collection of paintings and sculpture and became great friends), photographers Edward and Bret Weston, Man and Juliet Ray (who became friends for life after our first encounter), actors Vincent Price and Edward G. Robinson (who had unusually fine collections), and Professor Lionello Venturi, an Italian refugee and art historian who came to see us after visiting the Arensbergs' great collection. He was fascinated by the works of Louis Eilshemius, so Walter advised, "If you want to see Eilshemius, visit the Kaufmans," which he did.

On his first visit to our home Man Ray didn't approve of our collection, as we did not have any surrealist works, but upstairs he saw the only painting I had ever made. One afternoon in New York, in 1930, I had visited Avery's studio, and Milton unexpectedly said, "Why not paint something, Louis?" I accepted the challenge, asking, "What do you think I should paint?" Milton suggested, "Make a portrait of Berkman" (Aaron Berkman was in the studio). I set to work on a small cardboard Milton handed me. I made Aaron's chin and jaw red (presuming he had tender skin, like myself) and not being able to draw an ear drew a clock on his three-quarter profile—and his short disorderly black hair made a nice pattern. Milton commented, "That's not bad, Louis, paint something else." I demurred, as I felt one Kaufman artwork was sufficient! Years later Annette framed it and placed it in my room. Man, seeing it, exclaimed, "That's the only interesting painting you have! Who did it?" I replied, "I have no idea—it just amused me to pick it up."

Other visitors we met at the Arensbergs were the composer Edgard Varèse, writer Henry Miller, Mexican surrealist painter Roberto Montenegro, Abraham Rattner (an artist refugee from France), and writer Clifford Odets. Arensberg was annoyed when Odets stated, "No writer would ever permit his work to appear under another name." Evidently he ignored the fact that Balzac, Stendhal, George Sand, George Eliot, and many other writers chose to write under pseudonyms.

Walter and Magda Pach visited the Arensbergs and our home. Walter had a delightful story: when he helped organize New York's famed 1913 Armory exhibit, there was much publicity about Duchamp's *Nude Descending a Staircase.* One afternoon a lady asked to meet the director. Pach was amused when she requested, "I'd like to have a lady show me that Nude!" Walter Pach wanted to paint Annette's portrait but somehow our schedules never permitted that to happen.

We enjoyed meeting Kenneth MacGowan at another Arensberg soirée. He was greatly interested in pre-Columbian art and came to visit our collection. Danish painter Knud Merrild became another friend, though he returned to Copenhagen after World War II.

We introduced painter Mark Rothko to the Arensbergs when he visited us in Los Angeles and also drove him to Stendhal's gallery, for he was searching for a dealer. When the Averys visited us in 1938 we took Milton, Sally, and March Avery to the Arensbergs' home, which delighted them. The Arensbergs, however, never could appreciate Avery's paintings or the subtle masterpieces of Pierre Bonnard, for neither artist belonged to categories counseled by their friend and mentor Marcel Duchamp, an enigmatic genius. He aided them, however, in acquiring works by Chagall and Dali, cubist works, and Brancusi sculptures (including some of his own chefs-d'oeuvre).

When David and Mary Burliuk made a jaunt to Los Angeles, we introduced them to the Arensbergs. It pleased Walter that Burliuk was fascinated by his theory that Bacon's authorship of Shakespeare could be proved by numbers (he had two secretaries counting each word, according to some mathematical system). Burliuk translated, to Arensberg's delight, the Russian writing on their important early cubist Marc Chagall (painted soon after his arrival in Paris). This canvas depicted a poet, his head upside down, pen in hand, having just written "Every Day the Same Old Thing." Burliuk, enchanted by the Arensbergs' large Douanier Rousseau *Jungle Scene*, made a small watercolor copy of it, which he presented to them as an appreciative souvenir of his visit to their stunning collection, and it is now permanently on view in the Philadelphia Museum of Art. Unfortunately it is not well displayed, for they entrusted the installation to Marcel Duchamp, who separated the Brancusi sculptures and pre-Columbian works from the paintings, with the result that the magical juxtaposition and atmosphere of the Arensberg ensemble was missing.

Another lifelong friend we met at Stendahl's gallery, who often was at the Arensbergs, was pianist and art dealer Theodore Schempp. After study at Oberlin, Ted gravitated to Paris to study with Alfred Cortot. He bought a small apartment in a building where Georges Braque lived, and soon realized his true métier was art. He became an established modern-art dealer and trusted source for museums and collectors, dividing his time between France and the United States. This was at a time when significant collections could be made with modest means. No one then could imagine the soaring prices those paintings would reach in today's market; the Arensbergs paid a only few thousand dollars for Picasso and Matisse paintings that now cost millions. Schempp had a fine Steinway piano and enjoyed playing it and attending concerts. We bought a few small paintings from him.

The Arensbergs helped Dr. Karl With, a distinguished German art historian, museum director, and Orientalist, to enter the United States with his bride, Gerda, a painter. We became close friends and later collected Gerda's work (their son Christopher became curator at the National Gallery of Art in Washington, D.C.). Karl had assembled Baron von der Heydt's outstanding Oriental collection, which now forms Zurich's Rietberg Museum in the Wesendonck mansion, where Wagner composed his first draft of *Tristan und Isolde*. We often visited that fascinating museum during the 1940s. When we purchased two Khmer heads from visiting London-based Quaritch Wales, we hired Karl to authenticate a large head from Gump's collection. This was the first money he earned in the New World.

We drove Lucille and Bernard Herrmann to meet the Arensbergs, and though they admired the fine English antique chairs, they were put off by the profusion of modern French, German, and Spanish paintings, hung in the manner of nineteenth-century galleries in two or three rows on the walls, along with Oriental rugs, pre-Columbian stone and pottery statues, and most of Brancusi's sculptures. As I drove them home, Benny cautioned, "Look out, Louis, or your house will someday look like that!"

Mrs. Louise Arensberg played piano, and they both always attended my Los Angeles recitals. She had great charm, excellent taste, and quiet wit. One evening Mrs. Ruth Maitland, who had a fine art collection, and who greatly admired the Arensbergs' avant-garde works, was recounting her experience as a judge for a Los Angeles exhibit. Impressed by a banker on the committee, she repeated several times, "Louis, he has a heart of pure gold," until Mrs. Arensberg sweetly murmured, "That's usual for a banker, isn't it?"

The Arensbergs once traveled five days by train to New York only to make some purchases from Brummer's gallery. They returned home via train the same night! They suggested we visit Brummer on our next trip to New York, for he had remarkably fine Romanesque and pre-Columbian sculptures. This proved a fascinating encounter for us. We purchased a fine Totonac thin stone head in profile. Brummer recounted his debut as an art collector. "I was extremely poor in Paris, slaved for a year, skimping meals, to buy a Romanesque statue, and later found out it was fake," he said, adding, "one benefit of collecting is the knowledge one painfully acquires." He continued, "Douanier Rousseau's portrait of me was not a commission, I was a model. He paid me almost nothing for posing for him. I remember Guillaume Apollinaire asking Rousseau, 'Why have you painted petite Marie [Laurencin] so huge in my portrait?' Rousseau replied, 'You're a great poet and deserve a great muse.'"

The lively conversations, personalities, and general ambiance of the Arensberg soirées remain vivid memories. With these friends and the opportunities to attend the Pasadena Playhouse performances of Shakespeare's rarely produced plays—*Timon of Athens, Troilus and Cressida, Cymbeline,* and *Coriolanus*—we never considered Hollywood a cultural desert.

The literary giant Irving Stone, and his wife and editor, Jean, were also friends of the Arensbergs, but we first met them the summer of 1953 when I was head of the violin department at Santa Barbara's Music Academy of the West. They visited the academy to address faculty and students about their research for his biographical novels. They loved music and attended an academy concert of baroque concertos (most of which I had discovered) that I played and directed for string orchestra, with Annette as continuo. We became friends for life.

Shortly after meeting Milton and Sally Avery, I had become profoundly influenced (as were many of my generation) by Irving Stone's richly humanized *Lust for Life,* a historical novel about Vincent van Gogh. At this period van Gogh's significance was not widely recognized. This compelling book led to a reevaluation of van Gogh's oeuvre and made publishing history, for after rejection by seventeen publishers it sold millions of copies. Irving's small publication advance paid for their wedding!

I gave my copy to Annette when we met; she found it equally engrossing, and we both were artistically enriched by Irving's subsequent novels, including *The Agony and the Ecstasy* (life of Michelangelo), *Passions of the Mind* (Freud), *Sailor on Horseback* (Jack London), and lives of Darwin, Heinrich Schliemann (who discovered Troy), and Camille Pissarro. I greatly admired Jean's sage reply to persons fanatically enraged by Irving's account of Darwin's theory of evolution—"Why can't you believe that God created cells that can grow and change?"

Both Irving and Jean supported libraries and lectured at colleges, universities, and music schools. They were passionately concerned with education. They enjoyed congenial visits with friends, and we were fortunate to spend many occasions with them, including anniversaries, family weddings, and Passover seders. They invariably combined Jews without family and gentiles to partake of this traditional dinner to celebrate "justice and freedom from slavery." One evening a gentile man sitting next to Annette remarked, "I never knew Jews had happy holidays"—for this was a gala celebration!

Both Annette and I always thought Irving's great literary work deserved a Nobel Prize for the scope and quality of his remarkable achievements as well as his perfection of a personal form, the biographical novel. We shared many interests, and they enriched our lives with their example and friendship. At his memorial service in 1988, publishers, musicians, art collectors, and motion picture and theatrical people paid tribute to his life and myriad accomplishments. But the most moving tribute was paid by Jean, who rose and simply said, "Irving exists in his books." His and Jean's remarkable union (like ours) exemplified an Arab proverb, "Marriage is a garden of delight," for we both had partners who could share in the pleasures of achieving our best work in our chosen fields.

We appreciated the opportunity to meet and become friends of the great French composer Darius Milhaud, who with his wife and son escaped from the Nazi oppression in Paris. He usually sat in a wheelchair due to a lifelong rheumatic problem. His distinguished Spanish Jewish antecedents had arrived in Provence in the fifteenth century. His mother's Italian family were descendants of Jewish Princess Bernice, loved by Emperor Titus (who was forbidden by Roman law to marry a foreigner). Milhaud's wife, Madeleine (a Parisian cousin), was a talented actress who coached a generation of stars, including Irene Worth. She was also a peerless cook. Their son, Daniel, was studying painting with Italian refugee Corrado Cagli.

We met Cagli at Milhaud's Mills College cottage, as well as visiting composer-conductor Manuel Rosenthal and his wife, Claudine Verneuil, an excellent soprano who protected and supported him during the Nazi occupation of France. After France's liberation, Manuel became conductor of l'Orchestre National de la Radiodiffusion Française, and instituted scheduling five orchestral rehearsals for every new composition that was programmed. He had broadcast all of Stravinsky's major orchestral works (banned during the occupation). We became good friends, and I was soloist with Manuel when he became conductor of the Seattle Symphony Orchestra.

Shortly after they arrived at Mills College Annette and I were presented to the Milhaud family by his student, Charles (Sandy) Jones. I premiered Jones's Sonatina for Violin and Piano in Los Angeles, Boston, and New York, which led to its publication by the American Music Center. (My subsequent premiere of Gail Kubik's Sonatina also led to its publication by the AMC.) Jones became a lifelong friend in Oakland, Los Angeles, New York, and Paris. We shared love of music, violins, painting, and excellent cuisine. He was always urbane and pleasant, with the manners of an English lord.

Milhaud was committed to students and to the new in music, arts, theater and poetry. He listened with infinite patience to young efforts and viewpoints. He greatly admired and aided Erik Satie. Milhaud's appreciative ear welcomed his European contemporaries Debussy, Stravinsky, Sauguet, Poulenc, Honegger, and Hindemith. He conducted the Paris premiere of Schoenberg's *Pierrot lunaire* in the 1920s.

In 1937, I was studying Milhaud's *Concertino de Printemps* and wished to play it for him before my public concerts. The Milhauds invited Sandy and us for lunch at their Mills College cottage. Their son Daniel was seated at a nearby table with a young female student. During a lull in our conversation, we overheard her defiantly ask, "So, what is a work of art?" Twelve-year-old Daniel loftily replied, "Everyone knows a work of art is a mystery." I have never heard a better definition!

Milhaud was clear and precise about musical performance. We worked over the concertino carefully. Milhaud suggested I invite Igor Stravinsky to my next Los Angeles concert, which I did. Stravinsky graciously came backstage to congratulate me as a serious musician, especially pleased by my performance of Beethoven's Kreutzer Sonata and Milhaud's concertino.

We had many subsequent visits with the Milhauds in the Bay Area, Los Angeles, Paris, and London. Milhaud had studied and played violin as a youth, thus he had intimate knowledge of its possibilities. He thought concertos should be difficult in order to display performers' virtuosity. We shared enthusiasm for painting, theater, belles-lettres, and music, and never lacked subjects for engrossing conversations.

During one unforgettable conversation with Robert Russell Bennett in Los Angeles, we discussed various orchestrators for George Gershwin's Broadway musicals and some of his later ambitious orchestral pieces. Gershwin's curious association with Joseph Schillinger's system (a complex mathematical approach to analyzing and composing music) seemed to have aided him in his own orchestration for *Porgy and Bess*. Then I asked, "Who did the imaginative, colorful, and delicate orchestrations for Willard Robison's WOR *Deep River* programs? They seemed to be just woodwinds and strings, and they fascinated Annette and me." Russell replied, "Everyone in the trade knew they were the work of William Grant Still. He's a very gifted composer and a fellow member of ASCAP. He's most pleasant and charming, and lives here. Why don't you call him? He's in the phone book."

I called Still and made a date to meet at his home on Cimmaron Street. We were warmly welcomed by Still and his wife, Verna Avery (a pianist and writer about music and dance of Russian Jewish descent). To my dismay, Still said, "I've always composed for a specific event or performer. I've never met a concert violinist before so it never occurred to me to write for violin." Verna suggested, "Some of Still's piano pieces might also be played on violin." She sat down at their piano and played a few. One, "Blues" from the *Lenox Avenue Suite* commissioned by CBS, captivated us both. I asked, "Mr. Still, would you make a fiddle arrangement of this piece?" He modestly replied, "You know the instrument better than I do, Louis, why don't you make it, then play it for me and we'll decide what to do."

My harmony and composition classes at the Institute often came in handy. I made an arrangement; with a few changes I placed the melody an octave higher, and added harmonics and a few double stops. A couple days later, Annette and I performed it for the Stills, who were very pleased with my work. Annette and I performed this "Blues" piece widely in Europe and North and South America. It always received enthusiastic audience and critical response (usually we had to repeat it). Still later I orchestrated an accompaniment for my violin version for a CBS *Invitation to Music* program in New York, conducted by Bernard Herrmann, who greatly admired Still's music.

I also performed this arrangement as an encore with the National Orchestral Association at Carnegie Hall, conducted by Leon Barzin. Robert Simon of the *New Yorker* stated: "Mr. Kaufman and the Orchestra added the 'Blues' movement from William Grant Still's *Lenox Avenue Suite* to the great approval of the audience." This attractive and engaging work caused Russell Bennett to comment, "Ravel must have looked down from Heaven and smiled when Billy wrote that." I performed "Blues" on a few national programs over NBC and WOR.

Then Still composed a Suite for Violin and Piano, which he dedicated to us both. Works created by distinguished African American artists inspired this work. The first movement is "African Dancer," suggested by Richmond Barthé's large bronze statue in New York's Whitney Museum. The lovely slow movement refers to Sargent Johnson's handsome colored lithograph *Mother and Child,* at the San Francisco Museum of Modern Art, and the lively, jazzy third movement is Still's reaction to Augusta Savage's small bronze sculpture *Gamin.* I premiered the Suite at Boston's Jordan Hall and New York's Town Hall in March 1944 with pianist Vladimir Padwa, then played it at a Modern American Music Festival in Los Angeles with Annette. In 1945, I broadcast it with the Standard Symphony conducted by Henry Svedrofsky, and in 1946 broadcast it in New York with the WOR Symphony, with conductor Emerson Buckley.

I suggested to Still, "You know there's only one tone poem for violin,

William Grant Still and Louis Kaufman; this historic photograph broke the color barrier of "separate" photographs when it was published in the *New York Times* and *Newsweek*, 1943.

by Ernest Chausson. It would be a most attractive work for violinists if you would compose in that form." Billy immediately agreed and composed an imaginative, expressive tone poem, for violin and piano or orchestra, entitled *Pastorela*, inspired by California's varied landscapes, which we widely performed and later recorded for Orion Records. I also played his *Summerland*, a piano piece I arranged for fiddle.

Another friend, opera singer Herta Glaz, came to visit the Stills with us. She sang his *Songs of Separation*, based on works of African American poets, at many of her concerts during the 1940s and 1950s. Our friendship and association with Still had unexpected, socially significant results. The *New York Times* and *Newsweek Magazine* published articles with photos of Still and me looking over his music. Reliable reporters told us that this was a premiere event, for neither publication had ever before printed photos of white and black musicians together. Robert Bartlett Haas, head of UCLA's Art and Humanities Extension Department, suggested, "Louis, I know you and Annette are friends of the Stills. Please invite me to dinner when they next dine with you." We became close friends of the Stills and often dined at each other's homes, and watched with delight as their children, Judith Anne and Duncan, grew up.

Duncan Still became a research scientist and Judith Anne a writer and English teacher. She married a marine engineer, Lawrence Headlee, who was killed in a sea disaster caused by faulty equipment. Young Judy suddenly was widowed with four small children, but Lawrence's employer denied compensation to Judith and her family. I recounted this tragedy to Judge Gus Solomon, who remembered a recent similar case in New Jersey where the family won. Judy's lawyer looked up the case and won for her a generous settlement, which provided for the children's education and a Caribbean cruise for her parents. Judith was not able to meet them on their return, so Annette and I met Verna and Billy at the harbor and drove them home.

We admired Verna and Billy personally as well as musically. I have always believed two people who love each other devotedly and work together can accomplish as much as twenty others. Still's music, based on beautiful melodies like those of Mozart and Schubert, was ennobled by his love of God, people, and humanity. The genuine modesty of this gifted composer was expressed by words he placed at the end of his compositions: "With humble thanks to God, the source of inspiration."

At one of Rudy and Pauline Polk's chamber music soirées, I was delighted to meet Efrem Zimbalist again. He was in a very friendly and expansive mood, and told Annette and me of his Russian childhood memories. Reminiscing about Professor Auer's class he began, "I clearly recall being astonished when nine-year-old Mischa Elman appeared at an early-morning class lesson in Saint Petersburg. You undoubtedly know Jews were not permitted to stay overnight in that Imperial city. We older students (I was fourteen) were curious to know who arranged this for Mischa and his father. Auer politely asked the lad, 'What would you like to play for me?' Mischa answered, 'What would you like to hear?' The professor, annoyed by such brash innocence, replied, 'Play something by Paganini.' Mischa performed a Paganini caprice brilliantly! Whatever Professor Auer requested, Mischa played with exact intonation and remarkably beautiful, velvety sound. Auer immediately enrolled him in our violin class. I remember how definitely Mischa changed Auer's conception of tone and technique. He closely observed what Mischa had learned from his violinist father, who was the son of an Odessa klezmer-fiddler."

Zimmie continued, "After only three years' study with Professor Auer, one day Mischa disappeared from class! Auer became furious when a student from Odessa brought him a newspaper clipping announcing that young Mischa Elman would perform three concertos in Odessa! Enraged that Mischa and his meddlesome father had departed so unceremoniously—and dared to announce that Mischa would perform in concert works the lad had not studied in class—Professor Auer expelled Mischa from the Conservatory. This barred Mischa and his father from returning to Saint Petersburg.

"However, Auer's curiosity overcame his anger. He traveled to Odessa to hear the concert and discreetly sat in a back row. He was so pleased by Mischa's performance that he went backstage and embraced Mischa, saying, 'I forgive everything—you may return to my class.' Papa Elman replied, 'Thank you very much, Professor, but it's not possible. Mischa has engagements in Germany and is going to be soloist with Nikisch.' This was unheard of! The famed conductor Arthur Nikisch was known to detest child prodigies!"

Zimmie concluded, "Perhaps Mischa should have continued to study with Auer to profit from the professor's long experience and musicianship." A few weeks later at a private luncheon with Mischa and his wife, Helen, I related Zimbalist's conversation with us (omitting his concluding remarks) to Elman. Mischa, very surprised and pleased, said, "So *I* am the source of the Russian school?" I assured him Zimmie could attest to that! He was old enough to remember Auer's comments before and after his arrival in Saint Petersburg!

# Bernard Herrmann—
# Another View

*Other Friends, Anthony Collins—Herrmann's
Rebirth and Apotheosis*

Orson Welles's masterpiece *Citizen Kane,* with Bernard Herrmann's innovative score, greatly impressed Annette and me, so I was especially pleased to meet and work with Herrmann, an enthusiastic young conductor, on his score for Welles's next film, *The Magnificent Ambersons.* A highlight of the score was a nine-minute violin solo with only woodwind accompaniment to underline Richard Bennett's long soliloquy about the Ambersons' decline, which we recorded in one take. (However, later the scene and its music were eliminated, and the film was dramatically cut and given a "happy ending." Herrmann protested this mutilation of his score by removing his name from the screen credits. Roy Webb was hired to patch up a musical conclusion to close this botched production.)

After that first encounter, I reported to Annette how stimulating the day's session had been and how fascinating Bernard's comments about music, composers, and conductors had been during orchestral breaks. About 10 P.M. that evening, Bernard was walking in our neighborhood (he had rented a house nearby) and observed our lights on. He knocked at the door and entered to say how very pleased he was with my performance of the long solo (he, too, played violin). Attracted by our paintings, sculptures, and books, he became engrossed in speaking about music, art, and books, only departing about 2 A.M. We were equally

Lucille Fletcher Herrmann, Bernard Herrmann, with baby Wendy and Dorothy (Taffy) as residents in the Kaufman home, April 1946.

entranced by his conversation and thoughts about the vast universe. He mused, "Imagine an ant in this living room . . . could it envisage the size of your house with many rooms, on a block with several houses, in a city containing hundreds of thousands of buildings, the extent of Los Angeles County, the state of California, the entire United States, Canada, Mexico, Latin and South America, the Pacific and Atlantic Oceans,

Asia, Africa, and Europe?" Benny continued, "Whenever I am annoyed that some music isn't well played, I think of the universe's infinity and how insignificant such matters are!"

We became close friends of Benny and his wife, the screenwriter Lucille Fletcher, and admired their adorable little girl Dorothy (Taffy) and baby Wendy, who arrived a year later. With Lucille and Benny we browsed in bookstores and visited the Huntington Library and Art Collections. The museum's impressive collection of English paintings delighted Bernard and Lucille, who greatly loved England and its arts. They introduced us to the delights of travel, painting, and musical books of the Sitwells.

Bernard became obsessed with composing an opera based on Emily Brontë's *Wuthering Heights,* and over many years would perform excerpts for us, playing on a small rented upright piano, and singing all the roles in his hoarse, cracked smoker's voice. Lucille had created a libretto using Brontë's own words as much as possible. Benny couldn't bear the idea of any cuts being made in the completed work, so he refused several opportunities for its production, including one with Julius Rudel conducting the New York City Opera.

I found it bracing to work on Benny's next score, *All That Money Can Buy,* based on Stephen Vincent Benet's *The Devil and Daniel Webster.* This inventive score featured a reel that no *one* violinist could perform. I played "Pop Goes the Weasel" with a few virtuoso tricks several times. Benny then imposed these sound tracks on top of each other, creating a dynamic sonic montage for the violinistic Beezelbub, Mr. Scratch! This effective score won the coveted Academy Award for Herrmann. Jascha Heifetz asked Benny, "Who was that violinist?" Amused, Benny replied, "Oh, a Hungarian fiddler I picked up."

Bernard, a fascinating, stormy personality, enriched America's musical life with his New York CBS broadcasts of rarely heard American, English, French, Russian, German, and Austrian composers. He generously invited refugee composers to conduct their own music with the CBS Symphony, among them Erich Wolfgang Korngold, Igor Stravinsky, Darius Milhaud, and Anthony Collins. Bernard premiered works of Charles Ives, Gerald Finzi, Edmund Rubbra, and Ralph Vaughan Williams, and revived nineteenth-century composers Joachim Raff and Hermann Goetz, whom George Bernard Shaw considered more gifted than Brahms! During the afternoon rehearsal of Goetz's symphony, Benny suddenly asked the orchestra to stand up while playing. He had read that all orchestral strings (except cellos), woodwinds, horns, and so forth, stood during performances until conductor Hans von Bülow let them sit, and he wondered if standing would result in a different sound.

The orchestra flatly refused. Herrmann persisted, "Please, just play a few bars standing." Benny and I were surprised how much better everyone played, suddenly displaying increased vitality. They performed like artists, not "routiners."

Benny suggested, "You ought to look up Goetz's violin concerto, Louis, and we'll play it together." I found a first edition of this early Romantic concerto in one movement with orchestral parts and score in Europe. (The International Music Company in New York published my edition of this attractive concerto in 1989.) Fate did not permit me to premiere it with Benny; my first and only performance of it was in Glasgow with the BBC Scottish Symphony and conductor Ian Whyte.

I told Benny that Stokowski had based his orchestra's string playing on the tonal expressiveness of Mischa Elman. Bernard sent me the Khachaturian violin concerto, in the Russian edition given to him by Am-Russ (the American outlet for Soviet composers), urging me to learn it, and we broadcast this work for CBS. Am-Russ then asked me to edit the violin part for an American edition. Their new edition, however, merely photographed the Russian violin part, ignoring my work—a penny-pinching economy. NBC soon after asked me to broadcast the Khachaturian concerto with their orchestra, conducted by Frank Black, "sans fee." I asked why they expected me to perform gratis and received the disingenuous reply, "All soloists with our orchestra gain so much prestige that even Szigeti and Stern have contributed their services!" I responded, "That may be because they live in New York, but I live in Los Angeles, and since CBS has always paid me, I do not think it fair to them to accept your magnanimous offer!"

I have always thought it unreasonable that managers, printers, stage movers, and piano movers are paid without protest, but soloists and composers are considered mercenary for expecting big corporations to pay them for their services. It is both a duty and a pleasure to offer one's performance for charity, or to help composers receive recognition. But I did not consider NBC with its enormous profits entitled to gratis performances!

Annette and I gave our services freely to entertain troops during the Second World War. We played almost weekly at the Hollywood Masquers Club, which brought in marines and army soldiers for a good dinner and an evening of entertainment—often one-act plays by Synge, O'Casey, and others, performed by the Irish Abbey Players who were often employed by Hollywood studios for character roles. My solos fit in between acts or changes of scenes. On cross-country tours we performed at Army and Navy hospitals. One dramatic event occurred on New Year's Eve, at the Veteran's Hospital in West Los Angeles. After we concluded with Schubert's "Ave Maria," an attractive nurse pushed over a lad in a wheelchair, who told me, "Thanks, I really liked that." A few moments later the nurse returned saying, "He was gravely injured by a bomb blast and hasn't spoken in six months." His emotion at hearing the music led him to speak naturally without realizing his trauma-induced silence was over!

Benny frequently invited me to broadcast concertos with him at CBS, and often in New York we visited art galleries, museums, and bookstores together. On one trip, we escorted Lucille and Benny to Milton and Sally Avery's Greenwich Village studio. They were deeply impressed by Milton's quiet self-possession and his large handsome landscapes and still-lifes. But like other collectors, dealers, and musicians whom we brought to the Avery flat, no one was tempted to acquire any Avery works. Annette and I always found them so alluring that we would buy one or two irresistible portraits, landscapes, or still-lifes.

One evening, we invited Bernard and Lucille to join us at the Metropolitan Opera for Debussy's *Pelléas et Mélisande*. Our box seats overlooked the orchestra and conductor, Julius Rudel. Benny, not pleased by the performance, groused *sotto voce* during the opera. Lucy tried to shush him, although Annette and I did not mind that he felt so strongly; we were used to artists and composers having highly personal reactions. Milhaud couldn't bear Brahms; Toch considered French music *schlagobers* (whipped cream.)

In December 1943, Benny wrote to ask if we knew of any house in our neighborhood available for rent during March and April. It was always a grave problem for us to leave our home unattended or with unreliable housesitters. So we offered our home in exchange for their East Fifty-seventh Street flat during our next Eastern tour. On 28 December, a telegram arrived, "Delighted with your wonderful offer. Will arrive myself February third or fourth and would appreciate it if I could stay with you for the week. Lucy and children following February 15th will stay in house until you return. Everything in apartment all right for you here in New York. Will write full details. Love and thanks, Bernard Herrmann."

It was highly stimulating to have Benny as a houseguest. We visited Dawson's bookstore, a large shop on Seventh Street, and he joined us for a chamber music party at the Polks', where his nonconformist opinions about Toscanini and other famed virtuoso conductors and soloists jolted Rudy, Pauline, and their friends.

Hollywood studios were not used to classical composers. Benny made a big fuss about composers' royalties. Miklós Rózsa and Anthony Collins agreed, for they came from England where the Performing Rights Society protected composers. They were all surprised to discover that Hollywood contracts for film scores gave most rights to the studios, including future reuse for recording or broadcasting. Herrmann, Rózsa, Collins, and Waxman helped their Hollywood colleagues obtain royalties from performances of their own music. Benny insisted on orchestrating his own music, and many Hollywood arrangers and orchestrators resented this; they felt they were being put out of a job. After a rather stormy period, they accepted Benny's position.

After a cross-country tour, we comfortably settled in the Herrmanns' attractive New York flat with English antique furniture, a fine piano, and fascinating library. We enjoyed Lucille's March letter:

> We certainly are enjoying your house. We've never stayed in one we liked better. The days aren't long enough to drink in all the pleasure it affords. As for the spiritual side, we are eating our way slowly through your library. The Steinway is now resounding with Siamese music, as Benny has finally gotten up steam. Echoes of gamelan gongs, and xylophones fill the air, as well as Oriental scales. The funny part of it all is that you get used to the Oriental idiom so quickly. Also how much it sounds like Debussy and Ravel. Benny is really enjoying the score, though, as it is a real change from romantic music. The picture, *Anna and the King of Siam,* was rather a disappointment, but one learns to overlook that finally, and go ahead with one's own ideas. This morning Bobby (a maid) is here cleaning, and Benny was composing Oriental motifs. They rang in her head so long, she began whistling them as she went about her work—a true tribute to a composer! The most wonderful thing about your house, as far as the children are concerned, is the balcony—which has become a secondary nursery. Wendy's basket is out there all day and she seems to like listening to the birds, and watching the eucalyptus trees, as she is very good. Taffy has learned to stay out by herself, and sits on chairs, surrounded by tracing books, paper cutouts, crayons, all sorts of inducements to keep her occupied. I like it because they are protected from everything, and I can keep an eye on them, as I work in your bedroom, Annette.

We had established a first night in New York ritual: going to Greenwich Village to visit with Milton and Sally Avery and their gifted daughter, March, to see what Milton had been painting since our last visit and to catch up on gallery news and artists' lives before celebrating together at a nearby Basque restaurant we all loved.

The nights before my New York recitals, Annette and I, along with Sally Avery, would attend a Broadway play. I knew I had prepared my programs as well as I could, and the absorption in plays of Sidney Kingsley, Elmer Rice, and Tennessee Williams, productions by Orson Welles's

Mercury Theater, and best of all Shakespeare freed me from tension and provided inspiration. Sally always requested passes for my concerts for their artist friends who loved music but couldn't afford tickets. So my audiences always included David Burliuk, Chaim Gross, Mark Rothko, Adolph Gottlieb, George Constant, Nicolai Cikovsky, John Graham, Wallace Putnam, Raphael Soyer, and many other Avery friends.

In spring 1946 I played several concerts in Upstate New York, New Hampshire, Connecticut, and Massachusetts, which necessitated three Boston visits (one to play at the great Isabella Stewart Gardner Museum). Leaving Herrmann's flat, I hailed a cab to Grand Central Station. The talkative driver, noticing my fiddle case, said, "You know, my son studies violin. I like violin music, but it worries me—he doesn't want to practice." I assured him as we left the taxi, "When he makes some progress it will be more interesting for him." Returning to New York four days later, I hailed a taxi. It was the same driver, who also recognized me. As we entered the cab, he remarked, "As I was telling you—I can't make my kid understand you gotta practice." We discussed his problem until we disembarked at Herrmann's flat!

The Averys introduced us to Louis Michel Eilshemius in his brownstone house, which he shared with his elder brother (whom he referred to as "Old Fogey"). This handsome aged artist (admired by Marcel Duchamp, Jean Charlot, David Burliuk, and the Averys) had been hit by a taxi; after his recovery, he refused his doctor's advice to exercise, not believing he could, and remained seated in a wheelchair until his death. He was fond of the Averys, and Milton made a stunning portrait of him, which we bought and later presented to the Smithsonian's National Collection of American Art in Washington, D.C. Milton and Sally were enthusiastic about a charming "frieze of female nudes" which we bought that afternoon. Eilshemius was suspicious of checks and wanted cash payment. I dashed down to the street, found a bank, and mounted the stairs to pay him.

He spoke very intelligently about painting with Milton and me, remarking that most artists use too many colors. He stated, "five primary colors can be varied for most works." Learning I was a violinist he asked, "Why don't you play some of my music?" I walked over to his upright piano and looked over some of his printed songs. I found two that could be played and replied, "I'll return tomorrow with my fiddle." This pleased Eilshemius, who added, "George Gershwin bought some of my paintings, but HE never played any of my music."

I bought three of his rather artless self-published books of poetry and two of his printed songs before we departed. The next afternoon, I played the charming naive melodies very softly with mute, while Annette accompanied me unobtrusively on Eilshemius's out of tune piano. He was moved to tears, and as he wiped his eyes he remarked, "No one has ever played my music so beautifully." This time I was prepared with cash. I entered an adjoining room filled with stacks of his paintings and selected two beautiful large canvases, which we bought. Bernard Reis had recommended a fine framer, Lowey; we deposited our Eilshemius paintings at his shop before returning to the Herrmann's flat.

On a subsequent New York visit Annette and I persuaded Russell and Louise Bennett to visit Avery's studio, as I thought he should pose for a portrait. Russell had a most distinguished head. Milton made a stunning El Greco-like portrait of Russell, fascinated by his patrician appearance. Unfortunately the Bennetts did not acquire it—and I was reluctant to buy it—in case they might eventually wish to have it!

Milton, Sally, and March introduced us to Dikran Kelekian, an expert and dealer in modern French paintings, ancient Near Eastern ceramics, Coptic weavings, and early Greek and Egyptian bronzes. While we were there, Marsden Hartley arrived, for he collected small early Greek and Etruscan bronzes. Kelekian was extremely fond of March, whose artistic sensibility was outstanding for any age. He was surrounded by an impressive display of portraits of himself recently made by several New York artists. Those I considered the most outstanding were by Marsden Hartley, John Graham, and a chef-d'oeuvre by Avery, a portrait of Kelekian studying a wonderful small bronze, with a background of simulated Coptic rose-colored weavings. (*Ed. note:* In 1999 Annette saw this painting in the collection of the Metropolitan Museum.) I have always thought Milton's portraits were some of his finest work and greatly underestimated by collectors and critics. I have often wondered what happened to those excellent portraits, especially the painting of Kelekian.

Another letter dated 10 April 1946, from Lucille, bears quoting in part:

> I haven't written you in so long, you must feel completely cut off from home and hearth. However, I have had a vision of you endlessly traveling, and I was haunted by the thought that whatever I wrote you would vanish into the Dead Letter office. Your letter with the San Francisco address came today, and now I shall catch you there, so you will know our plans, and be sure of things here. All is well and has been ideal. We certainly hate to part with your house. It has been the very nicest place we have ever stayed at, and indeed the whole atmosphere this trip reminded us vaguely of our honeymoon days—the same peace and quiet. We have enjoyed every minute of it. But all things must end and I suppose I shall be glad to see New York again. Benny never is. . . . As you know, he shall

have to stay out here three weeks longer until May fourth or fifth to do the recording and dubbing. . . . Bobby is coming twice this week to set the house in order, and I am trying to find Mr. Green to tune the piano, although so far he has been very elusive. Everything is in fine working condition, and tell Louis the ants have kept away as have the mosquitoes, spiders, and any number of bugs. Barry cut the grass and straightened the beds of the garden yesterday. It looks very lovely and smells even better. The white irises are all in bloom, and the colored stock and snapdragons are all out. You have some roses, too, clambering over the arbor.

Benny's eyes are beginning to give out; he has been orchestrating so feverishly these last two weeks. He sits in the dining room, working at the table, and the wooden settee is piled high with music paper, rulers, etc. He has only five more sequences to do but they still keep changing the picture under him, which drives him almost crazy. He expects to start recording next Wednesday.

I finally sold my *Sorry, Wrong Number* to Anatole Litvak for a very tidy sum, and expect to do the screen treatment on it, as soon as I return to New York. It must be ready by June twenty-first. This will be my first venture into that medium, so I'm quite excited. We have much to tell you, but that shall have to wait until we gather round the silver teapot on Monday next.

Love to you, and happy journeying and wonderful performing.

Always affectionately, Lucy

As I look back on those cross-country tours, they merge into a blur of trains, hotels, auditoriums, and colleges, where we tested the acoustics and piano, then played a concert for enthusiastic audiences. It was a great comfort to have Annette's companionship and spirited collaboration. Wherever there were museums to visit she was eager to join me.

When we returned to Los Angeles Benny gave me his working sketches for his score for *Anna and the King of Siam*, saying, "I want you to have them, they were inspired by your Buddhist sculptures." Annette and I considered them too valuable for our library, so in 1957 I wrote to William Lichtenwanger at the Library of Congress Music Division, asking if they would like to have these film-music sketches. Bill was pleased to accept them. This gift was perhaps the first film music to enter that august archive, which so generously aided me to locate rare musical works.

Annette and I were delighted to exchange residences again the next year and enjoy the Herrmanns' Fifty-seventh Street flat as our New York home.

Bernard introduced many Russian compositions and performed several works of Charles Ives with great understanding and sympathy. He suggested that I write to Ives for copies of his four sonatas for violin and piano. When I did I promptly received a charming letter from the composer with the hand-bound scores. Years later I premiered the Third Sonata for the BBC with Irish pianist Frederick Stone. Benny introduced major English works by Edmund Rubbra, Vaughan Williams, and Gerald Finzi. Years later, on an English trip, Benny drove us to visit Rubbra's country home. Rubbra told me that Bernard conducted his Sixth Symphony with total comprehension of his intent unequaled by any other conductor.

In New York Bernard and I broadcast Gerald Finzi's *Introit* for violin and chamber orchestra. This led to my later friendship with the composer and his family, who lived in Newberry, England. Gerald conducted a group (including many English ladies) in performances of mainly eighteenth-century music. When Annette and I visited England we occasionally visited the Finzis' home nearby, and I would perform a Bach or Vivaldi concerto with them.

Bernard greatly admired the compositions of William Grant Still, so I asked Still to orchestrate his Suite for Violin and his tone poem *Pastorela*, which I premiered on Bernard's *Invitation to Music* program at CBS. Later, in London, Bernard convinced a British publisher, Novello, to republish Still's *Afro-American Symphony*.

Bernard was also very enthusiastic about Robert Russell Bennett's violin concerto, which he dubbed *In Popular Style*. We performed it a few times on CBS in New York and later premiered it at one of Bernard's three performances with the London Symphony Orchestra.

I also broadcast the Saint-Saëns Third Concerto with Bernard and the CBS Orchestra. One unfortunate performance was a broadcast of the Chausson Concert for Piano, Violin and String Quartet, Opus 21, with pianist Rosalyn Tureck, which sounded excellent in the studio. I had an air-check made, and we were shocked to realize that the CBS sound engineers had reversed the dynamics of our performances. The tender Sicilienne was louder than the stormy dramatic finale, which was cut down to mezzo forte. I remembered Russell Bennett's dictum, "Every musician should kill a sound engineer, they kill so much music!" Fortunately this disastrous situation has ended; more musically responsible sound engineers are now engaged. European recordings never suffered this situation, for they always had musicians, usually composers, to supervise sound and dynamics during classical music broadcasts and recordings.

Benny introduced us to the gifted English composer and conductor Anthony Collins. English producer Herbert Wilcox brought him to America to compose music for films starring his actress wife, Anna Neagle. In New York, our friend Hannah Bierhof welcomed his devoted

Anthony Collins—composer/conductor—1945.

housekeeper/nurse, Harriet Last, known as "Cissie," who was accompanying Tony's young sons, Tony Junior and Terry, and helped them join their father in Los Angeles. Cissie gave a mother's love and lifelong devotion to the lads, who had been abandoned by their mother, an opera singer. We became close friends of the Collins family.

Bernard urged us to consult his friend Dr. Maurice Bernstein, Orson Welles's stepfather, for our medical needs. Dr. Bernstein's first wife had been Mischa Elman's eldest sister, Minna. After his divorce he had married the widowed Mrs. Welles, and encouraged Orson's early interest in the theater. He loved classical music and was an amateur cellist. We became his patients. We also became good friends of Maurice and his charming third wife, Hazel Moore, and spent many enjoyable dinners and evenings with them.

Shortly after returning from New York, we dined at Musso and Frank's, a Hollywood writers' hangout. As we were leaving, Harold Clurman (stage director in New York), dining with friends, hailed me. "Louis, Aaron wrote me that you gave a *great* performance of his violin sonata with him. It's his only work I haven't heard. Would you play it for me some evening?" We set a date for the next week and I gave him our address. I had recently performed Copland's sonata with Swedish composer and pianist Ingolf Dahl, a professor of composition at the University of Southern California, for a Los Angeles Contemporary Music Festival, so I asked Ingolf to play it with me again. Before playing the sonata that evening, we shared an early restaurant dinner with Ingolf, his wife, Bernard Herrmann, and Franz Waxman, who were also interested in hearing Aaron's violin sonata.

Clurman arrived promptly, unexpectedly bringing along Charles Chaplin, Chaplin's fiancée, Oona O'Neill, and Clifford Odets, whom we had met at the Arensbergs. Mr. Chaplin, descending the three steps to our entrance foyer, slipped and fell to the floor. We were all aghast and rushed to help him, but he gracefully rose unaided, saying, "Don't worry, this is the way I've made my living!"

Ingolf and I played Copland's sonata, which Clurman and the musicians enjoyed. Benny asked, "Why don't you and Annette play César Franck's sonata?" Odets superciliously said, "Oh! Franck's music is too obvious—like Roxy's Music Hall." Benny flared up, "How *dare* you relegate Franck, a great original composer, to such a low level! You have NO idea of Franck's noble symphony, symphonic variations, his dramatic piano quintet, and remarkable string quartet; his sonata is a *masterpiece!*" Odets lapsed into silence, realizing he was out of his depth in such musically erudite company. Chaplin with great charm and tact took over to recount hilarious tales of his Hollywood experiences. Oona buried herself in some art books; she was very young, and perhaps not so interested in the past of her husband-to-be.

Benny asked, "Louis, where are those wonderful Balinese records you bought when we visited San Francisco?" We had recently driven with Benny to San Francisco to see the World's Fair and browsed in book and record shops. Annette quickly located the French Decca discs. Chaplin, hearing this evocative gamelan music, rose from a chair and began to move his head, neck, arms, fingers, eyebrows, legs, and feet in traditional Balinese court dance. He had captured every detail of their slow elegant gestures when he had toured Southeast Asia. It was sheer magic. His slow, expressive movements corresponded to the essence of these highly trained ritual dancers. Chaplin then told us fascinating stories of his traveling experiences. It was an unforgettable soirée.

We had engaged our architect friend Lloyd Wright to enlarge an upstairs bedroom. This became an upstairs sitting room and bedroom for Annette's parents, so they both could relax and visit with us for as long as they wished. Benny was very fond of Annette's mother. At one dinner at our home, she mentioned to Benny and his wife, Lucille, "This is a specially happy occasion, my children's twenty-fifth wedding anniversary." Benny semijokingly offered to Lucille, "We'll never make that!" (They didn't. We never commented on their stormy relationship.) The next day Benny presented us with a gift of two large eighteenth-century English serving spoons, which we treasure.

We were very fond of Benny's mother, who came from New York a few times to visit, as did his daughters, Taffy and Wendy. Benny, pleased that when they came to dine Annette had everything ready to serve immediately, commented, "It's great to dine at the Kaufmans, when you are invited for seven o'clock, you are served at six-thirty!"

Our close friendship with Benny endured through his three marriages, with brief visits in New York, Los Angeles, and London. I always urged him to record his own music and to perform his symphony in London, which he would stormily reject, saying, "New York critics gave me the raspberry when I played it." I persisted, "Benny, London is different—critics there will admire you for your creative gifts, and that will aid your conducting career." I constantly urged him to record all his works and eventually he did. He in turn always urged me to perform in London.

A letter from Benny, dated 15 October 1951, written at Tony Collins's Hollywood home, reveals his nature:

> My dear Louis and Annette,
> It was good to get your very nice and kind letter and also to know that all goes well with you both. We miss you both ever so much and wish that time and space did not separate. We are now living in a charming house in the Silver Lake district and we are planning to stay here the winter. The children spent the summer here with us and a grand time was had by all. I have finished the Opera [*Wuthering Heights*]down to the eyeteeth and have been able to get it off in time for the La Scala contest.

Now the other copies are at the binders, and so the end of the track has been finally reached at long last, and now the heartbreak of getting it on the stage begins. I feel that it is the best I can do and to keep on it longer would be to kill it with improvements. So here goes.

I do wish to take this opportunity to thank both of you for your faith, encouragement, and deep friendship during the creation of this opera, for you see it is not only my own creation but also that of my friends, who suffered so long under my torments and doubts and whose help and faith I needed so very much, so again, dear Louis and Annette—thank you—THANK YOU. I was kept busy this summer writing a new picture for Fox, *The Day the Earth Stood Still*. I wrote mostly for electronic instruments: theremins, electronic organs (three of them), and also for electronic violin, cello and bass, harps, piano, and brass. Do go and see it, when it shows, as I am sure you will enjoy it. Please excuse the awful typing and spelling, but I assure you it is a million times better than my scrawling.

Now that the opera is out of the way I have been turning my attention to resuming my conducting efforts and getting my opera produced, the best plan I can think of goes as follows, and please keep it as a confidence. I plan to stay the winter here and try to do two pictures in a row, save a good part of the money, enough to live a year upon and go next fall to Europe. Take a flat in London and see what I can do about getting concerts and the opera put on. I feel that the USA is a dead end for me, and what I need is a lot more of concerts abroad to impress them at home, but most important of all, to get the opera on. I am sure that I can get recordings to do in England, radio dates, etc., but that I must be prepared to hold out a year at least. What do you think of this?

I am sure that we could do many concerts and recordings together, and that I could offer the European concertgoers a new type of program and performance. But the most important thing would be that it would give me a new renewal of my creative life, and so perhaps the concerts I so long ago promised you would be forthcoming. Please not a word of this to anyone. Please keep on writing to me care of Collins as I live only a few minutes away and pick up mail there every day.

My mother was very ill this past summer and had a very serious operation, but she has made a complete recovery. Thank God. Heard Heifetz the other day, he played a piano recital upon the violin, all transcriptions, reminded me of a brain surgeon doing a corn operation. I guess that type of musical life isn't my dish. The boys said that he played better than he ever did in his entire life, but what a waste of time on such rubbish and cheap music.

Waxman, [with] whom I am not on speaking terms, returned from Europe and informed the press the world was waiting for the Waxman. . . .

But enough of these revelations. Keep well, and let me have the dates of your being in New York and if you come this way we have a very special Kaufman guest room awaiting you—AND I MEAN IT.

Love Benny and Lucy

Bernard became irascible in his last few years of life. He was portly, gray-haired, had high blood pressure and weakened lungs from continual smoking, but he always was extremely pleased to see us. We found it tragic that he was obviously so unhappy with his musical life, which made us extremely sad after our London visits. Then suddenly, young filmmakers, impressed by his effective scores for Welles and Hitchcock, "discovered" him and enlivened his life with their overwhelming enthusiasm. International acclaim followed quickly and has flourished to the present day. Young Steven Smith wrote a compelling biography of Herrmann, *A Heart at Fire's Center*, which has received great praise.

In Los Angeles in 1967, Lucien and Mary La Porte (cellist and violist colleagues and friends) invited several friends to their home for luncheon to meet Benny and his fiancée, Norma, and to hear Benny's *Wuthering Heights*, recorded in London in 1966. It was a lovely sunny afternoon. Annette and I were thrilled and excited to listen to fine voices interpret the various roles and the beautiful orchestral sound of this inspired work! Benny gave us an autographed copy of this excellent recording. But most people have a short attention span, and by the time the third act started, everyone had evaporated except the La Portes and us. That must have been a painful experience for the aging Benny. I told him, "You know the attractions of sunny days here. They wouldn't have stayed to hear Mozart, Wagner, or Verdi!" In any event this recording caught the notice of Stefan Minde, conductor of the Portland (Oregon) Opera, who eventually decided to produce it for a world premiere in November 1982. Alas! Benny died in his sleep in December 1975 after completing a Hollywood film scoring, so he never saw nor heard *Wuthering Heights* in an opera house.

The Portland premiere coincided with a "Louis Kaufman Week" arranged by the Portland Community Music Center to honor me, for Annette and I have supported the Center with funds, bows, and fiddles for over forty years. Judge Gus and Libby Solomon, who introduced us to the school, hosted a lovely dinner party for us with many guests at a large hotel.

Craig Reardon, a young fan of Herrmann's who traveled to London to interview Benny a few years before his "rediscovery," flew up to Portland for fourteen hours to dine with Annette and me before the performance and attend the opera with us and the Solomons. He caught an early morning flight back to Los Angeles. At my suggestion Craig gave his Herrmann interview notes to Steven Smith for the Herrmann biography.

Minde wrote a most appreciative and moving note for the opera program, opining that it would be fine if it proved a success, but regardless, it would be historically significant. We considered it a smashing success! The capacity first-night audience was transfixed by the poetry and drama of the music. The cast included Victor Braun, a handsome stage presence who sang with passion and colored his voice wonderfully, from the young ardent Heathcliff to the embittered old man. We had heard him sing Jupiter in the Richard Strauss opera *Die Liebe der Danaë* in Santa Fe and also as Loki in the Wagner *Ring* in Seattle.

The Cathy, Barrie Smith, was also ideal in appearance and sang well in spite of a cold. Chester Ludgin as the drunken Hindley sang a remarkable aria expressing his hatred of Heathcliff, which recalled the intensity of Moussorgsky in color and drama! I was deeply impressed by Herrmann's beautiful, tender, expressive orchestral interludes.

The stage director, Malcolm Fraser, scenic designer Carey Wong, and costume designer Saundra Kaufman were uniformly excellent. We were enchanted and moved by the opera.

The audience listened intently and at the conclusion gave the conductor and cast a tremendous ovation. Minde directed with most sympathetic understanding and precision. The opera came alive in the theater! Annette and I felt that the premiere justified all the anguish Bernard had lived through in composing it.

We had a heartwarming reunion in Portland with our dear friend Lucille Fletcher Wallop, Bernard's first wife, who had written the splendid libretto, Benny's daughter Dorothy (Taffy), who had become a successful author of biographical novels, and his brother Louis and sister Rosie, whom we hadn't seen for many years. What a wonderful week!

Mr. Ernest Bean and his wife Ellie, the manager of the Royal Festival Hall in London, replied to our account of Bernard's *Wuthering Heights* on 28 November 1982 from their Dorking home:

Dear Friends:
I can't tell you what pleasure you gave us in sending your account of the world premiere of Benny's opera. A pleasure deepened, yet tinged with sadness that he was not here to see the realization of his dreams. We put on the records of *Wuthering Heights* after reading the booklet and your vivid account of the premiere and were more deeply moved than hitherto by the way the music brought to life the genius of Emily Brontë

in another dimension. . . . How we wished he had been sitting in our home as the records were played as he was when we had that unforgettable day when we got lost in the Yorkshire mists . . .

Next day we played the records of the Torelli *concerti grossi,* which you sent us after your visit to Sussex—which put us still further in debt. As ever,

Ernest and Ellie Bean

# 17

## Concert Opportunities — Works Progress Administration
### *Music — Art — Theater — Trail-blazing*

Werner Janssen, distinguished composer and conductor, arrived in Hollywood to write film scores. Ann Harding, his wife, who starred in 1930s films, accompanied him. In New York, Annette and I had enjoyed dining at his father's excellent Hofbrau Restaurant. Burning with zeal to conduct, Janssen founded an exceptional chamber orchestra. He persuaded me to join as concertmaster for one season with the bait that I would be featured soloist. Thus I played Saint-Saëns's *Havanaise* with his ensemble in Los Angeles, Santa Barbara, and San Francisco. Extremely enthusiastic and appreciative, Werner telephoned me at 3 A.M. after the San Francisco concert to praise my performance!

Nathan Abas, born in Holland, a colleague from Kneisel's class, came backstage after that concert and invited me to visit his office the next day. He conducted the Works Progress Administration (WPA) Bay Area Symphony and directed the Project's choruses, bands, and other musical groups. He accomplished this with such fairness, diplomacy, and efficiency that there were no complaints from white or black personnel — an unqualified success!

Nathan asked if I would play Beethoven's concerto with him at a WPA Oakland concert. I instantly replied, "It would give me great pleasure, Nathan, to perform with *you* under *any* circumstances." He explained, "WPA concerts are meant for *everyone*. Tickets are priced at twenty-five cents, no reservations, first come, first seated. Word has gotten around that concert and symphony managers will not engage professionals who play for our 'low-cost' programs." "I've never considered great music simply a 'commercial' affair, so you can definitely count on me." He set a date, and Annette and I drove up to Oakland for most enjoyable musicmaking.

Alexander Fried, the *San Francisco Examiner*'s noted music critic, wrote:

13 August 1941

### WPA Symphony Experiment Held Success
#### Four thousand warmly greet concert — conductor lauded

Under Abas's direction, the orchestra has attained surprising quality. It is disciplined, flexible. It has good tone and spirit. It is an ensemble any musical public might enjoy. . . . Honors were shared by the superb solo that Louis Kaufman, noted Hollywood violinist, played in the great Beethoven concerto. His performance had technical mastery, beautiful tone and emotional vision.

Delighted by this auspicious result, Nathan proposed repeating this concert at San Francisco's famed Cow Palace, which seated twelve thousand persons and was customarily used for sports events or political conventions. I replied, "Schedule a date and I'll be there!" A few months later, Annette and I boarded a Southern Pacific daylight train, accompanied by our friend Nicolas Moldavan, visiting from New York. We listened en route to the radio reporting Winston Churchill's announcement that England would join forces with the Soviet Union to defeat the horrors of Nazi-dominated Europe! Nicolas explained how the flat terrain of Western Russia would make the German invasion terribly costly in Russian lives and cause unimaginable devastation. The overwhelming force of German tanks could advance without any natural barriers. When the war ended in 1945, we learned that over twenty million Russians had perished.

Arriving in San Francisco, we found the Cow Palace sold out. Nicolas, Annette, and Nathan's wife, Elsa, only managed to find seats in the balcony's very top row. After Beethoven's *Egmont Overture* and a violin concerto, Nathan conducted Richard Strauss's *Death and Transfiguration*, which matched our emotions over the war raging in Europe. The audience and press acclaimed us enthusiastically.

William Smith, young director of the WPA Federal Music Project, chanced to attend this successful event. Excited by such dramatic fulfillment of the Music Project's intent, he inquired, "Mr. Kaufman, would you be willing to play with other WPA orchestras?" Evidently, they all had problems obtaining soloists of a caliber to attract audiences. I accepted this opportunity. I had observed how difficult it was then for young Americans to gain experience in playing or singing with full orchestras. European pianists, violinists, cellists, and opera singers arrived as veterans in this musical arena. Young American instrumentalists and singers, used to performing with piano accompaniment, could be confused by hearing flutes, violins, horns, or other unfamiliar orchestral sounds.

After my performance of a Brahms concerto with Nathan's orchestra in Oakland, he invited me to tour in other central California towns. Annette and I would drive to San Francisco, visit the museums and the Gump's store, and board the tour buses with Nathan, Elsa, and orchestra for Taft, Watsonville, Fresno, Modesto, and Bakersfield. Nathan and Elsa discovered excellent Armenian or Basque restaurants for dinner. It was exhilarating to share the Beethoven or Brahms concertos and fine symphonic repertoire with enthusiastic, eager audiences in high school or municipal auditoriums packed to the rafters. Don Dudley, the orchestra's press director, was a gifted journalist who later founded and edited a lively music magazine, *Opera and Concert*. We remained good friends, exchanging many visits in San Francisco and Los Angeles. Nathan, an amateur photographer of remarkable ability (who later turned professional) introduced us to the photographs of Edward Weston and Ansel Adams, his mentors.

Dr. James Sample, adroit American conductor, invited me to play Saint-Saëns's Third Concerto with his San Bernardino WPA Symphony. This performance lead to an enduring friendship with Jimmy and his artist wife, Ernestine. After study in Paris with Pierre Monteux, he became Monteux's assistant conductor in San Francisco. Later he conducted orchestras in Honolulu, Portland, and Salt Lake City.

While playing concerts in Kansas, we visited Robert Russell Bennett's sister and her husband, and were pleasantly surprised to learn that famed muralist Thomas Hart Benton and his wife were their neighbors. They presented us to this distinguished artist. What a privilege to see Benton's workshop and works in progress! I expressed my admiration for his murals at New York's New School for Social Research. I learned that Benton created small wax figures and forms in a box to judge perspective and composition before creating his paintings and murals. I later read that some artists of the Italian Renaissance used this same device!

Later in the 1970s, Jimmy, conductor of the Erie (Pennsylvania) Symphony, telephoned an SOS when his soloist, Michael Rabin, was taken ill (he died a few days later). We flew early the next morning to Erie, where I performed the Mendelssohn and Saint-Saëns concertos and a solo recital with Annette. Everyone seemed pleased by our performances.

Thanks to William Smith's introductions, I crossed the United States playing the Beethoven and Brahms concertos with many WPA orchestras. Some of these groups later became civic symphonies, including those in Salt Lake City, Newark, and Brooklyn, which led to my being reengaged at regular concert fees by these associations. One memorable concert was with Philadelphia's WPA Symphony, led by Guglielmo Sabatini, and included several Curtis Institute of Music students. Later Guglielmo invited me to play with the Newark Symphony. He moved to Beverly Hills with his wife, Leona, where our friendship flourished with his unforgettable Italian dinners, prepared from his mother's Abruzzese recipes. Alas! Poor Guglielmo died too soon, from an exhausted heart.

In another outstanding collaboration I played the Brahms concerto in Brooklyn, New York, with the excellent conductor Emerson Buckley, who years later won worldwide celebrity conducting orchestras for Luciano Pavarotti in films and concerts.

My "karma" was propelling me out of Hollywood anonymity. A call from Marks Levine, director of the National Concert and Artists Corporation (NCAC), who heard the broadcast of the Brooklyn concert and was enthusiastic about my performance, invited me to his Fifth Avenue office. Marks had managed the Musical Art Quartet when I was the violist. His pianist brother, Mischa Levitzki, had brilliantly played César Franck's Quintet with our quartet at a Town Hall concert.

He ushered us into his large office and began, "You know there are good and bad things about our management, but we think you would fit in at reasonable fees. You have a built-in accompanist, Annette. Can you get away from Hollywood for a definite season?" "We'd be delighted, Marks. March to April are tax-assessment times for film studios; they clear all decks to avoid taxes on works in progress that don't earn income. I have a string quartet in Los Angeles, which also could be available for West Coast concerts."

Levine countered, "Not a chance! We can get bigger fees for you alone than for quartets. They are hard to sell! We can only book you. We never know what will happen. I couldn't do a thing for my brother. We'll prepare a contract for you to sign tomorrow and we'll see what we can do for you next spring." This put me in a different category. Now we would have access to the NCAC-controlled Civic Concerts circuit throughout the United States. At this time NCAC and Columbia Artists, its larger competitor, were the leading concert managers.

We proved to be reliable during the years of our association. We never arrived late for any concerts they booked, in spite of rains, blizzards, or floods. Only Syracuse, New York, was an unfulfilled date, due to a blizzard

National Concert and Artists Corp. press photograph of Louis and Annette, 1944.

that closed roads and stopped trains and all traffic. I called the committee chairman to explain what he already knew: "Impossible to enter your closed city. I regret not being able to perform for you, but will be happy to return next year."

A furious Mr. Bottorf, head of Civic Concerts, called me on our return to Manhattan, trumpeting, "Don't ever interfere with our arrangements!

You had no right to offer to play in Syracuse next year! *We* decide who will play in our cities next year!" I calmly answered, "I have no desire to interfere with any of your plans. I only wanted to explain that we had no objection to playing for them." As it happened, Annette and I never did perform in Syracuse.

The National WPA Program was a most important cultural development for our country. Although its severest critics considered it "boondoggling," this modest financial aid to needy writers, artists, actors, dancers, and musicians was a tremendous boon for the public as well as for artists. Milton Avery, David Burliuk, Stuart Davis, Ben Benn, Arshile Gorky, Joseph De Martini, Jack Levine, Philip Guston, Anton Refregier, Mark Rothko, Raphael and Moses Soyer, Lawrence Lebduska, and many others all welcomed the small funds to buy canvas and paints. They decorated walls in post offices and courthouses, many constructed by formerly unemployed carpenters, bricklayers, electricians, et cetera. The project created a splendid *Index of American Design* based on colonial motifs.

For the first time, national attention was paid to Native Americans of Santa Fe and Taos; and Zunis, Hopis, and Navajos created sculptures and produced handsome watercolors and drawings of native ceremonies and dances. I particularly admired Patrocino Barela's woodcarvings.

The Federal Theater Project enjoyed spectacular success. Annette and I were captivated by Orson Welles's imaginative productions of Christopher Marlowe's *Dr. Faustus* and later Shakespeare's *Julius Caesar* in modern dress. We were part of the enthusiastic audience for Marc Blitzstein's *Cradle Will Rock* when he played his score on an upright piano, having run into bureaucratic problems! Los Angeles mounted fine plays, ranging from classics to Kafka; and San Diego built a Shakespeare Old Globe Theater to perform Shakespeare plays. The Pasadena Playhouse offered great historic German plays and all of Shakespeare's Greek and Roman plays. The WPA Theater delighted a vast new audience, including people who had never before seen live actors on a stage.

Why should concerts, plays, works of art, and minimum aid to America's unemployed workers be accused of "spending us into a terrible debt"? We observed the beneficial results of new schools, hospitals, and public buildings constructed by WPA artisans.

It was both comic and tragic to read Hallie Flanagan's book, *Arena*, describing the demise of the WPA Theater Project she ably directed. The day after Congress voted its cancellation, she was clearing her desk before returning to Vassar College when her phone rang. A senator asked if she could do something to help his nephew who wanted a stage career.

Tactfully she replied, "I would have been pleased to help, but yesterday the Senate voted to terminate the Theater Project." "Oh!" exclaimed the dismayed senator, "I didn't realize that was what we voted on!"

Historians of the 1930s are evaluating all art work of this stimulating period, trying to trace what happened to paintings, sculptures, murals, watercolors, and engravings that were produced for such minuscule sums. Unappreciated frescoes by Arshile Gorky were badly damaged and mostly destroyed. Many works disappeared. Why was this national artistic contribution treated so negligently, without protest from museum directors, art galleries, or artistic groups?

Annette and I have never forgotten many excellent concerts we heard of works by American composers: Paul Creston, Charles Wakefield Cadman, William Grant Still, Leo Sowerby, Edward MacDowell, Virgil Thomson, Aaron Copland, Roger Sessions, Walter Piston, Quincy Porter, John Alden Carpenter, Robert Russell Bennett, and Ernst Bacon, among others.

The evening of 19 March 1940 Russell and Louise Bennett invited us to attend a splendid WPA concert, presented by Mayor La Guardia of the New York City WPA Music Project in cooperation with the Metropolitan Opera Association, in the old Thirty-ninth Street Metropolitan Opera House, conducted by Izler Solomon. The concert opened with Leo Sowerby's overture *Comes Autumn Time,* then Bennett's prize-winning *Abraham Lincoln* symphony, followed by *Dark Dancers of the Mardi Gras;* a fantasy for piano and orchestra, played by its composer Charles Wakefield Cadman; *A Poem for Orchestra* by Harold Morris; the *Overture, Work 22* by Robert Delaney; and concluding with *Saturday Night* (a barn dance) by Robert Sanders. We haven't heard any of those excellent compositions performed since! The WPA orchestras performed classical, romantic, and contemporary repertoire. They also provided American conductors with orchestras with which they could rehearse and learn their craft. This was a forecast of what creative Americans—all over the country—could achieve in the arts!

Whenever we returned to New York, my faithful friend Hannah Bierhof would invite us to lunch in her small flat on East Seventy-second Street. The last luncheon was in her ninety-sixth year. On one memorable occasion after the Second World War, she presented us to Jacques Thibaud, the famed French violinist. Thibaud graciously permitted us to see his fine Stradivarius violin, but I was distressed to see its table under the bridge covered by layers of rosin. He evidently was not aware that this should be cleaned off frequently before damage was done to the varnish.

He enthralled us with the account of his courage during the German occupation of France. His wife, Marguerite, was Jewish, and he forbade her to wear the yellow star or leave the flat without him. One day he returned to find that she had gone out alone. He decided to shave and lathered his face. The doorbell rang, he opened it to see two Gestapo agents who demanded he leave with them immediately. He hurriedly wiped his face and descended the staircase, stamping noisily to alert the concierge of his escort. They drove him to Gestapo headquarters at the Majestic Hotel, where he was placed standing in a small dark closet with no room to sit down in. After two hours worrying about Marguerite, he was led to the well-appointed office of Herr Abetz, the Gestapo director. He was graciously greeted by the German officer, who offered him a comfortable chair and cigarette. Jacques sat and politely refused the cigarette. Herr Abetz began, "I hope, Monsieur Thibaud, you have been well treated here?" Jacques knew Abetz was well aware of his arrest and reception, and replied, "Very well, thank you." He wondered if this meeting concerned his wife. Abetz continued, "We've picked up an Argentine Jew who claims he is a violinist here to study with you." Hoping to save the lad, he replied, "That is true, but I've told him to return to Argentina, as this is not a time for foreigners to study in France. You should extradite him immediately to Argentina." Abetz said, "I've wondered, Monsieur Thibaud, why you haven't offered to tour in Germany. Our people love French musicians and greatly admire your artistry." Thibaud answered, "I appreciate their generous consideration, but I am old now and not at my best technically, so I am not willing at this time to tour abroad." Abetz countered, "You perform in Paris and our soldiers attend your concerts. What is the difference?" Thibaud said, "I am pleased that your soldiers enjoy my programs, but I am playing for French audiences who don't mind that I am no longer at the top of my ability." Abetz replied, "You know, Monsieur Thibaud, there are ways to compel you to play in Germany." Jacques crossed his wrists as if they were chained and said, *"Comme ça oui, mais pas comme ça,"* as he mimed holding an imaginary violin and drawing a bow down across its strings. Abetz thanked him for coming and he was permitted to return home. There he was greeted by Marguerite, who had walked across Paris on foot to try to help their sick grandchild.

My spring tour of 1946 ended with concerts in colleges and cities of Washington and Oregon. En route to San Francisco by train, we encountered three members of the noted Lener String Quartet (Sandor Roth, viola; Josef Smilovits, second violin; and Imre Hartman, cello), recently bereft of their first violin (Jeno Lener). These cheerful Hungarians regaled us with amusing anecdotes. Hartman related, "The great Hungarian violinist Jeno Hubay, a splendid virtuoso and teacher, had a passion to conduct, although he lacked ability and talent for directing orchestras. At a Budapest Musical Academy concert, Hubay conducted the premiere of a Bruckner symphony. The long work ended with a shimmering effect of only strings, with horns intoning the main theme. Alas! Strings shimmered, but no horns played. Backstage, Hubay raged at the horn players, "You've disgraced the Academy, the orchestra, you've ruined Budapest's musical prestige! How in Heaven's name did you forget to play?" The first horn protested, "Maestro we were waiting for you to give us a signal." Hubay exploded "Dummkopfs! HOW could I give you a signal, didn't you see I was busy conducting!'"

Hartman's charm and expertise made cello studies very fashionable in Mexico City, where he and his wife lived. Smilovits and his wife were art collectors and ran a successful antique shop in Mexico. We were delighted with these new friends.

Soon after our return to Los Angeles, a cable arrived from Mexico City inviting me to join Hartman in May for two performances of Brahms's double concerto under Carlos Chavez's direction. I immediately accepted. We flew to Mexico City and fell in love with its broad elegant *avenidas,* handsome architecture, excellent restaurants, and art galleries and museums of pre-Columbian art. Annette and I had met Señor José Clemente Orozco and his wife at Durand-Ruel's New York art gallery and they were pleased to know we had bought one of his large paintings (from Stendhal). Orozco had lost an eye and one hand in a terrible childhood accident, but he surmounted the problems of limited vision to master perspective and composition, and created masterly frescoes at Dartmouth College, Claremont College, the Palacio de Bellas Artes in Mexico City, and at various government buildings in Mexico City and in Guadalajara. I considered him to be Mexico's and North America's Michelangelo. By chance on this trip we encountered Orozco's son at an art gallery. I invited him and his parents to hear Hartman and myself play the Brahms masterwork. It may have been their first attendance at a symphony concert; they sat with Annette. Señor Orozco seemed pleased with our performance, and asked Annette at intermission, "Will they play again this evening?" Annette explained, "Only the orchestra will perform."

Chavez and his wife invited the Hartmans and us to lunch at their home. He was a fine composer and excellent conductor. The second concert was on Sunday afternoon: A few of Hartman's pupils came backstage and although they were enthusiastic about the concert, said frankly they had enjoyed the broadcast more than hearing the concert in

Backstage after an afternoon concert in Mexico City's Belle Arts Auditorium. *From left:* Louis, conductor Carlos Chavez, with the orchestra manager and cellist Imre Hartman.

the hall. Imre and I were surprised that the natural sound of balance between orchestra and soloists was less effective to young listeners, who had become so used to distortions of recordings, where soloists are heard in a prominence that composers did not dream of.

The three ex-Lener Quartet players visited me the morning of our departure to ask me to become their first violinist. They had very good connections with the leading impresario, Ernesto Quesada, and felt we would be both most congenial musically and very successful in the musical Americas. I truly regretted that my Hollywood work and concert obligations made it impossible for me to accept such an interesting and gracious offer.

# 18

## Vivaldi Discovers Me—
## We Meet Francis Poulenc—
## Historic Recordings

> The perfection of life is to carry out in maturity the dreams of one's youth.
>
> Alfred de Vigny

Vivaldi, Venice, and eighteenth-century music were equally remote from my thoughts in autumn 1947, when Fate's voice came prosaically over the telephone. The New York caller, James Fassett, Columbia Broadcasting Systems' music director, asked, "Louis, would you play Antonio Vivaldi's *Four Seasons* concertos next spring instead of the Lev Knipper concerto you're scheduled to play with Benny Herrmann?" "Jim, I'd prefer to introduce the Knipper, I don't know the Vivaldi concertos." Benny, in Jim's office, broke in, "Louis, I have to be in Hollywood, so Alfredo Antonini will conduct that program. He's just received these Vivaldi concertos from a Milanese publisher. I think they're very interesting. You should learn them." Alfredo joined in, "I've heard you play, Louis, and I'm sure you'd play these concertos as I think they should be played." I was convinced. Jim promised to airmail the scores, which I could study while touring.

Two days later, another fateful New York voice, Dr. Samuel Josefowitz, called. "Louis, can you suggest some solo concertos requiring small orchestra that you could record for us when you reach New York?" Sam, co-owner with his violinist brother David of Concert Hall Records, which specialized in unusual repertoire, had bought my recording of Khachaturian's violin concerto from Jacques Rachmilovich, conductor of the Santa Monica Symphony. Jacques, a Russian Jewish refugee in Italy, fled to southern California when Mussolini joined Hitler's axis. In Los Angeles he realized his lifelong dream to become a symphony conductor. After studies with Dr. Otto Klemperer and Albert Coates, Jacques founded the Santa Monica Symphony, which has survived to the present. Needing soloists to attract audiences, he engaged pianist Shura Cherkassy and me. I performed with his orchestra several times, playing Beethoven's concerto and Mozart's lovely *Symphonie Concertante* with Paul Robyn, violist of the Jacques Gordon Quartet and later the Hollywood String Quartet. After performing the Saint-Saëns Third Concerto and Aram Khachaturian's concerto, I recorded them for Disc Records and RCA (reissued in 1994 on CD by Biddulph Records in London).

Shortly after the Khachaturian recording, Jacques had a disagreement with RCA and sold that recording to the Concert Hall Society. They reaped outstanding reviews and impressive nationwide publicity, for this was the first Khachaturian to be heard in the United States. Sam was delighted at my suggestion of unknown Vivaldi concertos (which I was to broadcast for CBS) and, since few Vivaldi works were then known to the concert and recording world, accepted the project immediately.

The urgency of his request was due to James C. Petrillo's decision as president of the American Federation of Musicians (AFM) to ban all recordings after 31 December 1947, unless record companies accepted his terms (mainly that royalties for discs manufactured and sold domestically be paid to the AFM, rather than to orchestral performers). Large companies, like RCA, Columbia, and Decca, decided to resist the ultimatum, having a quantity of unreleased discs. Smaller companies worked feverishly to build up stocks before Mr. Petrillo's threatened deadline.

Sam Josefowitz engaged string players from the New York Philharmonic, and Dr. Henry Swoboda, a Czech refugee, as conductor, and secured the last four nights of December 1947 at Carnegie Hall starting at midnight to record. Carnegie Hall was completely booked by the major companies and orchestras! He also scheduled an afternoon recording session at Carnegie Recital Hall to record Aaron Copland's Sonata for Violin and Piano with Aaron and myself.

The Vivaldi scores arrived from CBS one day before Annette and I boarded the train. I studied the concertos undistracted in our private compartment. Long before reaching New York we both had fallen under the spell of Vivaldi's music.

These fascinating concerti were possibly the first instrumental program music in concerto form. Each concerto was a musical setting of a sonnet describing the year's seasons with particular festivals, hunts, dances, etc. *La Primavera* (Spring) portrays birdsongs and the joy of budding nature. *L'Estate* (Summer) depicts languid heat and sudden storms; this storm is a forerunner of the one in Beethoven's *Pastorale* symphony. *L'Autunno* (Autumn) portrays a hunt, with violin double-stops to suggest hunting horns, a wine festival with drunken vintners, and a mazurka (predating Chopin!). *L'Inverno* (Winter) depicts icy winds, frozen landscape, falling on ice, and the comfort of a warm fireplace during a gentle rain, concluding with "warring" winter winds. The music's vitality and instrumental virtuosity also revealed Vivaldi as a master melodist and uncovered new aspects of this enchanting Venetian master.

Glancing through a *New York Times* while I practiced, Annette read that noted French composer Francis Poulenc had just arrived for a United States tour with singer Pierre Bernac. This seemed arranged by fate for my benefit! I had programmed the premiere of his violin and piano sonata, written in memory of Spanish poet-dramatist, Federico García Lorca, for my approaching December recital at Carnegie Hall.

Annette dashed off a letter to Poulenc's New York manager, giving our itinerary and requesting an interview and rehearsal with him wherever our paths might cross. I mailed it at the next train stop in New Mexico. By rare good luck, a reply awaited us in Chicago, stating that Poulenc, en route west, would arrive in Chicago one day before we were to depart east for New York! A rendezvous was set for 5 P.M. that day. Poulenc graciously consented to play his sonata with me during the few hours between his arrival and his rehearsal with Bernac before their Chicago evening concert.

We arrived at a Michigan Avenue hotel at 4:45 P.M. with violin, music, and some trepidation. I only remembered photos of Poulenc at age nineteen! Poulenc was not in his room, so we waited in the lobby, facing the entrance, hoping to recognize him. Suddenly, a tall, thin, handsome gentleman with slightly graying hair rushed through the doors and approached me, saying, "*Ah, vous êtes Kaufman!* I recognize you by your violin!" (We spoke French with Poulenc.) Immediately captivated by his warm friendly smile we trotted along behind him, attempting to keep up with his long strides as we went in search of a room with a piano. In a large mirrored ballroom, amid the tawdry disarray of gilt chairs, jazz band equipment, and drums, we saw a battered gilded piano. Poulenc sat down to try it, while I took my violin from its case and Annette found the music.

We plunged into intensive work, playing the sonata through twice,

Louis, Francis Poulenc, and Annette, 1947.

stopping only to discuss nuances he wished emphasized. The sonata, a tribute to his friend García Lorca, contains Canto Hondo phrases (Gypsy "deep song") and impressions of the music halls that Lorca loved. The andante was titled with a line of García Lorca's poetry, *"La guitarre fait pleurer les songes"* (The guitar makes dreams weep). Poulenc told us that García Lorca, a gifted musician, often sang his verses accompanying himself on a guitar. The finale's tempestuous energy is suddenly stilled by a loud chord-like shot and cold silence, described by Poulenc as *"comme glace"* (like ice). Fascists assassinated García Lorca by mistake during a raid in a gay neighborhood in his native Granada; the entire Spanish-speaking world had admired the genius of this remarkable writer. Poulenc urged me to play the sentimental phrases with greater freedom and intensity to stress their emotional character. After our second runthrough, Poulenc seemed very pleased, and wrote a note on my music, *"Pour Kaufman qui joues si bien cette sonate"* (for Kaufman who plays this sonata so well)—and on the piano score, in large letters underlined three times, *"Mettre beaucoup de pédale!"* (use lots of pedal!).

I mentioned I was to record his sonata in Paris for Capitol Records and asked if he could record it with me. He replied, "I am under exclusive contract, so cannot record for other companies, but I look forward to playing it with you in concert." With quick handshakes with us both he added, "I definitely want to see you in Paris; *au revoir*," and then hastily vanished. Annette and I packed up music and fiddle in a rosy glow.

The New York premiere of Poulenc's *Sonate* with pianist Erich Itor Kahn went off very well. Kahn, a German refugee and a sensitive artist, had lived in France. My Carnegie Hall program, including Khachaturian's concerto (with piano) pleased the large audience and press, with the exception of a Brooklyn critic who commented that though I was an excellent violinist, I lacked any idea of what Poulenc had in mind!

We stayed at the Wellington Hotel, just a block from Carnegie Hall. We could only work between midnight and four o'clock in the morning, so we lived our lives in reverse during this exhilarating week. We went to bed at 6 P.M. and rose at 11 P.M., in time for a hurried breakfast before walking to Carnegie Hall to begin daily rehearsals and recordings at midnight.

The night before our first session New York had a famous snowstorm, one of the worst in a generation. Earlier in the day only light snowfall was expected, so it was not considered necessary to alert the city's efficient snow-cleaning forces. Everyone was completely unprepared for the avalanche of soft white snow that steadily fell and within a few hours gave New York the aspect of a large country village.

During the afternoon, Aaron Copland and I recorded his Sonata for Violin and Piano. He was in great form and we polished it off efficiently. When the producer announced we needed a few more minutes of music to fill up one side of the record, Aaron remembered composing a nocturne for violin and piano in 1925, which would provide the right time. Annette called Schirmer's Forty-third Street music shop. They had one copy! She said, "Save it for me. I'll be right there!" She donned a coat, ran out to grab a taxi on Sixth Avenue, reached Schirmer's, obtained the music, and exited into the suddenly heavy snowfall that had stopped all buses, taxis, and subway service. She gamely walked back to Fifty-seventh Street against a heavy wind and blinding snow, returning in less than one hour from starting out. Aaron and I quickly rehearsed and recorded this effective nocturne. Everyone seemed pleased with the playback, and this recording has always had most favorable reviews!

The previous afternoon I had rehearsed with harpsichordist Edith Weissmann, who lived in the West Seventies. Her fine Steingraeber instrument was one of eight harpsichords this maker had created in

Louis and Aaron Copland at a New York City hotel before recording Copland's Sonata.

Weissmann's native Germany. Annette and I were surprised to find the harpsichord smothered in scarves of silk and wool, with added blankets for protection, although like most New York apartments, her flat was warmly heated. The idea of taking this precious instrument to Carnegie Hall filled her with dire premonitions, for the weather had turned very cold. She gloomily predicted it would not stay in tune after leaving her warm studio to travel through the cold to Carnegie Hall and back.

The next day automobiles were stranded in streets that had vanished under a white blanket. The city was literally paralyzed. Street cleaning forces started to work as quickly as possible, but there was so much snow that traffic was only permitted to travel north and south. No east or west turns were allowed. This was Madame Weissmann's day to take her Steingraeber to Carnegie Hall! She rode on the truck with it down Broadway to Fifty-sixth Street, but the harpsichord had to be placed on a handcart for the remaining few blocks! During the journey Madame Weissmann, armed with a thermometer, continually checked the temperature of the precious instrument. Once the instrument was installed at

First recording of the *Four Seasons* at Carnegie Hall: Henry Swoboda, conductor; Edith Weissmann at harpsichord with Edouard Nies-Berger; and Louis Kaufman, first violin.

Carnegie Hall, she would not go home to rest, remaining next to it from early morning until midnight when our work began.

The string orchestra, members of New York's Philharmonic, despite fatigue from unexpected last-minute sessions with Leopold Stokowski plus their regular schedule of concerts, remained alert throughout our recordings and were greatly impressed by the quality and charm of this fresh music. As the hours sped by on the brilliantly lit stage of the darkened auditorium, our attention never flagged and our excitement increased. We all credited this to the exhilarating vigor of Vivaldi's concertos. Bernard Greenhouse, first cellist of our string group, was particularly impressed with the harmonic structure and programmatic vividness of the *L'Autunno* concerto's adagio. He remarked, "They just discovered everything in the eighteenth century!"

Edouard Nies-Berger, the New York Philharmonic's organist (a friend and associate of Dr. Albert Schweitzer, who edited some of J. S. Bach's organ works), had predicted that cold weather would create pitch problems for Carnegie Hall's organ. However, his consummate artistry made that instrument sound like a reedy baroque organ, and it stayed in tune. Fate was definitely on our side during those four nights, for all the instruments remained in tune in spite of inclement weather! My devoted Annette always assisted in any manner possible when I recorded, and during the Vivaldi she turned pages, standing next to Nies-Berger and Madame Weissmann. The final night our usual three-hour session was extended to rerecord *Primavera*'s first movement, for after that session the engineer found an improved microphone placement. The *Four Seasons* recording was completed at four o'clock the morning of 31 December 1947, the very last day recordings would be permitted by the AFM, for negotiations had failed and the strike was now a reality!

Dr. Swoboda, sound engineer David Josefowitz, Sam Josefowitz, Annette, and I listened to playbacks before leaving Carnegie Hall. As the rain adagio of the *Inverno* concerto was heard, Emil Hauser, a violinist in the original Budapest String Quartet, who was listening as a guest of Dr. Swoboda, remarked to Annette, "These records will go around the world!" She smiled, thinking his praise quite exaggerated.

We returned to our hotel about six o'clock the first morning of 1949 emotionally and physically exhausted, with the melodies and captivating rhythms of Vivaldi dancing through our minds. They haunted us for many days.

The program notes that accompanied these recordings were written by the distinguished musicologist Dr. Alfred Einstein, who was so enchanted by the test pressings that he insisted on keeping them for his private collection. I learned from Dr. Einstein's notes that the *Four Seasons* were the first four concerti of a group of twelve termed by Vivaldi *Opera Ottavo* (my eighth work), bearing the title *Il Cimento dell'Armonia e dell'Invenzione*. *Cimento* was obviously an archaic Italian term and difficult to translate. A year later in Paris, the cultural attaché of the Italian embassy told us it might mean wedding or welding. By chance, our friend, Jonathan Griffin, poet-dramatist and English diplomat, translated it precisely. He had picked up an eighteenth-century Italian-English lexicon at Sotheby's and told me *cimento* was a medieval jousting term for a trial of strength or skill. I therefore translated the eighth opus as "The Conflict between Harmony and Invention," which became widely accepted.

Dr. Einstein's notes did not mention whether the remaining eight were for solo violin or for varied instruments (like Bach), or whether they still existed or where they might be found. Dr. Einstein had acquired a large body of Vivaldi data from his friend Dr. Ludwig Landshoff, a noted scholar, one of the first to research Vivaldi's life and oeuvre.

Louis with Alfredo Antonini rehearsing the *Four Seasons*, in Antonini's flat in New York City.

In June 1948, Annette and I shared great pleasure in meeting Alfredo Antonini, a gifted Milanese conductor who had urged me to learn these Vivaldi concertos, and his wife, Saundra. They became our instant and devoted friends. We rehearsed and performed the U.S. broadcast premiere of the Vivaldi for CBS in the Byzantine Renaissance Saint Paul

Chapel (on the Columbia University campus), a warm, resonant acoustical space. CBS forwarded a telegram from Pikesville, Maryland, an unexpected message from a dear friend:

> Congratulations to you and CBS for a most beautiful performance of the Vivaldi. Best greetings!
> Sincerely,
> Adelyn D. Breeskin

# 19

# En Route to France
# via Honolulu

My American tour in spring of 1948 concluded with the Khachaturian concerto, a premiere for the Oklahoma Symphony with conductor Victor Alessandro, before we returned home to rest a few days in Los Angeles. I was then engaged to perform with the Honolulu Symphony. En route to Honolulu, we lunched with my manager, Alexander Haas, at the Palace Hotel in San Francisco. He brought along Mr. and Mrs. George Stroud, Honolulu concert managers, thinking they might engage me for concerts on other Hawaiian islands. Alex introduced me, "This is Mr. Kaufman, who is to be soloist with the Honolulu Symphony." Mrs. Stroud abruptly stated, "You won't be paid if you play with the symphony!" I replied, "We don't care about the money, we'll enjoy swimming." Undaunted, Mrs. Stroud retorted, "The water is too cold." Her husband looked as if he wanted to disappear. I added, "It's always agreeable to see friends in any case." Mrs. Stroud, enraged by my indifference to her remarks, sharply persisted, "Well, my husband George writes concert reviews, and you won't get a good review when you play."

Alex, quite shocked by such hostility, attempted to change the conversation, saying, "Markova and Dolin have just returned from the islands and had fine success." Mrs. Stroud hissed, "Those Russian communists." I politely said, "You are quite mistaken; although they are exceptionally fine ballet dancers, Markova is English, her name is Marks, and Mr. Dolin is Irish."

Still trying to calm the waters, Alex tactfully continued, "Yehudi Menuhin has returned from a most successful tour in the Orient and the islands." Mrs. Stroud stated, "Another communist!" Undaunted, I quietly but firmly replied, "Mr. Menuhin is a remarkable violinist, musician, and humanitarian. I have heard countless true stories of his extraordinary generosity to musical colleagues and important composers such as Bartók and Enescu. You are indeed ill-informed, Mrs. Stroud, he is not interested in political theories."

Annette and I enjoyed delicious Crab Louis salads, speaking with Alex as both Strouds sat in dismal silence, merely coldly nodding when we said goodbye.

We flew to Honolulu and were welcomed with beautiful leis of fragrant jasmine by our dear friend Ben Hyams, former musical commentator for CBS and devoted to Bernard Herrmann, and Fritz Hart, Australian composer and conductor of Honolulu's symphony, with his wife, Marvell. I recounted Mrs. Stroud's odd conversation, saying they would certainly dub us communists. Ben explained that they hated anyone who appeared in Honolulu who was not under their management. He arranged for us to play for patients of the Army and Navy hospitals, as we had done on the mainland throughout the war and after. Ben, who worked for Hawaiian Factors, ran a series of illustrated interviews with us that flooded Honolulu with news of our activities, to lessen any damage from the Strouds. It worked: we had only sympathetic press!

Our new friends Karen (a violinist in the symphony) and Chuck Mau (a successful lawyer) hosted a fabulous Chinese banquet for us at their home, and we made many new friends. Annette chanced to sit next to Wiley Allen, editor of the Honolulu daily newspaper. She recounted, "We met the Strouds in San Francisco. They certainly do not make friends for your symphony." She then related that amusing (to us) conversation. Laughing, Allen replied, "We all know the Strouds, they won't even accept our checks for their concert series. We'll see that old George has the night off when Louis plays!"

Annette and I played a recital in the lovely courtyard of the Honolulu Academy of Arts. Robert Griffing, its director, had wide knowledge and appreciation of Western and Asian arts. He and his wife, Marjorie, told us a fascinating tale. His father, living in Paris before World War I, met Paul Cézanne, liked his work, and bought four of his paintings. His wife disliked them so strongly that he was obliged to sell them. Later he told Bob, "It's all for the best, you would have become arrogant if you'd inherited those valuable canvases."

Fritz Hart made it a pleasure for me to rehearse and perform the Saint-Saëns Third Concerto. That concert included his suite *Isolde of the White Hands*. After Fritz's death, Marvell, a curator of the Honolulu Academy of Arts, donated his musical manuscripts to the National Library of

Australia. We met Russell and Milton Cades, lawyers from Philadelphia and enthusiastic music lovers and art connoisseurs (Russell played viola in the symphony), and Val Ossipoff, an excellent architect who designed beautiful modern homes. Val built a gorgeous hillside home for Milton with a fabulous view of the Pacific Ocean.

Their friends Geoff Lloyd and his wife loved Monteverdi's music and invited many friends and ourselves to join them at their home by the sea to listen one afternoon to Monteverdi's fascinating opera *L'Orfeo* recorded in Italy.

We bought a few paintings by local artists William Stamper (from Ohio) and John Kjargaard (from Denmark), which we still enjoy. Our farewell saw us laden with beautiful fragrant leis from the Harts, Griffings, Maus, and Hyamses, who all came to say *Aloha*.

During our few days at home, I suddenly decided to have our phonograph equipment changed so we could play the new long-playing records. Annette suggested, "Let's wait until we return from Europe," but I felt strongly compelled to take care of it immediately. So my "karma" sent us down the fourteen-mile drive to Alfred Leonard's record shop on Wilshire. After we discussed and bought new equipment, Alfred remarked, "It's curious that you should happen to come in just now; someone in my office has just been asking about you. He wants to meet you!" Without giving me a chance to ask who it might be, Alfred led me to his office and presented me to young Dario Soria, head of Cetra-Soria Records. Years later I mused that perhaps Vivaldi's spirit may have been directing the Fates that were prodding me into completely new paths.

With a friendly smile, Soria said, "I've long admired your playing. My company is marketing a *Four Seasons* recorded in Italy conducted by Bernardino Molinari" (my recording had just received *Le Grand Prix du Disque* 1950 in the concerto category). He continued, "I like your Vivaldi better than mine. I come from Northern Italy, where our cooking is close to the French. Southern cooking is characteristically made with too many tomatoes and too much garlic. I feel the concerto I'm selling is like that. I like yours better, Mr. Kaufman. Are you free to record for me?"

I was definitely free and delighted at the prospect of playing more Vivaldi. The problem was, what to record? I knew the prolific Venetian had composed some two hundred and twenty-five concertos; very few were published or available in America. Were they to be found in Italy?

I suggested, "Alfred Einstein's program notes for Concert Hall said that *Le Stagioni* are the first four concertos of a series of twelve of Vivaldi's Opus 8. These concerti might be an ideal project. You also have the first four, but I do not have the music for the other eight."

After the meeting with Dario Soria that began our search for Vivaldi, 1948. Photograph by Alfred Leonard.

Soria amiably offered, "Gian Francesco Malipiero, a dear friend of my family, has edited the complete works of Claudio Monteverdi. He lives and works near Venice, where he is now engaged in editing Vivaldi's complete works. I am sure if you could visit him when you are in Europe, he would be happy to show you all the Vivaldi manuscripts. You could study the entire Vivaldi works in the archive! I'm not returning directly to New York, but I'll send a letter to your hotel before you leave for Europe and enclose a personal letter of introduction to the Maestro." He added, "If you do find the eight concertos of *Il Cimento* and they are written for violin, you could record them for me in Italy. I heartily congratulate you for your venturesome performances of new and baroque works, which I've greatly enjoyed." I thanked him and promised to let him know the results of our search so recording plans could be arranged. Annette and I considered this promised letter of introduction as a passport leading straight to the complete Opus 8. It never occurred to me there might be any difficulties ahead!

We had only six days to put our affairs in order: pack trunks (to be sent via boat) for our long voyage; store all furniture, rugs, music, books, large art collection, and new record-playing equipment; rent our house; get smallpox vaccinations from Dr. Bernstein (required for our return to the United States); and purchase air tickets to New York and Paris. An agent had trouble finding a tenant for our home—Californians demanded a swimming pool and a wet bar. But two days before departure, Hollywood writer Hy Kraft and his interior decorator wife fell in love with it. They had just sold a Beverly Hills Spanish home and were anxious to pay two years rent in advance. They gave me a check for the full amount. We had not expected such a windfall!

Sam Josefowitz, on a brief visit to Los Angeles to court his future wife, Natasha, visited us one evening, just before we started to put everything in storage. Sam, an ardent book collector, impressed by our paintings, mused, "I've never thought of buying art, I think I'll do it. What would you suggest that I collect?" Knowing of his interest in commerce and value, I suggested, "Impressionists are at top value." (How wrong I was in 1950!) "But the postimpressionist school is very undervalued and of great quality: Gauguin and his associates in Brittany, especially at Pont-Aven, like Maurice Denis, Sérusier, Caillebotte, Pissarro, Maufra, Luce, Pétit-Jean, Ranson, and others, are all sure to appreciate greatly." This was the only hint Sam needed to acquire, during the next few years in England, Belgium, France, and Switzerland, a uniquely comprehensive collection that is now world famous!

Annette and I attended an all-Milhaud concert in Los Angeles. We visited Darius and Madeleine backstage and I expressed my great admiration for his effective and masterly second violin concerto. Milhaud told us he would conduct a program of his symphonic music at the Theatre des Champs-Elysées for the French radio in autumn, and since we would be in Paris, invited me to play the second concerto with him. I mentioned this to Richard Jones of Capitol Records, and his company decided to record the concerto and the entire Milhaud concert to use their "frozen credits" in Europe. This would give us five rehearsals for the recordings!

Annette and I thought our final night of cleaning out all closets would never end. About 11 P.M., we were surprised and touched when dear Anthony Collins and his devoted housekeeper, Harriet Last, arrived to say goodbye and godspeed. They set to work with us, and by 1 A.M. the house and garage were cleared and our bags packed for our long voyage to Paris and then Italy!

We slept at a nearby hotel and boarded an early flight, so tired we dozed all the way to Chicago, where the plane took on more passengers. Annette's loving mother managed to reach the boarding area to embrace us, wish us a safe journey, and give Annette a beautiful topcoat. Comfortably installed in a New York hotel, I began practicing seriously for my CBS broadcast of the Khachaturian concerto with Benny. Annette and I had become friends of the great tenor Richard Tucker when he sang with the Metropolitan Opera in Los Angeles and New York. He and his wife, Sara (Jan Pearce's sister), had visited our home for a Romanian dinner (Richard was Romanian), and I had given him some useful career information about artist management. While we were in New York Richard invited us to attend, as his guests, his splendid performance as Alfredo in *La Traviata*. Sara invited us to Brooklyn the next evening for a remarkable seafood dinner where we met Richard's personal manager, Thea Dispeker, who became a friend. Learning she was en route to Paris, we made a date to dine together at La Coupole café in Montparnasse. Thea introduced us to Mr. and Mrs. Justin Tannhauser, at their New York flat, and we were astonished by their impressive collection of important French impressionist and postimpressionist paintings, which much later they bequeathed to the Solomon R. Guggenheim Museum.

Then my Vivaldi quest nearly ended! My vaccination became infected, my left leg turned scarlet, and swelled to double its size. Annette was very alarmed and called a doctor, who predicted dire consequences if I did not rest in bed. However with rest, penicillin, and ice packs, I managed to play the Khachaturian concerto. Only Benny knew anything was amiss. I was pronounced well enough to travel.

After the CBS broadcast, which included a marvelous group of Mussorgsky songs sung by the excellent Russian soprano Maria Kurenko, Jim

Fassett and Oliver Daniel invited Benny, Madame Kurenko, Annette, and me for tea at their nearby flat. Oliver, wishing to compliment the singer, said, "What a great pleasure to hear such a finished artist as yourself, Madame." Immediately incensed, Kurenko shouted, "What do you mean *finished?* I am not *finished! My* voice is youthful. I never sing *better!*" We all joined to reassure her of Oliver's admiration, explaining "finished" also expresses complete artistry and highest accomplishment. Our English language can be confusing and difficult for Europeans!

Benny appeared early the next morning at Air France to see us off, insisting "Louis, you must play in London." Dario Soria had kept his promise. I had his letter of intent to record Vivaldi's remaining eight concertos of Opus 8, and his letter of introduction to Maestro Malipiero with his Venice address.

Our plane was less than a quarter full, so Annette and I had a good rest. We landed at Orly the next morning and were soon in a taxi riding down the tree-lined boulevards of Paris—our first visit since the end of the terrible war and Nazi occupation! We observed many small bouquets of flowers affixed to buildings, which marked sites where French *résistants* had been executed during the liberation of Paris. Our friend Leo Mueller, a Czech refugee conductor in Los Angeles, had recommended a pleasant hotel on Avenue Wagram, where we settled down for a few days' rest. In the meantime, Annette had sent a letter to Maestro Malipiero that we were en route to Italy, and his cordial reply awaited us at the Paris American Express office. He would be in Venice for only a few hours on 16 July before leaving for Rome, so we were to telephone him at the conservatory between 4:30 and 6:30 P.M. to make an appointment to visit him at his home in Asolo. It seemed Opus 8 was almost in our grasp.

I determined nothing should stop me from this rendezvous and changed all our plans so we could arrive in Venice before 4:30 on the fateful afternoon of 16 July! Though I wanted to go to Venice immediately, I had to stop en route in Zurich for a few scheduled recordings for Concert Hall.

Our second evening in Paris, we arrived at La Coupole in Montparnasse, as planned. Thea Dispeker awaited us at a table, accompanied by her Australian friend Marjorie Osborne, a resident London impresario. After a delicious dinner, Marjorie suggested, "Let's visit my good friend Cecil Robson, who lives a few steps from here and is a great music lover. Cecil heard Toscanini conduct in Milan. He became so captivated by Toscanini's performances that he stayed in Milan for ten years to attend all of the Maestro's opera and concert performances. He has a marvelous record collection!" She called, and Robson invited us to visit his white two-story dwelling at 75 rue Notre-Dame-des-Champs, half hidden behind a wall that enclosed a charming garden and another house (where I had visited painter Othon Friesz in the 1930s).

Cecil, a tall, modest British gentleman, welcomed us warmly. He was charming and considerate, never selecting which recordings to play, but inviting his guests to choose what they wanted to hear. He had splendid record-playing equipment and an enormous record collection containing every Romantic or classical symphony or opera in interpretations by Toscanini, Bruno Walter, Weingartner, et cetera, as well as musical comedies, solo violin, piano, and vocal works. He adored all music and theater. During World War I, he "adopted" a young Polish couple who faithfully remained with him through and after World War II to care for his house and garden, prepare and serve dinners, and generally arrange his comfortable life.

Both Marjorie and Cecil became our valued friends during the years we spent in Paris. We spent countless evenings over the years with Cecil and friends, listening to music and attending French plays. Floor-to-ceiling bookshelves filled with interesting books about art, history, music, novels, and plays lined his spacious salon, which also had a large grand piano. Ostensibly Cecil lived by translating English plays into French or French ones—Anouilh, Marivaux, de Musset, and others—into English. Often these productions were unsuccessful or the producer would prove dishonest, but his fees were never adequate to pay for his lifestyle. His London-based family supported him, we learned years later. Cecil had served as Major General for British Intelligence in Egypt, and his brother and father felt he deserved recompense for serving brilliantly in two major wars.

At one of Cecil's occasional open house gatherings of assorted writers, musicians, poets, actors, diplomats, painters, and ballet dancers, we met Jonathan Griffin, an English diplomat and poet. No one was formally introduced at these coteries. Jonathan seemed isolated in a comfortable chair. We introduced ourselves and enjoyed a lively conversation about music and theater. We discovered we shared enthusiasm for Mozart, Wagner, and Strauss operas, and for various singers. Cecil and Jonathan knew everyone in *le tout Paris:* statesmen, journalists, playwrights, actors, artists, and musicians. We often met Jonathan at Cecil's when we would listen for hours to great recordings, and we began to dine together at small nearby bistros. We attended Alfred de Musset's great play *Lorenzaccio* and plays of Paul Claudel, Federico García Lorca, and Ionesco with him. One evening at Jonathan's home we met Felix Aprahamian, a London music critic who was visiting Paris for a few days. He

later became a good friend when we visited London. Jonathan introduced us to the novels of Nikos Kazantzakis. Our long uninterrupted
friendship with Jonathan included visits he made to California as our
houseguest. We made visits to his London home in the 1970s and 1980s,
and our unique relationship endured until his death in 1990. He greatly
enriched our lives.

# 20

# En Route to Venice via Zurich— after Visiting Poulenc

One very warm July afternoon we waited in line over an hour at the crowded French National Railroad Office to buy tickets to Zurich, and then learned we must return three days later to obtain seat reservations! Annette and I slowly walked to the Café de la Paix for a cold *citron pressé* (lemonade). Legend has it that everyone will meet someone he knows there! Suddenly André Walton, a French friend from San Francisco, loomed over us, saying, "What are you doing here?" I explained our predicament and invited him to join us. André offered helpful advice. "Why should you bother with trains? You're Americans! You can buy a four-horse-power Renault seating four for $895 with delivery in three days. We French have to wait a year for delivery, there is such demand. As tourists you are also privileged to obtain reduced-price gas coupons." (Gas is very expensive in Europe.) I demanded, "How are roads? Are garages available? Are gas stations frequent?" André laughed, "French national roads are excellent, garages and gas pumps frequent. I've returned to France, as my factory, confiscated by Germans during the Occupation, has just been returned to me. Also my wife and I agreed it would be better for our daughters to be educated here. Incidentally, my real name is Waldberg. By chance, I am en route to Dijon, and if you buy a car this afternoon, let's celebrate our reunion there. It's a famed gastronomic center. You should stay at the Hôtel des Cloches."

We immediately realized this opportunity would be the ideal solution for all our transportation and sightseeing in Europe. I canceled our train tickets, and then André drove us to Agence Renault. We selected a blue four-door model with scotch-plaid seat-covers, heater, windshield wipers, and a roof rack. Its horn was a hearty tenor, so we dubbed it "Gustave" in homage to Flaubert, whose style and craftsmanship we both admired. Gustave exceeded all expectations, providing accommodations for friends, reliability in winter and summer, and attracting friendly encounters with little boys and old men interested in our small auto, for cars were not plentiful in Europe at that time.

That same evening, we joyfully celebrated this acquisition by attending Poulenc's opera *Les Mamelles de Tirésias* (with Guillaume Apollinaire's libretto) at the Opéra Comique. During intermission, we encountered Poulenc, eating an *éskimo glacé* (chocolate-covered ice cream bar) in the foyer. He seemed as happy to see us as we were to meet him, saying, "Do come to luncheon at my apartment tomorrow," adding as he wrote down his address, "I've made some changes in my sonate that I want you to follow when you record it." Annette and I, and a capacity audience, found the opera enchanting. The performance sparkled with the ideal soprano, Dénise Duval. Poulenc told us, "I discovered her at the Folies-Bergère!" He was happy his opera was paired with a short Puccini work, which guaranteed a sold-out hall.

We picked up Gustave early the next morning. Our first ride was to rue des Médicis where Poulenc's flat overlooked the Luxembourg gardens. After ringing a few times for the nondescending *ascenseur,* the concierge appeared with "*Ah, M'sieu-Dame,* I'm sorry, but the elevator is out of order today." We were sorry to climb six flights of stairs to Poulenc's flat. He warmly welcomed us as I reported, "Our luck to arrive the only day your elevator is out of order." Poulenc smiled, "It hasn't worked for months! She likes to tell my guests it just happened." In his salon, we were pleased to meet Arthur Gold and Robert Fizdale, duo pianists (and later authors). Poulenc played for us recordings of his Requiem Mass in memory of his late artist friend Christian Bérard, and recordings of Gregorian chant sung by the famed Monks of the Abbey of Solesmes.

Poulenc presided over a delicious lunch, a gastronomic treat with excellent wines. Annette and I were fascinated by Poulenc's attractive sunny apartment, filled with fine antique furniture and vases of beautiful flowers he had purchased early that morning at the nearby flower market. His piano and salon displayed photographs of his friends Jean Cocteau, Federico García Lorca, Wanda Landowska, Darius Milhaud, Erik Satie, Nadia Boulanger, and many noted musicians and singers. I was delighted at this opportunity to go over with him his revised version of his violin sonata in memory of Lorca. We set up a date to broadcast it for the French radio in the fall, in memory of violinist Ginette Neveu, for whom it was composed.

Early the next morning, I joined the French Automobile Club to obtain the obligatory passport booklet for Gustave to enter and leave European countries. I also bought maps and a Michelin Guide, recommended by André for reliable data about hotels, restaurants, and garages. Then we set off for Zurich, via Dijon, at last en route to Venice!

There was very little traffic in Paris or on the national routes at this period. We drove through beautiful countryside and tree-lined highways, then entered the hilly terrain of Burgundy with well-kept vineyards and attractive clean villages that we could never have seen from train windows. In midafternoon, I drove into the charming city of Dijon, capital of powerful fourteenth-century Dukes of Burgundy, and home of eighteenth-century composer Rameau. His contemporary, Charles de Brosses, president of the Dijon Assembly, made a grand tour of Italy and wrote entertaining descriptive letters to his friends at home. I picked up a two-volume set, Charles De Brosses's *Lettres d'Italie*, published in Dijon. We later enjoyed reading his account of Italian artists, architects, and musicians, and his report: "Vivaldi made himself one of my intimate friends in order to sell me some of his concertos very dearly . . . he is a *vecchio* [old man] who has a prodigious fury for composition. I hear he can compose a concerto with all its parts more quickly than a copyist would be able to copy it. I find to my astonishment that he is not esteemed as highly in this country as he merits, where people have heard his works for too long a time, and where the music of the preceding year no longer pays!"

One of our greatest pleasures on tour is visiting museums and artworks. After settling in a spacious room at Hôtel des Cloches, we walked to the nearby fourteenth-century palace of the Dukes of Burgundy, now a museum housing art works of the elegant Burgundian school and the monumental marble ducal tombs with impressive mourning sculptures by Claus Sluter. The nobility of his sculptural forms approached that of Michelangelo's masterpieces.

We met André about 8 P.M. on the terrace of a celebrated cafe to enjoy a Burgundian dinner with fine regional wines. French newspapers were filled with news of the Nuremberg Trials. To our astonishment, André was unalterably against them, insisting, "They are only trying criminals who lost the war. What about criminals who burned Dresden? Whose atomic bombs destroyed Hiroshima and Nagaski? Are Allied criminals to be allowed to burn populations alive, while Axis powers are considered outlaws for the same crime?" Annette and I both protested, "André, you are French, of Polish and Jewish parents. How can you be against a court established to set norms of permissible behavior, to punish those guilty of genocide, inhuman experiments on children and adults? There must be a legal standard of behavior reestablished!" We disputed in a heated but friendly manner around our outside table until 2 A.M. in the beautiful starry night, with the exotically colored tiled roofs of Dijon's cathedral and ducal palace gleaming in the bright moonlight. Annette and I were passionately convinced the Nuremberg Trials would establish a legal organization to prevent future war crimes. How naive we were, what a vain hope that still was in 1993, after genocidal crimes in Cambodia and Bosnia-Herzegovina.

Early the next day, I drove into Zurich, settling at Hôtel Bellerive au Lac, facing Zurich's large lake bordered by attractive trees and flower-lined walks. If only the whole world could avoid wars and conflicts like the wise Swiss have done for hundreds of years! I enjoyed practicing in our comfortable room, occasionally glimpsing canoes and sailboats on the sunlit lake. Annette and I visited the excellent Kunsthaus with splendid French and Swiss masterworks.

As scheduled I recorded two American sonatas: Quincy Porter's second and Carmargo Guarnieri's second, with pianist Artur Balsam in the resonant ballroom of the Grand Hotel Dolder. We planned to press on the next day for Italy, but an early-morning call awakened me. It was David Josefowitz asking, "Louis, will you record the first violin part of a Telemann three-violin concerto today?" I did not know the music, but the project interested me, so I said, "Let me have the music as quickly as possible." Annette and I waited impatiently on the verandah of the fashionable Grand Hotel Dolder, drinking tea.

At last a lad approached at five o'clock, handed me the music, and led me to a pantry adjoining the ballroom (where two violinists were rehearsing with a string orchestra conducted by Dr. Henry Swoboda) so I could hastily study my part.

At 5:30 P.M., a recording engineer peered in and asked, "Are you ready to record, Herr Kaufman?" I replied, "I'd like to have a run-through with the violinists" (Peter Rybar, Czech concertmaster of Winterthur's Symphony, and Anton Fietz, Austrian concertmaster of Zurich's Radio Orchestra). Fietz spoke only German, but Rybar knew some German, French, and English, so our speedy rehearsal presented no difficulties; phrasings, bowings, and actual demonstration solved subtle details of performance. Annette was amused to watch us fiddlers solving fine points of ensemble while white-coated waiters and white-aproned chambermaids passed in and out of the crowded pantry. By 6:30 P.M., we were ready to rehearse with the orchestra, and by 8:30 that evening the recording was completed. Everyone seemed pleased with the result.

Early the following morning we were en route to Italy! The road lay over the Saint Gotthard Pass and we both delighted in the fresh mountain air and the unspoiled beauty of Swiss lakes and mountains. However, we saw large American and larger European cars stalled by overheated motors. Even Gustave couldn't proceed to the summit. I turned around and coasted down to a depot, where a small efficient train took passengers and their cars through the Gotthard tunnel every few hours. We regretted not being able to drive through the snow-capped heights, but enjoyed the comfortable ride through the long dark tunnel. A fellow passenger told us what a great engineering feat this tunnel was and how many workers had lost their lives during its construction. We left the train at Airolo completely refreshed. After a delicious meal on the verandah of a hotel overlooking beautiful Lake Lugano and more gasoline for Gustave, we completed our journey through the Swiss Ticino, crossed the Italian border, and arrived in Milan in time for a late dinner in the galleria near the Duomo.

To make certain we did not overlook the possibility of finding a modern edition of Vivaldi's Opus 8, we visited all of Milan's music publishing establishments the next day. One-way streets had not begun, so I could drive directly to their entrances. I soon learned that *Il Cimento* was unknown. When I inquired if Alceo Toni, who edited the *Four Seasons,* might know about them, I was told his Carisch edition was made thirty years ago, he was very old, and it would be best to avoid him. He had been an active collaborator with the Germans and was now in ill repute in all circles! He had even denounced antifascist Italians, causing their execution!

I looked over about sixty newly printed Vivaldi concertos at Edizioni Ricordi from the Istituto Italiano Antonio Vivaldi, edited by Antonio Fanna, under supervision of Maestro Malipiero. Out of this group I selected thirty scores and also accompanying instrumental parts. It became apparent that our search would be much more difficult than I had originally thought.

# 21

# Unfinished Business

*Meeting Malipiero*

As I drove through the beautiful flat countryside of Northern Italy, with the Italian, Swiss, and Austrian Alps in the distance, we were obsessed with Vivaldi's personality, having seen Ghezzi's caricature of him, made in Rome in 1723, showing his broad forehead, large inquiring eyes, and very large arched nose over a generous mouth.

Vivaldi's career as opera composer and violinist carried him to all parts of Italy and far beyond his native land. About 1728 he was in Vienna, where he composed the twelve concertos of his Opus 9, *La Cetra*. He returned to Venice, dying on 28 July 1741, so impoverished that there were not sufficient funds for his funeral. I surmised that his elaborate, extravagant operatic productions might have caused his financial ruin.

We stopped off to see museums in Bergamo and Verona, and also in Padua, where Giotto's frescoes in the Scrovegni Chapel were being restored. At Vicenza, we visited Palladio's Teatro Olympia, with a permanent Renaissance stage set that gives the trompe l'oeil illusion of deep perspective. I often told Annette, "Vivaldi must have seen this," or "Vivaldi might have played here." We enjoyed an unforgettable lunch in Verona with native Valpolicello wine, said to be the favorite of Virgil. It became one of our favorite *vins du pays*.

It seemed almost incredible to us that Vivaldi's immense output should have practically vanished, nearly forgotten for two hundred years. Yet here we were, parking the car and entering a gondola in Venice, hoping to find a mere eight concertos from only one opus! We settled into the Grand Hotel de Monaco on the Grand Canal. I immediately telephoned Maestro Malipiero at the Conservatorio. Although he was very pleased

Caricature of Vivaldi by Ghezzi.

to hear from me, unexpected matters demanded his attention, so he invited me to visit his Asolo casa on his return from Rome.

Venice still retains its eighteenth-century appearance: beautiful churches and palaces by Palladio and Sansovino look down on busy passengers in modern dress, passing through canals on *vaporetto*s (water buses), *rapido*s, and *motoscafo*s that dart through the canals. We visited

San Marco, the Doges' Palace, and the Correr Museum, and enjoyed the same ambiance that Goldoni, Vivaldi, Tiepolo, and Canaletto shared.

On the day of our visit with Malipiero, I picked up Gustave at the garage and drove to nearby Asolo, a beautiful ancient village with one of the oldest edifices in Northern Italy, a well proportioned castle with Etruscan foundations, later Roman additions, and early Renaissance embellishment. Although damaged by an earthquake, it remains impressive. Malipiero's estate covered an entire hillside, with stone walks and a semi-open brick and wood barn that resembled fourteenth- and fifteenth-century paintings of the manger where the Magi visited the Virgin and Child.

Maestro and Signora Malipiero warmly welcomed us. His handsome, white-haired appearance recalled Titian and Bellini portraits of ruling doges, who were among his ancestors. Although they spoke French with us, Signora was English and the Maestro knew English but was more comfortable with French. While dining, our conversation was mainly political. The Malipieros had actively aided the Allied forces; they helped many Yugoslav Jewish families, who were difficult to hide as they liked to walk about and did not speak Italian well enough to escape notice of the Germans. They were always sent on to safety, but left their pet dogs and cats with the Malipieros. Maestro and Signora Malipiero lived surrounded by eight dogs; five belonging to the Maestro liked music, so they were called *musi-chiens*! His wife had three cats that did not like music or the Maestro's dogs! I explained that Dario Soria was interested in recording the eight concertos that follow the *Four Seasons*. I wanted to know whether all the concertos of Opus 8 were composed for solo violin, or if some concertos were written for other instruments. To my dismay, Maestro Malipiero stated, "I myself have been trying to obtain that same music for *twelve* years and do not know. I am, however, certain that Opus 8 is not in Italy. I have written to all the libraries and have requested data, asked some friends who went on voyages to inquire about these concerti, but I have never received a reply! Of course, the war cut me off from the civilized world. I withdrew to Asolo for the duration. In any event the letters I sent, as well as the friends, all seemed to disappear into some mysterious limbo and nothing has ever been heard from them. I strongly object to all Italian editions [this may have been contra Toni?] as they are all bastardized!"

However, I had no intention of giving up, so I pressed on: "I have a small Renault and would go any distance to find the music, Maestro, if you could offer the slightest idea where to continue the search." Maestro replied, "I am not altogether sure where one might go, but it seems to me that since some of Vivaldi's music had been published during his life in the Netherlands, it might be possible to find a first edition somewhere there. My friend Paul Collaer, head of the Radio Flamande Music Section in Brussels, is passionately interested in early Italian music. He has produced Monteverdi's *L'Orfeo* and Antonio Cesti's *Il Pomo d'Oro* operas for Radio Flamande and might know where to find Vivaldi's editions." He added, "There are wonderful libraries in Belgium and Holland; it might be the best idea to look there."

Even this vague clue gave me hope, as Maestro sat down at his desk and wrote a letter of introduction for me to Collaer. As he sealed it and handed it over, he added, "Don't you disappear, Monsieur Kaufman. Let me hear from you!" I solemnly promised, "You will be the first to know if we find the music, and if we have such good luck, we will send you a microfilm."

In spite of our eagerness to resume our search, we decided to abandon temporarily our detective role and become tourists. This was our first visit to Italy since our honeymoon, and it was equally thrilling. With the freedom provided by Gustave, we could stop in any village to see any cathedral or museum without being limited by train or bus schedules. There was little traffic, and thanks to the dependable Michelin Guide, we stayed at inexpensive hotels and enjoyed excellent cuisine in modest restaurants or trattorias.

Florence had been severely damaged by the retreating German army, which destroyed every bridge over the Arno except the Ponte Vecchio. A New York friend, Carla Castaldi-Rava, accompanied us to visit San Miniato and the Church of the Carmine to admire the remarkable Masaccio frescos. She also introduced us to excellent restaurants. What a great experience to again visit Michelangelo's Medici tombs and enjoy the masterworks in the Uffizi and Pitti Palaces.

I have always been fascinated by the works of Benozzo Gozzoli, a pupil of Fra Angelico, and his magical *Procession of the Magi* in the Riccardi Palace chapel. How extraordinary that the splendid Botticellis were unappreciated for many years until the English Pre-Raphaelites proclaimed the genius of his line and composition!

Jacques Rachmilovich (conductor of the Santa Monica Symphony) was vacationing nearby at the seaside Forte dei Marmi, so we decided to make a quick jaunt to see him and his wife, Marussia. We drove there for an enjoyable lunch on a terrace overlooking the sea. Jacques invited us to attend his forthcoming concert in Rome with the Santa Cecilia Orchestra.

The Santa Cecilia Academy, founded by the Renaissance composer Palestrina, performed under Jacques's direction a most unusual program, comprising Rossini's overture to *La Scala di Seta*, Bizet's Symphony in C,

Samuel Barber's Adagio for Strings, and four Etudes-Tableaux of Rachmaninoff, orchestrated by Respighi. They also performed two interesting Roman premieres by Glinka—"Kamarinskaya" and "Jota Aragonese." We greatly enjoyed hearing Jacques's concert in the historic Baths of Caracalla, under a starry Roman night sky, with the floodlit Coliseum nearby. Jacques introduced us to an untalented "filmmaker" who wanted to use my recording of Vivaldi's *Four Seasons* for his documentary about a visit to Rome. He proudly showed us his idiotic work. He had merely photographed the fountain at the Piazza del Popolo from its four sides; since they are identical, his film was absolutely static!

I called Madame Elsa Respighi, widow of composer Ottorino Respighi, and she welcomed me warmly. She had attended the concert in Mexico when Imre Hartman and I had performed the Brahms double concerto. She gave me an autographed photo of her late husband, with whom she had studied composition. We did some sightseeing with her, visiting the church in Saint Ignacio Square where Tosca meets Cavaradossi in the first act of *Tosca,* and driving past Castel Sant'Angelo, from whose crenellated parapet Tosca leaps into the Tiber. Madame Respighi gave me some early solo violin works of her husband that evening after dinner in the Piazza Navona.

After this enjoyable reunion with friends, we decided it would be quicker to return to Paris via Turin over the Mont Cenis Pass. I was pleased that there was a train to "tunnel" us through. We spent the night in a little village, Cesena, in a charming small inn. We walked along a fresh mountain stream in the dusk, wondering if Paul Cézanne's forebears had come from this hamlet. We later learned they had.

Early next morning, we discovered train service had been discontinued during the summer months! So Gustave bravely climbed Mont Cenis Pass. When we stopped at the Italian customs house in the lonely mountains, I expected only brief formalities: "Whiskey? Cigarettes?" So I was surprised when a young officer demanded, "Bring your violin case and that valise into the customs house." He barely glanced at the valise, but then asked me to open the violin case, suddenly saying, "Play something!" I thought he suspected me of not being a fiddler, but a smuggler of jewels or drugs, so that my violin would rattle as I picked it up. I played a popular tune, and the officer said disdainfully, "Not that! Play something good! Play Paganini!" I obliged with "La Campanella," which pleased the officer. His colleagues inside, attracted by music in the mountain stillness, came out; a shirtless man in the process of shaving and a couple of dogs drifted in, as I played a Paganini "Capriccio" to this strange audience, accented by irate horns of the cars piling up at the customs barrier.

At the conclusion, the customs officer paid me extravagant compliments and accompanied me back to our car, where he congratulated Annette on her husband's artistry. He told us that he had been a violinist before the war, but had injured his hands and could no longer play. Suspect us of being smugglers? Nonsense! He was bored with his job and wanted to hear how an American violinist played! We sympathized with the plight of this unfortunate colleague, but the incident seemed very amusing to us as we continued on our way.

We stopped in Grenoble, Stendhal's birthplace, to visit its remarkable museum that contained one of the most beautiful paintings by Rubens that we had ever seen. This painting of Santa Cecilia covered almost an entire wall. The museum also had an excellent collection of modern French paintings. The curator had only modest funds for acquisitions but very discriminating taste, and he bought works of Modigliani, Braque, Soutine, Utrillo, and others when they were young and comparatively unknown.

I returned to Paris exhausted, and wanted to postpone travel for a while to devote myself to studying Milhaud's second concerto, which I was to perform and record in October, with the composer conducting. But Annette was possessed by a sense of urgency, due to the approaching *fermeture annuelle* (closing for summer vacation), and she wanted to push on to Brussels at once. Perhaps this was the guiding hand of our impatient "friend," Signor Antonio Vivaldi, but her overriding idea was to get to Brussels immediately! As usual, we compromised. I was allowed two days rest in Paris, and then we started off again on the *route nationale*, this time heading north to Belgium!

# 22

## Brussels con Moto

*Paris Recordings—Arrival in Brussels—
Fateful Meeting with Paul Collaer*

<br>

D riving into Brussels's North Station area, I quickly found a modest hotel, then immediately telephoned Radio Flamande to speak with the music director, Paul Collaer. His secretary politely answered, "Monsieur Collaer is out of the city for two days, he will return Saturday morning." I replied, "I have a letter for Monsieur Collaer from Maestro Malipiero." She answered, "Oh! If you are a friend of Maestro Malipiero, I will give you an appointment for Saturday at 11:30."

Annette and I spent this waiting period visiting Belgian cities with artistic masterpieces: Ghent's Saint-Bavon altarpiece by the brothers Van Eyck, and in Bruges, a large retrospective exhibit of masterworks by Hans Memling and Gerard David. One afternoon, we seemed to be alone in Ostend's huge retrospective of Belgium's great modern master, James Ensor, until we observed an elderly white-haired gentleman sitting near the exit. I thought this thin stooped figure might be Ensor himself, but hesitated to disturb him. Ensor's enormous masterpiece, *Entry of Christ into Brussels,* dominated the exhibit. I was surprised to see this masterly painting forty years later in 1992 at the J. Paul Getty Museum in Malibu.

On this first visit to Belgium, we were greatly impressed by Brussels's imposing Grand Place, with intact handsome medieval houses still serving as public buildings and restaurants. Brussels's royal churches and museums were filled with incomparable fifteenth-century masterpieces by Rogier van der Weyden, Peter Paul Rubens, Anthony Van Dyck, Pieter Brueghel, Hans Memling, and Gerard David. Restaurants, delicatessens, and pastry shops were filled with delicious temptations. The people were friendly, polite, and seemed well satisfied with their world.

Saturday morning, I drove to Radio Flamande's site at Place Eugene Flagey to find the large area filled by a Saturday morning open-air market, with beautiful vegetables, fruits, flowers, and items of clothing for sale under temporary colorful, covered stands. I parked nearby, and we walked through the stalls, arriving for our appointment well before 11:30 A.M. Collaer was occupied, so we waited impatiently in an outer office until he briskly ushered us into his large sunny office at precisely 11:40. I presented Malipiero's letter, which he quickly read, saying, "I can't imagine what Malipiero was thinking of to give you such a vague letter." He handed it to me; it briefly stated, "Here are Monsieur and Madame Kaufman who are searching for Vivaldi's Opus 8. Dear friend, would you please aid them to find it in the Netherlands?" Collaer dismayed us, saying, "There are many libraries in this part of the world. I wouldn't know whether to suggest you look in Antwerp, Liège, Louvain, The Hague, Amsterdam, or even here in Brussels." He continued, "I don't know if the music exists at all. But supposing Malipiero is right in thinking the Netherlands . . . it might lie hidden in any of the libraries of two dozen cities!"

Frankly, I hadn't expected Collaer to have it in Radio Flamande's library, but I remembered Malipiero had implied he would know where it was. We were deflated at this wreck of our hopes. Collaer, sensing our dismay, suggested that we might be helped by the librarian of the Conservatoire Royal de Musique de Bruxelles Bibliothèque (Royal Music Conservatory of Brussels Library). He then telephoned the news that we were en route there. He exclaimed, "Rush to the Library, it closes for *fermeture annuelle* at noon!" It was now ten minutes to twelve! I started to thank him, but Collaer stopped me with, "*Dépechez-vous vite vite* [Hurry, quickly, quickly]," and pushed me out the door. We raced downstairs and hurled ourselves into Gustave, only to realize I hadn't a notion where the Bibliothèque was. In desperation, I started off down the street and stopped to ask the only person I saw, a street cleaner sweeping up debris from the just-closed market, who kindly directed me.

The next few minutes were like a movie chase scene, as I careened around corners at alarming speed, and drove up to the Conservatoire just as noon was striking in the tower of the cathedral across the street. The door was not locked, but the concierge firmly shouted, "Closed!" I just as firmly replied, "We are expected!" and asked, "Where is the library?" The seated concierge replied, "Third floor to the right." We raced up five flights of stairs (Belgians number their floors from the third floor) to the Bibliothèque to find it empty! We sat down to recover our breath. After a few seconds, a pleasant young man entered to announce, "The library is closed." I introduced myself, saying Collaer had telephoned about our visit. He replied, "I would be delighted to aid you, if possible, but can only spare a few minutes, as I must take a tram to catch my train." I promised, "I've an auto. I'll drive you to the station [I would have driven him to his destination, if necessary!] if you will answer one question. Do you know the whereabouts of Vivaldi's Opus 8?" He calmly replied, "It's here!" He disappeared into another part of the Bibliothèque and returned holding a slim green parchment-bound volume marked *Violino I.* It looked so small, so thin, that on opening its cover and seeing *La Primavera* (the first Spring concerto of the *Four Seasons*), I said, "These are the *Four Seasons*! I am looking for eight concertos that follow these." The young man replied, "*Non, Monsieur,* there are twelve here." And so there were! I couldn't believe my good fortune! I demanded, "Do you have the *solo principale* part? The *Violino II,* alto, cello, and continuo part also?" After each request, the young man returned with the exact part. It was all complete! My first glance assured me they were all scored for solo violin, although Vivaldi indicated the ninth and twelfth concertos could alternately be played by oboe. I asked, "Is it possible to have all the parts copied on microfilm?" He answered, "Yes, but you must go to the main post office, fill out a special form, and pay the charges in advance to the post office, who will then transfer the form and funds to the Bibliothèque, which is not permitted to receive funds in direct payment." We three quickly counted all pages of the various parts.

I drove our new friend to the station, where he boarded his train. Then Annette and I deeply acknowledged our good fortune to have stumbled onto the very spot where the music had safely rested throughout wars and invasions, including the two devastating wars of our own century!

I drove to the central post office and Annette helped me fill in all the necessary forms. I paid for two microfilmed copies, one to be sent to Maestro Malipiero and the other to myself in Paris. Face to face with the formidable questionnaire in both French and Flemish, I realized why persons sent by Malipiero to look for Opus 8 had never been heard of again. I filled in my name, place of birth, origin of my parents, their names, our legal address, purpose of request, what documents I wanted, number of pages, et cetera. It took up most of the afternoon, and was too much bother for anyone not as obsessed as ourselves. That same evening we sent off an airmail letter to Maestro Malipiero to recount our success thanks to his clues, and a letter to Dario Soria to inform him the eight concertos were for violin! I also expressed thanks to Collaer for his friendly assistance. Their "shots in the dark" had led me straight to the mark!

Annette noticed the Bibliothèque's edition had been printed by Michele Carlo le Cene of Amsterdam, so we proceeded there, to see if we could locate a complete score of Opus 8. We settled in at the American Hotel in Amsterdam, where we took the opportunity to look at paintings in the nearby Rijksmuseum, as well as fabulous Rembrandts in The Hague's Mauritshuis, and Frans Hals's works in nearby Haarlem. What outstanding artists the Netherlands produced!

It seemed fitting that on the exact site of Le Cene's eighteenth-century workshop there was now a modern newspaper, *De Telegraf.* We learned that eighteenth-century editions were small—only a dozen to twenty copies would be considered a large edition—for wooden plates soon wore out. There were few patrons for expensive printed music. Kings, dukes, counts, or church dignitaries were the only possible clients, as musicians were lowly household servants wearing livery. This explains the scarcity of early editions. A great amount of music, art, and books was destroyed in wars and revolutions. A full orchestral score was never printed; only individual parts for players. The eighteenth-century conductor was also solo violinist and composer, leading from his original handwritten score. The orchestral conductor only arrived on the musical scene in the nineteenth century.

The director of The Hague's Royal Library informed me there was not one copy of Vivaldi's Opus 8 in the entire country, although he had received many requests for it. Could these have been earlier inquiries from Maestro Malipiero or his friends?

In the meantime, Collaer received our note and promptly visited Brussels's Bibliothèque to see the Opus 8 parts. On our return to Paris, I found a letter from him inviting me to premiere these concertos in Brussels for Radio Flamande. I soon received my microfilm copies in Paris. Maestro Malipiero told me the Istituto Antonio Vivaldi would reimburse me for microfilm, should I find the material. However, I ordered the microfilm as my gift to the Vivaldi archives. Malipiero's effusive and heartwarming letter of thanks repaid us for our long journey and minor discomforts en route. I never dreamed these events would reverberate into a widening circle of concerts for me in Europe, England, and the Americas.

The day after our return to Paris we encountered Diana Gibbings at Café de la Paix. Diana had written press releases at CBS in New York when I broadcasted the Khachaturian concerto with Bernard Herrmann and the Vivaldi *Four Seasons* premiere with Alfredo Antonini, and she had a summer job as correspondent for the *Continental Daily Mail* (an English newspaper in Paris). Over a cold *citron pressé,* she asked, "What are you doing in Europe?" Still exhilarated by our recent treasure hunt, I told her the whole story. The next day her paper carried a few paragraphs about our adventure, which was picked up by the European and American newspapers. Paul Collaer later told me that when he was in Venice, he read about it in *Corrriere della Sera*. It made quite a splash!

A *Time* magazine reporter actually went to Brussels to check out the story and met Collaer on the steps of the Conservatoire Royal, just as he was leaving. "Is it true," the reporter demanded, "that some Americans found some Vivaldi material here?" Collaer replied, "They certainly did," and showed the journalist the separate parts of Opus 8 he was carrying.

I was dismayed to learn much later that the chief librarian of the Bibliothèque was offended by this unsought publicity. He considered it a criticism of his institution because the reports made it appear he did not know the contents of his library. *He* knew the contents of his distinguished library, but unsuspecting scholars might have had difficulty in finding items, for they classified the library's contents by *date of acquisition!*

Neither Paul Collaer nor I ever received the Opus 8 parts from Italy for the Belgian premiere by Radio Flamande. Not one to be put off by such a problem, Collaer ordered the Radio Flamande copyists to prepare a score and parts from the Le Cene 1725 edition.

When I studied Opus 8's first four concertos, I had been surprised that Vivaldi's Autumn concerto's third movement was a mazurka, a Polish folk dance form that most musicians believe was introduced into classical music by Chopin. Now I realized from his dedication that the movement's double-stop violin chords evoked hunting horns and that the mazurka was a tribute to his patron's Polish estates.

Concerto 5, *Tempesta de Mare* (Storm at Sea), depicts troubled waves and lightning of Adriatic dimensions. Its form was daring, for the three movements are connected, without a final cadence until the third movement's conclusion. This dramatic idea of contrasting calm and stormy seas was executed long before nineteenth-century composers used this device in solo or symphonic works. Mendelssohn's connecting of the first and second movements of his violin concerto has been pointed out as a stroke of inventive genius.

At a later performance of Gluck's opera *Orfeo ed Euridice* that we attended in Brussels I thought Gluck might have heard the *Tempesta* concerto in Venice or Vienna. He utilized the same type of scale passages and rhythms in his music for Orfeo's descent into Hades in search of Euridice. Was this a mysterious artistic coincidence or was it patterned on Vivaldi's *Tempesta*? Due to Vivaldi's great Viennese success, this work could well have influenced young Gluck!

In Concerto 6, *Il Piacere* (Pleasure), the gaily syncopated allegros frame one of Vivaldi's most lyrical and beautiful *sicilianos*. It always delights listeners by its unexpected pianissimo ending. The seventh and eighth concertos are in the same three-movement form, distinguished by melodic and harmonic invention with diversified rhythms. The largo of Concerto 11 has Handelian grandeur, and its grave is a noble aria that so impressed me that I discussed it in detail with Maestro Malipiero a full year later. The tenth concerto, *La Caccia* (The Hunt), effectively uses double stops to express hunting horns for solo violin, as does the third movement of the *Autunno* concerto. This may indicate that Count Marzin was devoted to the chase, or merely that Vivaldi liked to write violin double stops (playing two or more notes at one time on the violin) to suggest two or three hunting horns. If the violin could not equal the horn's sonority, it could offer more beautiful tonal texture! The extraordinary eleventh concerto's first movement is a majestic fugue, which gives the solo violin bristling technical difficulties to solve, going into higher registers than any other violin literature at that time. Strong dissonances played by the solo violinist against the firm noble melody of the fugue in the whole orchestra dramatically suggest the *Cimento* between Harmony and Invention that inspired Vivaldi's title for his *Opera Ottavo*. The twelfth concerto joyously sings the victory of Harmony!

In October 1949 Paul Collaer and the musicians of Radio Flamande were busy with rehearsals for a radio production premiere of Darius Milhaud's setting of Paul Claudel's version of Aeschylus's *Eumenides*. I was also given generous rehearsal time with string orchestra, harpsichordist, and conductor Léonce Gras for the premiere broadcast of Concertos 5 through 8. Annette and I attended as many of the Milhaud rehearsals as fit in my schedule. Milhaud and Madeleine were there, as excited and thrilled with the power and beauty of this inspired work as we were. Milhaud had the ingenious idea for the Goddess Athena's great aria of having three sopranos sing in unison to express Athena's noble utterances!

My broadcast was, like Milhaud's, a full dress affair with invited audience. Collaer graciously invited the head librarian of the Bibliothèque, but his pique about our "finding" the first edition at his library and resultant news flurry caused him to reply, "I am not very interested in Vivaldi's music, and regret I have a previous engagement." However, the audience, musicians, and Collaer were enchanted by this "new" music, and I was launched in Europe as an apostle of the Venetian Orpheus. The BBC and Czech Radio both requested permission to transmit this program to their audiences. After this auspicious concert, the Collaers invited the Grases and ourselves to celebrate quietly at their residence on rue des Tilleuls.

There we were pleased to learn Collaer had written the fine Darius Milhaud biography we had recently bought and read. We discovered we shared many ideas and enthusiasms with the Collaers: the archeology of Mexico; music of Milhaud, Satie, and Monteverdi; early Flemish painters, sculptors, and musicians; and folk arts and folk music. We talked long into the night and became friends.

Dario Soria received our letter describing our visit to Malipiero and research adventures in Brussels. He replied from Venice enthusiastically that he hoped to record the eight concertos soon in Italy. A telegram followed:

> Tirenelli reports Turin Orchestra not available until October. Meeting Tirenelli and Radio head here this weekend. Hope to arrange recording remainder Vivaldi Opus 8. Advise your October availability.
> Greetings. Soria Hotel Gritti

Two weeks later came another telegram:

> Very sorry report Cetra decided not to record Vivaldi since it does not fit Company's present plans and commitments. Sorry not to see you before leaving but will be in Geneva a few hours.
> Thanks again all your interest trouble. Soria

Shortly afterwards I heard his disappointed voice, via telephone from Geneva: "The directors of Cetra wish to concentrate all their efforts and funds on the more profitable field of opera, and cannot envisage any instrumental recordings of such magnitude as the Opus 8."

Since I was now released from this commitment, I proposed the idea to Concert Hall, which David Josefowitz accepted. In August 1950 I recorded these concertos in Switzerland with strings from the Lucerne Festival Orchestra and Radio Zurich. However, Maestro Malipiero had written to me just before the Brussels broadcast, "You have noticed perhaps there is an indication *organo*. I am convinced this also means harpsichord and I shall realize the bass in such fashion that one may be able to play it with organ or harpsichord." Malipiero's realization of the figured bass has never arrived to this day! Harpsichordist Theodore Sachs had to play the continuo from the figured bass of the original edition loaned to us by Radio Flamande.

In his notes for my *Four Seasons* recording, Alfred Einstein wrote:

> In the field of instrumental music, Vivaldi seems to be the first indeed who tried to illustrate the Seasons—the model for so many imitations.... His music is based on four sonnets by an unknown poet, perhaps himself,

because they are not lyrical masterworks. If we believe him to be the author, it is only because they are written from the point of view of the composer.

As I read these charming sonnets in the 1725 edition, I felt certain Vivaldi wrote them, for his music illustrated them most effectively. The title page of that rare edition intrigued us both:

Il Cimento dell'Armonia e dell'Invenzione
Concerti
a 4 e 5
Consecrati
All'Illustrissimo Signore
Il Signor Venceslao Conte di Marzin, Signore Ereditario de Hohenlibe,
Lomniz, Tschista, Krzinetz, Kaunitz, Doubek, et Soweluska,
Cameriere Attuale, e Consigliere di
S. M. C. C.
da D. ANTONIO VIVALDI
Maestro in Italia dell'illustrissmo Signor Conte Sudetto,
Maestro de Concerti del Pio Ospedale della Pieta in Venetia
Maestro Capella de camera de S.A.S. Signor
Principe Fillipe Langravio d' Hassia Darmistah Opera Ottava
OPERA OTTAVA
Libro primo
a Amsterdam,
spesa di Michele Carlo Le Cene
Libro No. 520

SPRING
Spring is here, and full of happiness.
The birds salute her with their lilting song,
All fountains flow at the warm breath
of little breezes, softly murmuring.
Now come, mantling the sky in cloak of black
Lightning and thunder, to announce the Spring
While following these, again little birds
Return to make melodious enchantment:
And so, upon the pleasant flowering meadow
With tender whispering of leaf and branch
The goatherd sleeps, beside his faithful dog.
While to the festive sound of Shepherd's pipe
A shining apparition, Nymph and Shepherd
Dance on the beloved roof of Spring.

### SUMMER

Under the harsh, hot season, the man droops.
The herd is languid, and the pine tree burns,
The cuckoo showers its notes upon the air,
Soon sings the turtledove, and the little finch.
Come sweet Zephyr, but contending brusquely
Comes North Wind close beside.
The shepherd weeps because he fears
The fierce North Storm and his own fate;
Snatched from his weary limbs is all repose
By fearful lightning and thunder's roll
and angry flight of gnats and flies.
Ah, more's the pity, all his fears come true:
A thundering sky, with thunderbolts and hail
Beheads the trees, crumples the grain.

### AUTUMN

Country lads enjoy with songs and dances
The happy fortunes of abundant harvest.
When they've had their fill of Bacchus's cup,
The merry feast ends with all guests sleeping.
It summons lively chatter, dancing, song,
This pleasure-giving, temperate Autumn air,
This season which invites us to sweetest sleep
And wakes from sleep to even sweeter pleasure.
Forth go the hunters to chase at dawn
with horns, with guns, with staffs to beat the woods.
Before them flee the game whose tracks they follow.
Now frightened, wearied of the deafening noises
of muskets, beaters, wounded now as well,
The poor beast, spent with running, sinks and dies.

### WINTER

Frozen, shivering in the snowy cold
Under the harsh blows of a fearful wind,
Stamping your feet again and again and running
All in a world of ice, with chattering teeth,
Spending the days quietly, content by the fire,
While others go out of doors in the pouring rain,
Or walking upon the ice with cautious step,
Slowly, carefully, in fear of falling;
Then stepping out strongly, slipping, falling at last,
To scramble up once more and running hard
To race, while the cracking ice breaks, gaping wide

To hear bursting through door of iron, the winds,
The South, North Wind, all the Winds at War.
This is Winter. And yet, what joy it brings.

Upon our return to Paris, I devoted all my practicing to Milhaud's Second Concerto. The metronome indicated an extremely rapid tempo for the third movement, which had wide leaps on the fingerboard. I constantly worried about that. In the long dusk of Paris evenings, as Annette and I walked up and down the length of the Champs-Elysées, then rested at a sidewalk cafe, I would frequently tell her, "I can't play it cleanly at that speed, Milhaud will have to find another fiddler." In the meantime, Capitol Records scheduled my recording of four Vivaldi concertos in Milan. Their resident agent, Serge Glykson, a Russian who spoke English, informed me that Roger Désormière, a gifted conductor of modern and eighteenth-century music, was not available for my recordings. "Why not?" I asked. He replied, "Much too expensive—but don't worry. I have a Russian friend who conducts at the Folies-Bergère. He will be excellent." Annette and I took a dim view of this news. Milhaud had recommended Désormière and he had been engaged to supervise all the Milhaud recordings—First Symphony, *Concertino de Printemps,* and Second Concerto.

I read in *La Semaine de Paris* that Désormière was to conduct l'Orchestre National de la Radiodiffusion Française in scenes from Henri Sauguet's *La Chartreuse de Parme* at Théâtre des Champs-Elysées with singers from the Paris Opera. What an opportunity to hear Sauguet's opera and meet Désormière!

We attended, and enthusiastic about both music and performance, went backstage, introduced ourselves as friends of Milhaud, and congratulated him on his splendid performance. I invited him to join us at a bistro across the Avenue de Montaigne. I apologized for asking what fee he requested from Capitol, for I wished to have him conduct for my scheduled recordings. I added, "Glykson told me it was impossible due to your excessive demands." Surprised and pleased by my frankness, Désormière (Déso) replied, "I attended school with Glykson, so I told him to pay me whatever is customary." Glykson did not know we spoke French! I immediately informed Capitol that Déso's fee was modest, which eliminated Glykson's plot to aid his Folies-Bergère pal!

Shortly after we attended a concert Désormière conducted at the Salle de Conservatoire for La Société pour la Musique Oubliée (forgotten music) of early French and Italian songs and instrumental works, including an attractive Vivaldi concerto for two violins, with original Vivaldi cadenzas. I obtained a copy of this work and later recorded it in Switzerland for Concert Hall with violinist Peter Rybar, concertmaster of Winterthur's orchestra.

Dr. Grenzebach, of the high-quality German record label Telefunken, arrived from Germany with some nine hundred kilos of equipment. There was complicated financing for these recordings. His company could not pay Capitol for records sold in Germany so they paid for the cost of recording these records as well as for the Milhaud works. I was to record four Vivaldi concertos I had selected in Milan: one titled *Senza Cantin* (without the E string), another in E-flat with a most beautiful operatic adagio, the third titled *Dresden* (with woodwinds, unusual for that period), and the fourth a double concerto for violin and cello. The personnel included Jacques Neilz (first cellist of l'Orchestre National) and Antoine Geoffroy Déchaume as continuo-clavicinst. Glykson, representing Capitol Records, brought along Jo Bouillon (violinist husband of Josephine Baker) to be in charge of recording.

We began rehearsing in the large Cinema Rex at 10 A.M. with Désormière conducting. When we started recording, Bouillon, from the sound booth, shouted, "Violin too loud." This announcement was repeated for one-half hour as I attempted to play softer and softer. "Violin still too loud." Both Déso and I found this an unbearable strain. Déso finally exploded, "We can't work in the dark, you must let us hear a playback." As the recording started to play, I shouted, "You have not connected the orchestral mikes." Technicians immediately came on stage to connect the microphones. Bouillon, who obviously resented me for being an American, did not know much about recording equipment. We had to rush to record the four concertos, as the Cinema Rex opened at noon to show films. I told Grenzebach about a nearby recording studio where I could assemble the tapes quickly, and he agreed to this arrangement. Bouillon offered, "I am willing to help you, Monsieur Kaufman." I was too annoyed by his lack of knowledge and hostility to reply. Annette quietly said, "We don't need your help, Monsieur Bouillon."

The next morning we assembled at Cinema Rex to record Martinů's *Concerto da Camera*. Annette sat in the audience next to Grenzebach. As Martinů's vigorous music sounded in the spacious hall, Grenzebach turned to Annette, saying, "This is modern music isn't it?" Trying to be helpful, she replied "Yes, Herr Grenzebach, like Hindemith." He arose quickly and canceled the recording. For at that time he knew eighteenth-century music would sell but modern music did not!

I was puzzled by this development until we visited Martinů in Switzerland, where he was the guest of Paul Sacher. I told him how very disappointed I was at not being able to record his concerto. He smilingly replied, "When I was a very poor lad in Czechoslovakia the State Radio often performed a work by Italy's eighteenth-century composer Padre Martini. Each time it was played they sent me a small royalty. I needed those small mistaken payments and thought it was very justifiable that an old master wouldn't mind helping a struggling young composer. Evidently Grenzebach accepted my concerto, thinking I was an eighteenth-century composer!"

Meanwhile, I practiced the Milhaud concerto diligently, and I was extremely worried about his metronome indication for the final movement. I was very impatient for Milhaud to return to Paris in September to discuss this with him.

The day that Darius and Madeleine arrived in Paris, I phoned and Madeleine answered, "Come right over." Before playing I stated, "I'm worried that you won't be pleased by my performance of the last movement." Milhaud gently said, "Let me hear it, Louis." I started playing. Milhaud asked, "Where's the fire?" I played a little more slowly, and Milhaud stated, "It is too fast." I played still more slowly and Milhaud stated, "It's still too fast." Relieved, I said, "Oh, I can play it easily at this tempo, but what about your metronome mark?" Milhaud calmly replied, "Oh, my metronome hasn't worked properly for ten years!" Madeleine, Annette, and I laughed heartily!

A few days later the orchestral rehearsals began. Thanks to Manuel Rosenthal, Milhaud had five rehearsals for the symphony, including two rehearsals for his violin concerto.

The all-Milhaud concert at the Théâtre des Champs-Elysées in Paris featured his First Symphony, *Opus Americanum*, composed on the theme of Moses (its title referring to Milhaud's "residence-in-exile" in the United States), and his second violin concerto. This was my introduction to Milhaud's myriad friends and admirers. It was also a celebration of his return to a free France and was enthusiastically hailed by the capacity audience and the press. Backstage I met composer Henri Sauguet, who spontaneously offered, "Kaufman, I am going to write a concerto for you." (A few years later he did compose a *Concerto d'orphée* for me.) Our friends Manuel and Claudine Rosenthal attended, and I met the Romanian composer Marcel Mihalovici and his pianist wife, Monique Haas, the Hungarian composer Harsanyi, and his devoted friend, pianist Ina Marika. All these gifted people became our friends.

A later French radio concert devoted to works of the Paris School, conducted by Harsanyi, gave me the opportunity to premiere in France Martinů's *Concerto da Camera* for violin, piano, and strings with pianist Ina Marika.

Our Milhaud recordings were scheduled at the Salle de Chimie of the Sorbonne. Unheated until October, the hall was extremely cold. Glykson was in charge of recording equipment and fortunately Désormière was on hand to supervise balance. As usual with Glykson we had trouble getting to hear playbacks. We later discovered that Glykson kept much of the blank tape sent by Capitol for Milhaud's recordings, and diverted it to his own use for illegal recordings of Gypsy, Mexican, and Russian bits and bobs to be sold to American film companies.

Annette said to Milhaud at the day's end, "I admire your great patience with these delays," and he smiled, "One must have patience. I have learned it in teaching." Milhaud was an excellent, precise, and dynamic conductor, with a mystic sensitivity to whatever I was thinking. During rehearsal, at one moment during an orchestral tutti I was not sure where to enter, and Milhaud, sensing this, made a jovian gesture to me which was caught for all time by an observant French photographer. But later, knowing I was secure in my entrance, he never repeated that cue to me. Blanketed with woolen scarves and confined to his wheelchair, he must have suffered the cold more than Annette and me, for we could move about. One morning we rehearsed and recorded the charming *Concertino de Printemps*, then the second concerto, which took most of the afternoon.

We heard Milhaud's opera *Simon Bolivar* at the Paris Opera in a handsome production designed by Fernand Léger, and at the Opéra Comique we saw his tragic *Pauvre Matelot* (Poor Sailor). About this time La Monnale (the French department of medals) issued a portrait medallion of Milhaud, with his signature and right hand reproduced on the reverse side. I was deeply touched that he gave one to me, one evening after we shared Madeleine's deliciously prepared dinner. It was a French holiday tradition to bake a cake enclosing a small object, and I received a slice containing the trinket—which made me a "king" of the soirée.

We continued to visit Milhaud and Madeleine in various parts of Europe and America over a period of many years. One summer afternoon we arrived in Florence and noticed a poster announcing the Maggio Musicale Fiorentino was presenting that same evening Milhaud's *Minute Operas* (three delightfully witty versions of Greek mythology) and Sauguet's opera *La Voyante* (The Clairvoyant). Our hotel concierge managed to get us excellent seats in the Teatro Municipale. The next day we

Louis rehearsing Milhaud's second concerto at Théâtre des Champs-Elysées with Darius Milhaud conducting, fall 1949.

had a celebratory lunch with the Milhauds and took photos of this happy musical event.

After Milhaud's death, we flew to San Francisco to attend an all-Milhaud concert at Mills College. This was the official dedication of the Milhaud Archive at Mills. Madeleine made an unforgettable speech telling of the appreciation the Milhauds had for this secure haven of joy and happiness while working with colleagues and students. We are benefactors of the Paris Société Darius Milhaud, and also members of the Cleveland Milhaud Society in Ohio.

# 23

# More Poulenc, More Brussels
## *Paris Premiere of* Il Cimento dell'Armonia e dell'Invenzione

One must always strive to do what one thinks is impossible.
John Banville (Irish writer)

On the anniversary of Ginette Neveu's birth Annette and I attended a remarkable concert of Mozart's and Fauré's Requiem Masses at the Salle Pleyel by L'Orchestre Pasdéloup, sung by members of the Paris Opera. The audience was asked to stand for a minute of silence in Neveu's memory. In November 1950, before returning to Brussels for the premiere of Vivaldi's Opus 8, Concertos 8 through 12, I was scheduled to perform for Radiodiffussion Française — Francis Poulenc's sonata dedicated to Federico García Lorca for violin and piano, with the composer. Our broadcast was in memory of Neveu, a great violinist who died in an air crash. Annette packed up valises and music for our Brussels journey, as we were to leave directly after the broadcast, stopping to find a comfortable hotel en route.

We met Poulenc at the entrance of radio headquarters and searched for an available studio. Poulenc opened a studio door, and a slim young lady seated at a piano stood up and fled, saying, "Excuse me, I think this is your studio." Poulenc and I began warming up, trying various passages. Shortly before broadcast time, a stylish young female announcer entered with her unleashed poodle. This well-trained little dog patiently stood at her side throughout the program. After her crisp, precise announcement from behind a podium, she noticed Annette was turning pages for Poulenc and decided she would turn pages for me! Her high-heeled shoes clattered loudly on the hard tile as she walked back and forth from her mike. Whenever she moved away from her stand, her little dog yelped loudly. How strange, I thought, that sound engineers nonchalantly accepted this extraneous noise! At one busy section in the piano part, Poulenc surprised Annette by removing his glasses with his left hand, examining them, and replacing them while continuing to play. I wondered why the bass part was missing for a few bars! In any event, the broadcast had poetic emotion, brio, and precise announcements, mentioning the performers in tribute to Neveu and her pianist brother, who had perished with her in the crash.

The sonata ends quietly, depicting the death of poet/dramatist Lorca with a loud final chord. As the reverberations ended, we heard some lively syncopated orchestral music seeping in from an adjoining studio. Poulenc looked at me, saying, "*Tiens*, it's my music." A red light above the door indicated that no one should enter during the live broadcast or recording in progress. Ignoring this, Poulenc opened the door, rushed in (we trailed after him), and informed the conductor, "That's not the tempo!" Then he coached the vocalist, stating she did not pronounce some words as he wished! Everyone, of course, recognized him and appreciated his comments. I murmured to Annette, "This is like a René Clair film." After about five minutes of Poulenc's helpful suggestions everybody thanked him and he returned to our studio, embraced us warmly, and departed with a cheerful, "*Au revoir, a bientôt.*" We packed up my music and fiddle and again drove north to Brussels.

The Brussels broadcast of Vivaldi's last four concertos of Opus 8 for Radio Flamande had a studio audience. We both eagerly anticipated another interesting visit with the Collaers.

Although the Le Cene 1725 edition noted that Concertos 9 and 12 might be alternately played by solo oboe, Collaer and I opted for solo violin. I was impatient to hear these final concerti with chamber ensemble, for I was always fascinated by the sonority of Vivaldi's tuttis. Concerto 12 was a revelation. The score looked rather dull, with a great deal of solo and tutti in unison. I feared it would prove the least interesting of the series. But when I first heard it, I was swept off my feet, for the joyful unison playing with a Rossinian crescendo and compelling rhythmic drive was one of the most exciting musical effects of eighteenth-century violin literature, as *Armonia* triumphed over *Invenzione!*

I became convinced that Opus 8 might have been conceived and perhaps played by Vivaldi at the Ospedale della Pieta in one long concert and should be played as an entity. Without the cumulative effect of the preceding ten concertos, the tremendous climax of the eleventh and twelfth concertos could not be fully appreciated. I determined to present a concert of the entire Opus 8 as soon as possible, but realized I must wait until we returned to Paris.

In late May we vacationed in Italy, going first to Milan and then Venice, and we again visited Maestro Malipiero in Asolo. I had picked up a copy of his violin concerto in Switzerland and wished to discuss it with him. During luncheon we discussed Vivaldi's Opus 8. I mentioned the resemblance of the noble largos of Concertos 8 and 11 to the grandiose largos of Handel. Malipiero replied, "Oh no, Handel lived seven years in Venice and was influenced by Vivaldi, as was Johann Sebastian Bach. I have seen Vivaldi scores with five- and eight-part counterpoint, written with the greatest inspiration and mastery. I think Vivaldi wrote more simply for solo concertos to give more freedom to soloists, not for lack of skill in elaborate forms!" He continued, "Most musicologists only love the dust of eighteenth-century music and resent performers who share it with a wider public!" We discussed his concerto at length before leaving. I never had an opportunity to perform it. Unfortunately, Malipiero then presumed I had no real regard for his work, not realizing the lack of interest I encountered whenever I proposed performing or recording his concerto.

I decided to visit Count Chigi's palazzo in Siena. Thanks to the efforts of his secretary, former violinist Olga Rudge, it had become a center of musical studies and Vivaldi research. I called Miss Rudge from Florence and we were invited for the next afternoon. The ceiling of the elegant salon of the Palazzo Chigi depicted a Sienese victory over Florentine forces in the twelfth century. We were most graciously welcomed by Count Chigi and Miss Rudge, who were responsible for printing quite a few Vivaldi violin sonatas and concertos from original manuscripts. Olga's lover, poet Ezra Pound, had chanced to find in Dresden's library eighty Vivaldi manuscripts. He made photostats of the whole collection and mailed them to her, as he knew of her intense interest in works of this great master. What a splendid achievement to have saved these musical treasures for the world, for they would surely have been destroyed in the war. For a few years, Olga generously sent me periodicals of Chigi musical activities and beautifully engraved Vivaldi sonatas and concertos. In return, I sent the Accademia Chigiana my recordings.

After our October return to Paris, Annette and I discussed with Cecil Robson and Jonathan Griffin the possibility of performing the entire Opus 8 in a public concert. They were so very enthusiastic and sure that a Paris concert would be well received that I proposed the idea to Hervé

Dugardin, owner of Editions Amphion and distributor of my recording of *Les Quatres Saisons* (which sold extraordinarily well). Hervé immediately accepted the suggestion, offering to finance such a program if I would share costs. I agreed. The Salle Gaveau was booked for 21 October 1950 with a string orchestra (members of l'Orchestre National de la Radiodiffusion Française) and Aimée van de Wiele as harpsichordist.

Hervé Dugardin and his wife (she was a Singer sewing-machine heiress) gave a cocktail party in their elegant Left Bank apartment in honor of our arrival in Paris. They invited musicologists and informed discophiles of France. I was fascinated to meet Marc Pincherle, president of the French Musicological Society and a distinguished authority on violin music and performance. His masterly books about Corelli, Vivaldi, and Leclair were milestones of information about these great eighteenth-century violinist-composers. He arrived with his violinist wife, Diane. This was the first of several later pleasant meetings with the Pincherles. They were among the few French people we encountered who did not consume any alcoholic drinks, not even wine!

Pincherle told us he had been influential in presenting me with the *Grand Prix du Disque:* "I thought it time that someone be honored for playing Vivaldi with the instrumentation of his time." He had one slight reservation, thinking I did not ornament slow movements adequately. I replied, "Like Darius Milhaud, I strongly feel no phrase should be ornamented unless it has first been stated." Both Pincherle and Malipiero agreed with me that too little ornamentation was preferable to too much, otherwise one could never know the composer's original melody!

Pincherle continued, "We have to be thankful for the great interest in Bach set off by Mendelssohn, for in trying to discover more about this genius's life and work, musicologists began to fish around and brought up Vivaldi, Bonporti, Telemann, Torelli, and many unjustly forgotten composers of this fruitful era."

That afternoon, we also met Armand Panigel, editor of *Disques* magazine and founder of the Société Charles Cros that annually awarded the *Grands Prix du Disques,* and his wife, Sabine, who became cherished friends. Sabine, alas, died a few years later of cancer, but our friendship with Armand endured over forty years, until his recent death. He served with French Intelligence Forces in Cairo under our friend English Major General Cecil Robson in World War II. He and Sabine met in the resistance. Panigel eventually collected over 350,000 recordings and 35,000 films (French, Italian, German, American, British, Swedish, Russian, etc.). Then he established, with the help of Michelle, his devoted second wife, the Armand Panigel Foundation in Saint-Rémy-de-Provence, which splendidly houses these treasures. We all shared enthusiasm for Asian cuisine, recordings, and films. We spent an unforgettable weekend with the Panigels in 1991 listening to historic records.

Although Cecil, Jonathan, and Hervé Dugardin were as excited as we were at the prospect of presenting the Opus 8 twelve concertos, several musicians thought we were plain crazy and didn't hesitate to inform us. A whole evening of Vivaldi? Twelve concertos in one sitting? Only one work? Who would attend? And if anyone did, they would depart after the first four! Several prophets of doom called; finally I began to have misgivings, but posters were ordered, tickets printed, musicians engaged, so I continued rehearsals and hoped for the best.

Dismayed that the first posters began to appear on kiosks only three days before the performance, I became worried and had dismal visions of the stage orchestra outnumbering the audience. We would not have the consolation of a "papered" house, for Dugardin had firmly ordered, "No free tickets!" In any event, the first tickets were sold the next day. Another problem developed at the first rehearsal two days before the concert: I discovered we lacked one viola part and one second violin part for each of the *Four Seasons* concertos. Annette had not counted every part when the copyist delivered them to Dugardin's studio. Too late for them to be copied by a professional, Annette volunteered to sit up most of the night to copy out twelve movements for these two stands of players, so we were ready the next morning for the full string ensemble's second rehearsal. Friday night Marc Pincherle telephoned Dugardin to add his voice to the naysayers: "The French public might not like anything so excessively long as the entire Opus 8! Why shouldn't Kaufman play only seven programmatic concertos?" Dugardin strongly recommended that I accept Pincherle's judgment. I replied, "Hervé, the posters have advertised performance of twelve concertos; to play fewer would be misrepresentation. If the audience wishes to depart after hearing four or seven, that's their privilege. But I intend to play all twelve."

Saturday morning, when a taxi deposited us at Salle Gaveau for the final rehearsal, Annette and I were elated to see a long queue stretching from the lobby box office out to the street. By evening, not only were all one thousand seats filled by interested music lovers, but also there were two hundred standees at the back of the hall! Monsieur Valmalete, the concert's manager, also had thought no one would attend and had ordered only two hundred programs, which had to be shared by twelve hundred people!

The attentive audience inspired me and the orchestra, and Opus 8 was rapturously applauded at the conclusion of the joyous twelfth concerto.

World premiere of Vivaldi's Opus 8 in Paris's Salle Gaveau in 1950, Louis Kaufman conductor/soloist, Aimée van de Wiele harpsichordist.

The ovation was so prolonged that Dugardin was worried the musicians would be kept after midnight; in that event we were liable for overtime pay, plus taxi fares home, since the Métro stopped running at midnight! I asked him, "What can we do to stop the audience's cheering?" Dugardin replied, "Play an encore, and they'll depart." So the strings and I repeated the final intoxicating allegro of the twelfth concerto. The audience left just in the nick of time.

The next day the Paris press was universally acclamatory, the pessimists were put to rout, and Opus 8 was a huge success. Radiodiffusion Française had recorded the concert and scheduled the first French broadcast of two full hours of Vivaldi on New Year's Day 1951 on the national radio network.

The emotional and physical strain (as conductor and soloist I had played all tuttis as well as solo parts) and unremitting stress for us both had been formidable! The day after the concert we stayed in bed, too exhausted for *any* activity. We were invited for dinner that evening with Darius and Madeleine Milhaud. Milhaud had told Annette after the concert, "Go back and tell Louis, I wish he had played twenty such concertos! It is extraordinary how he found the exact rhythm, sense of each phrase and style for each concerto and movement! Bravo for him!"

Cecil Robson and Jonathan Griffin were overwhelmingly enthusiastic about the concert when we visited with them the following evening.

About this period, Jonathan, browsing at a quai bookstall, bought a narrative entitled *The Inquisition at Goa*. He became fascinated by King Sebastian's tragic loss of his sixteenth-century Portuguese empire. Based on this great historical theme, Jonathan began work on a remarkable poetic drama, *The Hidden King*. Later he read parts of it to us in Paris and once again when we were together in England. This great drama was produced splendidly at the Edinburgh Festival of 1956 with the remarkable actor-writer Robert Spaight in the role of the unfortunate King. Spaight, an impressive and handsome actor, had premiered T. S. Eliot's *Murder in the Cathedral* in London and also in Paris (in French), with equal success.

A few years later, Spaight directed Shakespeare's *As You Like It* for Los Angeles's Sacred Heart College with a remarkable cast of students. Spaight invited us to the premiere, at Jonathan's suggestion. I congratulated him on his remarkable achievement, for the production would have been noteworthy in London! He answered, "Louis it was easy, they were a clean slate, no bad habits of speech or action to overcome!" He brought a group of nuns to our home to see our art collection. Noticing we had Sir John Rothenstein's great book about Indian art, he borrowed it, as he was engaged in writing Rothenstein's biography. We became friends. The following season, he again directed and performed at Sacred Heart College as Shakespeare's *King Lear*. Annette and I considered him the greatest interpreter of Lear that we had ever seen. Some professional actors so impressed by the previous year's production asked to be included in the cast. Kathy Crosby created a sympathetic and lovely Cordelia.

# 24

# Introducing Vivaldi to America

*Opus 9 Reveals Another Masterpiece — the Paris Premiere of* La Cetra

Impatient to have Vivaldi's Opus 8 known "at home" on returning to Paris, I wrote to Walter Naumburg of Town Hall's Music Committee relating the enthusiastic response to Vivaldi's music in Brussels, where we had discovered the manuscript, and in Paris. I inquired if the prestigious Town Hall Music Committee might be interested in an American Vivaldi festival concert.

Since winning the Naumburg Award in 1927, I had remained in friendly contact with the Naumburgs and always invited them to my New York concerts, for they were truly interested in the careers of their prize-winners. My letter reached them at Rio de Janeiro's Copacabana Hotel on 22 August 1949, and elicited an immediate reply. They were thrilled about my Vivaldi discoveries, but since their concert series had been discontinued they referred me to Thurston Davies, vice president of Town Hall.

We flew from Paris to New York in early December for a meeting with Town Hall's Music Committee. Davies and the members unanimously approved of a Vivaldi Festival, comprising two concerts on 25 April and 9 May 1950. Thomas Scherman, conductor and board member, offered his services and those of the Little Orchestra without fee, and everyone else followed suit. I had hoped the concerts might include the entire Opus 8, but Scherman and others thought this work too long and, with Dr. Carleton Sprague Smith, he selected a more varied program, which proved very wise.

I was severely taken to task by a few American musicologists for my pilgrimage to Europe to find Opus 8, for they asserted I could have obtained a copy from the Music Division of the Library of Congress! I had never thought of looking there, since Dario Soria had directed me to Maestro Malipiero and the Istituto Antonio Vivaldi in Venice! However, the grateful letters I had received from Malipiero proved my integrity to the committee.

Annette and I set off for Washington, D.C., to visit the Library of Congress Music Division. There we met and became friends of William Lichtenwanger, who showed me their copy of Opus 8, which lacked *all* second violin parts of the tutti. Their edition had fascinating variations from the Brussels Vivaldi edition that I had photocopied, and included a handsome engraved portrait of Antonio Vivaldi as frontispiece, dated 1725, establishing the date of Le Cene's publication. Someone had obviously removed that engraving from the Brussels Bibliothèque copy. This detail proved useful later, when I broadcast Concertos 5 through 8 of *Il Cimento dell'Armonia e dell'Invenzione* for the BBC's Third Program with harpsichordist Boris Ord. After my London broadcast, an irate musicologist wrote to the BBC disputing the 1725 date, insisting that it could not possibly have appeared in print before 1732! Annette and I deeply respect musical scholars, but some perpetrate errors by quoting sources they have never seen in the original. The Library of Congress copy also included a loose optional part for the principal violoncello, *La Pioggia* (The Rain), the second movement of the Winter concerto. A difficult running accompaniment to suggest rainfall, this version was lacking in the Brussels copy, so pizzicatos by violins and violas in the tutti accompaniment depicted raindrops. When I premiered Opus 8 in Rio de Janeiro in 1952, I used this optional part for the first time, and was very pleased by the effect.

The Music Division Library had another version of Vivaldi's Opus 8 in a later John Walsh English edition, where I noticed an error which all subsequent editions followed. When Vivaldi placed "T" over a note, he meant *trillo*. Walsh and later editors thought "T" indicated *tenuto* (hold). So the beginning of the Winter concerto was played as long sustained notes to represent all frozen and still—but should have been played as agitated trills, which Vivaldi indicated to represent shuddering with cold.

Lichtenwanger was so very helpful, I thought this an opportune occasion to ask, "Do you have any other Vivaldi concertos?" Pleased by my interest, Lichtenwanger replied, "We do," and soon returned to hand me another Le Cene edition of twelve Vivaldi concertos, Opus 9, titled *La Cetra* (The Lyre). Since there was no score, I had to carefully scan all individual parts of the twelve concertos before evaluating this work. It took most of the afternoon, but convinced of its outstanding interest, I ordered photostats to be sent to our Paris address.

Leaving Washington, D.C., with knowledge of a new discovery to work on later, we took a train to Boston, where I premiered Vivaldi's *Four Seasons* with the Zimbler String Orchestra at Jordan Hall on 1 February 1950, as a prologue to New York's first Vivaldi Festival. The Boston audience and press were delighted with these charming works, and I greatly enjoyed working with these excellent musicians and harpsichordist-composer Daniel Pinkham.

Annette and I had first encountered Dan at Editions Amphion on Avenue de Montaigne in Paris. He was explaining to Dugardin's aide how to spell Massachusetts. I asked, "Where do you live in Massachusetts?" "Boston." We love Boston, its museums and its great symphony, so we discovered many shared interests with Dan, and our friendship has continued to the present. His family brilliantly merchandised Lydia Pinkham's Pills, but Dan preferred composing music, playing organ and harpsichord, and enjoying the fine arts and gourmet cuisine.

Our composer friend Gardner Read, Annette, and I often performed his violin piece *American Circle,* and his wife, Vail, arranged a party for us after the Zimbler concert. Gardner played recordings of his music and showed us some of his recent compositions. Among the guests was Nicolas Slonimsky, who had written liner notes for my recording of Ernst Toch's Opus 64 Piano Quintet performed by the Kaufman Quartet with the composer as pianist. Moses Smith, a former Boston music critic who had produced the recording, was also at the party. Smith had recently published an engrossing biography of Serge Koussevitzky, which that enterprising conductor of the Boston Symphony had tried to suppress. Nicolas, who had a lively sense of humor, shared some of his fascinating experiences with the conductor. Dan Pinkham offered an anecdote: At a Boston Symphony rehearsal of a Bach work, Putnam Aldrich, harpsichordist, was realizing the continuo's figured bass, when Koussevitzky stopped him with, *"Qu'est-ce que vous faites là?"* (What are you doing?) Aldrich replied, " Maestro, I'm realizing the figured bass." Koussevitzky exploded, "That's not necessary. Bach only put the numbers there to explain the harmony—you are not to invent patterns!" The general virtuoso conductor at that period was not familiar with eighteenth-century continuo performance.

In April 1950 we returned to New York for rehearsals with Thomas Scherman and his Little Orchestra for the first Vivaldi Festival concerts in America. For the 25 April program I played Concertos 5, 6, 7, and 8 of

*The Town Hall Music Committee*

presents

# A VIVALDI FESTIVAL

★ TOWN HALL

APRIL 25 • MAY 9

TUESDAY EVENINGS AT 8:30 P.M.

★ ★ ★

*Two Outstanding Programs*

FIRST AMERICAN PERFORMANCES

★ ★ ★

## THE LITTLE ORCHESTRA SOCIETY

THOMAS SCHERMAN, *Conductor*

WINIFRED CECIL, *Soprano*

LOUIS KAUFMAN, *Violinist*

PHYLLIS KRAEUTER, *Cellist*

## THE COLLEGIATE CHORALE

Direction: DOROTHY DICKHAUT, *Manager*
TOWN HALL CONCERT DEPARTMENT

Town Hall Vivaldi Festival concert announcement.

At rehearsal for first Vivaldi concert in New York's Town Hall. *From left:* Louis Kaufman (violinist), Winifred Cecil (soprano), and Thomas Scherman (conductor).

Opus 8. Scherman conducted *Al Santo Sepulcro,* Winifred Cecil sang *Ingrata Lydia,* a cantata for soprano and strings, and Edward Sadowski and Robert Nagel played a Concerto in C Major for two trumpets. This program was not sold out, but a large audience and press were enthusiastic about the music. Sydney Beck, my teenage friend from Morris High School in the Bronx, now the distinguished librarian and musicologist of the New York Public Library on Fifth Avenue, wrote authoritative program notes for both concerts. We were pleased to have a reunion with Thea Dispeker, who managed the Little Orchestra, and to meet Miss Cecil, who had lived for some years in Italy.

On 26 April, I was delighted to receive a letter from Naumburg.

Dear Louis:

Mrs. Naumburg and I, as well as the other members of our box, all of them very critical musical enthusiasts, were delighted with last night's concert, for which you and your good wife deserve all credit since you instituted it.

We were particularly pleased with the last of the Concerti and especially did I admire your playing of the Arpeggio passages, which was so suggestive of Bach's Chaconne. As I told your wife, I don't see how you find the time to keep up your technique as you do with all the travels, which you are undertaking constantly. Olin Downes gave us a nice send off, I think. With kind regards to you both,

Yours sincerely
Walter W. Naumburg

The second concert was aided by a large notice in *Newsweek* of 8 May 1950 stating in part:

Last week in New York the Town Hall Music Committee presented the first of two all Vivaldi programs. It was probably the first festival of its kind ever held in the United States and it brought out nearly a full house to hear six soloists and Thomas Scherman and the Little Orchestra present nine Vivaldi works of which four violin concertos played by Louis Kaufman, now a Vivaldi exponent, received their American premiere performances.

After this praise from the New York press, our second concert on 9 May drew a capacity house and reaped equally enthusiastic acclaim from the audience and press. This program comprised my performance of Concertos 10 and 11 of Opus 8 and a double concerto for violin and violoncello, which I played with cellist Phyllis Kraeuter (another Naumburg prize winner). I had recorded this concerto for Capitol Records with French cellist Jacques Neilz and conductor Roger Désormière. Scherman directed his Little Orchestra in the Concerto in C for woodwinds and strings, then the oboe version of Vivaldi's ninth concerto of Opus 8, played by Bruno Labate. The festival concluded with a stirring performance of the *Gloria,* with the Collegiate Chorale, Beverly Lane, soprano, and Virginia Paris, mezzo-soprano.

It was very gratifying to Annette and me that Davies of Town Hall's Music Committee, elated by the quality of the music and resultant success, publicly stated, "I wish we had scheduled three such concerts to honor Vivaldi." What a brilliant triumph for the inspired Venetian pioneer of concerto, symphonic, and choral forms, at his first American Vivaldi Festival!

Back in Paris I studied Opus 9 seriously, and it seemed even more fascinating and of greater significance than Opus 8. Even so, I had no idea I had again come upon a work as rare as Opus 9. I learned there are only three known copies of it in the world, the other two in the British Museum and in Vienna. Marc Pincherle, who had known of its existence, had never seen it or heard it. He told me, "If my Vivaldi book should ever be translated into English, I would wish to write a whole new chapter on *La Cetra* to state what an important new light it throws on its composer."

During 1728, Vivaldi was presented to Emperor Charles VI at the Viennese Court. Charles VI gave Vivaldi a gold chain and a considerable sum of money and conferred on him the title *Chevalier* (knight). Vivaldi, in return for such handsome favors, composed *La Cetra*, dedicating it to *Sacra Caesara Cattolica Real Maesta de Carlo VI Imperatore e Terzo Re Della Spagna de Bohemia de Ungaria* . . . et cetera.

In general form, the Opus 9 concertos follow the three-movement form of Opus 8 and were published in Amsterdam by Michele Carlo Le Cene in 1728. *La Cetra* became so well known that imitators produced similarly titled works. Alessandro Marcello even used Vivaldi's title.

I wrote to Paul Collaer about my enthusiasm for the important Opus 9, and by return mail he invited me to give the first radio performance of this long neglected work for Radio Flamande in November 1951. I sent him photostats, and Radio Flamande's staff copied out all the parts for the string orchestra and continuo and made a score for the conductor.

As I studied the solo parts of Opus 9, I encountered *scordatura* (untraditional tuning) in Concertos 6 and 12. The orchestra tuning remains normal. By changing the pitch of two strings, a new acoustical effect was possible for the soloist, especially in arpeggiated figures.

At the successful Brussels premiere, Annette and I were again overwhelmed by the masterly writing and beautiful sonority of the tutti passages as well as the power, vitality, and enchantment of the ensemble. Vivaldi's inspiration and originality seemed endless.

After returning to Paris, I discussed this remarkable *La Cetra* with Hervé Dugardin. He suggested, "Let's join forces again in a Paris premiere!" So Editions Amphion made the same arrangements at the Salle

Gaveau for Friday evening 7 December 1951 for the first public complete performance of Antonio Vivaldi's Opus 9, *La Cetra,* to a sold-out Salle Gaveau. Again I was soloist and conductor of the strings for l'Orchestre National de la Radiodiffusion Française, with Antoine Geoffroy Dechaume as clavecinist, and again Valmalete managed the concert. Marc Pincherle again wrote program notes.

During the final rehearsal with strings and harpsichord of *La Cetra,* an amusing misconception occurred. I was rehearsing the group in some difficult places, skipping from one movement to another, without continuity, to polish rough passages while Annette listened in the dark auditorium to judge acoustical balance. Suddenly Monsieur Fort, the orchestra's manager, appeared to tell her a strange man was sitting at the back, and asked, "Should I ask him to leave?" It was too dark to see the man clearly, so Annette decided he could remain. Was he a critic or musician, or a friend of Dugardin?

A bit later, I asked Annette to go to the back of the hall to hear whether a certain effect was audible. The mysterious stranger had Marc Pincherle's Vivaldi book open to the thematic catalogue, which he was straining to read in the dark. She thought it was too bad if he thought to follow my rehearsal from that table while I was jumping from section to section. Then she forgot about him. Our rehearsal concluded on schedule.

What a pleasure to be told by many of the orchestra's players that they enjoyed playing this music with me. One said, "We play so many notes of music during the year that one concert is almost lost in a sea of performances." They thanked me for my quiet manner of working with them, for although we all worked intensely to cover thirty-six movements of these twelve concertos in two rehearsals of two-and-one-half hours, they realized I worked harder than anyone, for I played all solos and tuttis in eighteenth-century style.

Late that afternoon I was resting before the concert, when Marc Pincherle telephoned, very upset. It seemed a musicologist acquaintance had been at our morning rehearsal and had phoned him to say that his thematic table in his great Vivaldi book was all wrong regarding Opus 9! Pincherle was very worried about this, and I was mystified about the musicologist until Annette remembered the unknown man at the rehearsal. I called Pincherle to explain what had happened and assured him his thematic table was absolutely correct, with the exception of a single dotted sixteenth note and one thirty-second note, which had been printed in the table as two sixteenth notes. Greatly relieved and pleased with this news, he declared, "I will insert the dot and correct the small notation error in future editions."

Announcement of the performance of Opus 9 at Salle Gaveau in Paris.

The *La Cetra* premiere concert duplicated the great success of the Opus 8, with a sold-out auditorium and many standees at the back, and an equally long and loud ovation at the conclusion of the music. Darius and Madeleine Milhaud sat in a box with Annette and applauded wholeheartedly. This time Valmalete had printed almost enough programs! Radiodiffusion Française recorded the concert and it was broadcast a few months later in a series of programs for the entire country, then later repeated by Paris-Inter.

A Señor Iriberri from Argentina came backstage to congratulate me, and expressed interest in having me play concerts under his management in his country. Henri Sauguet attended this concert with Alice B. Toklas, and they were both very enthusiastic about the music and my performances. Miss Toklas invited Sauguet, Annette, and me for tea.

A few days later Sauguet joined us in visiting Miss Toklas at 5, rue Christine, and we were greatly impressed to enter the art-filled apartment she had shared for so many years with Gertrude Stein. We admired the excellent Picasso paintings on the walls, especially his great portrait of Gertrude Stein, which she bequeathed to New York's Metropolitan Museum. There were fine Juan Gris paintings and a few works by Sir Francis Rose, who was visiting at the same time. (We later learned he was a cousin of our dear friend Jonathan Griffin, but their relationship was broken during the 1945 war.)

Miss Toklas warmly welcomed us, served excellent tea and delicious cookies, and regaled us with amusing anecdotes. She reported, "Claribel and Etta Cone, during their Paris residence, subscribed to the *Baltimore Sun,* which featured cartoons of the Katzenjammer Kids. Picasso chanced to see these cartoons, which fascinated him. He asked if he might have them. The Cones replied, 'Certainly.' So each week he arrived to obtain Katzenjammer cartoons and with Spanish pride in return gave Claribel and Etta one of his original drawings, which explains the great number of Picasso drawings in the Cone collection at the Baltimore Museum of Art."

Miss Toklas was very pleased that Picasso had designed cubist patterns for her petit point embroidery of covers for backs of two small antique chairs. Sauguet invited us and Sir Francis to accompany him to a performance of Marc-Antoine Charpentier's Mass at a small church on Ile de la Cité in back of Notre Dame Cathedral. Soloists from the Paris Opera sang the inspired music of this great composer, a contemporary of Bach and Handel. Annette and I were deeply impressed by our first hearing of Charpentier's beautiful melodies and masterful writing. After this moving experience, we accompanied Sir Francis to his nearby flat, which he had rented to General Eisenhower after the liberation of Paris. We entered a charming, elegant eighteenth-century building and mounted the stairs to his sparsely furnished apartment, where we admired his huge paintings, crudely depicting crucifixions in a style between Graham Sutherland and Bernard Buffet.

# 25

# Unexpected North African Tour
## *Paris Friends*

In late October 1951 my Paris manager, Fritz Horowitz, called to ask if I would play a few concerts in North Africa in November. Obviously someone had canceled. I was not pleased to be informed that Annette could not travel with me. The French administration would pay only for my concert services, hotels, and travel. I would have to rehearse and play with French radio staff pianists, and perform with local symphonies. Annette urged me to go, saying, "We'll do sightseeing another time. I really should remain in Paris to attend to all details of the Vivaldi Opus 9 concert premiere on December seventh." We both realized my rehearsals with local pianists would not allow time to visit local museums or tourist sites, as we customarily did. Nevertheless, Jonathan Griffin introduced me to some North African writers and musicians who volunteered details about interesting sites that I must see.

On 2 November Annette accompanied me to Gare des Invalides, where I left her to gray wintry skies while Air France transported me to sunny Casablanca. The exotic lands I visited had elegant French homes, hotels, and government buildings surrounded by palm trees and exotic mosques with chanting muezzins.

I was met at Casablanca's airport by Monsieur Fina, manager of Radio Maroc, who delivered me to the station, where I boarded a train to Rabat. André Girard welcomed me, and we drove to the hotel and later to a reception arranged by Jacqueline Capek of Radio Maroc. This affair was to welcome Girard as their new symphony conductor and myself for the first concert of their season at La Mamounia Salle of the Conservatoire on 6 November.

During the reception, I was interviewed for *L'Echo du Maroc* and stated, in part, "I have been slightly reproached for being only interested in Vivaldi and to deprecate other composers. I really do not have preferences. I only care about the quality of the music and the composer's sincerity. Nevertheless, I think Vivaldi deserves his place, for he changed the direction of music from extremely cerebral and complicated to an expression of clarity, joy, and vivacity. He is an ancestor of Offenbach! He remained close to life, never heavy or boring. His music is undoubtedly difficult to play, and for that reason, he was considered the Paganini of his time!"

The afternoon of 6 November, I recorded the César Franck sonata and an adagio of Tartini with a staff pianist. I had a tight schedule of rehearsals with these pianists for broadcasts or recordings for later transmission, plus orchestral rehearsals and performance of the Beethoven concerto in Tunis and the Saint-Saëns Third Concerto in Casablanca. For the Rabat concert at the Théâtre Cinéma Royal, I performed Vivaldi's *Four Seasons* with the excellent conductor M. Girard. Then I went on to Tunis.

One morning, I escaped to wander for an hour in Casablanca's Kasbah. Tempting small shops faced narrow spice-scented streets, with the occasional camel lurching by. I bought two ancient silver brooches for Annette at a colorful small shop. One had beautiful Sufic writing, which troubled me until I learned it merely stated, "Allah is Supreme." Annette was delighted with it and wore it almost constantly. Years later, at London's Heathrow airport, she lost it. Quite upset, she telephoned the lost and found department at the airport, described the brooch, and discovered to her joy that some kind gentleman had found it, and impressed with its unusual quality, immediately delivered it to the lost and found, who returned it to her. She still treasures it.

I regretted I did not have time to visit the site of ancient Carthage and other Roman ruins. I hoped to return soon with Annette to explore the museums and cities of this fabulously colorful part of the world. I have always thought Roman theaters, bridges, viaducts, walls, churches, arenas, and temples fascinating. The Romans saved Greek cultural achievements for our world, their sciences as well as Greek poetry, drama, and literature.

How grateful I am that Annette and I took full advantage of our opportunities to see the world when we were mature enough to appreciate Roman, Greek, Italian, French, English, and the varied European and Asiatic cultures. We could savor the arts and crafts of indigenous American, pre-Columbian, and African societies, as well as the world's theaters, dance, operas, and concerts. We both found travel enjoyable and learned immensely from these numerous voyages, accumulating a remarkable treasure of books and art, and gaining precious friends and memories.

Among our close and devoted friends in Paris were the highly respected Ségal family. Our friends Belle and Nicolas Moldavan, on a Paris visit, invited us to join them for a dinner party at the Neuilly home of writers Ben and Norma Barzman. There we met Dr. Simon Ségal, a dentist, art and antique collector, and amateur cellist. Widowed during the war, Simon was a friend of Casals and many musicians, painters, and sculptors, and was a true bon vivant. His sisters, Marie, also a dentist, and Cécile, a dermatologist, were also well known for their generous hospitality and helpfulness to musicians and artists fortunate to be in their circle of friends. Annette and I were for many years members of that happy group. After Simon's death, Marie lived in his spacious flat on Faubourg Saint-Honoré, which faced the Salle Pleyel. It had a large splendid office, which she shared with her sister Cécile, brother Joseph, also a dentist, and nephew Jean, a nose and throat specialist who took special care of me. I often had sinus and throat infections in the cold, damp weather of Europe and England.

The Ségal family owned a vacation cottage in Brittany and often spent weekends there. Marie would give me keys to the Paris flat, and on those weekends Annette and I practiced, using their fine Pleyel grand piano, surrounded by paintings of Renoir, Utrillo, Luce, Kisling, and Friesz and elegant Louis XV and Louis XVI furniture. I had carte blanche to use the piano when none of the doctors was in the office, as I was then editing and realizing figured basses of Telemann sonatas and Vivaldi concertos for publication.

When Marie returned from Brittany late on Sunday, she would prepare a light supper for us, which we would eat in their beautiful modern kitchen. We often attended plays, concerts, and operas with Marie and Cécile and visited art galleries and various events with them. One evening we invited them to a French light comedy. Before the play began, pianist Artur Rubinstein entered the auditorium with his wife. The audience, noticing them walking to their seats, began to applaud as if they were royalty.

Petite, slim Marie was always attractively coifed and smartly dressed. Her appearance would hardly suggest her immense courage and strength during the German occupation. She told us one day over lunch her brothers, proud of their Jewish heritage, stated, "We will go to the authorities and put on the ordered yellow star." Their father slammed his fist on the table and roared, "I forbid it! You shall not make yourselves victims of those monsters!" As they were a family of blonds with blue eyes it was easy to obtain false identity and ration cards as Protestants. They avoided interrogation thanks to their nurse, Madame Marte, who alerted them whenever the Gestapo made unexpected sweeps looking for Jewish patients!

Marie worked in the resistance with nuns of the rue Nôtre-Dame-des-Champs, and they jointly helped many Jewish, Polish, and other dissidents to escape deportation and annihilation. Marie recounted, "A federal judge, father of a dear friend at the Sorbonne, told me, 'If you are captured, Marie, give them some information, even false, but don't be silent or they'll torture you.'" Near the end of the occupation she was arrested but she denied everything. "When they showed me a photo of a colleague in the resistance I stated, 'I've never seen him. I have a precise memory of every patient and anyone can have my address and phone from the telephone book.' I was so authoritative that they released me. I learned later my colleague had been shot immediately, which was why I was not confronted by any conflicting witness!"

Annette and I were invited to a large formal dinner party at Marie's elegant apartment and we volunteered to play some sonatas for this occasion. There were many noted guests, including New Yorkers, and our French friends painter Jean and Jacqueline Hélion, Philippe Dupuy of our violin world and his mother, Madame Georges Dupuy, film director Jules Dassin, and Steven and Sophie Green. Steven's mother had studied violin with Kneisel and they became close friends, as did Maurice and Colette Bret. The Brets owned a quartet of fine Italian instruments, and I played string quartets at their flat with cellist Robert Salles (I had recorded the Chausson *Concert* when Salles was cellist with the Pascal String Quartet) and a Romanian violist, Rafael Wallfisch, whom Yehudi Menuhin had aided greatly, giving him a fine viola.

Perhaps the most distinguished guest was Dr. Frédéric Joliot-Curie, son-in-law of Marie Curie, pioneer of radium research. Marie told us that Pierre and Marie Curie, working to discover radium, often picked up bits of it and put it in their pockets, having no idea of its deadly danger. They both died from the effects of radiation poisoning. Joliot-Curie was an eminent nuclear physicist and also an enthusiastic lover of classic music. After Annette and I finished playing, Joliot-Curie asked, "Would you please play some solo Bach works?" I was happy to comply with the Chaconne. Later Joliot-Curie expressed his pleasure at our performances and my playing of Bach's masterpiece. He explained, "Bach is the composer I cherish most above all others. As a scientist, I am particularly fascinated by the supreme and logical beauty of all his music." I asked, "How would you explain the almost mystic perfection that triumphantly permeates Bach's oeuvre, outside of glib terms such as genius?" Joliot-Curie replied, "We know Bach was a profound student of numerology and Hebrew mysticism. The Kabalah seeks keys or paths of enlighten-ment in the mysterious world of the unknown. Perhaps Bach might have been helped to achieve contrapuntal perfection by using a mystical key that made it possible to solve the most obscure problems. You know, my colleagues and I are often against a blank wall, hopelessly baffled, groping in research until we stumble on to or dream our way to a 'key' that un-locks the door to a significant solution. Then once we've solved the im-possible problem, it seems so natural to everyone that we almost think it was obvious!"

As a musician who was passionate about art, I was fascinated to read that composers George Frideric Handel and Arcangelo Corelli were avid art collectors. Corelli is reputed to have bequeathed some five hundred works of art to his patron Cardinal Ottoboni in Rome. How intriguing it would be to learn which artists and works (sculptures, engravings, paintings, drawings) he collected in Bologna where he lived or in Rome where he enjoyed fame! Romain Rolland, in his study *Handel,* relates: "Sight was for him a source of inspiration, hardly of less importance than hearing, I do not know of any great German musician who has been such a visual [performer] as Handel. He hardly ever went out without going to a thea-ter or a picture sale. He was a connoisseur . . . some Rembrandts were found after his death." French nineteenth-century composer Ernest Chausson had a remarkable collection of impressionist artists.

We again encountered Theodore Schempp. He was enthusiastic about a new artist tenant in his apartment house, a neurotic Russian painter named Nicolas de Staël. Eventually Ted created an international market for his work.

Schempp also introduced us to Jean Hélion. We were attracted by Jean's integrity as an artist and the strength of his personality. He was then married to Pegeen, daughter of art collector Peggy Guggenheim, whom we had met in New York at her avant-garde gallery during the war years.

Pegeen developed grave mental problems. Hélion tried to interest her in painting as therapy and provided medical help, but to no avail. Her sui-cide was a great sorrow to him and their two small sons. Jean, who began his career as architect, was later drawn to painting. His abstract works achieved great success in London, Paris, and New York. During World War II, Jean was captured by the German army and spent over two years in a prison camp. In 1943 he published a compelling book about his expe-riences and dramatic escape, titled *They Shall Not Have Me*. Jean told me, "During that terrible prison experience I discovered how beautiful a human face, a tree, or a leaf is. I could not return to an 'abstract' vision." His former friends, colleagues, and art dealers dropped him! He continued to write about art and life in the tradition of Eugène Delacroix. He utilized to advantage his early abstract discipline and created series of images of still lifes, men with umbrellas, store fronts with mysterious recumbent men, men reading newspapers, and then heroic street scenes, markets, and demonstrations, recalling the scope of Poussin and Delacroix.

Jean and his second wife, Jacqueline, loved music, and he painted musical instruments and often listened to music while he worked. He considered music one of the most important arts and told Annette and me, "Music is the singing heart of life." I always invited them to my Paris concerts and gave them cassettes of my recordings. He gave us two paintings, one a self-portrait in his atelier, the other a seascape, inscribed on its back (in French), "This painting is for Annette, not Louis, but my affection is for them both."

We took Sam and David Josefowitz and other friends to his studio. Over the years we bought several of Jean's smaller works and three self-portraits. During our later visits to Paris we often dined with them, joining Ted and Odile Schempp for couscous. During a large winter exhibition in Denmark that Jean and Jacqueline attended, he caught a fatal pneumonia. After his death Jacqueline oversaw publication of his important journals, published by Galerie Maeght, and arranged international exhibits of Jean's oeuvre including a very impressive exhibit in 1993 in Valencia, Spain, which Annette and I visited.

Ted Schempp introduced us also to Alexandre Istrati and his wife, Natalie Dimitresco. They had arrived in Paris as poor young painters on scholarships from Romania. By chance they rented a room in Montparnasse close to the studio of the normally unfriendly Romanian sculptor, Constantin Brancusi. The unassuming, charming Istratis were soon welcome in Brancusi's atelier; they not only spoke his native language, but Natalie helped him with household tasks and they both pitched in to move the heavy stands for his sculptures. Brancusi also enjoyed Natalie's delicious Romanian cuisine. They became the children he never had. Years later, on their arrival in Los Angeles, we invited Ted, Odile, and the Istratis for dinner. Annette prepared a moussaka, rice, salad, French cheese, wine, and fresh fruit for dessert. Natalie laughed, saying, in French, "My mother was so worried that we wouldn't eat well in the faraway U.S.A.! How surprised she will be when I write her that we had an excellent Romanian dinner on arrival!"

Constantin Brancusi was very anxious to have the story of his life and work written and published. Alexandre and Natalie devoted nine years (during Brancusi's life and after) to this research and writing. In 1986 Flammarion produced a handsome volume with text and photographs by Natalie and Alexandre and a foreword by Pontus Hulten, director of the Musée Beaubourg. After Brancusi's death the couple convinced the Paris authorities to have the square behind his atelier renamed Place Brancusi and gave his entire atelier and its contents to the Musée Beaubourg.

We deeply appreciated their friendly dedication to us, when they gave us a copy of their book.

Pour nos chers amis Louis et Annette Kaufman avec toutes nos amitiés dans le souvenir de Brancusi.

Natalie Dimitresco
Alexandre Istrati
Paris, le 28 Novembre 1986

Jean Pougny. *Cellist.* 1919. Watercolor and gouache.

David Burliuk. *Fisherman*. 1928. Oil on board.

Lawrence Lebduska. *Portrait of a Collector (Louis Kaufman)*. 1932. Oil on canvas.

Lawrence Lebduska. *Portrait of Annette*. 1932. Oil on canvas.

Milton Avery. *Portrait of Chaim Grosz.* Oil on canvas.

Milton Avery. *Portrait of Louis Kaufman*. 1932. Oil on canvas.

Milton Avery. *Self-Portrait*. 1949. Oil on canvas.

Gerda Becker. *Joseph and His Brothers*. 1969. Oil on board.

# 26

## We Meet Samuel Barber in San Francisco—Drama in Holland

### Friendships with Artists

I n Paris, early in the spring of 1951, we visited David and Tanya Josefo-witz, shortly before we left for a brief American tour. David asked me to record Samuel Barber's violin concerto later that year in Zurich, where he would produce more records. He added, "While you are in the States, Louis, try to find a good general conductor for our future catalogue and your Barber concerto."

During our New York sojourn, we met young Samuel Barber, who arrived with his orchestral score and a tape of Serge Koussevitzky's performance with violinist Ruth Posselt. We studied the score together as we listened to the tape, which he gave me as a guide for the conductor, and he commented on what he did and did not like in that performance. Barber seemed very pleased that I would be recording his concerto for the first time.

I always consulted composers whose works I intended to play whenever possible so that I could be sure to carry out their intentions. I had learned that musical notation, at best, is approximate. Musical notation is a series of symbols subject to different readings. Not everything can be exactly indicated in print. By its very nature the musical art is evanescent and small variations of emphasis or shading can convey a subtlety of expression opposite of that intended by the composer. Tradition guides us in classical and romantic works, but contemporary music leaves wide scope for interpretation. The first few performances of new compositions are crucially important, as they influence whether audiences and critics accept or reject the work. They also provide a model, especially on records, for future interpreters.

On 19 July 1952, I received a letter from Capricorn, Mount Kisco, New York (Barber's home):

> Dear Mr. Kaufman,
> I am glad to hear of your recording my violin concerto, and thank you for your interest in this work. Shall I be able to hear a pressing of it shortly? Please let me know for I am naturally eager to. It was kind of you to look me up on your New York visit and I appreciate your good will in trying to observe my intentions in the concerto: but I am sure your natural musicianship would have served you just as well! Cordial greetings to you and your wife.
> Sincerely yours,
> Samuel Barber

While in New York we unexpectedly encountered Alice Garrett on Fifth Avenue near Fifty-seventh Street. Although she was as vivacious as ever, she appeared rather thin and emaciated. She explained, "I am following a special health diet," and invited us to join her for tea in her Hotel Pierre penthouse suite. She confided, "Although the Ambassador bequeathed Evergreen House to Johns Hopkins University, I continue to live there. As the University refuses to put in adequate heating, I've decided to spend cold periods here in New York. The estate now belongs to them, so I'm not going to pay for heating." Her penthouse was charming and cozy. She had hung some of her favorite modern French and Italian masters, including a stunning Picasso. I observed some Jackson Pollocks of exceptional quality in one room and congratulated her on such a remarkable collection of his works. Alice burst into hearty laughter, explaining, "All these 'Pollocks' are my own works. I do two or three a day when I have time. I give them to my friends as presents."

This posed interesting questions. What would happen to these presents in the future? It was disquieting to see how easy it was to mimic Pollock's undisciplined process and the techniques of other similar "squirters," "stripers," and color practitioners. What a travesty that minimal efforts are considered "art," taking great space to say nothing. Ironically, Alice Garrett had collected art with great taste and had studied art seriously with Zuloaga. She was more conversant with art in general than were most of the Abstract Expressionist school.

My reliable "karma" unexpectedly provided a conductor for David Josefowitz while we were in San Francisco! Backstage after our San Francisco
concert we met music lovers Dr. and Mrs. Peter Joseph, who graciously
invited us to their home for dinner the next evening. There we met Esther Joseph's charming mother, widow of the great German architect
Erich Mendelssohn. The two had lived for a time in London as refugees
from Germany and were close friends of another refugee composer, Walter Goehr, who now lived there. We knew Goehr's film score for the English film *Great Expectations*. They assured me that Goehr was a compe-
tent conductor, so I sent off this news to Josefowitz, who later met
Goehr and engaged him to record a wide repertoire for Concert Hall
Records, including my recording of the Barber concerto.

When Annette mentioned we would be in Holland in the fall for some
Vivaldi broadcasts, Mrs. Mendelssohn urged us to call on her dear friends,
Dr. and Mrs. Salomon, who lived in Amsterdam, and give them her best
wishes. She continued, "Fraulein Paula Lindberg, our housekeeper in
Berlin, used to sing at her work. Her voice was so unusually beautiful that
Erich and I urged her to study seriously, and we paid for her vocal lessons.
She became a successful opera singer and later married a widower, Dr.
Salomon, who had a young daughter, Charlotte, who died tragically dur-
ing the war." She cautioned us, "*Never* mention the daughter."

Years later we learned that Charlotte Salomon was a most gifted artist, and had been sent by her parents to what they considered a safe haven
in France, the home of her grandparents in Provence. After the fall of
France in 1940, she created a compelling series of captioned goaches,
which she titled *Life? Or Theater,* depicting her life's story and the tragic
fate that was in store for Jews at that period. She confided this artistic
treasure to an American woman in the area before she was rounded up by
a Gestapo raid and sent to Drancy (where Max Jacob had been imprisoned) and then to Auschwitz, where she was murdered. Her work has
been widely exhibited in Europe and America and is in a memorial museum in Amsterdam.

On reaching Amsterdam, I called Dr. Salomon, who graciously invited us for tea. This distinguished couple welcomed us to their comfortable home, and were greatly pleased to have news of Frau Mendelssohn and learn of Esther's happy marriage and their pleasant life in San
Francisco.

Before my Vivaldi broadcasts in Hilversum, Dr. and Mrs. Salomon
invited us to an evening musicale at their home. We felt obligated to attend, as we felt they were alone in the world. When we arrived, there was
such a large group to hear an Italian popular singer that we decided to

leave early. As I drove out of the city lights of Amsterdam, an impenetrable fog (what the Dutch term a "mist") surrounded our car like a blanket. Canals on either side lined the narrow two-lane road to Hilversum. I was afraid to continue. I got out of our car to determine which way to go and discovered I was on the wrong side of the road! Getting back in the car, I pulled over to the right side and stopped. I could barely see a few feet ahead.

Annette suggested, "Let's just sit here until morning when the fog may lift." I answered, "We can't, we'd freeze if we remain here several hours." Just then a Dutch man stopped his car in back of us, walked to my window, and asked, "May I help you? I saw your French license, are you lost? Where do you want to go?" I offered my deepest thanks and explained we hoped to get back to the Heidepark Hotel in Hilversum, as I had a rehearsal next morning for KYRO (the Catholic radio). This kind gentleman replied, "I drive this road daily and could almost drive it in my sleep. I live in Bussum and am returning there with my daughters. A few kilometers ahead, the road separates, one way to Bussum, the other to Hilversum. If the mist doesn't clear off, I'll lead you to Hilversum. I'll drive slowly, just follow me." He returned to his auto, passed us and we started off at a snail's pace, as he had to be sure of the road!

At the road's juncture, he stopped (as I did) and said, "There's a coffee house here and I've been under such strain I'd like to stop off and rest a while. Will you join me?" "I certainly will, but I insist that you and your two daughters will be our guests." It had been an equal strain for Annette and me to follow the dim red rear lights of his car! We enjoyed a very pleasant chat and coffee break with these new friends. Our Dutch good angel said, "This is one of the deepest mists I've ever encountered. I'll take you to your hotel." We continued our slow drive to the Heidepark Hotel and I again fervently thanked this good gentleman and his daughters, who had to drive twice as long through that terrible fog to reach Bussum.

When I arrived in Switzerland to record the Barber concerto, I met Walter Goehr and found him to be a remarkable musician with a curiously difficult personality. He had studied with Schoenberg and arrogantly dismissed Barber's romantic and beautifully orchestrated concerto as "silly music." He was annoyed that I asked him to listen with me to Barber's tape of the Koussevitzky-Posselt Boston performance. He stubbornly refused to listen to it. However, I did my best to follow the composer's excellent suggestions, and this recording has received excellent praise. In January 1992, the *London CD Review* printed an article by Bill Newman entitled "Barber Solitary Romantic" and listed all recordings of his compositions. Of the violin concerto, Newman wrote, "It has become one of Barber's most performed works. Despite several fine modern versions, I like Louis Kaufman's performance with the Lucerne Festival Orchestra/Goehr best of all!" I was to meet up again with Goehr a few seasons later in London.

# 27

# South American Adventures

Before leaving Paris in early March 1952 for a brief United States tour, we visited Fritz Horowitz's office and encountered his son Michael Reiner, who reported, "My father has booked a concert tour for you in Brazil, Uruguay, and Argentina, for next May and June. He received very fine reports about your North African tour. Either Iriberri in Argentina or Luis Gonzaga Botehlo in Brazil will get in touch with you in New York about definite arrangements." Horowitz joined Michael in wishing us success and safe journeys. We left Paris without receiving information about fees, travel arrangements, or number of concerts. No word arrived from the South American managers before we left New York.

After a few concerts en route, we reached Los Angeles, where we stayed with Anthony Collins's family in Hollywood. My friend Maurice Abravanel called from Seattle, where he had unexpectedly been engaged to conduct their symphony. He graciously invited me to play the Mendelssohn concerto on 13 March. I flew up to Seattle the next day for an enjoyable experience. On 12 March, we both were interviewed on a radio broadcast. Maurice stated that symphony concerts have a profound moral effect on young people; they never vandalize the halls for classical concerts, whereas rock concerts sometimes end in riots, which leave auditoriums and stadiums in shambles.

Soon after that concert Annette and I spent an engrossing week in Salt Lake City, where Maurice was resident conductor, rehearsing and visiting with him and his wife, Lucie Carasso. At that time I discussed the importance of preserving on records his outstanding performances with his orchestra. How delighted I was that these conversations resulted in his series of remarkable recordings of Handel oratorios and Mahler symphonies that received highest praise. In 1992 I sent him a review from London praising his conceptions of Mahler as preferable to all others recorded to that date!

On 22 March, with the strings of Salt Lake City's Symphony conducted by Abravanel, I premiered Vivaldi's twelve Opus 8 concertos in Utah's University Concert Series with Annette providing continuo. It was an outstanding success! After playing eight concertos, Maurice turned to the sold-out auditorium, saying, "You have already earned your wings and can leave if you like, we are enjoying this music so much, we will play the remaining four concertos!" The enthusiastic audience stayed; only one critic, who had to make a deadline, quietly departed. The next night, we repeated the program at the university in Provo, Utah, an equal musical triumph for us all!

My "karma" stepped in to help when we arrived in Portland, Oregon. We attended an excellent concert of their symphony conducted by Dr. Theodore Bloomfield. The highlight of the evening was a Brahms piano concerto performed superbly by our friend Rudolph Firkusny. Afterwards we all dined at a nearby cafe. I mentioned the vague situation of my South American tour. Firkusny, who had had very great success there, advised me, "They have excellent musicians, and São Paulo is a city of pianists." He continued, "Don't go, Louis, until the manager gives you round-trip airline tickets—New York to Argentina and back to Paris—with a *guarantee* of living expenses, hotels, local travel, food, et cetera, *plus* a percentage of net proceeds of *all* concerts." I thanked him most gratefully for this valuable information, which Michael Reiner should have given me in Paris. I immediately sent off a cable to Botehlo in Rio de Janeiro that same night with all of Rudy's suggested demands, giving our return address care of Tony Collins's family in Hollywood.

Very early the next morning we flew to Los Angeles in heavy rain that covered the entire Pacific Coast. We arrived late in the afternoon, with barely time to change into concert attire. The Collins sons, Tony Jr. and Terry, along with Cissie, drove us to our concert. We entered UCLA's Royce Hall barely in time for the concert.

Thanks to experience and discipline we managed to carry through that recital with professional expertise, in spite of extreme stress and exhaustion. On returning to the Collinses' home, I was delighted to find Botehlo's cable, stating, "Pick up Brazilian visas, airplane tickets, and two letters of credit for expenses at New York Brazilian Embassy. You need doctor certificate of good health, police guarantee for 'good conduct,' and bank assurance you will not be public charge in Brazil. Botehlo."

Dr. Bernstein provided medical reports, Chase Manhattan Bank assured we had sufficient funds, and Los Angeles Police Headquarters issued a certificate stating, "Mr. Louis Kaufman and wife, Annette, have not been convicted of a major felony in the past five years."

Annette politely inquired, "Wouldn't it be possible to state we do not have a police record and are law-abiding citizens of good character?" The officer replied, "This is the form *we* use, lady, we can't guarantee *anyone* for more than five years!" I pocketed the dubious document; fortunately no one ever requested it!

Our return to New York proved hectic. While I practiced, Annette packed our trunk with winter garments for boat shipment to Paris, and suitcases with clothes for hot or cold weather in South America, plus scores we might need for any type of orchestral performance or solo recitals. We visited our friends Saundra and Alfredo Antonini, who sadly told us, "You can't imagine how little classic music is being played at CBS now. You are lucky to be in Europe where good music is widely played by radio stations. I have only one orchestral program on Sunday mornings at ten devoted to musical comedy, Rodgers and Hammerstein, Jerome Kern, and others, but occasionally I play three minutes of Corelli or Manfredini. Louis, have you a Vivaldi concerto that is brief? I'd like to have you play with me. I'd have to put you down as pianist since the front office will ask, 'What do you want an "outside" fiddler for?'" I replied, "It's always a pleasure to play with you, Alfredo, I'd suggest the second concerto of *La Cetra*, Opus 9. I recently premiered all twelve concertos of this series in Paris and later they were broadcast over the entire French radio network. Each concerto takes only eight or nine minutes. The second is captivating, with a beautiful andante, and the finale is an ancestor of Rossini!" At the next Sunday's CBS morning broadcast I played this concerto, earning hearty applause from the CBS orchestra and Alfredo.

Monday morning, as Annette and I breakfasted at a Fifty-seventh Street drugstore counter, a smiling Mischa Elman approached, with "Louis! Where did you find that lovely Vivaldi concerto you played over CBS yesterday? I liked it very much!" I explained, "I obtained photostats of the first edition at the Library of Congress," and added, "We are leaving in two days for South America." Mischa warned, "Watch out there! Everyone has problems and difficulties with managers. Be careful!" I answered, "We are not sure what will happen, but it will certainly be an interesting experience for Annette and me."

On returning to the hotel, I found an urgent message to call Alfredo immediately. I did. CBS was in an uproar over my classical music broadcast. Jim Fassett and Oliver Daniel had called, threatening Alfredo with losing his conductor's post at CBS. I replied, "Don't worry, Alfredo, I'll go down to Madison Avenue and take the blame. Ciao!"

I taxied to CBS and met with Jim and Oliver, saying, "You must forgive Alfredo for yesterday's nine minutes of Vivaldi. I've been used to playing two hours of complete Vivaldi cycles of twelve concertos for the BBC, French, Danish, and Belgian radio networks and I had no idea that one nine-minute concerto would be so upsetting to listeners and personnel at CBS. It was all my fault and I'll never suggest any such idea to Alfredo or anyone else at CBS again!" Rather abashed by my remarks, Oliver defensively replied, "After all, Louis, it is a serious affair to change station policy."

Returning to the hotel, I called Alfredo with the reassuring news of my *mea culpa*. Annette and I considered that broadcast a pleasant *au revoir* to our families and friends across the United States.

Bernard and Becky Reis invited us to dinner at their home on West Sixty-eighth Street, filled with fine modern French paintings and sculptures. Other guests were Marc and Bella Chagall, Jacques and Yulla Lipchitz, and René d'Harnoncourt of the Museum of Modern Art, who had just returned from Brazil. Knowing we were en route there, Lipchitz spoke of his great annoyance with the São Paulo Museum, which had commissioned him to make an imposing sculptural figure for its facade. To save funds, they suggested his small maquette (model) be sent to them for casting in bronze. To Lipchitz's dismay the São Paulo foundry cast the statue in the small maquette dimensions and not to the actual proportions he had specified. Therefore the bronze figure on the huge facade of the São Paulo Museum is a miniature version of Lipchitz's heroic conception, creating an insignificant effect on passersby!

D'Harnoncourt related, "Everything in rich Brazilian homes is made of marble except the napkins! There are only very rich or very poor people. Some Brazilians work all year to buy one flamboyant costume to wear only once for the annual Carnaval! Rich Brazilian ladies purchase dresses in Paris at astronomical prices to wear only once or twice!"

David Tamkin's opera *The Dybbuk* and Prokofiev's *Love for Three Oranges* were being performed at the New York City Opera, and we attended both productions. David's opera was a great success. At its conclusion we stood up and cheered with the entire enthusiastic audience for about twenty minutes! It was staged and directed by Lazlo Halasz and splendidly sung. We sent a note to David in care of the New York City Opera to congratulate him for composing a masterpiece and for the good fortune to have had such an ideal cast, conductor, and stage director. We gave our address c/o Iriberri in Buenos Aires, and David's grateful reply awaited us from Universal-International Pictures on 28 April upon our arrival:

> My dear Louis and Annette—I am extremely touched by your kind letter and I am very happy indeed that you enjoyed *The Dybbuk*—At the present I am head over heels in the throes of grinding out pictures. Hope someday to be able to go back and write more music—Please call when you come back to Los Angeles—Both Peggy and I send our warmest greetings for you both—Thanks again for your beautiful letter and God Bless you both—as ever, David

John Coveney, Capitol Records' "A and R" (artist and repertory) representative, had engaged me to record a popular repertoire of violin favorites, carefully selected for maximum sales potential. I rehearsed with Paul Ulanowsky, a sensitive Viennese pianist who had accompanied Lotte Lehmann, for a recording session on our last evening in New York (16 April). Earlier that day we picked up our airplane tickets and visas at the Brazilian consulate in Rockefeller Center.

We enjoyed a relaxing and delicious Italian dinner with John, who supervised the evening recording, which went very well. John promised to send the completed recording to our families. We did not mention to anyone that this was our nineteenth wedding anniversary!

The next morning we embarked on a Pan American flight at 10:15 A.M., scheduled to arrive in Rio de Janeiro about 8 A.M. on the eighteenth. Planes traveled much more slowly in 1952. We had an hour stopover in San Juan, Trinidad, where we enjoyed a brief evening stroll and drank a local specialty, rum and Coca Cola, to toast whatever adventures lay ahead!

We were enthusiastically welcomed at Rio de Janeiro's airport by Luis Gonzaga Botehlo, who was as pleasant as the warm breezes we were encountering. Annette and I entered the awaiting taxi. Botehlo, a dark, stocky middle-aged man, requested, "Would you please get out and let me take photos of you arriving?" This became a pattern of our Brazilian sojourn. Wherever we were, visiting some site, or at a concert, Botehlo was always taking photos from high or low angles, with his Rolleiflex camera. He had an unusual eye for composing photos and took great delight in using his fine equipment effectively. Although exhausted by the long twenty-six hour flight, we willingly posed and then reentered the taxi.

As we drove along the beautiful South Atlantic shore to Copacabana Beach, Botehlo and I conversed at length about what I was to perform in

The Kaufmans arrive at Rio de Janeiro airport, 1952. Annette wears the Algerian pin.
Photograph by Luis Gonzaga Botehlo.

The Kaufmans in Rio de Janeiro with Luis Gonzaga Botehlo, 1952.

Brazil, Argentina, and Uruguay. Botehlo replied, "I am only concerned with Brazil. Sr. Iriberri will take care of Argentina and Uruguay." We were surprised to hear he had not booked any concerts for me in Brazil!

Botehlo explained, "I don't pay much attention to concert reviews from Europe or America. Everyone who comes here claims to have great reviews. I like to find out what an artist prefers to play and then arrange a concert. If it goes off successfully with the public and press, I then book a tour with confidence. Otherwise, I don't bother local managers or concert societies, so people know they can trust my judgment."

I replied, "That seems very sensible. I think the most interesting project for me would be an all-Vivaldi concert, which I have done successfully in Paris and Brussels, consisting of the entire twelve concertos of Opus 8, *Il Cimento dell'Armonia e dell'Invenzione*. Each concerto usually takes eight or nine minutes at most, which is not too long for a concert lasting about seventy minutes. They divide into three groups of four concertos with two intermissions; therefore it's not too fatiguing for either musicians or audiences."

Botehlo, who had read in the Brazilian press of the exceptional success of the Paris premiere, had hoped for this. He immediately agreed. "That sounds fine! I'll arrange it in a few days—how many string players do you need?" I answered, "Four first violins, four seconds, three violas, two cellos, and one double bass. Annette will play the continuo."

The taxi pulled up to the Lancaster Hotel across from Copacabana's smooth sandy beach. Botehlo again took photos of us entering the hotel. We removed our luggage from the taxi. Botehlo paid the fare, then followed us into the lobby. I signed the register; the concierge demanded our passports. I turned to Annette and discovered to our consternation that her handbag was missing! It contained our passports, visas, plane tickets, accompanying travel documents, currency, and the travelers checks we had purchased for Europe. She remembered placing it on the floor of the taxi at the airport when we got out to pose for photos. I quietly asked, "Annette, how could *you* do anything so foolish?" Botehlo was astonished, he expected me to shout or have a tantrum. He offered, "I'll return downtown and see if I can find that taxi, but I don't remember exactly where I picked it up on my way to the airport." He thoughtfully added, "Here's some Brazilian money," and pressed five hundred cruzeiros in my hand as he departed. I had no idea of the cruzeiro's value, but at that time it was possibly one hundred dollars.

We gloomily went upstairs to our attractive room, which faced the lovely beach. Ignoring the view, Annette and I soberly discussed our plight. We were foreigners, without any proof of U.S. citizenship! No visas for Brazil, no bank credit or travelers checks, not even a lukewarm police certificate! What would we do for currency in England and Europe? I decided to go as quickly as possible to the U.S. embassy to request they verify our lost passports from Washington, D.C., and authorize new ones to be issued in Rio.

Someone knocked at our door. Expecting to see Botehlo, I was delighted to see the taxi driver, who handed me Annette's handbag! He explained in Portuguese, which I barely understood, "I heard you speak English. After driving about and not picking up any passengers on the beach, I decided to eat. I parked my taxi, entered a small beach bar, had a snack, and in getting in my cab I noticed the handbag on the floor of the back seat. I opened it, saw the contents with some English writing, and knew it was yours." He had driven back to the Lancaster Hotel and requested our room to make sure we would receive it. We knew a few Portuguese phrases and enthusiastically chorused, *"Muito, muito obrigado"* (Many, many thanks). I thrust my five hundred-cruzeiro note into the driver's hand and we both shook his other hand vigorously. He seemed overwhelmed and thanked us with expressive gestures and gracious phrases!

We waited impatiently all afternoon for Botehlo's call or return, to relate this fantastic good news. Finally in early evening, after we had unpacked, an exhausted Botehlo appeared, announcing, "I searched all downtown and couldn't locate the driver." We both burst in, "Don't worry, Senhor Botehlo, the driver came here about an hour after you left and returned the handbag. We have everything! Passports, visas, money, travelers checks, certificates! Isn't it wonderful luck! We are so sorry you didn't call us, we could have saved you so much worry and effort and your valuable time!"

Botehlo, surprised and very pleased by his countryman's honesty, asked, "I hope you gave him a tip?" I replied, "Of course, I gave him the five hundred cruzeiros—he was most happy." Botehlo, aghast, exclaimed, "You gave him too much! He could not have earned that in a month!" I calmly continued, "Even if I was too generous, it was a good investment. The driver will be encouraged to be honest with everyone. I feel he deserved a great reward, as Annette and I would have been lost without the important necessary documents—not to mention the financial loss we would have had, for he returned all the money, which he could have kept. I had no other Brazilian currency—and had no idea of its value!" Botehlo agreed, "If he had found another client after depositing you here, that passenger could have taken the handbag and never returned it. The driver would not have been aware."

Botehlo then drove us to a cafe for supper with his assistant, Emma de Brito, and her lovely twelve-year old daughter, whom he obviously adored. We became good friends after our troubled arrival. Botehlo loved music and violinists. He recounted meeting Henryk Szeryng arriving in Rio on a boat of Polish Jewish refugees. He obtained clothes and a violin for him and arranged concerts that led to Szeryng's meeting Señor Quesada, an important Mexican manager. Quesada helped Szeryng acquire Mexican citizenship, which led to his world career. This gave us insight into Botehlo's infinitely kind and generous nature. Later that night as Annette and I strolled along the deserted Copacabana beach, the velvety sky and the stars seemed closer and brighter than any we had ever observed. My "karma" had protected us as usual!

Brazilian beds lacked springs in every hotel we encountered, but we always slept well on their hard surfaces. Our first Brazilian breakfast, like all the subsequent ones, consisted of fresh tropical fruits, fresh rolls, and excellent coffee. I observed Brazilians put three, four, or even five sugar cubes in a small cup of coffee! In spite of extremely warm weather, I practiced until Botehlo arrived in early afternoon to drive us to a Rio de Janeiro Symphony concert in the Municipal Theatre, a magnificent replica of Paris's Palais Garnier. We admired the marble decor and flying gold-trimmed cherubs that guarded the stage curtains. Botehlo hurried off backstage to engage musicians for my first concert as we found our seats.

A handsome young gentleman sitting next to Annette introduced himself as Henrique Mindlin, an architect originally from São Paulo. At intermission he charmed us with tales of his travels to the United States, France, England, Belgium, and Holland, expressing a passionate interest in art, music, and architecture. He had visited the Arensberg Collection in Hollywood, where he first encountered sculptures of Brancusi and Alexander Calder's mobiles. Later in France he met Calder and bought several of his amusing wire forms known as stabiles, which Henrique introduced to Brazil. Most buildings he designed featured Calder's mobiles hanging down stairwells or from ceilings or his stabiles set into walls. I told Henrique that Robert Russell Bennett studied composition in Paris when Calder first exhibited those wire forms. He told us other American students there coined the expression "wire-loose" to signify anything crazy and it quickly entered American slang.

Henrique's Russian Jewish parents had emigrated to Brazil. He continued, "Many German agents were here with the goal of bringing Brazil into the Axis hegemony to be used as a base against the United States. Democratic forces managed to swing public opinion to the Allies." We became close friends; he and his wife escorted us to view his elegant buildings in Rio, and drove us some sixty kilometers, to Petrópolis to visit the Royal Summer Palace. Brazil's nineteenth-century emperor, Dom Pedro, greatly admired our President Abraham Lincoln, and invited Africans of achievement to the royal residence—which contributed to Brazil's present-day lack of prejudice and happy acceptance of racial equality, each individual seen as a human being no matter what their economic status might be.

En route, I noticed a large number of bridges, side by side, leading nowhere. Henrique answered my questions: "Some builder obtained a government contract to construct twenty bridges to encourage opening up the jungle to inland Brazil [Brazilian cities customarily hugged the coast]. Instead of siting bridges to cross ravines or rivers he simply and irresponsibly built them on this nearby convenient plain." Mindlin told us, "Many of our architects lack engineering skills, so you'll often read in our newspapers accounts of new buildings collapsing." Curiously enough, we did!

Meanwhile, Botehlo had hired musicians for our Vivaldi concert. Annette played continuo on a piano, in keeping with the eighteenth-century practice of using any available instrument at hand for continuo: organ, lute, harpsichord, or piano (invented in Italy in 1709). Botehlo engaged

Rio's large Symphony Hall. It had excellent acoustics. We had two very good rehearsals with very well trained string players, mainly Russian or Polish Jews who had found a new life in Brazil. I supplied all the orchestral parts, which I had carefully edited for bowing, phrasing, and dynamics for my European concerts. I conducted and played all tutti as well as solo passages.

We learned to travel on bumpy, crowded minibuses that quickly took us into downtown Rio for rehearsals. The colorful sidewalks patterned in fanciful designs fascinated us. The oppressive heat did not stop our daily rehearsals. The Rio harbor was astonishingly beautiful and lush, with heavy tropical foliage that made the city appear almost a wild garden. Rio's citizens called themselves Cariocas, the word for colorful Brazilian parrots.

Deeply concerned by humidity in our ocean-front hotel room, which was affecting my violins (in spite of the silica gel that I had been advised to place in my fiddle case to absorb moisture), I asked the manager to move us to a room in back facing the high hills, which was less expensive. Botehlo laughed when I told him of this change. "All string players do that," he admitted, "but I like to give artists the oceanside room to show that I consider they deserve the best accommodations."

Our new room faced the *favelas*. The shanties lacked water, so people carried supplies and water buckets on their heads to the makeshift huts perched on high hills. The settlement echoed with laughter, lively conversation, and samba music, but Annette and I worried about such dangerous conditions. What possibilities for infections and epidemics! However, we were told the authorities had moved dwellers to proper housing, but they straggled back to the free and easy camaraderie they preferred.

The Opus 8 premiere in Rio de Janeiro created wide press and public interest. Vivaldi's beautiful melodies and lively rhythms were universally appealing. The capacity audience was as enthusiastic as the Parisian audiences were and demanded we repeat the joyous twelfth concerto as an encore. The critics gave us overwhelming praise, so Botehlo quickly organized several engagements for me in Rio, Belo Horizonte, São Paulo, Santos, and São Salvador, popularly known as Bahia, near the equator.

We flew to Belo Horizonte, capital of the state of Minas Gerais, as huge as Texas, with great natural resources, steel and mining industries, and mines of precious gems. I was engaged by Don Carlos de Carvalho to provide a week of musical coaching. De Carvalho was a department-store owner who became wealthy by instituting "hire purchase payment" (known as "extended payment plan" in the United States). A great music lover, Don Carlos decided to give his city a symphony orchestra. He wrote to Milan's Conservatorio for a conductor and string players and to the Paris Conservatoire for woodwinds. When the Italian maestro arrived, Don Carlos entrusted him with the year's budgetary funds. With this considerable sum in hand, the maestro decided Brazil was too far away from where he chose to be, so he promptly decamped to another part of the world, leaving the stranded orchestral players penniless.

Don Carlos paid their wages to a local radio station that was not interested in classical music but agreed to accept their services! Botehlo suggested that I coach the musicians for a week in baroque music performance, and then play a public concert.

During rehearsals, I immediately sensed an unfriendly spirit in the string orchestra, almost a miniature state of war between French and Italian musicians. Deciding to be peacemaker, when overly hostile asides were muttered, I genially stated, "Both Italian and French traditions have enriched the western musical world."

On two or three evenings, Don Carlos and his beautiful young wife invited us and a few leading players of the orchestra to a formal dinner, surrounded by their many children and white-gloved servants. After an elegant repast, we listened to classical phonograph records. When players made acrimonious remarks about French or Italian performers and composers, I would comment, "I find it provincial to decry the merits of varied interpretations. The world is fortunate to have varied views of familiar repertoire. There is more than one way to interpret *Hamlet*!"

Don Carlos and his wife drove Annette and me to visit the excellent concert hall designed by Oskar Niedermayer, one of Brazil's leading architects, who briefly studied and worked with Le Corbusier. Niedermayer designed many civic buildings in Belo Horizonte; most of his structures had colorful mosaic facades designed by Lazar Segall. Annette and I thought all Niedermayer's buildings resembled quonset huts, but we never mentioned this to his admirers.

A young French flautist from Rennes, Jean-Louis Le Roux, burning to conduct, asked if he might conduct a Handel concerto grosso and accompany me in Bach's E Major Concerto and Vivaldi's *Four Seasons*. I agreed to give him this opportunity and the program was a triumph! I had to play six encores with Annette. Don Carlos was delighted and deeply appreciative of my good influence on the combative orchestra.

The Italian concertmaster, Attilio Genocchi, had pressed me all week to lunch with him at his boarding house. I accepted just before flying to São Paulo, for I did not want to seem a partisan of either side in the Franco-Italian disputes. I was also aware that Genocchi could ill afford guests, but he obviously considered it important to entertain us and recount his colorful career in the Far East.

Genocchi's glamorous and charming landlady prepared a sumptuous Italian feast. In the beautiful garden setting, and in the company of her two ravishingly beautiful daughters, the lunch was unforgettable! We "paid" for this treat in the enchanted garden by listening to the almost incredible tale of Genocchi's life and career.

After completing his education in his native Milan, Attilio emigrated to Shanghai, China, where for a quarter of a century he was concertmaster of the Shanghai Symphony, soloist, and promoter of countless musical events for social affairs in the foreign concessions (Shanghai's districts for foreign nationals). He managed teas, engagement parties, weddings, anniversaries, and receptions, and provided small chamber orchestras and dance groups for various national associations. The fees and gratuities were generous, and he amassed a fortune.

The war with Japan and subsequent battles between Chiang Kai-shek and the Communists caused great inflation. Shanghai newspapers reported continual victories over poorly armed communist forces. Genocchi continued, "Shanghai was strongly fortified, similar to impregnable Gibraltar, with every type of armament, tanks, and anti-aircraft artillery, so everyone felt very secure."

Returning from work late one night, he glanced at a newspaper headline: CIVIL WAR ENDED! COMMUNISTS WIPED OUT. He thought, Thank God! Now we'll have peace and a normal life.

He continued, "The next morning when I walked out of my hotel I was astonished to discover the entire city was occupied by Communist Guards, ragtag and shoeless, on every street corner—all with modern weapons in hand. The city had been sold out during the night! The commanding nationalist general had sold Shanghai for 20,000 gold bars and fled abroad, after giving orders to all officers and soldiers under his command to deposit their arms and equipment in a central depot, telling them to return immediately to their homes, as the war was over! This arsenal was distributed to weaponless Communists troops as they entered the city! This same ruse succeeded with other cities that were sold for the Soviet Union's gold bars, and the Civil War collapsed quickly."

As an imperialist foreigner Attilio was in peril. Orders were sent to all hotels: No doors could be locked, so authorities could inspect contents at will. Genocchi realized anyone who lived in Shanghai for twenty-five years was bound to have jealous colleagues who might plant a dangerous book or incriminating letters in his room, then denounce him as a counterrevolutionary. He could be imprisoned or could even be shot immediately as a spy!

He immediately visited the Italian consul, saying: "I would like to return to Italy." The consul replied, "Naturally—fortunately there's a ship sailing tomorrow. I'll arrange for you to be on it, but only with the clothes on your back and your violin. Absolutely no funds can be exported!"

His laboriously acquired wealth was now valueless. He was wiped out! Arriving in Milan full of hope, he was crushed to realize that no one remembered him in spite of his fame in the Far East. He visited the Conservatorio and explained his plight to a sympathetic director, who queried, "Would you consider going to Brazil? We've received a letter from Belo Horizonte—they are forming a symphony and need a concertmaster." Genocchi gratefully accepted, and on arrival met with disaster, for the dishonest conductor disappeared soon with all the funds.

Annette and I expressed our deepest sympathy and offered best wishes for his future as we departed in the late afternoon. As we flew to São Paulo we wondered what fate had in store for Attilio Genocchi. I assured Annette he would be able to survive in any situation.

Brazil is an immense country. Train travel from Belo Horizonte would have taken twenty-nine hours; our flight reached São Paulo in two hours. Inland Belo Horizonte then was a remote, semideveloped region, while São Paulo was a thriving metropolis mainly developed by the "yeast" of poor Italian immigrants, who with intelligence and hard work became millionaires! They erected handsome skyscrapers, museums, concert halls, libraries, and schools to embellish this coastal city. Consequently, land there became outrageously costly. Botehlo met us and informed us that he had booked two concerts for me at the Cultura Artistica Society. I had an immediate rehearsal with Fritz Janks, a fine pianist, for the Chausson Concert, and the following morning and evening I had rehearsals with a string quartet.

I gave the South American premiere of Torelli's eighth concerto and played Bach's E Major Concerto with the accompaniment of string quartet and Annette as continuo; then concluded with Chausson's Concert for Violin, Piano, and String Quartet. This unusual program won great praise from the audience and press. My second concert was a regular virtuoso violin recital, with Annette at the piano, which was equally well received. Botehlo presented us to the society's president, Senhorita Mesquito, a charming, elderly Portuguese lady who supported cultural activities in this extraordinary city.

We went sightseeing with Botehlo, who was amused to learn why Jacques Lipchitz's statue on the São Paulo art museum's facade was so insignificant. The museum had a small group of very fine French paintings, including Modigliani's life-sized portrait of Leopold Zborowski, which we had admired at Zborowski's gallery in Paris during our honeymoon.

We later visited the remarkable Mesquito family bookshop. What an immense display of outstanding publications from Italy, Austria, Spain, France, England, Switzerland, and the United States—in every field! Senhorita Mesquito presented me with a handsome book devoted to the life and work of the Venetian eighteenth-century painter Canaletto, a charming souvenir of my concerts and our resulting friendship. Senhorita Mesquito invited me to return the following year to play six concerts for her society!

Annette and I became very fond of guarana, a refreshing fruit drink made from a native fruit. We thought it superior to most soft drinks in the United States and consumed great quantities, for the extremely warm weather made us constantly thirsty.

Botehlo flew back to Rio with us. We arrived just in time for my 11 A.M. rehearsal with the Municipal Orchestra conducted by Eleazar de Carvalho. We then returned to Hotel Lancaster for rest and a nap before performing the Bach E Major Concerto at 5 P.M. that afternoon. En route Botehlo reported, "The orchestra's musicians so enjoyed playing your Vivaldi concert, they've invited you to play at the annual May anniversary concert which is offered gratis to Rio de Janeiro's officials, the military, civilians, and the general public."

A large reception after this successful concert gave Annette and me an opportunity to see the mayor, various city officials, and military personnel wearing colorful sashes and large medals set with precious stones. Beautiful, fabulously coifed and elegantly robed Brazilian ladies accompanied them. We met composer Heitor Villa-Lobos, muralist Cándido Portinari, and composer Carmargo Guarnieri, who was delighted to know that I had recorded his Second Sonata for violin and piano with pianist Artur Balsam. He told us of exotic Macumba rites based on African ceremonies, which consisted of very slow, drug-induced movements that often led to loss of consciousness or violent shouting. His research into Afro-Brazilian music was fascinating, for he proved their folk music was based on fragments of Gregorian chant sung by Portuguese monks. Carmargo gave me a manuscript copy of his violin concerto.

Not having fluency in Portuguese, we spoke mainly French, almost universally understood by Brazilian musicians. Otherwise Vivaldi spoke eloquently for me, making us new friends. Francisco Mignone complimented me on my Vivaldi concert, saying, "It is remarkable how you have achieved such unity of style and precision with two brief rehearsals and have revealed the essential character of each movement of every concerto." Annette replied, "That's interesting, Darius Milhaud made almost identical comments after Louis's Paris premiere of Vivaldi's Opus 8."

We felt honored to speak with Heitor Villa-Lobos, whose masterful

Carmargo Guarnieri and Louis after the Municipal Orchestra concert in Rio de Janeiro, 1952.

personality dominated every occasion. A few years later we had the opportunity to meet again when the Los Angeles Philharmonic performed some of his major works.

The next day we lunched with Carmargo Guarnieri and he was most complimentary about my Vivaldi program. I told him in turn, "Aaron Copland is very enthusiastic about your compositions." Guarnieri, conductor of São Paulo's symphony, invited me to perform the Beethoven concerto with him on my return from Argentina.

Conductor Eleazar de Carvalho congratulated me effusively and invited us to dine with him the next evening. We waited over an hour for him, before realizing it was a custom to issue an invitation out of sheer politeness without any intention of honoring the engagement. Brazilians understand this.

Botehlo introduced us to Leo and Tilla Kowarsky, Polish emigrants from Belgium who were friends of Manuel Rosenthal. They overheard me ask Botehlo about the native specialty *feijoada* and interjected, "We'll make it for you—you can't trust what they put into it at restaurants!" This treat became my 10 May birthday fete. I dislike formal celebrations, but Botehlo knew my birthdate from official documents. Annette and I greatly enjoyed Tilla's delicious *feijoada* consisting of black beans, pork, smoked meats, rice, and spices. We drank many guarana toasts with Botehlo, Emma and her daughter, and the Kowarskys. Botehlo gave me a handsome leather wallet and presented Annette with a small inlaid wooden box, which she still treasures. It was a most festive occasion!

Botehlo announced, "You must have a Brazilian doctor's certificate of good health to enter Argentina." He accompanied us the next day to a doctor who had the concession. We entered a gloomy office where a doctor with big horn-rimmed glasses was seated behind an imposing desk. He said in a deep voice, "Please show me your tongues." We obliged, and he handed me two prepared stamped certificates attesting to our perfect health and requested a large fee, which I paid.

Next morning we flew north for six hours to São Salvador, near the equator. It was extremely hot, rainy, and humid! São Salvador, founded four hundred years ago and popularly termed Bahia, was the first city of our tour that still had beautiful baroque homes and churches with sculpted facades, constructed by the original Portuguese settlers. We were very disappointed that a fierce tropical storm prevented our visiting these sites. There had been sixteen continual days and nights of rain before our arrival, and the next two days of constant downpour were the dates scheduled for my concerts.

We had enthusiastic large audiences for both concerts. Evidently Bahia residents were used to inclement weather. After the second program, a taxi deposited us at our hotel. Soaked to the skin, we removed our dripping garments and drenched shoes. Then I decided to clean my violin's fingerboard. When I lifted the instrument from its case, I was shocked to see that my flat-model Guadagnini was swollen. The top was definitely higher from excessive moisture. I quickly removed the bridge and loosened all the strings to reduce strain and to prevent the tabletop of the violin from cracking.

Early next morning we flew back to Rio to almost equally hot but dry weather. Botehlo faithfully welcomed us with news of plumbing problems at Copacabana Beach. No running water was available at the Lancaster Hotel! He had managed to obtain a room at a more central hotel with working plumbing, so I could bathe and shave before rehearsing the Beethoven concerto that afternoon for a performance the next day with British guest conductor Richard Austin and the National Symphony. The performance was a most pleasant collaboration and well received by the large enthusiastic audience.

The following afternoon Botehlo flew with us to Santos, a large coastal city which mainly exported coffee. We arrived in the early evening, with only a small suitcase containing concert clothes and music. Botehlo hailed a cab that drove through deserted streets to the theater, which was dark and empty! Botehlo disappeared to find a telephone. Returning quickly, he reported, "They've changed the concert site without telling me! The audience is waiting for us at a theater in another part of Santos!" Our taxi raced there.

That theater lacked a dressing room, so Annette and I changed our street clothes to concert attire in the wings and walked onstage to perform. While we were playing Schumann's A Minor Sonata, both stage lights and footlights unexpectedly went out. Annette couldn't see the piano keys and didn't realize she knew the last pages from memory. We continued to perform in the dark and completed the sonata without errors, even with aplomb! The audience cheered and applauded in the blackout. Suddenly the lights came on and we concluded the concert with remarkable success. We played many encores and Botehlo beamed with delight. We had become very fond of each other and we all knew we could count on each other in any situation. We flew back to Rio late that same night for a well-deserved rest. I had played five concerts and had four orchestral rehearsals under trying conditions during this last week in Rio.

The next morning Botehlo and Emma accompanied us to Rio's beautiful airport. Their affectionate embraces were heartfelt. Botehlo assured me they would have more concerts for us on our return from Argentina. Since it was constantly humid and hot in Brazil, I was continually hot and thirsty. I did not realize until our arrival in Argentina's cold weather that I had a high fever!

Our airplane landed on Buenos Aires's snow-covered ground. Before we exited, a doctor and nurse, dressed in white medical uniforms, their faces covered by white masks, entered the plane to inspect and collect our meaningless health certificates. I weakly stood up from my seat, murmuring to Annette, "Help me walk," as I leaned on her shoulder. We slowly made our way to the airport lounge. Iriberri, a distinguished, gray-haired gentleman (who had attended my Vivaldi Opus 9 concert in Paris) was accompanied by his daughter and his aide, Señor Gonzalez, who all warmly welcomed us. After brief salutations, I requested, " Señor Iriberri, please call a doctor for me. I am very ill."

He departed immediately to seek a doctor, and Gonzalez drove us to the modest Hotel Regia, in the elegant city center. The room contained two small beds, a small desk and chair, a bureau for clothes, a radio, and adequate bath, plus an upright piano for rehearsals. This proved a restful, warm, comfortable haven for free evenings, as we could listen to excellent musical programs. Gonzalez, affable and helpful, told me that all public concerts in Argentina were broadcast.

A young doctor appeared, swabbed my inflamed throat, and gave me quinine, which seemed to relieve the symptoms. I examined my violin and noticed the table had become unglued. Gonzalez drove me to a nearby French luthier, Henri Viret, who reglued my violin, put it in clamps, and smilingly promised, "It will be ready for you to play tomorrow morning." Then Gonzalez and Señorita Iriberri escorted us to a late *churrasco* supper, an Argentine barbecue specialty consisting of generous assortments of meats grilled to order and served with various vegetables and salads.

The next morning I retrieved my violin from Viret, and that evening I gave the Argentine premiere of Torelli's eighth concerto, and also played Saint-Saëns's *Havanaise* with the radio orchestra, on a program sponsored by *El Mundo,* a leading journal. The radio producer told Iriberri this program was one of the most important events of their entire season!

Our tour took place during the last weeks of Evita Peron's life (which of course no one knew at that time). The regime was highly sensitive to any implied criticism; we were warned to never say that something offered for sale was too expensive, as the phrase could be considered critical of the regime and the customer imprisoned. One could safely remark, "the color doesn't please me," or "I don't like that style."

Gonzalez gave me a list of my future concerts: Two programs at Teatro Colón, the superb opera house, with an excellent accompanist, Carlo Rossi (from Milan).

Then nine concerts with Annette:

June 5—Sociedad Hebraica, Buenos Aires
June 10—Concert in Santa Fe
June 11—Concert in Rosario
June 12—Sociedad Wagneriana, Buenos Aires (they never played works of Wagner!)
June 16—Concert in Bahía Blanca
June 27—First concert in Montevideo (Uruguay)
June 29—Premiere concert of *Il Cimento dell'Armonia e dell'Invenzione* in Buenos Aires, Teatro Palacio
July 2—Second Montevideo concert

This schedule made it impossible to return to Brazil for more concerts. Annette immediately sent Botehlo this news.

Unexpectedly, David Josefowitz telephoned from Geneva, asking me to come to Holland for a Concert Hall project in mid-July, saying, "We want you to record the Mendelssohn concerto in Utrecht." I replied, "Why, David? There are so many fine recordings of that lovely work." "Don't worry, Louis, we have an idea that justifies another and it will sell very well. We have an excellent conductor, Otto Ackermann of the Zurich Opera." "I'll do my best, David. See you in Utrecht!" Then I attempted to find a flight to Paris from Recife. The trip from Brazil via Dakar to Portugal and finally Paris would be a twenty-hour journey. All Air France flights were sold out, so Annette and I were put on a waiting list.

Annette was delighted to hear me perform with Rossi in the magnificent Teatro Colón, which has fabulous acoustics. She thought I had never played better. Only she and Iriberri (and the doctor) knew I was burning up with fever. The audience of 3,500 people filled every seat, for this was part of the prestigious Iriberri Concert Series. During intermissions I rested completely (no visitors!), for I was extremely weak. Immediately after my 5 P.M. concert, which I performed only through sheer professionalism and willpower, we returned to the hotel and Annette put me to bed. Iriberri offered to let me cancel all Argentine concerts, but my sense of responsibility made me answer, "I'll carry through, I don't want you to have the loss of refunding tickets and associated concert expenses."

The Spanish doctor's daily visits and doses of quinine did not reduce my dangerously high fever. I perspired continuously; my pajamas and sheets were changed three or four times nightly. The doctor urged me to eat steaks (Argentine beef is world famous), but I only managed to swallow a few mouthfuls of the food sent to our room from a nearby cafe. Extremely worried, Annette requested another doctor, so Iriberri brought in Dr. Aaron Gorodner, an Austrian specialist. He gave me an injection, assuring me it would end my raging fever. When he departed, Annette read the discarded container used for my dosage, which stated, "This medication is effective for unknown infections. May cause convulsions." Not knowing what to do in such an eventuality, Annette watched me all night, but I slept quietly until morning. The fever was gone!

Dr. Gorodner appeared early and, pleased his treatment was so effective, stated, "I have no idea what infection you acquired in Brazil, it may be completely over or it may recur. To make sure you are rid of it, I'll give you another injection." He did, which vanquished the debilitating unknown ailment. However, this second injection caused an almost constant itching sensation that moved through my entire ganglion to my back, arms, legs, stomach, or top of my head, a condition which lasted for six months. The only and best treatment was being constantly busy playing, recording, and practicing so I could ignore this constant irritation.

One evening Señorita Iriberri drove us to the elegant home of a Spanish gentleman, an amateur luthier, anxious to show me his very peculiar work. He had constructed a violin but had made the top and back with the thickness of a cello. Finding this did not "sound," he made huge ridges in the top and back slabs to lessen strain. Then he applied many coats of very hard, glassy red varnish. He asked me to play it. Curious to know what this bizarre fiddle could produce acoustically, I played and found it to be harsh and strident—not a violin sound. I honestly said, "Señor, you have invented a new instrument, it does not have a violin sonority." Extremely annoyed by my frankness, he replied defensively, "Menuhin and other violinists have praised my violins." I quietly replied, "Violinists have varying opinions like everyone else."

Outside of Buenos Aires we encountered conditions never mentioned in Argentina's controlled press. It was compulsory to arrive at airports three or four hours before embarking so everyone's identity could be checked.

Arriving in Santa Fe, I noticed a group of men standing in front of the hotel entrance. I said to Annette, "How nice, they're here to welcome us." Descending from our taxi, I heard them mutter *"huelga"* and quickly realized they were on strike. They politely asked us not to enter. Soon we learned this was a nationwide strike of hotel and restaurant workers, ardent supporters of Peron, who had given them government sanction. I would explain in halting Spanish, "We are musicians in town for one night to play a concert and will depart in the morning, we did not know about your strike and have no other place to sleep." In every city, strikers let us enter, and we fraternally greeted them whenever we exited for rehearsals and concerts.

After we entered a hotel, we would find only the owner or manager of a cold building. This was winter, and there was no heat, for not one employee tendered any service! After signing the register, I would ask, "What room may we have?" The universal reply was, "Take any room you want." All rooms were unoccupied. They handed us sheets, blankets, and towels; then Annette would make the bed in an icy room. The bathrooms had only cold water; it was very difficult to shave. After concerts, we would change into street clothes, don sweaters and overcoats, remove only our shoes and huddle close to each other to keep as warm as possible in COLD beds. How we wished for English bedwarmers!

All the concert societies knew that restaurants were closed. Merchants, doctors, and lawyers graciously invited us for lunch or dinner in their homes. Audiences wore overcoats during these provincial concerts, for theaters were also cold, their personnel also on strike.

In Santa Fe, a large hole in the theater's backstage ceiling caused an icy, windy draft across the stage. Annette's music fluttered disturbingly, and her fingers became chilled. As we walked into the wings, Annette whispered, "I'm going to put on my topcoat or I'll freeze and not be able to play!" When we returned onstage, the audience burst into hearty applause on seeing her wearing an overcoat, for they shared our plight.

After the concert, I was told the theater ceiling had needed repair for quite some time, so I surmised maintenance staff were part of the strike.

Our Rosario concert had similar conditions, except I was dismayed there were no return flights to Buenos Aires for two days! We dashed to the railroad depot barely in time to board the overnight train with only third-class carriages, providing only hard wooden benches—no cushions available and no dining car! We traveled supperless, under constantly glaring lights on this rattling, bumpy train. Friends had told us that Argentine trains, originally built and managed by the British, were efficient and comfortable, but after Argentina took them over services rapidly deteriorated under corrupt administration.

Happy to be back again in Buenos Aires, we fell into our warm beds for a few hours of rest in the comfortably heated hotel room, before a scheduled afternoon rehearsal for my Friends of Music Society concert. A string orchestra and chorus had been engaged to perform some Bach cantatas directed by Viennese conductor Dr. Karl Prohaska. I was to perform three concertos from Vivaldi's Opus 9, *La Cetra,* which would be an Argentine premiere.

Prohaska impatiently remarked, "Mr. Kaufman, do these concertos have to be so long? Couldn't you make some cuts?" As I was tired, I replied, "Dr. Prohaska, they are compact in form. Each is only eight or nine minutes, but if you can find any superfluous bars, I wouldn't mind. In fact, you may cut me out of the concert all together!" The problem was solved! No cuts would be made.

At the rehearsal Bernardo Feldman, tall and thin with dark hair and a rakish mustache, introduced himself. He expressed great admiration for Vivaldi and myself, saying he had played violin as a lad and loved the violin.

The evening program opened with a dull Bach cantata for orchestra and chorus with the depressing refrain, *"Nein, nein, nein,"* which earned tepid applause. The Vivaldi concertos I played before intermission were applauded enthusiastically.

Bernardo came backstage with his charming wife, Ina, to congratulate me. I thought we should join them in the auditorium to hear the rest of the program. When we attempted to enter the hall from backstage, we were told, "The conductor has ordered no one to be permitted to enter the hall from backstage!" We departed with the Feldmans for a pleasant dinner and became good friends. Bernardo told me, "I have a knitwear factory that produces very fine goods but I cannot obtain an export license. Under the Peron regime, army officers sell all export licenses. If one attempts to bribe the wrong officer he could end up in jail! This explains the exorbitant prices for American cars, equipment, or products."

The next morning Iriberri asked, "Why did you disappear from the artists' room last night?" Evidently the rest of the concert proved pedestrian and many in the audience had wished to speak with me. Prohaska sourly remarked to Gonzalez, "Audiences are always more interested in soloists than in music!"

We enjoyed pleasant excursions and dinners with Bernardo and Ina. The Feldmans drove us to see Anton Bourdelle's imposing monument for Buenos Aires honoring a liberator on horseback, one of Bourdelle's most important achievements. Bernardo escorted us one morning to an excellent furrier who made a fine nutria coat for Annette, absorbing many of our nonexportable pesos. This kept her warm and comfortable during subsequent cold European winters and the remainder of our wintry Argentine tour. We purchased warm sweaters for ourselves and a pullover for Botehlo at Bernardo's factory.

Bernardo and Ina were anxious for us to hear a talented young Jewish pianist, Daniel Barenboim, whose parents had invited the four of us for a home-cooked Sabbath dinner. After the meal, twelve-year-old Daniel, seated in front of an upright piano in their living room, brilliantly performed from memory some Bach inventions and a Beethoven sonata. He turned and asked, "Señor Kaufman, why did you make a retard at the close of each movement?" I answered, "It is a convention used to indicate the ending of a work."

I advised his parents that Daniel's great talent would be stifled if they did not take him as soon as possible to better teachers in New York, London, or Paris. He needed the opportunity to study harmony and composition in an ambiance where great composers and performers lived and worked. We later learned they moved to Israel that same year. It is now evident what worldwide success this phenomenally gifted lad achieved thanks to the wise encouragement of his parents. His development as an outstanding pianist and conductor is a tribute to his extraordinary capacity for growth. In 1986, Annette and I went backstage to congratulate him for a splendid all-Wagner concert he conducted with the Chicago Symphony Orchestra, where he is now resident conductor. I gave him our Dybbuk Committee private recording of David Tamkin's opera *The Dybbuk,* expressing my hope that he might conduct it at some future time.

On 5 June, I played a recital for the Sociedad Hebraica with Annette's accompaniment. The program included Telemann and César Franck sonatas, Mendelssohn's concerto, Dvořák's *Four Romantic Pieces,* Anthony Collins's arrangement of a Jewish folk song, "Raisins and Almonds," Ravel's "Pièce en forme de habanera," and Paganini's "La clochette."

On 14 June we flew south to Bahía Blanca for a violin recital on 15 June. A charming doctor invited us to his beautiful Spanish-style hacienda. He told us it had been constructed in the eighteenth century by a man who believed the world was mad and built this solid home as a protection from the destructive society of his time. I agreed the world has not changed for the better; one still needs such refuges.

On Wednesday and Thursday, 25 and 26 June, I had two three-hour rehearsals with a string orchestra, with Annette playing continuo, for Vivaldi's Opus 8 premiere at the Teatro Palacio in Buenos Aires, plus rehearsal with Annette for our first Montevideo concert on 27 June.

We flew via seaplane to Montevideo, a charming, elegant seaside city, arriving at 6 P.M. in time to rehearse, change our clothes, and to play that same evening at 8 P.M. in their eighteenth-century "jewel box" theater. The seats and boxes were covered in red velour trimmed with gold braid and the sparkling glass chandeliers were gracefully handsome. The sold-out hall welcomed us most enthusiastically. Early the next morning we flew back to Buenos Aires in time for another three-hour rehearsal for Sunday's Vivaldi program.

That Sunday afternoon, 29 June, the premiere of *Il Cimento dell'Armonia e dell'Invenzione* was a huge success. The house was sold out, and *La Razon*, Buenos Aires's largest newspaper, termed it "the musical event of the highest artistic quality of the year." My farewell appearance at the Teatro Palacio, conducting and playing the entire Opus 8 with Annette as continuo, was an impressive triumph for Vivaldi's inspired music, Iriberri's management, and myself! Señor Iriberri, Señor Gonzalez, and Señorita Iriberri were greatly enthusiastic about this concert, and Gonzalez invited us to a farewell celebratory dinner.

Later that evening he and Señorita Iriberri called for us, after we had a brief rest and changed our clothes. During dinner Gonzalez asked, "By the way, Kaufman, did Botehlo pay you for your concerts in Brazil?" I replied, "Certainly." Gonzalez continued, "Michael Reiner wrote us that Botehlo should have given your payment to us, as we loaned Michael money when he was in some trouble in South America last year."

I said, "I know nothing about that. Botehlo never mentioned anything about Michael to me."

Gonzalez went on, "Michael requested that Señor Iriberri withhold your fees to repay his debt, but Señor Iriberri is very grateful to you for your very fine performances, your courage, and the integrity to continue to perform under the most trying conditions of your illness and the truly difficult conditions in our country. He intends to pay you the full fees." I answered, "Señor Gonzalez, I'm very grateful to Señor Iriberri and you for this very friendly consideration. Michael never told me he owed Señor Iriberri large sums." Gonzalez drove us back to the Hotel Regia and we exchanged friendly farewells. Although elated by the success of this final concert, we both fell into our beds exhausted by the strenuous, long day.

Early Monday morning, we visited Iriberri at his handsome Via Florida office to thank him for his kindness to us and for finding Dr. Gorodner, who had restored my health. Iriberri thanked me for the outstanding music I had performed under very difficult situations and handed me the full fee. He expressed his hopes to have me return soon for many more concerts. I added, "Señor Iriberri, we both look forward to our next visit with you and your colleagues in this outstandingly beautiful city."

Armed with considerable funds from Iriberri, we flew to Montevideo that afternoon for a good rest. I played my final Montevideo program with heartwarming success and concluded our South American tour on 2 July 1952. My "karma" had protected us. Evita Peron died soon after our departure and all concerts and public events in Argentina were abruptly canceled for a month of national mourning. This was a disaster for the Comédie-Française group with Jean-Louis Barrault and his wife, Madeleine Renaud, for they had just begun their tour. After we waited three rainy days in Montevideo for an airplane to Paris, Air France phoned. They were still booked solid, but KLM would honor our tickets to Paris, with brief stopovers at Rio de Janeiro, Dakar, and Madrid.

In Rio's airport we met Botehlo and Emma. I gave Botehlo the wool pullover. He was deeply touched by this small memento and remarked, "None of my other artists or friends ever thought of giving me a present." We've deeply regretted that fate did not permit us to visit these good friends again.

As we boarded the KLM airplane, we encountered Jose Iturbi and his sister Amparo (both pianists), who were very enthusiastic about my Sociedad Wagneriana program in Buenos Aires, saying, "What a marvelous sound! What violin do you play?" I replied, "Thank you—it's a 1775 Giovanni Baptista Guadagnini." I did not add the famous Jascha Heifetz quip: when he answered a similar query, he held his violin up to his ear and remarked, "Strange, I don't hear anything!" Obviously violins do not play themselves!

During our flight a French fellow passenger en route to Dakar introduced himself to congratulate me on our Buenos Aires Vivaldi concert, which he had greatly enjoyed.

Our early morning stopover in Dakar's oppressive heat only allowed time for croissants and coffee. We were served by tall, handsome Africans dressed in colorful long robes and white turbans while we waited in a spacious hall with open views of sand and brilliant blue sea.

After a brief stop in Madrid, we landed at the Paris airport in late evening. We picked up waiting mail and enjoyed one night of rest at "our" Royal Hotel. Next morning we walked to the nearby rue Lincoln garage, retrieved our small Renault from storage, and drove off immediately via Brussels to Utrecht, where Heinrich Krotoschin had engaged a room for us at the charming Hotel des Pays-Bas.

My "karma" permitted me to arrive in Utrecht one day before my scheduled recordings!

# 28

# Utrecht Recordings —
# War Crimes — Search for Spohr

Utrecht proved to be a beautiful garden city. The Hotel des Pays-Bas was extremely comfortable with an excellent restaurant. The nearby art museum fascinated us with its great collection of sixteenth-century Dutch Mannerist painters. I became obsessed by Maerten van Heemskerck paintings, which Rembrandt admired and collected, and began searching for his remarkable engravings. He was official artist for Charles VI of Spain. A few years later in London I acquired some complete series of van Heemskerck engravings in shops near the British Museum.

Early next morning David Josefowitz introduced me to Otto Ackermann, an extraordinarily fine conductor. We immediately began rehearsing the Mendelssohn concerto and discovered that our mutual concepts of the work fit like gloves. The rehearsal and recording were completed in two hours.

David wanted me record Saint-Saëns's Third Concerto the next day, but Ackermann wittily remarked, "Saint-Saëns *sans moi!* I must return to Zurich tomorrow." Later, Swiss critics in a blindfold test selected our Mendelssohn performance as "the best available at that period."

Krotoschin quickly obtained violinist and conductor Mauritz van den Berg for the Saint-Saëns. To save rehearsal time I invited van den Berg to dine with us at our hotel that same evening. As we discussed Saint-Saëns's concerto, I realized I was in very capable hands. He was obviously very melancholy, and told us about the Netherlands' tragic fate: central Rotterdam had been bombed ten hours after the Dutch government surrendered. Later, as the defeated Germans departed, they opened the dikes, so salty seawater ruined land that had been excellent for crops.

Finding us sympathetic listeners, he related his personal tragedy. "I was concertmaster of the Berlin Opera orchestra. My Dutch father married a Jewess. My wife, a Christian, was harpist of the Berlin Opera. One day shortly after Hitler became chancellor, she returned home to warn me, 'Nazi gangs will come for you tonight. We must leave immediately to join your family in Holland. We only can take your violin, my harp, and a small suitcase.' We fled, leaving behind most clothes and all music and books. In Holland, she protected me throughout the occupation. One night, having heard that I had been denounced for working [Jews were forbidden to work], she hid me in a safer place. The frustrated gang then searched out all the members of my family and executed my father, mother, brothers and sisters, and all our relatives—in all nineteen people." Like some other survivors, van den Berg was haunted by the idea that he was personally responsible for their deaths.

Annette gently offered, "Mr. van den Berg, you didn't murder anyone. The Nazis were insane people who tortured and killed Jews, Communists, homosexuals, and Gypsies. If they had found you they wouldn't have stopped looking for your family members. You would have been murdered and there would have been twenty deaths that dreadful night!" Her words seemed to give some solace to the unhappy man.

Early the next morning our recording of Saint-Saëns's Third Concerto in an ancient church went very smoothly. Van den Berg was an accomplished violinist and most capable, sympathetic conductor. After we approved playbacks, van den Berg remarked, "Louis Spohr composed three excellent *Sonate Concertante* for violin and harp which my wife and I often played. You'd play them ideally, Kaufman, and I wish I could give you the music as they were rare first editions—not easy to find—but all my music left in Berlin was destroyed."

This unusual instrumental combination appealed to me and I decided to try to find the music, which had been printed in the early nineteenth century by an obscure German press. I found an English translation of Spohr's biography and learned that he invented the violin chin rest and was the first orchestral conductor to use a baton. His first wife, Dorette, a leading harpist of her day, died very young. The violin and harp parts for *Sonate Concertante,* Opuses 113, 114, and 115, were printed separately. The violin parts were written in the popular key of D and the harp part in the key of E-flat, with a notice to harpists to tune down a half-tone.

I found one sonata in an Amsterdam secondhand music shop and then another in London at a small shop near Charing Cross. Annette found the third one in Paris. She had stopped in a music shop near Avenue Victor Hugo to avoid a sudden downpour. She casually inquired, "Have you any harp music?"—and by chance in an old folder there was the third sonata we had hoped to find!

I asked several harpists to play them with me: Lily Laskine in Paris, Eugenie Goosens in London, and Marcel Grandjany in New York, who all refused, using practically the same words: "I've heard about them, never came across the music, but it's just too much trouble to learn them at this stage of my career!"

After our return to Los Angeles in 1956, I met a very gifted harpist, Marjorie Call-Salzedo, who, intrigued by the project, learned the Spohr sonatas. We played them together at several local concerts and broadcasts. Her second husband, Ivan Boutnikoff, was a splendid musician and conductor who had the good fortune to become conductor for the orchestra of Hurok's Ballets Russes de Monte Carlo. As a musical present for his wife, Ivan made modern scores for Spohr's three *Sonates*. Marjorie edited the harp parts and I edited the violin parts, and the Theodore Presser Company published them. After those editions sold out, Presser returned the copyright to me, and the International Music Company in New York reissued these unique nineteenth-century works. In the 1970s when I discussed these rare Spohr compositions with Giveon and Marian Cornfield, who established Orion Records in Los Angeles, Marjorie had already retired from performing. They recommended an ideal harpist, Susann McDonald, who studied at the Paris Conservatoire and won its *Grand Prix* for Harp. We met Susann to show her the music. Enthusiastic about the virtuoso harp parts, she quickly mastered them. We recorded the *Sonates* in 1977 for Orion Records. Susann taught at the Juilliard School of Music and later became head of Harp Studies at Indiana University in Bloomington and for a time head of the International Harp Society.

# 29

# Paris — the Survivor — Maryan

The evening that we returned from Utrecht to Paris and the Royal Hotel, we took an after-dinner stroll down the nearby Boulevard des Champs-Elysées. A man arose from a sidewalk café and approached me saying, "Kaufman, you don't know me in Paris? I knew you in Brazil." He was Senhor Mizne, a so-called architect who passed off work of young architects as his own. Henrique Mindlin had told us about him. His game plan was to persuade Parisian art dealers to give him valuable impressionist or postimpressionist paintings in exchange for a flat on Rio de Janeiro's Copacabana beach, a safe haven if there was a communist takeover of *la belle France!* Not a likely prospect!

We accepted his invitation to join him and his pianist wife, Felicja Blumental (both were Polish), for tea. Mizne continued, "Kaufman, my wife is a great pianist and I'm anxious for her to have a fine career. We visited an impresario in London, who advised me she should do something spectacular, like playing all five Beethoven concertos with a London orchestra in one season. What do you think?"

I asked, "Does she know all five concertos?" Mizne replied, "No. But I can take her to Vienna for three months and she can learn them." Felicja seemed to take as dim a view of this as we did. (Several months later in London we noticed Felicja was scheduled to play a Rachmaninoff concerto. We attended, but poor Felicja, paralyzed by stage fright, played uncertainly and wandered off into silence. Heartsick at her misery we did not go backstage, but fled from the Royal Festival Hall. The reviews were courteous — the *London Times* wrote, "Miss B would be well advised to use a score in future performance.")

The commercially minded Senhor Mizne continued, "Kaufman, I've heard you have an art collection and know a lot about art. I've been told of

Burstein, a young Polish artist in Montparnasse, and I'd like to have you visit his studio with us tomorrow afternoon." Thinking it might be interesting, I replied, "I've an auto and we'll pick you up at your hotel."

The Miznes were staying at the elegant Parc Monceau hotel near us, and at 2 P.M. the next afternoon we called for them and drove to Montparnasse. The French government had closed all brothels at the end of World War II and turned one huge barrack-type brothel, "Le Sphinx," into small studios for poor young artists. We scanned the list of dwellers, found Burstein, mounted the stairs, and knocked on the door. It was opened part-way by a thin young Jewish lad with a crutch. He'd lost a leg. I inquired in French, "We would like very much to see your work."

He let us follow him single file into the cell-like atelier containing a single bed on the right, across from a wash basin and bidet on the left, separated from the room by a curtain. At the far end of the room a window faced a brick wall but gave adequate light. A table and chair were in front of the window. A few paintings and a large black portfolio were leaning against the left wall. Burstein placed the portfolio on the table to display its contents—thirty or forty drawings, watercolors, and gouaches.

Mizne, impressed by my obvious interest in Burstein's work, signed with his first name, Maryan, suddenly said to the quiet lad, "I'll give you five hundred francs for the whole lot!" (about one hundred dollars). Maryan's sad blue eyes became steely; he closed the portfolio and replied with quiet fury, "I'd kill myself first." Anger filled the small room; we could only leave in silence. I deposited the Miznes at their hotel. Then I sent Maryan a *pneumatique* (intracity message sent through tubes) from the post office across the street from our hotel. A nearby cafe delivered my message to Burstein, since he did not have a telephone. He called and I asked, "May my wife and I visit you tomorrow? We admire your work very much." He politely agreed.

The next afternoon I bought four of Maryan's oil paintings at the prices he asked. I also bought two copies of a series of lithographs he made illustrating Franz Kafka's *The Trial*, in memory of his father, mother, sister, and brother, who had perished in Auschwitz. This publication had a preface written by the French cultural minister, Jean Cassou. To celebrate together, I invited him to join us for dinner. He requested we wait for the arrival of his girlfriend, also named Annette. She joined us at a nearby Romanian cafe and he recounted his life's drama. Born 1 January 1927, he and his family were interned in concentration camps in 1939. He was in Auschwitz as the war was ending in 1945. The Nazi guards ordered all survivors to dig a great pit, then lined them up at its rim and shot them, hoping to hide their genocidal crimes against Jews from the world.

As the Russians closed in, the Nazi guards fled without having time to throw lime on the bodies.

Russian soldiers took Maryan, wounded but not dead, from the pit. After living in Germany for two years at a displaced persons camp (1945–1947), he was sent to Israel. From 1947 to 1950, he studied art at the New Bezalel School. Maryan moved to Paris in 1950, where he studied three years at the École des Beaux-Arts, specializing in lithography. His first salon exhibitions began in 1951. Annette and I had admired in his atelier a large canvas depicting Jewish ritual objects that he exhibited at the Salon des Sur-Independants that same season.

Rose Choron was in Paris, and we joined forces to visit Maryan's atelier. She bought six of his paintings (she later gave two to the New York Jewish Museum). Rose, the sister of Sam and David Josefowitz, became a close friend. We often visited museums and galleries with her in Paris, New York, and Switzerland (where she had a lovely lakeside home and garden in Etoy, close to Geneva).

Adelyn Breeskin visited Paris, and after a pleasant day with us visiting galleries, she enjoyed meeting Maryan, and bought a copy of his Kafka lithograph portfolio and a watercolor. Another friend, Mrs. Robert Tyler Davis, purchased a small oil painting. We visited a few art galleries with Maryan and his Annette, and I invited him to dine with us. Later we lost sight of them. I learned he moved to New York in 1962, where he exhibited at the Alan Frumkin Gallery. In 1976 the French government awarded him an honorary title, Chevalier of the Order of Arts and Letters. His frail body expired in New York on 14 June 1977, and he is buried in Paris at Montparnasse Cemetery. There were rumors he committed suicide.

After our return to Los Angeles, Irving and Jean Stone invited about twenty couples to dinner at the Skirball Museum and requested that they help the museum with funds and donate works of art. Annette and I contributed two Maryan paintings—a portrait entitled in Hebrew *Hamman the Terrible; Kapporat,* which refers to an Orthodox Jewish ritual in which one's sins are symbolically transferred to a fowl; and the lithographs he made for Kafka's *The Trial.*

The day we browsed in Paris galleries with Adelyn, she saw a small drawing by Paul Cézanne—a stunning, very finished self-portrait at the Galerie Louis Leiris. It was modestly priced, and Leiris agreed to reserve it for her. On her return to Baltimore, where she was director of the art museum, she was disappointed that the museum board had no interest in acquiring a small drawing. Adelyn decided to buy the Cézanne for herself and wrote to me enclosing her check to the gallery, asking that I pick it up and bring it to her on our return to America. By chance I was engaged by the Library of Congress's Nicholas Longworth Foundation to play a program of chamber music with my pianist friend Erich Itor Kahn at the Coolidge Auditorium on 25 January 1952. I replied by inviting Adelyn to the program, which I knew would interest her. Kahn and I played four contemporary American sonatas: Charles Martin Loeffler's Partita, Carmargo Guarnieri's Sonata, Robert Russell Bennett's Song Sonata, and Quincy Porter's Second Sonata. I was probably the only fiddler ever to arrive at the Library of Congress with an original Paul Cézanne drawing in my music case, which I delivered to Adelyn before the program!

# 30

# London Adventures in Music and Art

Marjorie Osborne had become our devoted friend and my informal representative in London. On a 1950 visit to London, from Paris, she warmly welcomed us. She had obtained comfortable, modestly priced quarters for our sojourn, in a large Knightsbridge flat of her Australian friend, Mrs. Nelly Stilwell. This pleasant Irish lady, a former opera singer, provided a spacious pleasant bedroom and private bath, and graciously offered me use of her salon and grand piano for rehearsals or to meet guests.

Bernard Herrmann had urged me to call his friend Edward Lockspeiser, in charge of foreign artists at the BBC, and he invited me to his office. As Annette and I walked to the imposing BBC building, we noticed a few nearby bombsites. I could not resist saying to Lockspeiser, "How dreadful and tragic that Luftwaffe pilots bombed your cities and civilians!" He replied, "We were lucky. In spite of bombers, we were always free, with our own democratic government, not 'occupied' like Europeans!"

Edward, friendly and engaging, was a fine musician and devoted Francophile. He wrote books and articles about music, and was an authority on Debussy. We became good friends. I later performed under his baton the Vaughan Williams *Concerto Accademico* in Paris for Radio France, a concert we later repeated in London at Chelsea Town Hall.

On a Paris visit, Edward, a friend of composer Jean Françaix, invited us to attend a broadcast, conducted by Roger Désormière, of Françaix's *Passion de Saint Jean* for full symphony orchestra, bass soloist, large heavenly choir, and small *infernale* (small jazz band and choir). The work closed with heavenly forces triumphant but the *infernale* group still bubbling underneath in impertinent coexistence! After the performance Edward introduced us to Françaix and I expressed our great admiration for his masterpiece and Désormière's stirring performance.

In London, we accompanied Edward to a reception in honor of Darius Milhaud at the French embassy, and were pleased to visit again with Darius and Madeleine, who presented us to their embassy friends, Réné and Thérèse Mayer. Felix Aprahamian joined us and recounted an amusing incident: "The Armenian word for 'Mister' is 'Baron.' A friend just back from Erivan visited my office and greeted me, 'Hello Baron Aprahamian.' After he left, a snobbish coworker, who previously had ignored me, hurried over to say, 'Felix, I had no idea you were titled!'"

Having a free afternoon, I indulged my fascination with ancient Rome by visiting one of the oldest Roman sites in England, Verulamium, now called Saint Albans. I was greatly impressed by the large Roman baths and fine theater, where both Romans and the local populace could enjoy Greek and Roman plays. Remembering Hollywood soirées at the Arensbergs, we visited Saint Albans' Cathedral to look for the tomb of the great statesman, philosopher, and writer, Lord Chancellor Francis Bacon. His effigy was carved in stone, slouched over in a chair in sixteenth-century formal dress, with a fanciful high hat decorated by a quill. It seemed to us a rather mysterious memorial to this important personage.

My first London performance was to play for the BBC Third Program four concertos of Vivaldi's Opus 8, *Il Cimento,* which follow the *Four Seasons.* I was to play all solos and tuttis and direct a fine string group, with noted harpsichordist Boris Ord (who taught a generation of English harpsichordists, including the remarkable Thurston Dart). Annette and I traveled by train to Cambridge for my private rehearsal with Ord in his quarters. We agreed on tempi and style and achieved a fine rapport. Then he accompanied us to admire beautiful King's College Chapel. Later we browsed in a bookshop, exiting at dusk to watch young lads rowing on the River Cam, before returning to London.

The BBC broadcast from a large studio, which permitted a small audience. We achieved an excellent ensemble and spirit and my performance gained us new friends. Janet Brandes Jessup introduced herself, as our San Francisco friend Don Dudley had asked her to review this program for his magazine, *Concert and Opera.* Janet was an actress, writer, vegetarian, and dedicated Richard Wagner enthusiast. She often waited in queues all night to obtain reduced priced tickets for a Covent Garden *Ring.* Her husband, Reg Jessup, an actor with the Royal Shakespeare Company, also loved classical music. Over many years we attended plays and operas together and shared experiences over dinners. One time Janet reported that, after acting in a play on tour, she became extremely weak. She visited a London doctor, who asked if she had been in a certain area. She had. He told her there had been a nuclear disaster in that region and immediately sent her to a hospital where all her blood had to be removed and exchanged, or she would have quickly died. Alas, dear Janet did eventually die from cancer. Aware of her imminent death, she sent us a precious letter to thank us for our long friendship, which had meant so much to her.

Don Dudley had written at length to Janet about our Vivaldi research. She found this engrossing and urged me to write a book about Vivaldi, offering her help. As a first step, Janet introduced Annette and me to Sheila Bush of Gollancz Press. During our first brief chat, I discovered Sheila shared our ideas and interests. She invited us to dinner at her flat. We shared a fascinating evening with Sheila, her husband John, also a Gollancz stalwart, and a few of their friends. We were a most congenial group, all sharing a passionate interest in music, opera, books, theater, and art. These friends greatly enriched our lives.

We enjoyed many memorable visits with John and Sheila whenever we visited London. They drove us to see stately English castles and Roman sites, and we attended plays, concerts, and operas together. We met them in Florence where we shared visits to museums, churches, and restaurants, and later they drove us to Arezzo, where we admired Piero della Francesca's murals and visited Vasari's house. They built a holiday villa in Greve, a Chianti wine center near Florence, on the estate grounds of Pietro Anichini, their good friend, where we shared a wonderful day.

John and Sheila had purchased a seventeenth-century cottage in Surrey and they invited us for a weekend. Since I was scheduled to broadcast immediately upon our return to London I brought my fiddle along and practiced. Their adorable blond daughter, Clarissa, at the tender age of three, had never before seen or heard a violinist. Fascinated, she watched me, then ran to tell her mother about it in another room, delightedly describing what she had heard as "squeak! squeak!"

I had performed Gerald Finzi's *Introit* for violin and orchestra with Bernard Herrmann and the CBS Symphony in New York, and Benny had sent a tape of our performance to Finzi. Annette and I made several visits to the Finzis' beautiful home in Newbury, which had an original Roman well in the garden. On several occasions I performed baroque concertos with his Newbury String Players, with Julian Bream playing continuo on a lute. During another visit I played string quartets with the family, with Gerald and I as violinists, Gerald's wife Joy as violist, and their son Christopher as cellist.

Britain and its country life could provide amusing surprises. Returning to Paris, after performing a Telemann concerto for the BBC (a brief voyage to London without Annette), I overheard a fascinating conversation behind me on an airport bus:

LADY: I think it's shameful that Freddie sold his family's portraits to the Russians.
MAN: You don't mean those great Van Dyck portraits? I knew he recklessly gambled but those are national treasures.
LADY: Oh! Indeed he did. He was horribly in debt at the club. I've been told the Russians offered 50,000 pounds which poor Freddie foolishly accepted.

As I listened, I thought that Russian museum directors were canny buyers. As we left the bus, I regretted not knowing which museum acquired poor Freddie's masterpieces.

In 1952, I was engaged by the BBC Third Program to perform the English premiere of the twelve concertos of Vivaldi's *La Cetra*, Opus 9, which I had edited. As conductor the BBC had engaged Walter Goehr, who had been such a challenging colleague in Switzerland. Goehr imperiously stated at one rehearsal break, "Kaufman, you play the tempo indicated throughout each movement. You don't know anything about eighteenth-century music; they changed tempos in every bar!" I replied, "Walter, the eighteenth century was a time of great symmetry. A movement marked allegro was as lively for its duration as a largo was slow!"

Annoyed that I was an American and a guest musician, who thus did not have to fear his displeasure as the English staff players did, he continued, "Everyone knows Paganini varied tempo in every bar!" I quietly answered, "Paganini lived one hundred years later than Vivaldi, and even if he took operatic liberties, I am sure a subtle rubato still guarded the composer's indicated tempo."

To my dismay, at the evening broadcast Goehr set a tempo for the opening tutti and when I entered at that tempo, he would abruptly take a slower or faster tempo for the next tutti. Since I had vast experience in following excellent, mediocre, and even incompetent conductors in Hollywood and in the concert world, he couldn't lose or rattle me, which was his intent. But I was very unhappy about the eccentric and arbitrary effect of that broadcast, with bizarre tempo changes during every movement! Annette sat with Eric Lavender, editor of the *Strad* magazine, and they both were aghast at the erratic tempi Goehr created with his rigid beat. Finally this unmusical performance was over.

**first public
performance
in England of
OPUS IX (La Cetra)
ANTONIO VIVALDI**

**ROYAL FESTIVAL HALL**
General Manager : T. E. Bean

*The London County Council in association with Louis Kaufman presents*

## OPUS IX *(La Cetra)*
### *Antonio Vivaldi*
*12 Concertos for Violin, String Orchestra and Harpsichord*

## *Louis Kaufman* (Solo Violin)
### The Goldsbrough Orchestra

Leader :
**Emanuel Hurwitz**

Harpsichord :
**George Malcolm**

(Harpsichord by Thomas Goff)

**Thursday, 25th September at 7.30 p.m.**

Tickets : 10/-, 7/6, 5/-, 3/6, 2/6 from the Royal Festival Hall Box Office (WATerloo 3191)
and usual agents

Announcement of first public performance of Opus 9 in England, 1952.

I placed my violin in its case and departed with Annette, without saying goodnight to Goehr. We took the Underground to our Marble Arch hotel. When we approached the Cumberland entrance, Goehr was waiting there; he had raced ahead in his auto. Smiling broadly, he cheerfully offered, "Great show tonight, Louis." I replied quietly, "It was a complete mess, and you know it," and we entered the hotel without saying another word.

The BBC at that time repeated Third Program performances on two consecutive evenings, so I was not looking forward to the second program. However, Walter had probably encountered criticism from others. He greeted me politely, and I replied, "Good evening," and waited for his downbeat. That broadcast proceeded normally. Walter held a small Buddha statue in his left hand during the concert and conducted with his right hand, maintaining steady tempos without arbitrarily abrupt changes. This disagreeable encounter convinced me that in the future, I should play and conduct in eighteenth-century style as I had in Paris.

I visited Bernard Herrmann's friend Ernest Bean, director of the Royal Festival Hall, to suggest a future public premiere of Vivaldi's Opus 9. I felt obligated to the great Venetian that his music be performed without bizarre distortions of his indicated tempos. Bean enthusiastically accepted my idea immediately. We had a delightful conversation about Benny's visit to the Brontë moors with the Beans to research his opera *Wuthering Heights*. Benny told them, "There are better Georgian houses in Beverly Hills than in England." Benny of course knew better but he often liked to shock his friends. Bean selected a date for the fall, booked the Royal Festival Hall, and had circulars printed.

This concert attracted a sold-out Festival Hall and was a triumph for Vivaldi, my colleagues, and myself!

In March 1953, Jonathan Griffin suggested we stay at Durrant's Hotel on George Street near the Wallace Collection, a treasure house of European masterworks. We liked this comfortable hotel and stayed there during several London visits. Durrant's was handsomely designed by Robert and James Adams. All second-floor bedrooms faced a quiet street, and a long series of bathrooms with tubs were across the hall. In fall and winter a small heater, activated by a shilling, provided minimum warmth. Durrant's also supplied hot water bottles that we deeply appreciated in our cold beds! We took all our meals there, including late cold suppers after concerts or theaters.

At this time, England's distinguished poetess Dame Edith Sitwell was also a guest at Durrant's, and her assigned table in the dining room adjoined ours. Her tall, thin figure and aquiline Plantagenet features were striking, as was her exquisite politeness to everyone. She never merely said "Thank you" when served. Even for a glass of water she would look up smilingly with, "How exceedingly kind you are to think of bringing this. Thank you very much!"

Miss Sitwell wore huge cabochon aquamarine rings on practically every finger of her elegant long hands. I have always been attracted by cabochon rings of semiprecious gems and purchased several for Annette in Italy, but she only wore one at a time! We were fascinated by the poetess but never wished to disturb her. She always smiled graciously to us and nodded and we smiled and nodded to her. We both felt it would be presumptuous to introduce ourselves.

Evidently she had recently returned from America, for one morning as she was leaving the dining room, an elderly lady, who sat near the door, asked, "Miss Sitwell, what did you think of Marilyn Monroe when you met her in Hollywood?" Slightly annoyed at this impertinence, she politely and icily replied, "I found Miss Monroe very intelligent and greatly enjoyed our conversation. She is a remarkable young actress." With queenly grace she proceeded through the door.

Most of the elderly ladies at Durrant's were friendly; one introduced herself as Clifford Curzon's mother. We had met Curzon on an Atlantic crossing to England. He and I performed at a ship's concert to benefit widows and children of seamen; he was most friendly and charming, and we admired his artistry and pianism.

Annette and I attended a magical Covent Garden production of Rimsky-Korsakov's *Le Coq d'or* as guests of the conductor, Igor Markevitch. We sat in the box of his Italian wife, a contessa. Distinguished counter tenor Hugues Cuénod, making his Covent Garden debut at age eighty, was a superb magician; Mattiwilda Dobbs was a most seductive Queen Shemakhan. We unexpectedly met Jonathan Griffin at the bar during an intermission and invited him to join us, along with Igor Markevitch and his wife, for cold supper and champagne, which I had previously ordered. We were alone in Durrant's dining area, but since Jonathan knew *tout le monde* in Paris and London, he stimulated lively conversation.

During this London sojourn on 16 March I played and conducted for the BBC's Third Program the premiere of twelve Vivaldi concertos that comprise his *L'Estro Armonico* (Harmonic Inspiration),Opus 3. These concerti were composed in three groups of four—each consisting of concertos for four violins, three violins, two violins, and concluding with one soloist. My solo violin colleagues were Emanuel Hurwitz, Granville Jones, and Neville Marriner, who went on to an international career as a conductor. Our harpsichordist was Thurston Dart, and Geraint Jones played the organ. I played all first violin solos and tuttis in all concertos and directed the strings of the Goldsbrough Orchestra.

The rehearsals and concert went off very well; we achieved a precise ensemble and vivacious spirit. I was pleased that Jonathan Griffin, John and Sheila Bush, and our friend from the *Strad* magazine, Eric Lavender, attended.

These inventive concerti, published in Amsterdam by Etienne Roger

GOLDSMITHS' HALL

*MONDAY 16 MARCH 1953 AT 7 P.M.*

# L'ESTRO ARMONICO

Opus 3

ANTONIO VIVALDI

CONCERTO IN D (*four violins*)
CONCERTO IN G MINOR (*two violins and 'cello*)
CONCERTO IN G (*solo violin*)
CONCERTO IN E MINOR (*four violins*)
CONCERTO IN A (*two violins*)
CONCERTO IN A MINOR (*solo violin*)

CONCERTO IN F (*four violins and 'cello*)
CONCERTO IN A MINOR (*two violins*)
CONCERTO IN D (*solo violin*)
CONCERTO IN B MINOR (*four violins and 'cello*)
CONCERTO IN D MINOR (*two violins and 'cello*)
CONCERTO IN E (*solo violin*)

| | |
|---|---|
| Solo violin and director | LOUIS KAUFMAN |
| Solo violin | EMANUEL HURWITZ |
| Solo violin | GRANVILLE JONES |
| Solo violin | NEVILLE MARRINER |
| Solo violoncello | TERENCE WEIL |
| Harpsichord | THURSTON DART |
| Organ | GERAINT JONES |

THE GOLDSBROUGH ORCHESTRA
Leader: Emanuel Hurwitz
*Harpsichord by Thomas Goff*

Announcement of the presentation of Vivaldi's *L'estro Armonico*.

in 1712, were both a source and inspiration for Johann Sebastian Bach's four harpsichord concerti. Bach transcribed Concertos 3, 9, and 12 for solo harpsichord and the eighth concerto for organ; however, the dry, plucked sound of four harpsichords, or the percussive playing on four pianos, can't compare with the thrilling overtones of four singing violins!

The extraordinary beauty of Vivaldi's adagios demand singing violins.

Nightingales sang exquisitely two hundred years ago and crows cawed. I could never accept the false notion that eighteenth-century composers did not mean *sing* when they wrote *cantabile* at the head of their adagios or lentos. There is no musical or artistic reason that elegant eighteenth-century music should be frozen, like insects in amber, in one type of performance. If provincial musicians in culturally backward regions played inexpertly, in a clumsy manner on inferior instruments with poor tonal quality, why should contemporary professional artists try to duplicate such wretched performances?

The London journal *Time and Tide* of 23 March 1953 noted:

Last Monday evening among the noble proportions, sumptuous coloring and ideal acoustics of the Goldsmiths' Hall, the BBC in collaboration with the City Music Society had the good sense to engage that prodigious but self-effacing violinist Louis Kaufman to direct a fine English ensemble in what was most certainly the first performance in this country of the whole of Vivaldi's Opus III. As the twelve superb concertos unfolded their infinite variety listeners realized that truly great composers are more numerous than we used to think. Vivaldi must now be definitely placed among them. To have revealed this is surely pure gain.

Mr. G. R. Hughes, Clerk of the Goldsmiths' Hall, Foster Lane, Cheapside, London WC2 wrote to the BBC:

We all thought that the concert on Monday night was one of the most memorable we have had at the Goldsmiths' Hall. I do not know who is responsible for reviving the memory and work of Vivaldi, but all of us here who heard the concert, including people who listened in, thought it was outstanding both for the work itself and for the playing.

Gerald Finzi sent his reflections from Newbury on 18 March 1953:

Dear Louis and Annette:
A hurried note to wish you bon voyage. I know how busy you are but try to keep a day or weekend for us when you come back. . . . The Vivaldi was a wonderful experience. They start rather dully and get better and better, and I still think that the Solo in A minor and the Two Violin in D minor are amongst the very finest — the great thing is to hear the music done as it was intended to be done and without any preciousness or old-world revival feeling.

Although one's own interest is primarily in the work of one's own age, performances of this sort make one realize that we have lost quite as much as we have gained in the last 200 years. . . .

Yours ever,
Gerald

An especially fortunate encounter was meeting Dr. Ernest Roth, the editor of Boosey & Hawkes Publishers on Regent Street, who not only supervised the publication of works of Benjamin Britten, Ernest Bloch, Igor Stravinsky, and Aaron Copland, but arranged concert and opera performances for them. He had attended my Vivaldi Opus 9 concert and, enthusiastic about the concertos, accepted for publication my realizations of the figured bass for continuo and edition of violin parts, with an orchestral reduction for harpsichord/piano made by my colleague Hans Brandt Buys (who had played continuo when I performed Opus 9 for radio KYRO in Hilversum).

Roth often lunched with Annette and me at the excellent Cafe Royale on nearby Regent Street. He was conversant with great painters, sculptors, and conductors, and we shared enthusiasm for the Italian Renaissance. He regaled us with reflections about western civilization and his amusing adventures with famous composers and conductors.

Roth recounted, "The Royal Society of Music conferred membership on Igor Stravinsky and a gold medal. Before the ceremony, Sir Arthur Bliss received a note from Stravinsky, asking 'Is the medal *real* gold?'" Sir Arthur did not reply, but requested a Russian friend to phonetically teach him a phrase. At the ceremony, when he presented the medal to Stravinsky, he stated in Russian, to the composer's astonishment, "It's real gold; if you wish you may pawn it!"

Roth later published an informative book, *The Business of Music,* which reflects comprehensive knowledge of the music publishing world, and his wit and appreciation of music and art. Roth also published my edition of six Telemann sonatinas for violin and piano or harpsichord. I had obtained photostats of a unicum edition in Brussels's Bibliothèque, with only a violin line and figured bass, and realized the figured bass. Annette and I played them for Milhaud, who found them charming and gave me some very helpful suggestions. Later I broadcast the six sonatinas for the BBC Home Service with harpsichordist George Malcolm.

After Roth's death, Ralph Hawkes returned the copyright and music of Vivaldi's Opus 9 concertos to me, explaining that Boosey & Hawkes felt their interest should be devoted to modern works. (*Ed. note:* In 1994 Annette Kaufman delivered the Opus 9 Vivaldi concertos to Mrs. Beebe Bourne, head of the International Music Company in New York, where they have been published.)

Marjorie Osborne had a wide circle of friends, many of whom became our friends, too. One colorful bon vivant was Cecil Robson's father, who had worked for a paint company. He suggested to the company the valuable idea that London transport buses be painted red, which would be visible during fogs, and was rewarded with a handsome fee for the rest of his life! He graciously invited Marjorie, Annette, and me to an unforgettably elegant and delicious luncheon at the Savoy Hotel.

We also became friends with Dr. Theodore Goodman, a musicologist, his mother, and his barrister brother, Arnold. Goodman's mother invited Annette and me, whom she considered homeless American Jews, to Sabbath dinners in their home whenever we visited London. Arnold, a great music lover and collector of Forain's graphic works, later became chairman of the Arts Council. A most charming gentleman, he inspired confidence and was generous with time for visitors. Some of his illuminating speeches to the House of Lords about political and artistic matters were published in *Not for the Record,* which we cherish. Lord Noel Annan stated in its preface, "Arnold Goodman knows that if you care passionately about liberty in one aspect—you are going to have to admit that liberty in another sphere is less important and there is no doubt which sphere he thinks the most important. It is the liberty of the individual." We always invited the Goodmans to my London concerts.

Our friends seemed pleased to show us England's treasures. Jonathan Griffin escorted us in a taxi to Hampton Court and guided us through its handsome rooms and lovely gardens, relating the history of its tenants from Cardinal Woolsey to the present. Anthony Collins drove us to Windsor Castle and led us through its royal rooms and chapel. He lived in a little cottage on a large estate near Thorpe, and when we visited him he always sent a car and driver to meet us at the railroad station. We usually ate a lunch prepared by Sheila Wilcox, the daughter of his producer friend Herbert Wilcox, in the lovely garden. At train time he would order a car and driver for our return to the railroad station. One day Tony led us to a little nearby church where Handel had played a tiny organ at Sunday services for ten or more years. Only some two dozen people regularly heard him play during the period when his operas no longer pleased Londoners! Tony was always thoughtful and kind to us. Every time we arrived in London he met us with a bouquet of flowers and would see us off to France or the United States with flowers and a friendly embrace.

Tony had composed a violin concerto for me, inspired by William Blake's *Songs of Innocence,* but fearing musicians' derision of sentiment titled it only "Opus 48." In February 1953, he was engaged by the London Symphony Orchestra to direct a few concerts, which gave him an opportunity to premiere his lyrical poetic concerto with me at the Royal Festival Hall. I had rehearsed Collins's violin concerto with pianist Frederick

Stone in various BBC studios. When Tony returned to London, we played it for him at an unoccupied BBC studio to receive his suggestions. Freddy loved the concerto and on meeting Tony was ecstatic with effusive, heartfelt praises. His Irish volubility overwhelmed Tony who, although pleased, turned to me and commented, "Louis, you see what we English have to put up with."

The premiere of Anthony Collins's violin concerto, on 3 March 1953, was warmly applauded and admired by a capacity audience, as well as the London Symphony Orchestra players. Annette reported that Tony and I took seven curtain calls.

I have always regretted the prejudice shown against symphonic works by composers who scored Hollywood films, such as Erich Wolfgang Korngold, Miklós Rózsa, Anthony Collins, and Bernard Herrmann. Only Aaron Copland escaped this, despite his having written scores for *The Red Pony* and *The Heiress* (I was concertmaster for both). This bias almost never appears when orchestral works of composers of film scores not made in Hollywood are performed (e.g., William Walton, Sergey Prokofiev, Darius Milhaud, and Dmitri Shostakovich). Was it pertinent in reviewing Tony's concerto to mention that he had scored a few Hollywood films? Many dull and ineffective concertos have been written by so-called composers who lack knowledge of orchestration. I believe writing for Hollywood films is not a criterion for judgment of musical works.

It is unfortunate that Tony was so dedicated to recording all of Sibelius's symphonies that he never recorded his violin concerto, which might have led to wider interest among violinists for this effective work. *Rimington's Review of Long Playing Records,* edited by Fred Smith, printed a long sympathetic interview with Tony, concluding, "Thank you Decca, for discovering Anthony Collins, and now let us have the Sibelius Second Symphony, some Delius, and perhaps eventually Anthony Collins's violin concerto with Kaufman, to whom the work is dedicated. Anthony Collins has made an indelible impression in the world of the gramophone. . . . I feel I can say with conviction that this 'Prophet' will not be without honor 'in his own land.'" I deeply regret that our mutual "karmas" did not permit this to happen!

Tony had joined an elegant, new (and short-lived) Musician's Club, with an excellent dining room and bar, on fashionable Audley Street, and often invited us to join him there. Over a delicious luncheon he recounted, "The Liverpool Symphony Orchestra wants me to be their conductor, but I have refused."

Rather surprised, I said, "Tony, Barbirolli chose to go to Manchester and has led that symphony to great accomplishment and fame. I am certain you could achieve a similar musical triumph in Liverpool." He firmly stated, "Louis, I think I deserve a London orchestra."

When we returned to London in January 1954 Tony Collins suggested we book small bedrooms at the White House Hotel, with central heating, small refrigerators, and private baths. This hotel had an excellent French cafe where we often dined, inviting friends to join us.

During this visit I was to conduct the strings of the Goldsbrough Orchestra and perform as soloist for twelve Giuseppe Torelli Opus 8 concertos, which I had edited. The first six are for two solo violins, and my associate was Emanuel Hurwitz; Concertos 7 through 12 were for one soloist. Julian Bream played lute continuo and Charles Spinks was harpsichordist.

I had recorded Torelli's eighth concerto in Zurich for Concert Hall, which aroused my interest in Torelli, and I performed it in South American concerts. When we visited the Library of Congress, I obtained photostats of the rare 1708 first edition, published posthumously in Bologna by Marino Silvani. It was titled *Concerti Grossi con una pastorela per il Santissimo Natale* and paid for by his brother Felice, a successful stage designer, who stated in a preface, "This publication is in memory of my brother now in Heaven."

The powerful Cardinal Richelieu, while visiting Italy, was charmed by a cultured Bolognese cardinal, Mazzarini, and brought him to France. There he became known as Cardinal Mazarin, and his *palais* and great library became the foundation of the Bibliothèque Nationale. Mazarin's entourage included Felice Torelli, as well as commedia dell'arte performers. Torelli's innovative stage designs for plays of Corneille and Racine are still reproduced in textbooks about that extravagant theatrical era.

Four performances, under the auspices of the City Music Society in collaboration with the BBC Third Program, took place on 11, 12, 27, and 28 January in elegant Goldsmiths' Hall (owned by the ancient artisans' guild). Torelli's concertos, which I performed and directed with the Goldsbrough Orchestra, shared each program with Scarlatti's *Il martirio di Sant'Orsola*, edited by Edmond Appia of Geneva, who conducted the Goldsbrough Orchestra with the Orpington Singers and five soloists. Charles Spinks played continuo for both the Torelli and the Scarlatti on a fine Thomas Goff harpsichord. Appia told Annette, "I am enchanted by Monsieur Kaufman's golden tone, he must play with me in Geneva!"

I consider the opening pastorale of the first concerto the prototype of all such pastorales, a siciliano rhythm with a hauntingly beautiful melody suggesting a lullaby for the Holy Infant. Then tutti violins play a halting, descending pattern to suggest angels descending from Heaven to surround his manger. The concluding joyous tarantella is a true instrumental "Alleluia" with Neapolitan exuberance!

On 27 January Gerald Finzi sent his impressions from Ashmansworth Near Newbury:

> Dear Louis and Annette,
> We were able to listen in to both the Torelli recitals. I am glad they were done in groups of three, rather than in groups of six, as six at a stretch can be too much for one's concentration. They again struck me as being on a general higher level than Vivaldi, though one could hardly say without Vivaldi's peaks, when one thinks of number eight or that wonderful slow movement in number eleven (or was it number nine). I thought numbers twelve and seven the least satisfactory of the lot, but they are a magnificent set as a whole.

Jonathan Griffin attended all four programs and was delighted with the music. During this London sojourn we visited Henley-on-Thames for lunch with Jonathan, his sister Joyce, and their father at their stately home. After a delicious repast, Jonathan read to us passages from his great verse play, *The Hidden King*. Annette and I were deeply impressed with the scope of Jonathan's great trilogy, which we consider historically significant. It was the focus of a conference at Harvard University at the invitation of Archibald MacLeish. Jonathan later reduced the trilogy to a single play, which was premiered at the Edinburgh Festival of 1956 with Robert Speaight in the role of the unfortunate King. Speaight, an impressive and handsome actor, had premiered T. S. Eliot's *Murder in the Cathedral* in London and also in Paris (in French), with equal success.

A few years later, Speaight directed Shakespeare's *As You Like It* for Los Angeles Sacred Heart College. Speaight invited us to the premiere, at Jonathan's suggestion. He brought a group of nuns to our home to see our art collection. Noticing we had Sir John Rothenstein's great book about Indian art, he borrowed it, as he was engaged in writing Rothenstein's biography. We became friends.

At this time I also performed Chausson's Concert for Violin, Piano, and String Quartet with the Leonard Hirsch Quartet and pianist Frederick Stone for the BBC. I had recorded this masterpiece in Paris with the Pascal Quartet, who had played and recorded it years before with Jacques Thibaud and Alfred Cortot. I was able to share insight into the French tradition of performing this work with my English colleagues.

On free evenings I worked on editing and realizing the figured bass for six Telemann sonatas for violin and harpsichord for publication (recently republished by International Music Company). I tried out these sonatas

Jonathan Griffin and Annette at "Barrymore" (Griffin's family home at Henley-on-Thames). Photograph by Louis Kaufman.

at Felix Aprahamian's Muswell Hill home, as a friend had loaned him a harpsichord. Aprahamian was a music critic and writer. One evening Felix and I played all of Bach's sonatas for violin and harpsichord. We finished very late, and the buses and Underground had stopped running. Annette and I slept with our clothes on in a cold spare bedroom, getting up early to catch the first train back to the West End for an early morning rehearsal.

We enjoyed copious, unforgettable meals that his darling mother, Araxie, prepared. Jonathan always said, "Felix is the best-fed man in England." Araxie gave Annette many of her Armenian recipes. Felix once asked me, "Louis, how did you capture such Armenian feeling in your recording of the Khachaturian concerto?" I replied, "Because I have consumed so much of your wonderful Armenian food!" We both loved and admired Araxie for her wonderful joyous attitude to life's problems.

Another afternoon *chez* Felix, I took part in string quartets with violinist Manoug Parikian, violist Harry Danks, and cellist John Kennedy. John was the son of Lauri Kennedy, with whom I had played quartets in Los Angeles. (Later Lauri returned to Australia and retired as an innkeeper; John's son, Nigel, currently has a crossover violin career mixing classical music with "rock," which I consider unbearably monotonous and noisy.) Harry Danks asked me to perform Arthur Benjamin's "Romantic Fantasy" for violin and viola with him at an orchestra rehearsal at Morley College. It was a congenial collaboration and I enjoyed learning this very fine work.

Annette and I usually attended the theater the evening before an important concert in London, Paris, or New York. I found it relaxing. I knew that I was as well prepared as I could possibly be and that last-minute practicing would not improve my performance. I recall many magical evenings in the theater: Orson Welles's great realization of Captain Ahab and his staging of *Moby Dick* in the style of Brecht; and *Julius Caesar* at the Old Vic, where we sat in the front row with Edward Lockspeiser and felt the intensity of the actors. How impressive Maurice Evans was as King Richard II in New York! (Sally Avery joined us.) We attended the first production of Tennessee Williams's *A Streetcar Named Desire* in New York, with the remarkable young Marlon Brando. In Paris we attended the Comédie Française's great production of Molière's *Le Bourgeois Gentilhomme,* which so delighted us that we attended four performances. We saw the gifted Gérard Philipe in Corneille's *Le Cid,* Cocteau's *Les Enfants Terribles,* and also his delightful performance in Boccaccio's *La Mandragora* at the TNP (Théâtre National Populaire). A Comédie Française presentation of Racine's *Britanicus* with handsome Jean Marais was memorable. He had achieved international fame in Jean Cocteau's poetic films. During the German occupation Marais had been a courageous opponent of vicious collaborators who wrote Nazi-slanted articles about theatrical events. We attended the premiere and were surprised that a small group of provocateurs hurled insults when he entered on stage, trying to disrupt his performance. His presence of mind and excellent diction quickly silenced them. When the performance concluded, he received a tumultuous ovation!

Frederick Stone and I decided to perform sonatas in public. We presented two programs at Wigmore Hall entitled "Aspects of the German Sonata from Bach to Hindemith." Freddy played harpsichord for the eighteenth-century works and piano for later composers. We performed Telemann, Bach, Handel, Schumann, Beethoven, Brahms, Richard Strauss, and Hindemith sonatas on Saturday afternoons at 3 P.M. on 28 April and 26 May. We had very good audiences and reviews. Jonathan Griffin and Bernard Herrmann attended. I invited them for tea at a nearby cafe. Benny was in an obstreperous mood, so Jonathan lost interest in him, remarking later to me, "*Les enfants terribles* are not amusing after the age of ten." That unfortunate encounter prevented a friendship developing between two dear friends who should have had years of enjoyable conversations!

After Milhaud's return to Paris concerts, Sauguet had told me he would write a concerto for me. He needed to find a sponsor for the work and only in 1952 did one appear when the West German Radio commissioned Sauguet to write an orchestral work. He composed a violin concerto and invited me to give its premiere in 1952 at the Festival of Aix-en-Provence. I had been engaged for that summer to head the violin department of the Music Academy of the West in Santa Barbara, California, so I could not accept his invitation. Sauguet decided to save the "premieres" for me so I could perform them at a later date (in order to have the funds supplied by the festival, the concertmaster would perform the concerto at Aix). I premiered the *Concerto d'Orphée* in London, Brussels, and Luxembourg. Sauguet attended the performances in Brussels and Luxembourg, traveling with Annette and me via train. After the Brussels concert, Paul and Madame Collaer had a lovely dinner at their home for our congenial group. As always at the Collaer table there was an empty place set for the departed Erik Satie, whom Collaer, Milhaud, and Sauguet greatly admired.

In Paris, Henri Sauguet introduced us to his London friend Leighton Lucas, a fine composer and conductor, and his wife, Edna. As a young man Leighton had danced in Diaghilev's corps de ballet in Paris. During

Louis with composer Leighton Lucas in London.

World War II he composed scores for British war films. He started to compose a concerto for Ginette Neveu, but abandoned the project when she and her brother were killed in an airplane disaster. He decided to complete the work for me; the violin part was beautifully written and his orchestration imaginative and poetic.

We performed Lucas's *Concert Champêtre* for Radio France in Paris. At our first read-through the French orchestra applauded him enthusiastically, which rather flustered Leighton, and they began to leave the stage. I immediately recognized their attempt to avoid rehearsing and said, "Leighton, call them back, they intend to leave the studio!" Leighton alerted the orchestra manager who called them back. A few recalcitrant members (horns, basses, etc.) refused to return to their places on stage. They stubbornly sat in the front row with their arms crossed in front of their chests in order to avoid being penalized for walking out. However, the broadcast was successful! I had observed on occasion that a few French orchestral players would decide they didn't like the music or a conductor and attempt to sabotage a performance. However, most orchestras have an ésprit de corps and try to play well in spite of whatever music is selected and often save mediocre conductors.

Leighton and I later broadcast his *Concert Champêtre* for the BBC, which led to its publication. His publisher arranged for us to perform this fine work, with Leighton conducting a London Proms concert at the Royal Albert Hall, where we both received high acclaim. Backstage visitors included Warwick Evans, cellist of the London String Quartet, and his wife, Lysbeth. Rudolph Dunbar, an African American conductor and my colleague from the Institute of Musical Art in New York, also came backstage, and we invited him for lunch the next day. We were sorry to hear he had encountered prejudice abroad.

Felix Aprahamian carried us off after the Proms Concert to meet his friend Mr. Elmassian and see his collection of fine French post-impressionist paintings. Elmassian related an extraordinary tale. After the war, needing a kitchen table, he visited an auction house on the South Bank. One of a few paintings stacked against the wall caught his eye, a handsome seascape, which resembled some Turners he had recently seen at the Tate Gallery. (Many Turners are not signed.) He decided to visit the Tate again on his way home. The next day he attended the auction, bought a kitchen table, and waited for the paintings. When the seascape appeared, he bid and bought it for three hundred pounds.

With Armenian enthusiasm Elmassian shouted, "I've bought a Turner!" London auctions are quiet affairs—usually one bids by holding up a card or raising a hand or nodding one's head. So everyone turned to stare with curiosity at the barbarian who had shouted. The painting's provenance was unknown and he spent many months showing this canvas to various London dealers and museums, where he was invariably told, "Very interesting, leave it for a few days"; then when he returned, they said, "Very difficult to decide who painted this interesting work." One evening, his doorbell rang. A noted West End art dealer arrived to say, "Mr. Elmassian, you have a Turner and I know its provenance. Museum directors and dealers don't like to have great works discovered by amateurs—it makes us appear inefficient. We have waited until interest in the matter is over. We have a museum client in Canada that desires an important Turner so we can offer you thirty thousand pounds for your painting."

Thus Elmassian acquired a great collection of fine French post-impressionist paintings with the proceeds from his fortunate discovery. I congratulated him on the great quality of his collection. What an agreeable experience to see and enjoy such handsome paintings to complete that musically satisfying concert!

In August Bernard Herrmann wrote from Hollywood, where he was working on a Hitchcock film. He was eager to resume his conducting career and asked for my help in finding engagements in London, the Low Countries, and France. He suggested that I contact Jack Henderson, musical attaché at the American Embassy and Herrmann's London representative, which I did, but he was not really an agent, just a friendly gentleman who told me how greatly he had enjoyed my concerts in London. Our mutual "karma" determined that Herrmann and I did join forces for the premiere of Walter Piston's second violin concerto on 8 and 9 April, two consecutive programs for the BBC's Third Program with Bernard conducting the London Symphony Orchestra, which went off very well. We received a nice note from Gerald and Joy Finzi, who had heard and enjoyed the broadcast.

Bernard conducted two programs with the London Symphony Orchestra in May at the Royal Festival Hall. His first began with Wagner's Overture to *Die Meistersinger,* then I premiered Robert Russell Bennett's Concerto for Violin and Orchestra (dubbed for this concert "In Popular Style"). Russell had composed a new, more brilliant and dramatic fourth movement, which Russell, Benny, and I thought was the best version! It received an enthusiastic reception from the large audience, press, and orchestra members. After intermission, Benny conducted Sibelius's Second Symphony and ended the program with Borodin's "March" and "Polovtsian Dances." On his second concert Peter Katin played Rachmaninoff's second piano concerto and concluded with Dvořák's *New World* symphony. Rehearsals for both concerts were stormy, as Benny was ill at ease with some of the orchestral players. I always thought Benny would have had greater success as a conductor if he had performed his own orchestral compositions, but I could not convince him at this period of his career. Nevertheless his great enthusiasm, his vitality, and his intuitive understanding of the spirit of the compositions made those concerts stimulating and memorable.

Gerald Finzi invited us to attend a rehearsal of his great choral work *Intimations of Immortality,* which was to be played at the Three Choirs Festival. Since I was in England on a limited-period Labour Permit, we could not remain to attend the festival. However, we attended a morning rehearsal at the Royal College of Music en route to the airport! Annette and I arrived with our baggage and violin just as Jean Pougnet was playing Elgar's violin concerto. I enjoyed meeting him and congratulated him on his fine performance and added how much I admired his recording of Delius's violin concerto directed by Sir Thomas Beecham. Ralph Vaughan Williams was seated in the auditorium and Finzi presented me to the distinguished composer. Williams graciously told me how much he enjoyed my recording of his masterly *Concerto Accademico.* Annette and I were thrilled by Finzi's impressive choral masterpiece, with its splendid writing for orchestra and choir—truly inspired vocal music! How we wished we might have attended the festival!

Louis with Henri Sauguet in New York City.

Noticing that the time for our flight was approaching and not wishing to disturb Finzi or Vaughan Williams, we tiptoed out of the hall without speaking to anyone. In the hallway I heard rapid footsteps behind me and turned to see Ralph Vaughan Williams, who wished to say goodbye. How embarrassed I was by our lack of courtesy! I murmured what an honor it had been to meet him and how grateful I was that he was pleased by my performance of his splendid work. We flew back to Paris in a rosy glow.

The following week it was heartbreaking to receive a letter from Joy Finzi with the news that Gerald had died shortly after the Three Choirs Festival. What a tragic loss! Everyone fortunate enough to have encountered this gifted, modest composer and conductor, who so generously aided many English composers and performers, were seized by a sense of irreparable loss. He had bravely lived under a "sword of Damocles," which only he and Joy were aware of—he lacked an immune system, and any infection could be life threatening! At the festival he had picked up an infant with measles, which sealed his fate. What poetic and beautiful music he gave to our world! How fortunate it was that he had heard his choral masterpiece performed at the important Three Choirs Festival.

During our fall and winter trips to London, we traveled via the night boat-train from Gare du Nord, departing about 10 P.M. The wagon-lit was transported across the English Channel and we had breakfast before arriving at Charing Cross station. On one such trip, on our way to the dining car we passed a compartment in which Picasso stood with Jaime Sabartes, looking out into the corridor (it was well known in Paris that Pablo Picasso feared flying). I have never seen such a penetrating gaze in my life. As usual, Annette and I respected a famous man's privacy.

Upon our arrival in London, we settled into our hotel and prepared for the BBC broadcast premiere of Henri Sauguet's *Concerto d'Orpheé*, which was composed for me. With Leighton Lucas conducting the Royal Philharmonic Orchestra, I thought it should be an ideal realization of Sauguet's masterly poetic work. The evening before this program, Annette and I attended a Royal Albert Hall Proms concert to hear the Royal Philharmonic Orchestra play an all-Sibelius concert conducted by Sir Thomas Beecham. Although the final work ended softly, the audience (ourselves included) was mesmerized throughout the evening by the fabulous poetry, passion, and vitality of the orchestra's performance under Sir Thomas's inspired direction! As the last notes died away we all applauded, cheered, and stamped our feet for ten minutes! Sir Thomas took many bows, included the orchestra, and finally, with a large smile to the still cheering crowd, "cocked-a-snook" (thumbed his nose) at the public to say, "Let us rest!"

The next day at my first rehearsal with members of the Royal Philharmonic, I mentioned to the concertmaster, David McCallum, "You chaps must have rehearsed like slaves to have achieved such an inspired performance last night. My wife and I were enthralled!" McCallum smiled, "We didn't rehearse. Sir Thomas arrived for the morning rehearsal, conducted a few bars, stopped, and said, 'You know these works. Just follow me tonight. Go home!'"

Sauguet's French publisher, Jean Pierre Heugel, came to London for that broadcast and was delighted with Leighton's direction of Sauguet's *Concerto d'Orpheé* and my performance, for Sauguet's music and operas were not known in England.

The Scottish sector of the BBC engaged me to play Hermann Goetz's violin concerto (in one movement), with an excellent conductor, Ian Whyte, in Glasgow. Learning a concerto with only piano accompaniment does not reveal the beauty of its orchestral color. Both Annette and I were enchanted to hear Goetz's almost Mendelssohnian perfection of orchestral writing. This is a work Fritz Kreisler should have performed and recorded for its expression of romantic poetry. (International Music Publishers in New York published my edition of this rare work.)

We stayed in the charming Saint George Hotel, which served excellent cuisine. In spite of inclement weather, we managed to see Glasgow's excellent art museum and nearby Edinburgh's great museum. They both had remarkably fine paintings.

In the 1970s one of our most enjoyable experiences in London was with Robert Spaight. Before dinner at Jonathan Griffin's, he and his wife invited us for a drink at the famed Garrick Club. The walls of the celebrated actor's club displayed great Zoffany and Hogarth paintings, and their historic silver plate was impressive. Hailing a taxi, Bobby Spaight—tall, with shoulder-length white hair framing his handsome patrician features—looked like Jove commanding the elements! That evening at Jonathan's we met Sir Robert Mayer, recently knighted for his important role in England's musical life. A German refugee industrialist, he established the Manchester Children's Concert Programs. Sir Robert also persuaded Jonathan's father to let Jonathan study harpsichord·with Dolmetsch and piano with Artur Schnabel.

We enjoyed great art exhibits at the Royal Academy in London, and became familiar with the British Museum, the Wallace Collection, the Courtauld Institute, and the Victoria and Albert Museum. We learned a great deal from exhibition catalogues and explanatory labels, which gave dates of artists' lives and the cities where they created masterpieces. We acquired interesting books about music and art and some fine old Italian and Dutch prints; also English eighteenth-century prints of Hogarth, Gillray, and Rowlandson, as well as those of more contemporary artists. I completely agreed with Dr. Samuel Johnson's opinion, "It is impossible to tire of London's attractions and delights!"

# 31

# Northern Exposure

Jacques and Marussia Rachmilovich unexpectedly surfaced in Paris during the spring of 1953 at "our" Hotel Royale (my recommendation had persuaded them). Jacques reported they had recently visited Sweden: "I met Dag Wirén, a composer in Stockholm who studied at the Paris Consérvatoire. He told me he has just written a violin concerto. Write to my manager there, Herman Enwall. I'd like to perform it with you."

I ordered the music from Skandinavisk Musikforlag and found it extraordinarily well written for fiddle, so I wrote to Enwall, who arranged the premiere for that fall. Fate and my "karma" could not solve conflicting schedules with Jacques, so Swedish conductor Sten Frykberg was engaged to conduct its premiere with me. I drove north from Paris via Holland and slept overnight in Hengelo, the last stop on the Dutch border. After an early breakfast we filled our car with petrol and drove across Germany all day, arriving in Denmark in time for a late dinner and rest at the nearest Danish hostel. This was the pattern of all our future trips. German custom inspectors, when examining our passports, always queried, "How long do you plan to stay in Germany?" My reply was always, "We are en route to Denmark." I later learned that Danes did the same thing. The memory of the Holocaust was too fresh in our minds to remain in Germany any longer than absolutely necessary.

The northern part of Germany that we traversed was dotted with farms and equipment, practically arranged but drab-looking. As soon as we drove into Denmark, we saw farmhouses with colorful shutters and window boxes with colorful flowers. We both fell in love with Copenhagen, a lovely city of canals, with its diverting Tivoli Gardens created by nineteenth-century writer-architect Georg Carstensen. It still offered free nightly performances of commedia dell'arte. The actors and acrobats are descendants of the touring eighteenth-century practitioners of that improvisatory theater who chose to remain in Copenhagen.

The Tivoli Gardens offered varied attractions, including a wide range of amusements, and an attractive choice of restaurants, from elegant service and finest cuisine to simple cafes with displays of tempting open-faced sandwiches. We had arrived during festive concerts celebrating the opening of a new concert hall (replacing a previous auditorium destroyed by German invaders). These celebration concerts were devoted to works of Danish composers and performers. After an excellent dinner we attended the evening program, which offered the Fifth Symphony of Herman Koppel. Danish violinist Henry Holt was soloist; after many years in England, as concertmaster of Manchester's Hallé Orchestra, he had recently returned to Denmark to head their conservatory's violin department. He masterfully played Carl Nielsen's beautiful violin concerto on his outstanding Guarneri violin. We went backstage to congratulate him.

The next morning we visited the violinmaker Hjorth's shop, where I saw a splendid Nicolas Lupot violin with beautiful soft red varnish. Lupot (1758–1824) is generally considered the French Stradivari. Hjorth refused all offers to sell this great violin, for he intended it to remain in his shop as a model for his descendants. Seeing this extraordinarily fine Lupot gave me an ardent desire to acquire one for myself. This wish was fulfilled in Paris a few years later when Philippe Dupuy obtained a splendid example of this great violinmaker for me. I used this Lupot in tropical concerts in South America and Tahiti.

Later we drove to Oskar Davidsen's Cafe, where hundreds of open-faced sandwiches of fowl, herring, eel, shellfish, meats, salads, et cetera, were enticingly prepared and consumed daily. We enjoyed both Tuborg and Carlsberg beers but felt obligated to drink Carlsberg, for their family founded a great art museum, the Ny Carlsberg Glyptotek, devoted to modern French and Danish artists and sculptors.

Leaving our car in Denmark, we embarked for Sweden on a large ferryboat with a spacious dining room, featuring a lavish smorgasbord on an immense table decorated with beautiful flowers and handsome china and silverware, offering smoked fish, herring, shellfish, cold salads, aquavit, various hot dishes, beers and wines, succulent desserts, and excellent coffee. We dined with much pleasure during the trip. I never tired of their tasty apple cake.

The ferry docked in Malmö, where a connecting train carried us to Stockholm. We settled in a mid-city hotel, the Eden. Early the next morning, I called Dag Wirén, who invited us for lunch at his comfortable home in Danderyd. His living room had large windows facing the Baltic Sea, and a huge lionskin rug with a large noble head. Annette admired this unusual rug. We were both surprised when Wirén's wife Noel replied, "I shot it myself, in India."

Then Dag sat down in front of his grand piano, and I took out my violin, and we played through and discussed his composition at length. A slow movement of tender sadness follows a dramatic first movement. There is an unexpected passage of swift excitement before it resumes nostalgic serenity. When I asked Wirén about this, he explained, "That section is like a dream, where many events are compressed, like film running at lightning speed, images that are almost impossible to recapture on awakening."

Annette and I thoroughly enjoyed a sauna in Stockholm, where separate steam rooms were available for men and women. We were scrubbed by strong matronly women armed with soapy brushes, followed by stimulating showers and relaxing massages. Greatly refreshed, we would meet and walk out into the bracing cool evenings to enjoy dinners.

After morning orchestral rehearsals, we visited Stockholm's fine museums of Viking, Greek, modern Swedish, and French art, all well displayed and informative. The Swedish king was fascinated by archeology and encouraged his people to be interested in the arts. One afternoon we visited the nearby isle of Skansen, an outdoor museum devoted to folk arts, crafts, and costumes exhibited in buildings of eighteenth- and nineteenth-century Sweden. Living artisans dressed in historical clothing were demonstrating trades: bakers, weavers, leather-workers, pottery and furniture makers, basket weavers, shoe and boot makers, and a pharmacist. The isle also had a celebrated restaurant.

We enjoyed a fascinating trip via bus to visit the Royal Palace of Drottningholm, surrounded by exotic chinoiserie structures, a pagoda-like tower, and an eighteenth-century opera house, where only eighteenth-century operas are performed. The orchestra players, singers, and conductor wear white wigs and dress in eighteenth-century costumes. We attended an enchanting matinee of Domenico Cimarosa's opera *Il Matrimonio Segreto* with excellent young Swedish singers. The orchestra rows where we sat were marked for cooks, waiters, valets, maids, gardeners, et cetera; boxes were reserved for the royal family and their guests.

The public concert broadcast of Dag Wirén's violin concerto premiere on 15 October 1953 had a fine success. *Svenska Dagbladet* on 25 October stated, "The most important part of the interesting symphony concert played on Sunday was performed by an outstanding foreign violinist. The international market for Swedish music has not yet become so big that one does not feel pleased and encouraged by marks of interest from abroad. Especially when the interest is concentrated on such solid value as Dag Wirén's violin concerto, which sounded so beautiful in the masterly and inspired playing of Louis Kaufman, which brought out all the brilliance and poetry of the work."

Stockholm's *Svenska Dagbladet* on 26 October reported, "Dag Wirén's Violin Concerto Opus 23 has an unbroken line of continuity and is so concentrated that one gets the impression that not one bar is unnecessary. For the solo part, Radiojänst had the good fortune to succeed in obtaining the American violinist, Louis Kaufman, who was on the same wave length as the work's quick pulse and astringent lyricism. He interpreted the andante with luminous warmth and developed the necessary brilliance and supple strength in the finale, so that the general impression was a marvelous performance technically and musically. Both the soloist, the conductor, and the orchestra had every reason to accept with clear conscience the very enthusiastic applause of the audience."

This premiere was later rebroadcast in many parts of Europe and England. As I have said before, I always consulted composers, whose works I wish to perform, for it gives me added assurance that I am performing the music as they would wish. Music is a unique art which, unlike a painting or a book that has a definite form, demands re-creation by a performer. Only then does it fulfill the composer's intentions. However, the symbols are not precise and there can be wide differences in interpretation.

Annette and I visited Radiojänst's record library to hear works by other Swedish composers, and I was impressed by André Gertler's fine performance of Lars-Erik Larsson's violin concerto and obtained the music. When I discussed Larsson's concerto with Per Lindfors of Radiojänst, he invited me to play it the following year.

Returning to Denmark to pick up our car, we went shopping for souvenir gifts for our families. We bought some amber rings in traditional Viking settings, and I bought Annette a beautiful amber necklace, rings, and earrings. We decided to visit the Danish Radio Headquarters, where music director Kai Aage Brunn greeted me with, "Mr. Kaufman! Congratulations! I heard you play on Swedish Radiojänst. What can you offer *us*?" I proposed a group of unknown Vivaldi concertos from Opus 8, which he found attractive, so he engaged me for the next season as soloist and conductor.

In January 1954, Annette and I returned to snow-covered and magically transformed Stockholm, where it became night in early afternoon, so that one needed electric lights throughout the day.

We met Lars-Erik Larsson, well known as a composer for Swedish films. In Paris we had attended a film based on Strindberg's play *Miss*

*Julie,* starring Anita Bjork, and admired Larsson's score. Larsson was a skillful conductor with charming, polite manners and was obviously adored and respected by the orchestra. The general musician's opinion was that his violin concerto was his best work. He told me, "I studied for a year in Vienna with Alban Berg, but I greatly disliked and resisted the tyranny of the twelve-tone school. However, after my return home, I found that I had been strongly influenced by the masterly richness of Berg's orchestration."

I played his concerto for him in an empty radio studio for his suggestions. He attended all my rehearsals with orchestra under Sten Frykberg's precise and dynamic baton, as well as the concert performance at Stockholm's handsome modern Concert Hall, which faces a large Carl Milles statue of Orpheus.

Larsson's gift for expressive melody attracted me at first hearing. I have always believed the violin is a singing instrument and should not be mistreated by modern composers as a percussive device. Larsson's first movement invokes a mysterious fresh Nordic atmosphere of lyrical enchantment. The poetic andante Pastorale charms with an engaging, wistful melody and mood. The allegro molto Finale has Viking energy. Its bravura captivates soloists, players, and listeners with intoxicating vitality. The two cadenzas, one by André Gertler and the other by the composer, are masterfully written. Since the orchestra and Sten Frykberg were so well acquainted with Larsson's concerto, our performance before a live audience was remarkably dramatic, spirited, poetic, and precise! We gathered flattering reviews and success with the large audience.

Larsson graciously invited Annette and me to a delicious luncheon on Skansen Island. We shared a lively conversation about life in Sweden and about the musically restricted conditions in the nearby Soviet Union, where audiences were barred from hearing works by Rachmaninoff, Stravinsky, and Bartók. He recounted, "When Johann Strauss visited Stockholm to perform his waltzes at the Grand Hotel's ballroom, he only brought second violins from Vienna, who knew the subtle rubato necessary for the 'oom-pah-pahs,' to accompany his melodies played by Swedish first violins!" As we drank a fine wine, Larsson mentioned, "Our laws are so stringent against drunk driving that if one has any moving traffic violation while under the influence, one's driving permit is revoked forever! So, after a dinner or party with whiskey or wine, we take a taxi home, then return the next day for our cars."

Back in wintry Copenhagen, my concert coincided with another program with Maryan Filer, a Polish pianist playing Chopin. Danish radio arranged a press conference for us both. Reporters featured photos and articles that Annette and I could not read. Radio Denmark called me to ask if they might give my phone number to Knud Merrild, an artist we had known in Los Angeles through the Arensbergs; I consented. Merrild and Kai Goetze, another Danish artist, spent a winter in Taos, New Mexico, where they were neighbors and friends of D. H. Lawrence and his wife, Frieda, and encountered the legendary Mabel Dodge. In 1938 Knud wrote a fascinating book, *A Poet and Two Painters,* about that Taos sojourn and a trip to Mexico with the Lawrences. Knud called, asking, "Are you the Kaufman I knew in Los Angeles?" "I certainly am! When may we see you?" "We'll be right over, I have my car here."

The Merrilds arrived and drove us to a delectable luncheon, then accompanied us to see the Royal Palace, telling us of their king's remarkable courage. When the Nazis occupied their country and ordered Jews to wear a yellow star, the king wore one. When the Nazi commander ordered the Danish flag taken down from palace grounds, the king firmly stated, "Can't be done! A Danish soldier would always raise it up again." The commander trumpeted, "Who would dare?"

The king replied, *"Myself!"*

The Merrilds took us to visit Denmark's impressive Viking museum before driving us to their home to show us his recent work. Merrild gave us one of his Flux paintings as a souvenir of our visit. Seeing newspapers there, I asked them to translate our interviews. Annette and I were fascinated to learn our visit coincided with a week of celebration by Jewish Danes honoring fellow Danes for saving their lives during World War II. One story was particularly striking: A brave Danish sea captain made frequent night fishing trips. One night in 1939 he saved a man struggling in the Baltic waters who turned out to be a German pilot shot down by Danish defense forces. Goering appeared in Copenhagen and pinned a medal on the Danish captain, which he accepted, thinking it might be useful if war broke out. During the German occupation of Denmark, this sea captain made almost nightly trips to fish and on every trip, his hold was packed with Danish Jews escaping to nearby Sweden. When he was occasionally stopped by Nazi patrols inspecting ships, the Dane pointed to his medal, saying, "How can you think a man like me would do such a thing?" He saved several hundred Jewish families throughout the war and was never discovered!

We attended Carl Nielsen's oratorio-like opera, *Saul and David,* at the Danish Opera. Although the work was lacking theatrical action, the excellent singers and instrumentalists made it an enjoyable musical evening. We listened to some of his symphonies and his imaginative oratorio, *Hymnus Amoris,* for soloists, women's and men's choruses, and a children's choir. We also attended a performance of Maestro Giulini conducting a Cherubini Mass. My Vivaldi concertos met with a fine success there and I was invited to return the following year to play Sauguet's *Concerto d'Orphée*.

The cold weather introduced us to a Danish winter specialty, *gule ærter*, a thick pea soup with hearty meat and vegetables, always followed by light crepe suzettes and a small glass of Cherry Heering, an after-dinner liqueur.

Danish bookstores were the most tempting and attractive we had ever seen. The United Nations reported Danes as the leading readers of the world. Their average reader consumed at least fourteen books per year. They had Danish, Swedish, Finnish, English, French, Italian, Spanish, German, and American books on every imaginable subject: science, poetry, music, philosophy, history, fiction, and all the arts and crafts of every country. When we left Copenhagen, Gustave was loaded with books.

Driving back to Paris was perilous on snowy and icy roads. Gustave held the road, but I often passed overturned trucks in Germany, too heavily laden for fast driving on icy autobahns. The evening we reached Holland, Annette mentioned, "You'll find it hard to believe but I counted seventeen overturned trucks today!" Our warm clothing protected us—I had purchased a heavy winter coat in Holland and Annette was snug in her warm Argentinian nutria coat. The small heater helped keep us quite cozy.

We stopped in Brussels to see the Collaers, who hospitably invited us to dinner and a surprise event later. After dinner they took us to a concert by the Choeur de Bourgogne (Burgundian choir in Brussels), young Belgian orphans educated by Catholic priests, supported by a Jewish gentleman and the Princesse de Ligne (from an older Belgian lineage than the present royal family). The lads were taught to sing Gregorian chant and songs of Flemish composers of the fifteenth and sixteenth centuries. Clad in handsome red robes, the boys gave an inspired program, which was a highlight of this trip.

# 32

# Miracle in Milan
## *Recording in Paris*

Recording is the only form of immortality attainable by a performing musician.

Bruno Walter

As usual in early August 1954, we were in Zurich. During a week of gray skies and incessant rain I recorded Stravinsky's *Duo Concertante,* Poulenc's *Sonate en memoire de García Lorca,* César Franck's *Sonate,* and the Brahms *G minor Sonata* with Hélène Pignari (official chamber-music pianist for Radiodiffusion Française), with whom I had broadcast in Paris. Hélène, a sensitive artist, suffered from headaches since her husband (director of l'Opéra Comique) was killed in the War. Annette and I did our best to keep her entertained and headache-free during rehearsals, recordings, and meals. We succeeded, and cheerfully delivered her very early to a Paris-bound train. Then, yearning for sun, we immediately drove off in pelting rain for sunny Italy, where we planned to meet Richard and Sara Tucker in Milan.

After crossing the Gotthard Pass via auto-train I drove through Swiss Ticino, with gray skies but no rain. As we descended the mountains, shortly before crossing into Italy, traffic suddenly stopped. A long line of autos waited for road-clearing crews, with huge equipment, to remove large rocks and masses of mud blocking the road. Cars quickly piled up behind our small Renault. We were wedged between autos and surrounded by mountains in the distance, which torrential rains turned into gigantic (temporary) waterfalls. The scene resembled Leonardo da Vinci's drawings of furious tempests. We were immobile for two hours; Annette and I read books we always carried in the back seats. Finally the road was cleared and I drove slowly down to Milan.

Cloudy but dry skies covered Milan. Richard had left a note at our hotel with his telephone number. I immediately called and he invited us to attend his afternoon recording for EMI at Teatro alla Scala—Verdi's *La Forza del Destino* with Maria Callas and Nicola Rossi-Lemeni—and later to join him and Sara for dinner. I parked my Renault near La Scala in a paid parking lot and we walked to Hotel Duomo to meet Sara and Richard. Richard did not speak before singing, so we talked only with Sara until we reached La Scala. Richard proceeded backstage and we joined Sara in a box that overlooked the orchestra, chorus, and soloists.

The conductor was Tullio Serafin. Richard sang Don Alvaro, Nicola Rossi-Lemeni sang Padre Guardiano, and Leonora was the celebrated Maria Callas. Walter Legge and his wife, Elisabeth Schwarzkopf, were supervising the recording. The orchestra was in the pit; the chorus was on stage with three microphones awaiting the stars. Richard was in great form and as always prepared to give his best performance, as was Rossi-Lemeni. For each take they both sang their arias perfectly with style and passion. Alas, Callas was not in her best voice. Her attentive husband was hovering near her on stage as she struggled with several takes. Her scale was very uneven, almost three voices—a low register, an excellent middle range, and very shaky at the top. She was well aware of this and railed at the excellent conductor and chorus.

She demanded Richard's mike, claiming hers was defective, then, still not pleased by playbacks, demanded Rossi-Lemeni's mike—but no improvement! We were embarrassed to see such a display of bad temper. Finally the long session was over and we presumed EMI would combine several tapes to obtain a good performance for Leonora.

We enjoyed a wonderful dinner with Richard and Sara, and Annette asked, "Did Callas ever have an even scale?" Richard replied, "We made our Italian debuts together at the Verona Arena and her voice was splendid. She sang beautifully and it was Maestro Serafin who conducted that performance and helped her Italian career greatly." Annette persisted, "What happened to her voice?" Richard replied, "Some people thought her voice suffered because of her great loss of weight! She was attractive but became obsessed by the idea of becoming very thin."

During our dinner and long conversation all lights in the restaurant went out for a few minutes due to a great rainstorm breaking over Milan. When the storm subsided we departed and arranged to meet the next day.

When Annette and I returned to our car in the parking area, I noticed that the window on Annette's side was open and realized the lock had been broken. My music case, which contained Annette's handwritten copies of the 1709 edition of the twelve Torelli concerti, was gone! In our haste to meet the Tuckers I had only taken my violin and our valises into our hotel and left my music bag in the car. We had taken the music to Zurich so I could edit all the parts for a recording I was to make in December for l'Oiseau-Lyre in Paris!

I called the guardian of the parking area, stating I had paid the required fee for supervision. He claimed he had just taken over; the man I paid had left. I asked for the nearest police station and he gave me directions. I arrived there to be told they were closing; it was almost midnight. "Signor, you must go the Central Milano Stazione on Via Benefratelli." Annette and I drove there. Signor Bofitto, the officer in charge and an amateur composer of popular songs, listened with great sympathy to my sad tale and fervently promised to help me. He immediately ordered extra policemen to watch the La Scala area.

I drove back to the hotel. The concierge suggested I place an urgent announcement in the *Corriere della Sera,* which would appear the next morning on the front page, not in the general want ads—but it would cost extra. I thanked him for such a good idea. The concierge composed the text: "Anyone who can return or offer whereabouts of music taken from a car on Via Silvio Pellico will receive a generous reward. Call Hotel Duomo."

The next day Annette and I drove all over central Milan to look at peddlers' stands of used music and books. No success! We shopped with Richard and Sara at elegant shops on Via Napoleone and I purchased six hand-painted Fornasetti plates decorated with ancient lutes. We drove the Tuckers to visit the impressive funereal sculptures in Milan's famed cemetery, which they found greatly interesting. All the while, I was terribly worried that the robbers, attracted by my case, might have burned or even thrown away the music, and in the rain the ink on the music pages would dissolve!

The next morning Signor Bofitto called excitedly and said, "Maestro Kaufman, come to my office *pronto!* We've arrested the robbers and we have your music here!" We drove off to Via Benefratelli, marveling at our good luck! Two plain-clothes police officers in the La Scala area had noticed two lads opening a locked car in the same way my Renault had been burglarized and arrested them. They confessed quickly. The announcement had saved my music! The boys had returned to their house on the outskirts of Milan before opening the heavy case, saw the music, which was valueless to them, and decided to burn it. But their sister, who had read the notice, counseled, "Wait a few days and we can claim the reward!"

We thanked the two charming plain-clothes policemen who retrieved our music and offered them the reward, which they graciously refused. I insisted, "You must buy the police force a glass of *vino* or whatever they like, it's only a small thank you for your remarkable recovery of a year's work of copying these scores."

Signor Bofitto, beaming at the quick success of his special team, asked, "May we take photos of you and your wife with the music?" He continued, "Our force is always being criticized by the press for inefficiency. This happy result could be very helpful for our reputation! May we write about this?" I replied, "Signor Bofitto, I consider this truly a *miracolo a Milano* to have these handwritten scores and parts safely returned! My wife and I will be most pleased to be of any help to you and your colleagues. You have been of such great help to us!"

The official police photographer took several pictures of us and sent out a highly embroidered release. They stated I was a conductor and composer who had my thirty operas stolen. The capable police had miraculously recovered every one! Pictures were published by every Italian newspaper, even the communist daily. What a lost opportunity! All that publicity would have sold out any recital Annette and I could have arranged, but we would not have dreamed of embarrassing the helpful police force by revealing that I was only a fiddler who had lost copies of twelve Torelli concerti! Signor Bofitto came to visit us in Paris and we enjoyed taking him to a fine luncheon. He brought us printed copies of his charming tunes, and we sincerely hoped to meet again.

We had a joyous celebration and farewell dinner with Richard and Sara Tucker at Tantalo's excellent restaurant in the Galleria. Everyone in the large room smiled at us, recognizing us from the fabulous newspaper photos of us both! How delighted and thrilled we were to have the Torelli scores and parts in our hands again. The music bag was gone forever, but I replaced it with a handsome new Italian case. When we returned to New York, Richard and Sara gave us a copy of the EMI complete recording of *La Forza del Destino* inscribed 8 October 1954:

> To Annette and Louis my dear friends with whom we spent a glorious time in Milan while making this recording.
> Sincerely,
> Richard Tucker

After some London concerts and broadcasts, I broadcast an entire concert of Charles Martin Loeffler's music in Paris with members of the

Pascal Quartet and Hélène Pignari—French premieres of his Partita for violin and piano, the String Quartet, and his lovely String Quintet for three violins, viola, and cello. I always thought the poetic and imaginative music of Loeffler should be more widely known and appreciated. Years before I had also played these lovely works in Los Angeles for the Pro Musica Society.

The last five days of 1954 were taken up with recording for l'Oiseau-Lyre the twelve Giuseppe Torelli concertos for one and two solo violins. I conducted the strings of l'Orchestre National de la Radiodiffusion Française with Ruggiero Gerlin from Naples playing harpsichord continuo; I also played the solos. The review I treasured was in the prestigious *Saturday Review*, written by Herbert Weinstock, entitled "Masters of the Baroque": "London, through the Editions de l'Oiseau-Lyre, continues to make available interesting music of the Baroque (well played and handsomely recorded). The twelve concertos of Giuseppe Torelli's Opus 8, for example, are superbly performed on OL 50089/90, the musicians being Louis Kaufman, violinist and conductor of the l'Oiseau-Lyre orchestral ensemble, Georges Alès, second violinist, Roger Albin, cellist and Ruggerio Gerlin, harpsichordist. Kaufman, evidently the moving spirit behind the recording, prepared the text from photographic copies of the original 1709 edition supplied by the Library of Congress. These concertos, six for two violins and six for solo violin, survive not only as pioneering works in establishing the long primacy of the violin as a solo instrument, but also as living music of great charm and substance. The anonymous explanatory and historical notes on the record sleeves are excellent." I can now state my dear collaborator Annette was extremely modest and would not permit her name to be credited for those notes she wrote in 1954!

We celebrated the New Year with our dear friends the Ségal family. We were served a traditional Paris New Year's midnight menu of oysters, roast duck, salad, cheese, lots of champagne, and wonderful fruits. What a satisfying year of accomplishment for us both!

# 33

# Return to Los Angeles
## *Korngold Memorial Concert*

In November 1956, we returned to Los Angeles and our empty house. I called the storage company and within a few days our home was again filled with rugs, furniture, Steinway piano, sculptures, paintings, music, and books. We soon added our European acquisitions, which arrived from storage in New York. After eight years of living in hotel rooms, what a pleasure it was to be at home surrounded by the acquisitions of many years and the books we loved!

One Sunday afternoon we visited the Los Angeles County Museum of Art and encountered Philip and Florence Kahgan. Phil had been musical contractor at Paramount and now was in charge of museum concerts. He was very pleased that I was home again and invited me to play some baroque concerts at the museum. I accepted on the spot, outlining programs and a title, "The Music of Vivaldi and His Contemporaries." He engaged an ensemble of six violins, three violas, two cellos, and a bass; Annette provided continuo. On 9, 16, and 23 December 1956 I played and directed concertos of Bach, Telemann, Torelli, and Vivaldi. The museum printed a handsome program and reproduced on its cover the Venetian *View of the Piazzetta* by Luca Carlevaris (1665-1731). Annette and I wrote program notes.

We resumed visits with Bernard and Lucille Herrmann. Benny urged me to resume recording for films. He told Alfred and Martha Newman we were back, and they invited us for chamber music. Al asked me to play again for his film scores. Therefore I again worked for a few seasons at Twentieth Century Fox. Frequently I played concerts on the West Coast, often chamber music with Annette and various colleagues at the

Los Angeles County Museum, and I performed Bennett's violin concerto with Bernard when he conducted a program with the Glendale Symphony. I played both the Brahms and Bloch violin concertos (the Bloch was a Los Angeles premiere) with the American Youth Symphony conducted by Mehli Mehta, as well as the Rózsa Concerto for Violin and Cello with Gabor Rejto and the same group. I also performed the Bloch concerto for its premiere with the Rochester Symphony, under the excellent baton of my friend Dr. Theodore Bloomfield.

Annette's dear father died suddenly in 1958 from heart failure, which deeply grieved us both. We made a hurried trip to attend his funeral in mid-winter in Bismarck, North Dakota. On our final evening, I insisted that Annette's mother come to live with us in Los Angeles. She was hesitant, fearing that she might be a burden, but we both were so persistent that she did move into our home within a few months. She was so tactful, charming, and pleasant that we were pleased to have her company at the concerts, films, and plays we attended, and she traveled with us to Europe and Asia.

We attended a concert at UCLA's Schoenberg Hall with Louis Kievman (who succeeded me when I left the Musical Art Quartet) and his wife, Elaine. This excellent auditorium had not existed when we had set off for Europe in 1948. Kievman and I were impressed by its ambiance and acoustics and thought it ideal for chamber music. I chanced to meet Dr. Robert Nelson, music department head at UCLA, whom we had met in Brussels when he was on sabbatical leave and I was performing Vivaldi concertos for Radio Flamande. I proposed to Dr. Nelson a series of chamber music programs devoted to the works of Mozart, Schubert, and Brahms. Then unexpected added support for the series came from Dr. Gustave O. Arlt, head of UCLA's Fine Arts Productions, who thought such programs would be a cultural boon to the community. Kievman and I decided to avoid string quartets, for they demand a long commitment to achieve a fine ensemble; we decided to play trios, quintets, sextets, septets, et cetera. The programs were called "Three Evenings with Great Composers," and we chose the name "Westwood Musical Artists."

The first concert devoted to Mozart included the Quintet for two violins, two violas, and cello; a Trio in C for violin, cello, and piano; and the Divertimento in E-flat for violin, viola, and cello. Subsequent programs were devoted to Schubert, Schumann, Dvořák, Brahms, and Mendelssohn. My colleagues were violinist Joseph Stepansky, violists Louis Kievman and Cecil Figelski, cellist George Neikrug, and pianist Emmanuel Bay. We also used the sensitive and excellent pianist Sidney Stafford as well as Lillian Steuber and Yaltah Menuhin.

Westwood Musical Artists—Louis, violin; George Neikrug, cello; Louis Kievman, viola; Emmanuel Bay, piano—rehearsing for their first musical concert at Kaufman's Los Angeles home.

Ernst Toch was in residence at the Huntington Hartford Foundation to compose a symphony and he and I met again at a local reception for Aaron Copland. Annette and I attended a seventieth birthday celebration for Toch at USC where I sat next to Lester Koenig, a dissident Hollywood writer who had formed the label Contemporary Records. A great admirer of Toch's music, Lester suggested that Westwood Musical Artists should record Toch's excellent Opus 18 string quartet for his label. Joseph Stepansky, second violin; Louis Kievman, viola; and George Neikrug, cello joined me in recording Toch's work and also the Spitzweg Trio for violin, viola, and cello. We were very fortunate to have Toch's supervision at recording sessions. His suggestions for tempi and dynamics were extremely helpful. Koenig tried to record significant works, but he often had trouble in finding distribution for his recordings.

Vernon Duke recorded some of his unpublished Society for Forgotten Music compositions for Lester's Contemporary Records label. The same players were engaged to record a Glinka string quartet and a very early Mendelssohn string quartet with remarkable counterpoint, which ends with a stunning double fugue.

Westwood Musical Artists survived for three years, but most Hollywood musicians did not like my insistence on at least three or four rehearsals for programs. After a Beethoven program, when we played his remarkable septet, some players informed me they did not wish to continue, so I ended the series.

In January 1959, Luzi Korngold, the gracious and lovely widow of Erich Wolfgang Korngold, called to request that I arrange a memorial concert for this important composer. I immediately accepted the honor, not anticipating the difficulties I would encounter. Dr. William Melnitz of UCLA's theater arts program, who had worked in theatrical productions with Korngold and Max Reinhardt in Austria and Los Angeles, was of great help. He reserved 7 June 1959 at Schoenberg Hall for the event, and Luzi formed a small steering committee: Mrs. Dorothy Huttenback (manager of the Los Angeles Music Guild), Melnitz, the Korngold sons, Ernest and George and their wives, and Annette and me. I proposed adding as chairperson Mrs. Willard Coe, a former voice teacher from Portland, Oregon, who had married a Santa Barbara millionaire, for she had wide experience in arranging benefits. She devised a form letter that our small committee sent out on 24 January. Annette as secretary received charming letters in reply from Korngold's colleagues: Dr. Bruno Walter wrote, "It gives me much pleasure to learn you are going to arrange a memorial concert for Erich W. Korngold and I will certainly attend." Fritz Kreisler replied, "I am most happy to join with you and the many friends of my old and dear friend Erich Korngold. The many pleasant recollections of my early youth, in which Erich played such a large part as a musician and great man will never be forgotten." Rudolph Bing stated, "I would be greatly pleased if you should add my name to your list of honorary sponsors." Lotte Lehmann responded, "It gives me great pleasure to pay homage to one of my dearest of friends whom I was privileged to sing and work with in Vienna. Those hours together are very precious memories for me. He will live on in his great works. I shall never forget him." Dr. Josef Krips wrote, "I shall be delighted and honored to serve on your Sponsors Committee, I am sure Erich Korngold's music will remain in the repertory for many generations." Other distinguished patrons were Mario Castelnuovo-Tedesco, Miklós Rózsa, Darius Milhaud, Ernst Toch, William Steinberg, Werner Klemperer, and Hal Wallis.

Despite such encouraging responses, Mrs. Coe found it impossible to obtain any star performers for the program. Both Jascha Heifetz and Gregor Piatigorsky ignored Mrs. Coe's appeal (Heifetz's superb recording of Korngold's violin concerto was a more lasting tribute than any transitory musical event). Members of Hollywood's large Viennese colony bombarded Annette with helpful suggestions, mostly why hadn't we asked Heifetz to play, or Maria Jeritza (who lived in New York) to sing, or

Lotte Lehmann? Someone even proposed we mount scenes from Korngold's operas with famous singers! Annette always expressed thanks for such counsel and would explain we had vainly tried to lure world-famous celebrities to perform.

John Crown, who taught at the University of Southern California, opened the concert with Korngold's Third Piano Sonata in C major, Opus 25, composed in 1931. Then a gifted contralto, Eva Gustavson (whom Toscanini had brought to America to sing Amneris in his *Aïda* recording), accompanied by pianist Dr. Gerhard Albersheim (we later met him again in Basel when I recorded a concert with Annette for Radio Basel), sang seven songs on texts by Shakespeare and other writers. For the finale, a quartet consisting of James Getzoff and myself, violins; Cecil Figelski, viola; and Kurt Reher, cellist performed Korngold's Third String Quartet, Opus 34, which Luzi particularly wanted on the program. Also at Luzi's suggestion, Annette and I played Korngold's Suite for violin and piano, based on his incidental music for Max Reinhardt's production of *Much Ado about Nothing*. Luzi's coaching helped us understand how Korngold wished it to be played. We enjoyed these visits with her, especially her anecdotes about their family. One evening she told us the following: When Erich was about twelve years old, Bruno Walter moved into the apartment building where his family lived in Vienna. He visited the Korngolds to complain that their son's piano playing disturbed him when he was studying scores, but Erich's talent won him over. When Erich composed a piano trio, Walter agreed to play it with the concert-master and the first cellist of the Vienna Philharmonic. When this trio played it at the Korngolds', Erich's father, Julius, who was Vienna's leading music critic, began to comment, "Too fast," or "Too loud," or "Slower." Each time young Erich would protest, "But Papa, I like the way they play," Julius would reply, "Quiet! You don't know anything about it!"

We all worried that we could not attract a large audience. Melnitz, concerned about lack of ticket sales, called Annette a few days before the concert to say, "UCLA is willing to let you off the hook and cancel the program." But Annette, remembering our experiences in Paris and London when we sold out the halls at the last minute, refused the offer. Fortunately we did achieve a capacity audience.

After intermission the actor Robert Ryan read a message from Bruno Walter. I was extremely uneasy, for I knew that Kurt Reher had been performing with the Los Angeles Philharmonic that same afternoon in San Diego, some 120 miles south. He had assured me he could easily arrive in time for our evening program. But even after Ryan's speech there was still no sign of Kurt!

As Annette and I walked on stage to perform *Viel Larmen um Nichts* (Much Ado about Nothing), I was anxiously hoping that Kurt had not been in an auto accident and would momentarily appear! However, I turned my concentration to performing Korngold's seductive suite. After heartwarming applause as we returned onstage to bow, I heard Kurt arriving back stage! By the time we took three curtain calls, he had his cello out of its case and proceeded to enter on stage with colleagues to play the string quartet! The concert was a fine success, with enthusiastic press.

We were deeply touched by Luzi Korngold's note of June 7, 1959.

> My dearest friends, Erich and I would not know how to thank you both: Annette for the tremendous work she did (and now on top of it, playing the piano so beautifully!) And Louis the inspiration and the great artist, whom we always admired. This little sketch to *Much Ado About Nothing* was the only manuscript I could find on this work. I hope it gives you a little pleasure. Erich extends his thanks with it to you.
> Very affectionately
> Luzi Korngold

Two valued life friendships developed from this event. Dr. Robert Bartlett Haas, head of UCLA's Arts and Humanities Extension, attended the program and came backstage to congratulate me and say, "This is the type of program we should do at UCLA!" Tony Thomas, a great Korngold fan in Toronto who rebroadcast the concert over the Canadian broadcast network, wrote how captivated he was by the performance. He later visited us in Los Angeles, and we became lifelong friends. We met in London, and one day when Annette and I had to perform he graciously spent the day showing Kew Gardens to Annette's mother. He eventually settled in Los Angeles and accompanied us to concerts and operas, including William Grant Still's opera *Bayou Legend.* He and his companions dined at our home frequently and we often met at Alfred Newman's home.

Tony was also a fine writer about films and film scores. He was devoted to Robert Russell Bennett and Max Steiner and admired William Grant Still's music. On Robert Russell Bennett's seventy-fifth birthday Tony recorded Bennett's *Song Sonata* with Annette and me, and also the *Hexapoda Suite,* which he coupled with a London recording of the Bennett violin concerto conducted by Bernard Herrmann. The recordings were issued on CD by Bay Cities; after the demise of this company, Tony resold Bennett's concerto to Musical Masterworks Society, which gave it an impressive distribution, to the great delight of Russell and Louise Bennett!

German novelist Lion Feuchtwanger and his wife, Marta (his cousin), invited us to attend a German film based on his anti-Nazi novel, *Die Geschwister Oppenheim,* and also for a few readings of works in progress by himself and friends. In his magnificent modern oceanfront house, Lion had assembled a superb library (his third, as his libraries in Berlin and France had been destroyed in the war), with a first edition of Holinshed's *Chronicles of England, Scotland, and Ireland* (a source for Shakespeare), incunabula of Josephus's *Antiquities of the Jews,* works of Horace, Cicero, and Suetonius, and complete works of many of the world's greatest writers. One huge volume of bound copies of daily newspapers, dating from the French Revolution, had been collected by Napoleon's brother Joseph. This volume was a goldmine of data on day-to-day political, social, and cultural events, including the founding of public art museums, the first printing of *The Rights of Man,* and lists of who was guillotined each day. After Lion's death in 1958 Marta bequeathed this valuable collection to the University of California, and the German government bought Villa Aurora (their home) to use for conferences. We continued to enjoy cultural events, concerts, and lectures with Marta.

Another dear friend, Ebria Feinblatt, also of Romanian parents, was head of prints, drawings, and works on paper at the Los Angeles County Museum. We became close friends and enjoyed attending many exhibits with her at the new Getty Museum in Malibu and also in Paris. Ebria became fascinated by our Gillray colored prints and arranged an exhibit of them at the Los Angeles County Museum; they were later exhibited at the Santa Barbara Museum. She introduced us to Gordon Gilkey of the Portland Art Museum's print department and to the great Leonardo da Vinci scholar Carlo Pedretti and his lovely wife Rosanna, who all became devoted friends.

The Dante Society invited Irving and Jean Stone, the Pedrettis, and ourselves to become members, and we greatly enjoyed the lectures and dinners they organized. Annette and I performed a program of Italian sonatas by Tartini and Veracini for one program. Ebria and Carlo generously gave us copies of their publications on Italian painters and fascinating research on Leonardo da Vinci.

We regularly attended the annual summer Shakespeare festivals at San Diego's Globe Theater in Balboa Park, which contained three museums, a superb zoo, a remarkable botanical garden, and pleasant cafes. In the shop of the San Diego Art Museum, I was attracted to a painting of Granada's Lion Courtyard in the Alhambra by Hinson C. Cole, a local primitive/naive artist. I asked about the artist and was given his address in Leucadia, a nearby oceanside village we had never heard of.

As I drove north to Los Angeles on the freeway, Annette noticed a small exit sign and said "Here's Leucadia—let's visit that artist." The address was the office for a huge trailer court. The manager directed me to Cole's trailer about a block away. We knocked on the door and introduced ourselves to a tall, ruddy, sandy-haired man. Cole told us he was a native of Arizona, a retired U.S. Army engineer who had constructed roads, bridges, and dams in Southeast Asia, China, India, and Latin America. Now a widower, he enjoyed traveling with inexpensive retired-persons tours to various exotic sites where he had worked during his Army services; he related with a western drawl, "I took photos of sites I worked in and the people, which I used as a source for my paintings." He painted indigenous peoples with sympathy and understanding. I bought six of his charming small paintings. We became good friends and, as usual, I managed to interest a few of my friends to also buy some of his works. Over the several years we were acquainted with Cole, he sometimes drove to visit us in Los Angeles, and on most encounters we purchased a few of his interesting works, including several Asian landscapes and a series of California and Arizona Spanish missions. One large historic painting of the Santa Barbara mission was painted as it might have appeared in 1820; we later gave it to the Smithsonian Collection of American Art in Washington, D.C. Cole confided the typescript of a book he had written about his experiences with a family in India to us. Annette and I had a true sense of loss when he died.

Sculptress Anna Mahler (daughter of Gustav and Alma Mahler) lived for a time in Los Angeles, as did her often-married mother, who, after Mahler's death, lived with painter Oskar Kokoschka, married architect Walter Gropius, and later married writer Franz Werfel. Anna created a large statue, "Theatre Masks," for UCLA's MacGowan Theatre and impressive portrait heads of Otto Klemperer, Schoenberg, and our friend Ernst Toch. His daughter, Franzi, inherited the fragile, discolored Toch plaster cast, one of Anna's important works, which she had given to Ernst on his seventy-fifth birthday. I suggested to Franzi that this plaster cast be preserved in more durable form. Annette and I drove with her to a foundry. She ordered two bronzes cast, one for herself, another for us to share the costs. We remained friends with Franzi until her untimely death in 1989 in an auto accident, after she had taken us to hear a performance of Toch's *Cantata of the Bitter Herbs*. (Years later in London, at Miron Grindea's home, I met conductor Anatole Fistoulari and his beautiful blond wife, not realizing, until much later, that she was Anna Mahler!)

During this period I played a number of film scores. I remember working on Alex North's *Cleopatra,* starring Elizabeth Taylor, and the scores for *The Sound of Music* and *Hello, Dolly!* at Fox, conducted by Lionel Newman. I also played in John Williams's inventive score for the hilarious film *John Goldfarb, Please Come Home*, starring Peter Ustinov, where my violinistic gyrations accompanied frantic chase scenes.

Annette and I enjoyed brief trips to England, France, Switzerland, and Italy with Annette's mother. But the most rewarding trip was in 1965 when we visited the Far East. I had long dreamed of seeing Angkor Wat and Angkor Thom in Cambodia. The Los Angeles Museum offered a trip to Japan, Thailand, Cambodia, Singapore, Kuala Lumpur, and Hong Kong, and so our trio embarked with a small group. En route Annette and I played a program at the Honolulu Academy of Art and saw dear friends Karen and Chuck Mau, Marvell Hart, Ben Hyams, and Robert Griffing, who told me of special sites to see and addresses of art dealers in Kyoto.

We were fascinated by the beauty of Japanese temples, parks, and museums in Tokyo, Kyoto, and Osaka, and enjoyed the wide range of entertainment and cuisine offered. But Cambodia offered the supreme experience of walking with Annette in the temples and seeing the huge beautiful statues, stone heads of Khmer gods and rulers, and sculptures of sinuous dancers on the walls. I had bought a camera in Japan and took countless photos. One evening remains fixed in my memory. A small group from our tour and a few tourists from the Cleveland Museum of Art attended an evening performance of Royal Dancers in the traditional sacred dance of Ramayana on the causeway leading to Angkor Wat. We had been provided with comfortable, high-backed wicker chairs and sat in the dark jungle. The beautifully robed young Royal Dancers danced on a red carpet bordered with flaming torches, which attracted mites and flying insects of all kinds, rather like a white diaphanous sheet that surrounded these slowly moving dancers. The torches illuminated their colorful golden costumes and elaborate headdresses, casting fantastic shadows. They wore the fixed smiles of gods and goddesses, so these tiny insects must have entered their ears, noses, and mouths! I was amazed at the impassive control of every gesture made by these small, perfectly trained dancers. No one attempted to protect his or her faces from these pests. They raised and lowered their legs slowly as they turned and moved their arms and heads and fingers as elegantly as if they were in a theater. Their intense concentration and exquisite perfection of movement was truly a magical experience. Our visit to Thailand gave us a deeper understanding of Thai culture.

Our friend Oscar Meyer, an erudite Hungarian art dealer in Paris, had given us the address of Connie Mangskau in Bangkok. We visited her fine studio filled with impressive ancient Thai bronze and stone sculptures. She greeted us warmly, and then asked, "What do you do for a Bar Mitzvah? I have a sister who married a Jewish man in Zurich. Their son is thirteen and all of her husband's family will be there, so she insisted I attend." I replied, "You only have to bring a present for the lad, a watch, a scarf, or a fountain pen." We bought four ancient Thai bronze figures from Connie; they are a permanent souvenir of our Southeast Asian journey.

# 34

## Adventures behind the Iron Curtain

As Annette and I walked down New York's Fifth Avenue in spring of 1967, I noticed in KLM's window an attractive offer to visit Czechoslovakia, Hungary, Romania, Bulgaria, and three cities in the Soviet Union for four hundred dollars, with all sightseeing, hotels, and airfares *prepaid*. It seemed an ideal and inexpensive way to show Annette Romania and to enjoy the museums of Prague, Budapest, Leningrad, Moscow, and Kiev! A friendly travel agent in Los Angeles offered an inexpensive flight to Frankfurt, telling me that all KLM flights stopped there en route to Prague; I planned to visit Holland anyway for their summer festival programs. Before returning home, I booked three spaces on the tours. KLM sent us three booklets with visas, air tickets for travel in Eastern countries, and hotel and sightseeing tour tickets (bus, etc.). The tour package included three large identity pins marked "ATA" (Americans traveling abroad).

Annette's mother was visiting North Dakota and decided to remain there for (supposedly) minor surgery, so she canceled her trip to Europe and later returned to Los Angeles. However, I kept her KLM continental reservations. In August, Annette and I boarded a charter flight to Frankfurt that arrived late at night. After a welcome rest in an airport hotel, we boarded the scheduled KLM airplane early the next morning, wearing our ATA identity pins, and were surprised to find the plane filled by a large company of young French tennis players en route to matches in Prague. Not another ATA passenger in sight!

When we landed in Prague's airport, a young lady, seeing our ATA pins, asked, "Mr. and Mrs. Kaufman?" I answered, "Yes." She helped us clear customs and led us outside to a waiting cab, saying, "I have to find another gentleman, so please wait here for my return." After half an hour, she returned, saying, "I couldn't find him but he wasn't supposed to be on that plane. You also were not on the right plane!"

Prague is a lovely city and we had a fascinating drive along the famed Moldau River and across the beautiful Saint Charles Bridge to our comfortable hotel. Our concierge, a lovely young blond who resembled Ingrid Bergman, welcomed us. I asked, "Has the ATA tour group arrived?" She seemed puzzled by my query, saying, "I have no news about them." We climbed the stairs to our spacious, pleasant room, deposited our bags, and then returned downstairs to request a taxi, as I thought it would be good to visit a museum. I learned that in socialist countries, taxis could not be hailed on the streets. One had to order a taxi, give one's name, and state where one wished to go; the driver then checked the client's name and destination, which was a way to know where tourists went and what they did! We spent a pleasant few hours visiting a historic museum in a palace overlooking the picturesque city.

When we returned to our hotel about 5:30 P.M., I asked, "Has the ATA group arrived?" "No."

Not being able to read or speak Czech, Annette and I decided to dine in our hotel's restaurant. As we entered the dining area, a man's voice called, "Louis Kaufman! What are you doing here?" There eating dessert were Miklós and Margaret Rózsa! I replied, "How good to see you! We're on holiday en route to Budapest. Miklós, may we bring or do something for your lovely aunt?" (We had visited with Miklós and his widowed aunt in Rome a few years before. His uncle had been concertmaster of Budapest's opera.)

Miklós answered, "We've just visited her, she doesn't need anything. Do go visit her, she'll be very pleased to see you, and look up my friend János Sebestéyn. He's an organist and harpsichordist, has a car, and will be very helpful to you." Miklós gave me their addresses and telephone numbers before they left Prague that same evening.

Early the next morning we boarded a Cedok (Czech tourist organization) bus for French and Spanish speakers to visit Karlstein. This historic castle resembles a fourteenth-century French chateau. King Charles, who established the third university in Europe (after Bologna and Paris), married a French princess who brought along a French architect! Our guide offered, "Many young couples choose to be married in its chapel."

The bus stopped en route for lunch at a rustic inn, where a confused discussion erupted: "Who paid for lunch? Who paid for entry to the chapel? Who paid only for the bus trip?" I had our coupon books, which paid for everything! A dark-haired young man across the table from us, wearing slacks and a pullover sweater without cap or hat, held up a book of coupons like ours. Annette offered, "You must be Señor Quinones, we waited half an hour for you at the airport yesterday!" The smiling señor replied, "I am from Puerto Rico, I'm a social science teacher." We discussed our KLM coupons and discovered we were booked on the same tour, hotels, and flights. We were now three ATA voyagers! Learning we shared interests in music, art, old churches, and palaces, we became friends. Quinones was very polite and helpful to everyone we encountered, aiding older passengers to descend stairs or buses. He had a very fair complexion and easily burned in the hot summer sun. Annette and I were protected by hats and Annette always carried an umbrella, so she often held it protectively over his head.

I thought him a bit too venturesome. The next morning over breakfast, he reported, "I marched in an antiwar parade last night and met some people who offered me a better exchange for dollars." I warned him, "Be careful, Quinones. Avoid involvement in political affairs and money-changing on the street—we're foreigners here and shouldn't do anything that might involve ourselves or our country in any trouble." While Quinones had been marching, Annette and I had attended an excellent chamber music concert in a lovely historic hall.

The next day, a Cedok guide led us in a walking tour of the Old City. En route I encountered Eugene Weintraub, United States representative of Russian Editions, who was returning to New York that evening after a Moscow visit, very disgruntled by his experiences there. He told me, "They know you from your performances of the Khachaturian and Knipper concertos. Here's the phone number of Grigori Schneerson, head of their Union of Composers Society. It's very hard to obtain telephone numbers in Russia; they haven't printed phone books for many years. Take some safety pins to close your drapes at night, and get sink stoppers, as hotels don't have plugs for wash basins or tubs!" This was useful advice!

Quinones joined us in visiting the historic Altenu synagogue, and a new synagogue whose walls were completely covered by names of persons executed by the Nazis, with dates of their births and deaths. Our guide indicated children's names six months or two or three years old, which made her cry. She explained, "I can't help crying whenever I come here!" We then visited the Jewish cemetery and a museum with fabulous Judaica, including silver torah finials, objects made by Jewish artisans, and sailor's sextants and maps. This collection had been assembled by a German general, who decided to save these treasures of destroyed synagogues as examples of what these "vanished people" had made and used. The "legendary Jews"—whom they intended to exterminate! Quinones joined us to visit a small museum which displayed a large collection of woven Torah covers, some brought from fifteenth-century Spain and Portugal.

That evening Annette and I, wanting distraction from the tragic scenes of the day, attended an original and entertaining theatrical event with multiple uses of the stage, juxtaposing live actors with film sequences of some of the stage actors! A most innovative and astonishing theatrical experience!

On our last day in Prague, Quinones and I gave our flight tickets to our concierge for confirmation before leaving to visit other Prague historic sites, including the small apartment of Franz Kafka. When we returned in late afternoon, the concierge was troubled. "Something is wrong with your tickets, I couldn't confirm your flight. You must go immediately to the Cedok office."

We were directed to a shabby second-floor office, where a very determined lady stated, "You have no right to travel with those tickets to Hungary. Since you, Kaufman, live in Los Angeles and you, Quinones, live in Puerto Rico, you were not informed! The New York tour was canceled—not enough passengers."

However, we had KLM booklets with air tickets and hotel and meal vouchers, which we had paid for! I quickly replied "Madame, our visas *expire* tomorrow. We do not have the right to *remain* in Czechoslovakia!" Astonished and upset by the thought of unauthorized foreigners remaining in Prague, she conceded, "We'll let you go to Budapest." Our coupons paid for our hotel rooms.

We reached the airport early. The airplane for Budapest was announced and passengers' names were called out for boarding, but there was no mention of our trio. Quinones and I rushed to the control counter to protest, "Why weren't our names called?" The controller stated, "We did call your names, but you didn't appear" (not true). The shuttle bus for boarding the plane had just departed so another small bus was called for us, and finally we were en route for Budapest! This mix-up occurred at every airport until we left the Soviet Union! We always arrived early at each airport and could only board by protesting, "Our visas have expired," and off we would go! No socialist country wanted to be responsible for keeping American tourists with expired visas within their borders!

Budapest was fascinating. The Roman ruins and museum on the banks of the Danube was an unexpected experience. I was impressed by a Roman water-pressure organ, which suggested that their music was more complex than I had thought possible! We attended the excellent Budapest Opera every night. The singers, orchestra, and conductors were outstanding. One evening we heard an all-Bartók performance of *Bluebeard's Castle* paired with a chamber orchestra work.

Annette and I visited Miklós's aunt, whose spacious and elegant apartment near the opera house had been her home for sixty years; however, she now had to share it with others. She was confined to a medium-sized room crowded with her bed and handsome antique furniture. She served us pastries and tea with elegant china and silver. We looked at her countless photos of Miklós as a child, young student, and adult, with photos of Margaret and their son and daughter, obviously the precious center of her life. She asked me anxiously, "Is he happy?" I assured her that I thought he was happy in his work and life.

I called Miklós's friend Sebestéyn, who graciously chauffeured us to museums, churches, and picturesque sights. The Fine Art Museum had international scope—excellent French, Italian, and English masterly paintings, as well as unknown (to us) Hungarian artists. One Celtic museum was most impressive. It contained a large iron cart decorated with human and animal figures. It was obviously made for a Celtic chieftain, and made us realize the Celts occupied a great deal more of Europe than we had previously thought! Sebestéyn and I spoke of our mutual admiration for Rózsa's music, and I invited him to dine with us at an excellent restaurant. He interviewed me for the Hungarian radio (in English) and broadcast some of my recordings. He gave me some of his own harpsichord records.

One evening, after attending an opera, Annette and I dined in our hotel's elegant dining room that featured an excellent Gypsy orchestra—the violinists played beautifully. A young blond lad of about twelve entered from the pantry, and the fiddlers urged him to perform. There were very few diners present. He had not brought his violin, so he tried various violins offered by older colleagues, selected one, and began to play and direct the group. I was delighted by his mastery of the fiddle and lovely tone. The regular concertmaster walked by our table and I asked, "Is he your son?" "No. He's our chef's son and has his own Gypsy youth group." Both Annette and I thought the lad capable of a virtuoso career!

The next day we flew to Bucharest, which brought back many childhood memories. One surprise: streets that seemed *so* big to me, like the Calle Victoria, now seemed small. I had an adequate understanding of Romanian language from my childhood, but had forgotten some verbs and vocabulary. We had not seen Quinones in Budapest and were pleased to join him again for sightseeing. Our young attractive guides were inefficient and unreliable! A Romanian friend, composer Marcel Mihalovici, a resident of Paris, had recommended some excellent garden restaurants with Gypsy musical groups, which we liked. He highly recommended the elegant cuisine of the Grand Hotel, where he had dined as a child, so we dined there in style one evening.

A Romanian king had visited Spain before World War I and bought some remarkably fine El Greco paintings with almost Matisse-like color. They were an unexpected treasure among the works displayed in Bucharest's Art Museum, which also contained an unimpressive early student sculpture by Brancusi. I was disappointed that when we passed the Georges Enesco Concert Hall we were unable to see its interior. I visited a music store and bought Enesco's string octet, which I had played at a Kneisel chamber music class. It was written before Arnold Schoenberg's more conservative *Verklaerte Nacht* string sextet and had unusual harmonic and melodic qualities.

Our hotel had a terrace cafe, where we enjoyed breakfasts under the trees, with a few impudent birds hopping onto our table looking for crumbs. Bucharest has many large parks and small Romanesque churches that were kept locked so we could not see their interesting Byzantine interiors. Their outer walls were decorated with elongated, painted religious forms.

We entered a shop well stocked with foreign delicacies, wines, liquors, and chocolates. I bought two bottles of cognac and some chocolates for future use. Summer in Bucharest meant no concerts, operas, or theaters to enliven our evenings. Our irresponsible guides arranged a bus tour to Sinaia, a forested mountain region that was the site of a royal summer lodge. The residence was bizarrely decorated with copies of sites the royals had visited as tourists! Then we were herded into a small hotel that offered a miserable repast, which our trio refused to eat. What a dismal excursion! We would have been better served to remain in Bucharest visiting parks and fine cafes.

After our usual visa dispute at the airport we flew to mountainous Sofia. Our very comfortable hotel had an excellent cafe where we ate all meals, and our room overlooked the small city surrounded by mountains. All museums were closed either for holidays or restoration. We did attend a performance at the elegant small opera house and heard Bulgarian singers, orchestra, and conductor perform Verdi's *Rigoletto,* a politically correct opera for socialist countries! Our local guide accompanied us on a walking tour to point out a very flamboyant, costly modern cathedral, most uninteresting for Quinones and us!

We arrived in the Soviet Union rather late at night, presented our passports and visas, and cleared customs, declaring honestly that we were not bringing in any books (a dangerous thing which might harm the minds of their citizens?). Then we were deposited in a waiting taxi. After a long drive through unlit roads with a mute chauffeur, we arrived at Moscow's Metropol Hotel, where rooms had been booked for us by Intourist. Annette pinned the drapes together and we fell into bed for a good sleep. Next morning Annette and I ate breakfast in a large dining room where the service was extremely slow! As we were leaving we encountered an upset guide. "Where have you been? You shouldn't have eaten there. You are part of an English-speaking group and must eat with them in a special small section!" I replied, "I'm sorry, we were not informed on arrival, we are delighted to join the group!"

Our group consisted of ten people, mostly Californians; one Canadian from Toronto, Lloyd Singer, an artist, became a dear friend. He later visited us in Los Angeles and we visited him in Toronto. KLM's booklet provided us with four daily food coupons while in the Soviet Union. Since all repasts were copious we didn't use all of the coupons. When we dined, we ate in our Intourist section apart from other hotel guests. The food was always waiting on the table for our arrival. The *zakuskas* (hors d'oeuvres) in Moscow were always modest portions of delicious unsalted black caviar and unsalted smoked salmon, which we considered special treats. A few members of our group did not appreciate them or any "strange" food. Some would only consume ice cream. Annette and I traded our ice cream for their untouched caviar and salmon! The soups, vegetable and borscht, were hearty and excellent. Chicken Kiev (breast stuffed with butter) was a frequent item.

I called Schneerson and invited him to lunch with us (our guide arranged this with the kitchen), and I paid for his lunch with unused coupons. He proved to be a charming middle-aged man, who arrived with a chauffeur and private car. After lunch he drove us to visit the house of the Union of Composers; however, no composers were present. He gave me some printed music (obviously works of students) and told me, "Khachaturian is in hospital with a broken leg." I sent him a bottle of cognac via Schneerson with good wishes for a speedy recovery, but never heard from Khachaturian! The chauffeur, an agreeable lad, drove us back to the Metropol and I gave him some chocolate.

Our pleasant blond guide led us through Kremlin museums and churches, which displayed impressive large icons and golden religious and secular objects. I found the large coat and boots of Czar Peter the Great especially interesting. He was extremely tall. Saint Basil's Cathedral with its fantastic design and colorful turrets was closed. How we would have loved to see its interior!

The Soviet government and university buildings all appeared to have the same blocky style. At the university, we were ushered into cramped dormitories in which a few students were studying. The university's formal gardens resembled Le Nôtre's French gardens. I asked who had designed them, but our guide had no information about gardens.

One rainy morning we were compelled to visit Lenin's Tomb and felt embarrassed that our group was pushed ahead of a great line of waiting Russians and other tourists to enter a cold cavernous tomb (it felt like a refrigerated room) lined with armed guards. We passed single file by a coffin displaying a waxy, yellow-faced Lenin. Stalin's tomb had been removed from Red Square by then. I noticed against a Kremlin wall the tomb of American writer John Reed, a native of Portland, Oregon. After that dreary experience we were herded across the huge Red Square to enter GUM, a famed department store, very unimpressive. A few persons were lined up hoping to buy umbrellas! Our guide (from Leningrad) was well educated and had traveled in the west. She told us she shopped in Helsinki's fine stores or in London because Russian-made clothing and shoes were very inferior!

Intourist provided opera tickets for Mussorgsky's *Khovanshchina*. Lloyd, Quinones, and a few others joined us. We sat in a special Intourist section in the orchestra reserved for their tourists. We all were enthusiastic about the singers, orchestra, and conductor, but since we couldn't read the Russian program we never learned the performers' names! The next morning our guide provided a bus, which delivered us to a small plane that flew to Kiev. En route we were served small dishes of excellent fresh strawberries.

We were met by a local Kiev guide who deposited our group in a new hotel, which was very shabby; our group discussed how strange it was that new buildings were so poorly constructed. Kiev was a lovely provincial city. Our Moscow and Kiev guides jointly showed us some ancient churches and monasteries, where Saint Demetrius and Saint Gregory had entered Russia from Greece and taught the natives Greek rituals and alphabet. The Kiev guide forcefully explained that these saints never existed because their graves were empty! This distressed Quinones, but I assured him, "No one doubts today that Wolfgang Amadeus Mozart existed, although his burial site is unmarked and unknown!"

A nice-looking young man asked our guides if he might accompany our group and speak English with us, as his university urged students to speak English daily. He told me he loved John Synge's poetry, which he had only read in Polish translation. He wanted very much to read the poems in English. When Annette and I arrived in London we sent him paperback copies of the Irish poet. A year later he sent us a New Year's greeting; evidently he had received our gift.

Our guide mentioned the Babi Yar massacre, but we were not taken to the site where Nazis murdered Kiev's Jews. We found it strange that we never saw any other people; as our guides herded our group through socialist parks devoted to recreation and culture, we saw only rose bushes and peacocks! I did observe Quinones speaking with a Gypsy in a Kiev park. Later I again cautioned him to avoid such encounters, which could possibly endanger our trip.

We joined our guide, Quinones, and Lloyd at a so-called "folk opera," which turned out to be a raucous rock concert! Our Moscow guide translated one refrain as, "Love turns the world, not Copernicus!" We really felt we had only skimmed a small part of Kiev's charms. As we boarded the flight to Leningrad our Moscow guide said to me, "That Kiev guide is crazy—she refused to speak Russian with me—only spoke Ukrainian." That was a nuance we had not understood!

We approached Leningrad from the airport in a motorboat with large windows that gave us our first view of the wonderful Hermitage Palace and the Peter and Paul Fortress. The blue palaces with white trim had unique beauty. Czar Peter the Great had engaged two eighteenth-century Italian architects, Rossi and Rastrelli, to construct his imperial capital on the banks of the Neva. It is one of the world's most elegant cities. Entire blocks of streets are lined with noble Italianate palaces, theaters, and churches with a harmony rarely approached elsewhere. Czar Peter, who had worked as a ship builder in Holland, created a wonderful city on the Baltic, hoping it would surpass the beautiful cities in western Europe!

We were guided through the imposing, elegant Hermitage Palace and were dazzled by its sumptuous use of malachite for large tables, tall lamps, great urns, et cetera. Lloyd joined us in paying an extra fee to see a fabled gold collection locked in a special suite of rooms. The gold works were of Scythian, Greek, and Renaissance dynasties and consisted of gems, necklaces, bracelets, urns, vases, and animal and human forms. We recognized Rembrandts, Titians, and Leonardo da Vincis, but since the paintings bore Cyrillic labels which we could not read, we could not identify several works.

The next morning, Annette and I returned alone to visit the more modest third-floor galleries, reached by climbing a small staircase. There we admired impressive twentieth-century paintings from the Shchukin and Morosov collections and the masterpieces of Matisse, Gauguin, Picasso, and others, which had been closed to all viewers until recently. Joliot-Curie told me in Paris that even foreign communist intellectuals were not permitted to see them. The repressive regime thought these paintings would have a deleterious effect on all viewers!

The following day our guide arranged a bus to transport our group to see the recently restored Peterhof Summer Palace and resplendent gardens (German shelling had greatly damaged both). We could only view the elegant exterior and fountains and were not permitted to visit its interior. Our guide rushed us through the enchanting park, where I paused to take photos of the attractive sculptures and lovely floral gardens. Annette waited with me, and when we looked about for our group, they had vanished! We are used to finding our own way, so we returned to the bus to await their return. When the guide noticed we were missing, she became upset and hustled the group back to the bus, quite annoyed by our independent return.

Another day, we again visited via bus Tsarskoye Selo (the Tsar's Village, renamed Pushkin)—a fabulous palace built for Catherine the Great. It had suffered great damage from the German invasion, but the restoration had been meticulous. Scraps of fabric had been sent to Lyon, France, where the original window drapes and covers for furniture had been woven. The same Lyon factory made complete replicas; thus the handsome rooms were as elegantly furnished as when the palace was constructed! However, its famed amber room, stolen by the Germans, has not yet been found.

The nearby Palace and Park of Pavlovsk was designed by the Scotch architect Cameron. In front of this harmonious English-style palace were two large bronze Italianate figures of Hercules leaning on a giant club and Pomona holding a sheaf of fruits and vegetables. Our guide recounted how a rather naive tourist asked her, "I know the man is Pushkin, but who is the lady?"

Quinones joined us in attending Verdi's *La Traviata* at the Kirov Opera. We sat in handsome individual armchairs covered in blue velvet. We were inspired to think that the great composers Rimsky-Korsakov, Borodin, Tchaikovsky, and Rachmaninoff might have sat in these same chairs to hear their compositions premiered. However, we were soon bored by a very poor performance. I presumed the regular singers were on holiday or touring. The soprano sang so out of tune that I suggested to Quinones that we leave. This was during the "White Nights," when daylight remained until almost midnight. We walked out after the first act, heading in the direction of a handsome Rastrelli church. We passed a few drunken men lying on park benches. We entered the lovely small church, and were surprised there was no flooring, only a hard dirt surface. It was almost filled by old women with scarves tied around their heads. Some were kneeling to kiss the dirt floor under the icons. Quinones, very disturbed by this, murmured, "The authorities shouldn't permit this, it's very unsanitary." I replied, "Quinones, their lives seem very unhappy—perhaps being here gives them comfort." We strolled back to our hotel at a leisurely pace, encountering very few people in the streets. We entered a cafe section to have a cup of tea and sat at a table with two pleasant Japanese men, who offered us their business cards printed in Cyrillic.

The next evening before our group went our separate ways, we all attended a very fine performance of Borodin's opera *Prince Igor*. Our farewell luncheon with Lloyd Singer and Quinones was at a grand hotel, where the Nazis had planned to celebrate their victory over the Soviet Union! Lloyd stated, "I'd like to return in ten years to see what changes have taken place." Quinones and I were not certain changes were about to occur and I added, "As the French say, there's always the *imprévu* that occurs!"

We said our farewells. Quinones flew to Helsinki with us, where we returned to the normal world of parks filled with young lovers, nurses with baby carriages, and older people relaxing on benches. We dined with Quinones, rejoicing that we had completed our "canceled" trip and remembering the pleasures of our joint sightseeing. Quinones was flying to Poland for the one-thousandth anniversary of the Catholic Church, and our morning flight would take us to Amsterdam for concerts and to enjoy great artists of the Netherlands.

We said our farewells as we parted at our adjoining rooms. What a pleasure to have window curtains that closed and stoppers in the sink and bathtub!

Early the next morning I answered a rap on our door and was astonished to see our friend Quinones, wearing a priest's collar and coat, his official hat in one hand. He explained, "I wondered all night if I should tell you who I am. I like you both very much and would like to see you again. I am Archbishop of Puerto Rico and I was traveling to observe church life." In a flash, I realized his strange encounters with people and in parades were a way to speak with disguised religious colleagues! He continued, "I couldn't have succeeded without you. I could not wear a disguised head covering so my valise only contained my priestly collar, hat, and coat. If I had been questioned, I would have proclaimed my identity. But thanks to your ingenuity in making our trip succeed, I accomplished my mission." I replied, "Monsignor, anytime you wish to travel incognito, do not hesitate to call us. It was an honor and privilege to be in your company." We exchanged addresses and for many years we sent each other Christmas and New Year greetings.

Annette's dear mother spent the last nine years of her life with us and often remarked they were among the happiest years of her life. We both were deeply grieved by her final illness in September 1967. Many friends joined us in mourning our great loss. The only sadness of growing older is that we are deprived of so many dear family members and friends.

# 35

# Recordings at Last— the Lebduska Mystery

In the summer of 1971 Yaltah Menuhin introduced us to Giveon Corn-field, owner of Orion Records, and his wife, Marion. Giveon had collected my recordings for many years, and he asked, "What could you record for me?" For thirty years all the record companies to whom I had proposed the music of William Grant Still had insisted that Still's music would not sell, but Giveon was delighted. Still attended all the recording sessions and contributed helpful suggestions. We recorded his Suite for violin and piano, *Pastorela*, "Blues," *Here's One*, *Ennanga* (an African word for harp) for violin, piano, and harp, and *Summerland* and *Danzas de Panama* for string quartet. The French mezzo-soprano Claudine Carlson, a close friend, recorded Still's *Songs of Separation*.

These recordings were issued on two LP records with the joint support of Dr. Robert Bartlett Haas and Mrs. Joan Palevsky. These two sponsors were also patrons of an anthology edited by Dr. Haas, *William Grant Still and the Fusion of Cultures in American Music*. Dr. Haas had asked us to introduce him to Still in order to propose this project, and Verna and Billy were willing and able collaborators. Annette and I contributed an essay about the violin works, and Black Sparrow Press published the book in 1972.

One early evening during 1972, I received an unexpected telephone call from New York from Mrs. Elizabeth Fehr, who asked, "Are you the Louis Kaufman who bought several Lebduska paintings in the 1930s?" "Yes, I am." She continued, "I was a close friend of Lebduska during his last years and I promised him I would write a book about his life and art. He

352

Lawrence Lebduska and his painting *Circus Horses*.

spoke warmly of your generous help. Do you still have those paintings?"
"Yes, although my wife and I gave four Lebduska paintings in 1964 to
Reed College in Portland, Oregon, in memory of my father and mother."
Mrs. Fehr said, "Paul Anbinder of Rockefeller Press is interested in pub-
lishing my Lebduska book. Would you please send me photographs of
your Lebduskas?" I agreed and Mrs. Fehr gave me her address.

After receiving my photos, she called again, enthusiastically stating,
"Mr. Kaufman, your Lebduskas are the finest I've ever seen! A friend of
mine, Mrs. Julia Weissman, thinks so also. She is here with me and
wishes to speak with you."

Mrs. Weissman explained, "I'm writing a book with Herbert Hemphill, an important collector of naive American art works and painters, to
be published by Dutton. May I have permission to reproduce two of
your Lebduskas in that book?" "Yes, indeed, which paintings have you

selected?" "I've chosen *A Collector* [that was my portrait], and an Oriental scene, *The Land of Pease.*" (Lebduska meant "peace.")

Julia, a passionate devotee of American folk art, soon became a good friend. Her book with Herbert Hemphill, *Twentieth Century American Folk Art and Artists,* was published handsomely by Dutton in 1974 and the edition quickly sold out! Mrs. Fehr sent me a gift—a very handsome colored lithograph she had produced from a Lebduska floral painting.

I heard from Sally Avery that Anbinder was interested in publishing an Avery book by Hilton Kramer for Rockefeller Press. His secretary wrote to me requesting photographs of several of our Avery paintings. Alas Anbinder then left the press and both the Avery and Lebduska book projects abruptly ended. Mrs. Fehr called again, proposing we try for a university exhibit of Lebduska's work with an illustrated catalogue and text by Julia Weissman, for she had prepared a resume of Lebduska's life and work. This would fulfill Mrs. Fehr's promised pledge to the late Lebduska.

I discussed this with Dr. Robert Bartlett Haas at UCLA, who had helped us with the Korngold memorial concert. He thought UCLA might sponsor a Lebduska exhibit and that he might be able to find a sponsor to provide funds for a catalogue. Bob was to lecture in Stockton, California, and Mrs. Fehr was to speak to a therapy group in Santa Cruz, not too far away. They met in Santa Cruz. We were en route!

Bob returned to Los Angeles and reported that Mrs. Fehr was a practitioner of primal scream therapy, based on the premise that birth is very painful to the newborn and causes later mental problems. Her cure advised patients to crawl on the floor and scream loudly. She had a group of patients in New York who were unhappy in America's troubled environment and wanted to emigrate as a colony. She was en route to select a suitable site in Venezuela. She entrusted Bob with a large leather portfolio containing colored photos of all the Lebduska paintings she had located, with names and addresses of their owners. Her farewell had been, "I fervently hope you will carry through with a Lebduska exhibit at UCLA and produce a catalogue!" Bob gave us the portfolio for safekeeping, and we still have it in a closet.

A few weeks later, our devoted New York friend Mrs. Terese Schwarz Milbauer sent us a brief *New York Times* obituary reporting that Mrs. Elizabeth Fehr had died from a mysterious ailment acquired on a recent South American voyage. A letter arrived shortly after this with a strange return address, "Forget Me Not Shop" (the boutique's owner? or an employee?), announcing, "I am Mrs. Fehr's heir." Terese checked this and discovered he was a group member, not an heir. Mrs. Fehr had one child, a daughter, who was also a primal scream practitioner. We wrote to ask her what we should do with Mrs. Fehr's case, which Bob had left with us since he was planning to leave UCLA (he now lives in Germany). Her answer came two years later, 16 April 1976:

> Dear Louis and Annette Kaufman,
> I have been involved in a dozen or more projects and simply did not have the time to put any thought into the Lebduska book. I have not forgot about it but simply have been delaying any decision or correspondence till work and legal matters were reduced. I definitely think it would be desirable for Dr. Haas to work on the manuscript provided that a legal contract is drawn up specifying the provisions of such a partnership. I will then be glad to send everything I have on Lebduska to you or Dr. Haas. Hope all is well with you.
>     Leslie Fehr Ferney

Julia Weissman came to see us in Los Angeles and reported that there was really no Lebduska text, just some rough notes! We have since visited with Julia in New York and San Diego to see museums and galleries and share fine cuisine. We both still hope to help establish Lebduska's reputation.

Sometime later, I received a call from a charming couple, Mr. and Mrs. Richard Dennis, who were en route from New York to Honolulu. Dennis, a young architect, and his attractive wife had been members of Mrs. Fehr's group. I invited them to dinner and we enjoyed meeting them. I had performed with the Honolulu Symphony three times and Annette and I had played recitals four times at the Honolulu Academy, so we had many friends there. I gave them several addresses, including that of Val Ossipoff, the architect we had met there, as I knew they would be compatible. Dennis informed us, "There has been a great disagreement in the group founded by Elizabeth Fehr. We know you are trustworthy; you have kept your Lebduskas! We have brought you several Lebduska drawings which belonged to the group, as we do not want to take them to Honolulu, so we want to consign them to your care." I replied, "We'll keep them for you until you decide what you wish to do with them." They briefly corresponded with us after they settled in Honolulu.

En route to Tahiti in 1974 Annette and I performed an all-Beethoven concert at the University of Hawaii. We tried to call Richard Dennis, and learned they had departed without leaving a forwarding address. Just disappeared! Undoubtedly searching for the ideal unspoiled area in the vast South Pacific. We still are guardians of Lebduska's paintings and hold in trust Mrs. Fehr's portfolio (her daughter did not want it) and the group's drawings until we can create interest in a Lebduska retrospective exhibit and book.

# 36

# Cousin Mico Kaufman, Sculptor

In autumn 1972, an unexpected letter arrived from Mico Kaufman, stating he had been born in Buzaŭ, Romania, the son of Herman Kaufman, my father's brother. After miserable experiences in Nazi labor camps during the Second World War, Mico left Romania to escape military service in the Russian Army on the last train possible, which was totally packed with people on top and under train carriages, fleeing to freedom. A few border guards could not stop this mob! With aid from Jewish charitable organizations he reached Rome. Hoping to become a sculptor, he passed entrance tests, won a scholarship, and studied for five years in that inspiring city. Mico then studied two years in Florence, where he fell in love with a Greek Jewish science teacher. After their marriage they sailed for America, with the help of a Jewish agency, and reached Boston. He eventually obtained work as a medalist there, earning a distinguished reputation creating elegant medallions of American historical, literary, musical, and political personalities. He was chosen to make the official presidential medallions for Presidents Reagan and Bush.

Mico knew he had an Uncle Isaac who immigrated to America and whose son Louis was a violinist. He tried unsuccessfully to locate me until a musician in Tewksbury, Massachusetts, where he had bought a home, suggested, "Write to the Musicians Federation in New York for information." In the letter Mico gave his telephone number. I said to Annette, "Of course he's my cousin. I remember going to my Uncle Herman's wedding in Buzaŭ when I was seven."

I phoned Mico and said, "I'm definitely your cousin, come visit us." He replied, "Louis, I am doing well, I don't want to ask you for help—I just want to have some family here!" He flew to Los Angeles a short time later and we had a wonderful time together. Annette and I drove him to

Pasadena to see the splendid Norton Simon and Huntington Art Museums, the Los Angeles Museum, and the Getty Museum in Malibu. Mico, surprised by our great interest in art, stated, "My Boston friends will find it surprising to know what I did in Los Angeles!" Greatly impressed by our collection, he said, "Louis, you know more about art than I do!" He brought us a present, a small wax-model portrait he had made of Arthur Fiedler, and gave us some of his handsome medallions.

I arranged a brunch in Encino with some cousins from Portland, Rose Kaufman and her handsome son Arnold Semler, with Blessing, his wife. Rose had known me from birth; my parents had stayed with her parents, Avram and Rebecca Kaufman, when they arrived in Portland. It was a jolly reunion.

We visited Mico in Tewksbury and we enjoyed seeing the Fogg Museum in Cambridge together. Annette and I had visited the great Winthrop collection of Chinese art at his New York home; Winthrop had graciously also shown us his important collection of Pre-Raphaelite paintings. He bequeathed this great collection to Harvard. We were delighted to show Mico the handsome installation of Winthrop's marvelous Chinese sculptures in Cambridge's new Sackler Gallery. Mico's studies in the Mediterranean world had not prepared him for the elegance and grace of China. He was delighted to experience this previously unknown world of art.

Mico drove us to see some of his large statues. In nearby Lowell he had created a remarkable large statue of young female mill workers. In Tewksbury he had sculpted a splendid fountain of Helen Keller and her teacher, Anne Sullivan (who once lived in the town), who holds Helen's hands in the water, representing the first word she learned. The Japanese, who are intensely interested in Helen Keller, sent a television crew to make a film about that statue. Mico also made a life-sized statue of Saint Joseph for a Catholic church in Lowell. His large statue of Claude Debussy, depicting on its base scenes from *Prelude de l'après midi d'un faune* and *Pélleas et Mélisande,* is on the campus of the University of Massachusetts–Lowell. The French government has allocated a small plot in front of Debussy's birthplace in Saint-Germain-en-Laye for this important memorial to the great composer. When the statue is unveiled Annette and I hope to attend the ceremony. (*Ed. note:* Annette, accompanied by Jacqueline Hélion, attended the unveiling ceremony in November 2000.)

In 1978 we met Mico in Paris and visited the Louvre and Musée Rodin together. Annette and I are indefatigable walkers, and Mico, not accustomed to so much walking, was quite exhausted. We introduced him to our Romanian friends, painters Alexandre Istrati and his lovely

Annette, Mico, and Louis in the Louvre, Paris, 1990.

Louis and Annette at Oberlin College after receiving Honorary Doctorates in 1985.

wife, Natalie Dimitresco, who were devoted friends and helpers of Constantin Brancusi. They lived in Brancusi's home near the Gare Montparnassse, which Mico found fascinating (the Istratis donated his studio and contents to the Musée Beaubourg). Mico was interested in learning about casting bronzes in Paris, and they gave him excellent information. Then we all walked to a nearby Algerian restaurant that served us a delicious couscous with lamb, chicken, sausages, vegetables, and chick peas, a new gastronomic experience for Mico. Alexandre had a brother, a doctor, still in Romania; Istrati bought him a car and sent him food. Evidently the Russians took all the rich Romanian agricultural produce, and Romanians found life terribly difficult; both food and heat were rationed in winter.

Mico came to Oberlin when Annette and I were awarded Honorary Musical Doctorates. It was an impressive ceremony—the commencement address was by William Goldman, author of many books and screenplays. We were with a very distinguished international group awarded Honorary Degrees: two Doctorates of Humane Letters, for Czech author Miroslav Holub and Russian poet Andrei Voznesensky, and Doctorate of Fine Arts for Madeleine Hours of the Louvre Museum. It was heartwarming to receive congratulations from my friend William Duncan Allen after the ceremony. Another friend, Dr. Theodore Bloomfield, along with Dr. Holub and Madeleine Hours, joined us for a delicious luncheon served under umbrellas in a lovely garden.

We visited the fine Oberlin Art Collection with Mico, and introduced him to Kirby Talley, its director. Annette and I gave a lovely Eilshemius seascape to the gallery. We then had a farewell lunch at the Oberlin Inn with Mico and our conductor friend from nearby Erie, Dr. James Sample, before Mico flew back to Boston. Our farewell dinner at the Oberlin Inn was with our friends John and Susan Harvith, who wrote a fine book, *Edison, Musicians, and the Phonograph,* and our good friends Grace and Howard Mims, who drove in a pelting rain from Cleveland to join us. In 1988 Annette and I donated our large collection of violin solos, sonatas, concertos, and chamber music to the Oberlin Conservatory of Music Library.

Annette found it fascinating that Mico and I resembled each other so much in appearance, mental attitudes, and habits of work, and that we both tried to do our best in whatever we did in our respective fields. Although my late brothers undoubtedly had the same Kaufman-Adler genes, we did not resemble each other physically nor share ideas of what is important in life. Mico and I, although born and raised worlds apart, shared similar views about the importance of art and how to make the best contribution to society that we possibly could.

# 37

## *The Dybbuk*—a Devil to Produce

An early morning call in 1972 from David Tamkin, to wish me well when I was in the hospital (for hernia repair caused by overdoing pushups), made me apprehensive. In spite of his attempt to cheer me, his despairing conversation about his unhappy life and the neglect of his operas caused me to worry about his future. We had not seen each other for some time.

When Annette arrived to spend the day with me, I said, "We must do something for David and his opera to raise his spirits." *The Dybbuk* was completed in fall of 1931 with a libretto by David's brother, Alex, based on S. Ansky's play. In 1949 David made a concert version of his opera for tenor and orchestra, which his friend Jan Pearce premiered with the Portland Symphony Orchestra, conducted by Werner Janssen. Pearce managed to interest Leopold Godowsky, Leopold Stokowski, and Artur Bodanzky in David's opera. Bodanzky promised to perform it with Pearce at the Metropolitan Opera but unexpectedly died. Stokowski's and Godowsky's enthusiasm for the work eventually influenced Laszlo Halasz twenty years later to produce it for the New York City Opera. Annette and I attended that thrilling performance in New York on our way to South America.

A few days after David's call, after my return home, Judge Gus J. Solomon called. He was on some routine federal cases in Los Angeles, and I invited him and his wife, Libby, to dinner. Over dinner we discussed David's unhappy state and we decided to form a *Dybbuk* committee. We could produce a record from a tape David had of the world premiere performance (Alex Tamkin's libretto) by the New York City Opera on

David Tamkin, 1972. Photograph by Louis Kaufman.

4 October 1951 that had been broadcast by Voice of America for overseas listeners only! This splendid performance, conducted by Joseph Rosenstock, had excellent singers: Robert Rounseville, tenor, as Channon; Patricia Neway, soprano, as Leah; Mack Harrell's noble baritone as Rabbi Azrael; and the impressive African American bass-baritone Lawrence Winters as the Messenger.

I asked Miklós Rózsa to be honorary chairman of the committee, which he willingly accepted, and my dear opera-loving friend Milah Russin Wermer to be co-chairperson. Our steering committee was composed of Irving and Jean Stone, Mrs. Marta Feuchtwanger, Dr. Paul and Milah Wermer, Nicolas Slonimsky, Oscar and Vita Tannenbaum, Rabbi and Mrs. Henry Fisher, and Annette and me. Judge Solomon could not participate actively, but he helped Annette (our secretary-treasurer) write letters to the New York City Opera and American Federation of Musicians for permission to issue a noncommercial record. Marta Feuchtwanger, our distinguished friend and sponsor, suggested this necessary condition. Knowing the perilous state of Tamkin's health (David had heart failure), both organizations gave us permission to privately print a limited quantity of LP records. Jean Stone, an active sponsor, suggested we donate them to members, sponsors, opera companies, and musical institutions.

We decided to request one hundred dollars for a sponsoring membership, which would entitle members to an LP copy autographed by the composer, with a libretto listing the cast, plus an additional LP of the Ben-Gurion speech "What Is a Jew," produced by Giveon and Marion Cornfield (owners of Orion Records). They could not find buyers for it at that time and offered it to us gratis! The committee chose an identifying label, Phoenix IX, since it was a resurrection of a historic performance. David informed us that nine was a significant number in the Kabbala, the mystical ancient Hebrew text that influenced many artists. Basic membership was fifty dollars and included an unautographed *Dybbuk* LP and libretto.

Milah and I sent soliciting letters to David's friends and ours. Annette quickly received about three thousand dollars from sponsors and members. The Cornfields contributed their services by producing an attractive LP package. The total production costs including mailing came to approximately $2,500. Annette asked Gus if she should return the remaining funds to subscribers and he advised, "Keep it for further *Dybbuk* use—stationery and postage."

Rabbi Fisher provided names and addresses of Jewish educational institutions in America and Milah was a source for opera personnel. She sent a copy to *Opera News* in New York, which resulted in a fine review of this private recording. Since the reviewer mentioned our address, we gained a few additional members. David Tamkin became happily busy helping Annette package and mail records to opera lovers and Jewish educational institutions. Two opera enthusiasts helped promote the recording: Carl Princi, a radio broadcaster of classical music, played the *Dybbuk* to a wide audience, and Fred Hyatt of KPFK not only broadcast our LP on David's birthday, but interviewed David and Paul and Milah Wermer, and later broadcast interviews with Annette and me on anniversaries of David's death. Fred has never lost his affection for David's *Dybbuk* and the world of opera, which he devotedly supports. Fred and his wife, Betty, became close friends.

Martin Sokol, after reading *Opera News,* requested a review copy, which we promptly sent him. He wrote a two-page article about the dybbuk in music—mentioning an Italian opera, *Il Dibbuk* by Lodovico Rocca, and Leonard Bernstein's *The Dybbuk* ballet. Sokol stated that Tamkin's opera, a musical drama, was "the most successful version"! Later Sokol wrote a comprehensive opera history, *The New York City Opera: An American Adventure,* published in 1981 by Macmillan, New York/London. This contained a fascinating chapter, *The Dybbuk and the Devil to Pay,* which related the entire history of the premiere of this successful opera and the subsequent debacle of Laszlo Halasz's career. Halasz was both dynamic and innovative. He eliminated prompters at City Opera and selected young attractive singers to create dramatic roles. During the 1951 season, he premiered four remarkable fresh and unfamiliar operas— Prokofiev's *Love of Three Oranges,* Wolf-Ferrari's *The Four Rustics,* William Grant Still's *Troubled Island,* and David Tamkin's *The Dybbuk*—in spite of the governing board's reservations and disapproval. According to board member Jean Dalrymple's book, *From the Last Row,* when the board refused to fund Tamkin's opera, an infuriated Halasz obtained funds and support (approximately $25,000) from Frederick F. Umbrey of the International Ladies' Garment Workers Union and Jacob S. Potofsky of the Amalgamated Clothing Workers of America, which enabled him to produce David's brilliant work. Dalrymple concluded that Tamkin's *Dybbuk* was "the biggest success and best money-maker the opera ever had." All five performances were sold out. Undoubtedly the garment workers were part of the wildly cheering audiences! Halasz ended his season triumphantly with $80,000 profit!

Then this macho Hungarian was accused of using autocratic methods in running the City Opera, bad manners, foul language, unjust methods of casting, politicizing opera (he programmed a Russian opera, an African American opera, and a Jewish opera), and throwing a baton at an orchestral player in Chicago! Without permitting him to answer these allegations in person, the governing board dismissed Halasz while Jean Dalrymple was in Europe. Two outstanding board members, Lincoln Kirstein (renowned dance authority and founder of the New York City Ballet) and my cellist colleague Gerald Warburg, resigned in protest at this injustice, believing Halasz should have been permitted to answer any complaints—especially after a season that was hailed as a series of artistic and financial triumphs, unheard of in the expensive world of opera! The rest is history. Anything concerning Halasz became taboo at City Opera and remains so to the present. Fortunately for City Opera, Leonard Bernstein and later Julius Rudel arrived to revitalize this remarkable opera company. David became very embittered by this contretemps, although his own rather difficult nature was responsible for impeding other performances in America and Europe. Also, he lacked both sponsors and funds. So he returned to orchestrating film scores for Hollywood.

While Annette and I vacationed in Europe, David Tamkin died on 22 June 1975. He was born in Russia on 26 August 1906 and his family emigrated to Portland, Oregon on 1 January 1907. We both were violin students of Henry Bettman, a pupil of Eugène Ysaÿe. Later he told us, "I changed to viola for I sounded like a snake on fiddle." His composition studies were with Francis Richter, Ernest Bloch, and for a brief time with Maurice Ravel. Tamkin composed chamber music and several symphonic and choral works. He orchestrated the charming *Children's Suite* of his neighbor, composer Joseph Achron. In 1962 David composed a three-act American folklore opera, *The Blue Plum Tree of Esau*, based on an original story and libretto by his brother, Alex, that has not yet been performed.

Vita Tannenbaum arranged a memorial service at a West Los Angeles synagogue. Many *Dybbuk* sponsors and members attended. Alex Tamkin and his wife, Sloan, came from New York. Judge Gus Solomon spoke movingly of our association from early childhood in Portland. Alex, who wrote both librettos for David's operas, tenderly spoke of their collaboration, mutual respect, and brotherly love. Dimitri Tiomkin sent a message from London, I said a few words about our lifelong friendship, and Annette read a letter from Miklós Rózsa sent from Italy:

> David Tamkin was a remarkable man. Remarkable not only for his creative talent and musical knowledge, but also for his artistic and personal integrity and for his loyalty to his friends. He had a tragic life. He was destined to become a great composer but unable to make a living he had to become a musical artisan in the Studios. He had to submit himself to their cheap commercialization and work with countless amateurs, whose music he had to patch up and make palatable. He did it without a grudge he was paid for it. He suffered from the indignities the Hollywood Studios can offer to serious artists, but his soul and his high artistic ideals remained untouched. He composed *The Dybbuk* as a young man and it was an outburst of youthful enthusiasm and energy, as Mascagni's *Cavalleria* and Leoncavallo's *Pagliacci*. But when these two operas were produced their young composers became immediately internationally known,

whereas David had to wait twenty years until his opera played in New York. It was a success, but for him it was too late. He went on with his work in the studios, more embittered than ever and his deep frustration must have been the cause of the malady that finally killed him. A great man passed away. With one great achievement and as Franz Grillparzer said at Schubert's funeral, "With ever greater hopes." We who loved him and were his friends, should consider ourselves lucky that our paths have crossed with such a noble spirit, who left one masterpiece for the world, which will perpetuate his name in the world of opera forever.

Miklós Rózsa

Santa Margarita Ligure

Rabbi Fisher closed the service eloquently, speaking about David and his *Dybbuk*, stating, "*Dybbuk* is a Greek term referring to an unsatisfied spirit that roams the universe seeking rest and solace for its unhappy life on this planet."

Shortly after this sad event, the *Dybbuk* committee and Alex Tamkin collaborated with publisher Boosey and Hawkes to produce a badly needed *Dybbuk* piano-vocal score—the conductor's score and all orchestral and vocal materials were and are available on rental. Then, with David's widow's permission, I gave all of David's musical creations to the Moldenhauer Archives in Spokane, Washington. Dr. Hans Moldenhauer and his wife, Rosaleen, established a music school in Spokane, where I had performed with Annette in the 1940s. He was an old friend of Heinrich Krotoschin, whom he had met while mountain climbing in Switzerland. Knowing of his musical archive and his book about Anton Webern (written with Rosaleen's aid and published by Gollancz/London), I presumed Moldenhauer would properly care for Tamkin's musical legacy. Harvard University Music Library later acquired most of the Moldenhauer Archive, including Tamkin's music.

In spite of all our efforts, it was not possible for our committee to obtain another opera performance. Milah did persuade Mehli Mehta to perform the *Dybbuk Suite* for tenor and orchestra, which was enthusiastically performed at Royce Hall in Los Angeles on 29 April 1984 with lyric tenor Joseph Gole, and well reviewed by the local press. Alex and Sloan again journeyed to Los Angeles to attend this performance. Our committee assisted by paying rental fees to Boosey and Hawkes.

In 1988, Bert Wechsler, a New York music critic, mentioned our *Dybbuk* private recording in a fascinating article he wrote about recorded American operas for *Opera News*. We were extremely pleased at this unexpected attention and invited Wechsler to join our committee. This gave us another opportunity to attract a new generation of opera producers.

Louis with Darius and Madeleine Milhaud in Florence, 1972. Photograph by Annette Kaufman.

"Hope springs eternal"—so we still await the time the musical world will eventually see and hear again Tamkin's *Dybbuk*!

We continued to visit Darius and Madeleine Milhaud in various parts of Europe and America over the years. One summer afternoon we arrived in Florence and noticed a poster announcing that Maggio Fiorentino was presenting that same evening Milhaud's *Minute Operas* (three delightfully

Annette and Louis at the University of Southern California concert given for William Grant Still's seventy-fifth birthday, 1975.

witty versions of Greek mythology) and Sauguet's *La Voyante* (The Clairvoyant) at the Teatro Municipale. Our hotel concierge managed to obtain excellent seats and we enjoyed the performance immensely. The next day we had a celebratory lunch with the Milhauds and took photos of this happy occasion.

After Milhaud's death in 1974, we flew to San Francisco to attend an all-Milhaud concert at Mills College. This event was the official dedication of the Milhaud Archive at Mills. Madeleine made an unforgettable speech, conveying the appreciation the Milhauds had for this secure haven of joy and happiness while working with colleagues and students.

In May 1975, our dear friend Dr. Paul Wermer, as president of USC's Friends of Music, arranged a celebration banquet and concert on campus to honor the seventy-fifth birthday of our old friend William Grant Still. About two hundred and fifty people attended, including Dr. Howard Hanson (Dean of the Eastman School of Music, who had conducted the premiere of Still's *Afro-American Symphony* in 1930), and who traveled from Rochester, New York, to pay tribute to Still. I performed his *Pastorela*, with Annette's accompaniment, and a college choir beautifully sang his arrangements of Negro spirituals. Dr. Wermer announced that the dinner's proceeds would be used to establish a William Grant Still Scholarship. Our friendship with the Stills ended only with their respective deaths, but endures with their daughter Judith Anne, who is devoted to writing and speaking about her father's life and work, publishing his music, and arranging performances and recordings of his compositions.

# 38

## From Sicily to Tahiti

In spring 1974 during a New York visit with Milton and Sally Avery, March (now an accomplished painter and sculptor) and her English professor husband, Philip Cavanaugh (a gifted photographer), were so enthusiastic about their recent trip to Sicily that I immediately decided to take the *giro* (a self-scheduled tour of the islands) as soon as possible. Adelyn Breeskin was there and offered, "I hear it's very dangerous and think you should reconsider." However, Philip insisted it was very safe and we should not worry.

We flew directly from Los Angeles to Rome, changed airplanes, and arrived in Palermo in early afternoon. A taxi drove us in brilliant sunshine to the outskirts of this ancient city with Roman and Norman walls, to the elegant Albergo Igea facing the blue Mediterranean Sea. Its art nouveau decor was unchanged from the days when European royalty and composer Richard Wagner vacationed there.

The dining salon, open on three sides to a flowering garden, provided a most delicious dinner. An ancient small round Greek temple, dedicated to the goddess of health, Igea (or Hygieia), overlooked the hotel and the calm sea.

At breakfast early the next morning, I was surprised by blood-red orange juice—a Sicilian specialty, which I presumed was tomato juice until I drank some. Then we set off via streetcar to visit Monreale, a hilltop Byzantine church with colorful twisted pilasters in mosaic surrounding the ancient cloister. Inside, fabulous golden mosaic-decorated walls related scenes from the Old and New Testaments, and in a central cupola was an imposing *Pankrator* (a Byzantine depiction of Christ).

Seeing a few taxis in a nearby small plaza, I hailed one to take us to the art museum, which displayed a famed group of metopes (carved friezes) from nearby Greek temples. The paintings were local in flavor. An anonymous painter had created an imposing memento mori depicting a skeleton astride a huge white horse, and there were some fascinating paintings in Spanish style. The museum has a splendid head of the Virgin by Antonello da Messina, who is reputed to have brought oil painting from the Netherlands to Italy. We also visited the Norman Cathedral, which contained an imposing tomb of King Roger, and the Norman Palazzo, with great early mosaics. Palermo has a famous ornate nineteenth-century opera house. How we regretted not to have heard a performance!

The *giro* tours offered stops of a few days, and if one wished to stay longer at any site, one could latch on to the next tour. We set off for Syracuse and en route admired an isolated Greek temple of Selinunte, situated on a hilltop facing the sea (as do all Greek temples). The next stop was Agrigento, which has remains of huge Greek temples dedicated to Hercules and to Hera, who has a wonderful temple near the sea. We arrived at sunset as the sun's rays transformed the stones into a golden glory.

Early the next morning our bus proceeded inland to Piazza Armerina, where second-century Romans had built a huge hunting lodge. The remaining floors, all in colorful Roman mosaics, are surrounded by a visitors ramp. The intricate mosaics depict scenes of hunting, fishing, domestic activities, and even bikini-clad young ladies.

Syracuse, on the coast, has a huge marble quarry, and a gigantic cave where Athenians were enslaved and imprisoned in arduous toil after their invasion failed. On the reverse side, facing the sea, they had carved out a complete arena with rows of marble seats and a stage area from one continuous slab of marble. Greek dramas were played in Syracuse immediately after being presented in Athens. Only Greek or Roman plays are permitted—no rock concerts! This is considered hallowed ground. There are remarkable baroque churches in Syracuse; one is constructed around a Greek temple, so one sees the original Greek pillars embedded in the walls.

We fell in love with mountainous Taormina, which provided a view of Mount Etna from a comfortable distance, since the volcano erupted dramatically during our visit. We viewed its rivers of flame and lava from our pleasant modern hotel veranda. It was most enjoyable to roam through the small picturesque village with small shops, bars, cafes, and flowering gardens of hillside cottages. It reminded me of Capri. An ideally situated Roman theater, where concerts and plays are still presented with a backdrop view of the sea and facing Mount Etna, made us wish we could have heard an opera or play there.

The *giro* offered a visit to the volcano, which we declined. Instead we spent the day taking a local bus to visit nearby Messina's cathedral, greatly damaged by a 1783 earthquake but with a gaily painted ceiling reminiscent of local colorfully decorated wooden carts. The museum's courtyard had an impressive, large golden-hued marble statue of a standing Poseidon, unfortunately damaged by the earthquake. On each side of this noble figure writhing statues represented Charybdis and Scylla, originally created by Michelangelo's pupil Montorsoli. This modern replica of Montorsoli's masterpiece is in the plaza in front of the cathedral, which faces the sea.

The museum also featured a large triptych by Antonello da Messina and fragments of statues by a great local Renaissance sculptor, Serpotta, which had been rescued from the earthquake-damaged cathedral.

Early the next morning the bus left Taormina. The only passengers were ourselves and a most congenial Dutch couple, Fersen and Babs Brikkenaar Van Dyk. In a few moments we discovered we shared interests in music and art. We invited them to dine with us at Villa d'Igea and we became devoted friends. We later visited them at their home in Bussum, in the Netherlands, and grew to know and love their son and daughter. They all visited us later in Los Angeles.

Palermo's airport was chaotic before boarding the return flight to Rome. Families brought heavy food packages for traveling members, crying and embracing each other as if their loved ones were going to the ends of the earth (maybe they were), running into the plane for a last kiss and hug—it was like a film! Finally the crew managed to clear out the invading Sicilian siblings and mamas, and we departed for Rome.

I had booked a room at Rome's Eliseo Hotel, recommended by an Italian friend. Full pension was required. We always enjoyed delicious food in Italian hotels, so were unprepared for a very inferior dinner, served on the covered rooftop. This was the only time we ever encountered mediocre cuisine in Italy. Not wishing to offend the waiter, we conversed in French. As we waited for the elevator a distinguished white-haired couple approached and after a long wait the man stated (in French), "Even the elevator doesn't work here!" Finally the elevator arrived, and as we descended, the gentleman introduced himself as Pierre Artur, editor of a newspaper in Rennes. Annette offered, "We lived in Paris; my husband is a violinist and he played a Vivaldi concert with Aimée van der Wiele, a harpsichordist from Rennes. We also met a flute player from Rennes in South America." Artur replied, "I have a daughter Thérèse who plays violin." Annette said, "This is extraordinary, we have met your daughter Thérèse, at the home of friends in Paris, the Ségals, who told us she had studied with David Oistrakh in Russia."

Gilles Artur, director of the Musée Gauguin in Tahiti, at the Kaufman house in 1972.

Artur answered, "That's not my daughter, she isn't that advanced; there is another Artur family in Rennes." We were now downstairs in the Salon, which had a beautiful view of the Borghese Gardens. Continuing our conversation, Artur offered, "I have six sons." Annette replied, "Felicitations!" Artur said, "Oh, you like Frenchmen?" Annette smiled. "I like French thought, Pascal." We spoke about sites in Rome we had visited. I told them about great Etruscan art and shared our out-of-the-way discoveries. A slim young Frenchman with a disapproving look approached, knowing his father spoke to everyone, and Artur presented his son Gilles, curator of the Musée Gauguin in Tahiti. Gilles explained, "My museum is not funded by the French government, but supported by individuals." Evidently deciding we were respectable, he graciously added, "La Princesse de Polignac has arranged for Yehudi Menuhin to play a benefit concert in Paris for my museum. I would like to invite you, but you must be in evening clothes." I replied, "I'm so sorry. It's not possible, as we are traveling lightly without formal attire—only tourist raiment—so regretfully cannot accept your kind invitation." I added, "If you ever visit Los Angeles where we live, I most cordially invite you to visit us, see our art collection, and dine with us." We exchanged addresses and hoped we might meet again.

Later Gilles telephoned from New York, saying he would stop in Los Angeles on his return to Tahiti. He added, "I have a film about my sojourn in Nouvelle Irelande [I presumed he meant the Hebrides in the South Pacific] and would like to show it to interested persons." We set a date. I called Dr. Haas at UCLA and he obtained equipment to show Gilles's film under good conditions. He invited some people interested in films and ethnology, and we invited our interested friends. Annette served moussaka, salad, good cheeses, fruit, wine, and dessert to about twenty-five persons. We welcomed Gilles, who was pleased to show his film and recount his impressions of the natives and their artifacts.

The silent film was an honest record of his two-year sojourn with these families, showing how they constructed canoes, homes, et cetera. Their women wore *only* decorated straw hats (based on some English ladies' wide-brimmed hats decorated with feathers and flowers, which had washed up on shore after shipwrecks); men wore only a small g-string, which might have been too controversial for educational television. Gilles had learned their language and eventually discovered they were cannibals, which the men had tried to hide from him. It was a jolly and entertaining soirée. Gilles remarked, as he was leaving, "Louis, I would like to have you come and play a concert for the museum in Tahiti." I replied, "That's very kind and I would certainly like to some time." However, I didn't take it seriously, considering it merely politeness.

A few weeks later, the phone rang during dinner. A French voice introduced himself: "Monsieur Kaufman, I am René Déssirer, I design museum installations and have just returned from Tahiti. Gilles Artur expects you in April and has arranged two tickets for you at UTA." Pleased to hear that, I asked, "How long will you be in Los Angeles?" He replied, "I'm returning to Paris tomorrow evening." We picked him up Sunday morning and visited the Los Angeles Museum, which had a loan exhibit of nineteenth-century French sculptures and paintings, and then I drove him to UCLA, which had a show of African art that greatly interested him. He had a brief rest at our home, where he was fascinated by our Khmer and Thai sculptures. After a restaurant dinner, we delivered him to an Air France flight. On our next visit to Paris, we visited the Déssirer flat and enjoyed a delicious luncheon with René and his lovely wife. He had a fascinating library, which included ancient Thai incunabula.

Gilles wrote asking me to play four Bach solo sonatas for the museum concert. He explained he had played violin as a youth, and he and his Tahitian friend Lenoble loved Bach. They thought it would be ideal to hear me play only Bach in the museum.

I replied, "Four long Bach sonatas might be too tedious for average Polynesians, French officials, and varied music lovers." I proposed playing Bach's D Minor Partita, with its superb "chaconne," and the G Minor Sonata with its masterly fugue, plus two Telemann solo sonatas, which are less concentrated and more cheerful for variety.

Gilles and Isabelle de Saint-Front (Belgian wife of Gilles's lifetime friend, artist Yves de Saint-Front) met us at the Papeete airport and drove us to the comfortable seaside Hotel Maeva. I had brought a small gift for the museum, a large bronze medallion by Belgian sculptor Constantin Meunier, depicting an aged Camille Pissarro, with long beard and wearing a cap. He had been a friend and mentor to Paul Gauguin. Although Gilles placed it in a locked glass case, it was stolen a few months later and never recovered! It remains a strange mystery.

We left our luggage in a large cheerful room and went off with Gilles to enjoy a tropical lunch and our first visit to the Musée Gauguin. The same evening we dined at his beautiful home beside the seashore, with his friends Monsieur and Madame Lenoble and charming Dr. Tauzin and his attractive wife. Dr. Tauzin had established a clinic and fine hospital in Tahiti.

One evening we dined at the home of the Lenobles with their many children. We listened to excellent French recordings of Bach's works. For another enjoyable excursion, Gilles's secretary, Françoise, drove us to the tenth anniversary celebration of the Tauzin hospital. Charming little girls and ladies, all with crowns of flowers on their heads, and informally dressed gentlemen were served by native waiters a traditional Polynesian banquet, consisting of roast pig, poi, breadfruit, and delicious fruits and wines. Tahitian poi was not like the Hawaiian version; the French chefs created something delicious, a sort of exotic fruit compote. Native musicians played dance music, and the French governor, Dr. Tauzin, and other staff danced with the little girls and the lovely ladies among the coconut trees and flowering vines and plants.

My unaccompanied solo concert in the museum's large exhibition hall was for a distinguished audience—the French governor, officials, friends, and attractively dressed natives. They listened attentively and patiently and seemed very pleased by my rather spartan program. Everyone (including Annette and me) greatly enjoyed the superb banquet Gilles had arranged to be served after my concert—with beef, lobster, shrimp, and crayfish from New Zealand, cold meats and salads, cheeses, fine wines, and tempting desserts. It was a gala event!

A few nights later Annette joined me in performing a more varied violin program at the French Cultural Center, for an informed and enthusiastic public. We were delighted to meet Yves de Saint-Front and visit his atelier. Yves's father, a famed naval officer, had courageously sailed alone in a small boat across the Atlantic Ocean to New York. He was also an accomplished painter of marine subjects, a French equivalent of England's great Turner, using the pseudonym Marin Marie. Yves's father was a lifelong friend of Pierre Artur, and their sons Yves and Gilles shared the same friendly devotion. I was very attracted by Yves's work. He was a most sensitive, subtle artist, and I found it remarkable that he could paint in Tahiti with fresh eyes—not merely imitating Gauguin. I bought two of his Tahitian scenes and have since acquired several more of his paintings, including some of his fine work from France—scenes of Paris, Trie-Chateau, where he and Isabelle lived for a time, and seascapes of Chausey, a group of islands off the coast of Normandy.

Gilles's secretary, Françoise, drove us all around the island, which was fascinating, as we traversed mountainous terrain and livestock farms introduced by French settlers. Gilles accompanied us to visit the impressive tropical garden built by an American near the museum. He invited us to accompany him on a visit to the nearby island of Moorea and pointed out some discoveries of Captain Cook. Seeing a large statue of Admiral Bougainville in Papeete, we learned this handsome officer took the beautiful vines to Europe and America. Our own garden's flowering bougainvillea had been named for this explorer. We truly had a marvelous time in this enchanting new world!

The next year, Gilles's father, Pierre, invited us to visit Rennes. This was our first glimpse of Brittany and of elegant Rennes with its excellent art museum. Pierre and another son, Oliver, drove us to visit fascinating villages and even to Mont-Saint-Michel, an architectural miracle! Annette and I climbed the many steps to the monastery's large dining hall. When we descended to join the waiting Arturs, we barely drove off in time to avoid the incoming tide. It was surprising how fast the tide roared in to separate the monastery from the mainland.

After our final pleasant family dinner at the spacious Artur residence, Oliver put his arms about Annette and me as we left saying, "Our doors are always open for you." When I mentioned his remark later to Gilles, he quipped, "Yes, to go out as well as to enter!"

Two years later we returned to Tahiti and delivered my André Lanskoy painting (containing portraits of André Lanskoy, Jean Pougny and his wife Kostia Terechkovitch, Guillaume Apollinaire, and Marie Laurencin), which Gilles was acquiring to replace a Lanskoy self-portrait lost in a devastating fire that destroyed many paintings of the previous Musée Gauguin. This time a piano had been set up in the museum garden and the Lanskoy painting was specially displayed. During our afternoon rehearsal a group of Japanese tourists visiting the museum stopped to listen as we played a Beethoven sonata. One gentleman approached the piano and deposited a tip for Annette. She said, *"Monsieur je n'accepte pas les pourboires* [Sir, I don't accept tips]." The polite Japanese visitor knew tipping was usual in France and refused to take back the coins. This led to museum merriment; whenever Annette wished to buy a cold drink, the staff would laughingly say, "The Japanese paid for you!" Our evening concert in the garden was a fine success and a joyous reunion with many old friends, the Saint-Fronts, Tauzins, and Lenobles.

A year later Gilles's oldest brother, André, and his charming wife, Zette, visited us in Los Angeles after a long visit in Tahiti with Gilles. We took them to an excellent production of Mozart's opera *The Marriage of Figaro* at the Music Center. They invited us to tour with them in Brittany the following spring. André, who was familiar with travel in this area, booked fine hotels for the trip. We met in Angers and visited the ancient fortress, where there was a remarkable collection of thirteenth-century tapestries. Then we accompanied Zette and André to a huge exhibition of modern tapestries by Jean Lurçat. Each day André drove us to lovely small churches and villages where Gauguin had painted during his sojourn in Brittany. We had a most enjoyable and jolly time sharing meals, sampling wonderful Breton crêpes, and sightseeing in museums and churches. We admired the local costumes of the women with tall starched-lace headdresses, with a unique pattern for each village in Brittany.

Attending an early mass sung in Gregorian chant at the elegant Italianate chapel of the Benedictine Abbey of Saint Pierre (located in the village of Solesmes, about one hundred and fifty miles southwest of Paris) was an outstanding experience. The white-robed monks knelt and moved with the grace of elegant ritual dancers. This community was responsible for the revival of Gregorian chant. We had first heard recordings of their service and remarkable singing at Poulenc's apartment in 1949.

Zette recounted a fascinating tale one evening. Before World War II, a young German tourist paid court to her for several weeks, and they often had pleasant picnics on the beach. When war broke out, he returned to France as a *Gauleiter* (Nazi district officer) in Brittany. He had been a spy mapping all the contours of the beach and locations of French military installations!

André had scant trust in the press and only read the sports pages. We all shared his enthusiasm for tennis matches. We so enjoyed the seafood treats, traveling and sharing experiences with these agreeable friends, that we were sorry to say *au revoir* at the end of this pleasant tour.

En route to Los Angeles, we visited London, where our friends John and Sheila Bush had arranged for us to play a concert to benefit the restoration of paintings at Dulwich College. Our rehearsal there was our first visit to that art collection, which comprised splendid early English portraits and outstanding Dutch masters. Clifford Curzon had selected their fine grand piano, which Annette was delighted to play. The large gallery was ideal for sound. We performed sonatas of Veracini, Beethoven, Brahms, and Ravel for a large enthusiastic audience. We were extremely pleased that our friends attended—Marjorie Osborne, Dr. Theodore Bloomfield (under whose baton I had premiered Ernest Bloch's concerto) and his wife Marge, Jonathan and Kathleen Griffin, and Miron Grindea (Romanian publisher-editor of *ADAM, an International Review*). Jonathan was fascinated by his first visit to this interesting art gallery. The director of the gallery provided a delicious buffet after our program, which gave us a fine opportunity to visit with our friends!

Sheila Bush drove us the next morning to Guilford, where we met Gilles Artur's sister, Françoise, and her husband, Geoffrey Lawman, a professor at Saint John's Academy. We had offered to play a benefit concert and had sent our program to the headmaster with a request to please invite our friend Dom Robert, a Jesuit priest at Saint Mary's Abbey. Robert, who made fine modern tapestries, was a friend of the Artur family in Rennes. He had attended my Opus 8 Vivaldi premiere in Paris with Henri Sauguet. When they came backstage to congratulate me, Robert said, "I have been inspired by your performance of *La Caccia* and will design a tapestry based on *La Chasse* [the hunt]." His tapestry *La Chasse* now hangs in the Lyon Art Museum, where we have admired it.

As we enjoyed the delectable lunch of cold salmon and salads, which Françoise had prepared, we conversed with her husband, their teenage son, and Françoise, who seemed embarrassed. She began, "I don't know how to tell you some unforeseen and upsetting news!" I reassuringly replied, "Annette and I are used to unexpected events, so please do not hesitate to say anything." Françoise continued, "Our headmaster has left not only his post but also the Catholic church, and until the administration of this college, which is in Brussels, decides on a new headmaster and learns why the 'apostate' departed, *anyone* who wrote to him is to be avoided.

Therefore our faculty, associate orders, nuns, and pupils have been forbidden to attend your concert!" I smilingly said, "Annette and I will be happy to play a program for you and your son in the chapel, we never worry about the size of an audience." I realized immediately that I was seen as a suspect "heretic American fiddler" who had written to the departed headmaster, sent a program, and hoped to "seduce" another priest, Dom Robert at Saint Mary's Abbey! Françoise knew this was absurd, but my good intentions could not be understood in faraway Belgium!

That evening, Annette and I, dressed in concert attire, played our program in the almost empty chapel. A few townspeople, remembering my concerts and BBC broadcasts, bought tickets, and perhaps six courageous nuns, a few brave faculty members, and several students sat in back rows. At intermission, an ill-at-ease gentleman from the academy apologized for the small audience, saying, "Mr. Kaufman, you are a very great artist. We all regret this misunderstanding and we wish to pay you for this wonderful program." I replied, "That is most gracious but I offered to perform gratis due to my long friendship with the Artur family and do not wish any remuneration. If you have any funds available please give them to any charity of your choice."

After our concert, Françoise graciously had arranged a small reception for the townspeople and a few students. We had very pleasant conversations. Françoise obtained a limousine to drive us back that same night to our London hotel. We never learned what occurred in this curiously medieval situation. Why was our concert thought to be dangerous to listeners? Was Dom Robert forbidden to attend? An unsolved mystery!

# 39

# Hazardous Travel

In May 1978 Annette and I began a European holiday in Vienna, Budapest, Athens, Crete, and Yugoslavia. During a few pleasant days in Vienna we visited the remarkable Kunsthistorisches Museum and the Albertina's great drawing and musical collections, where I was permitted to study the manuscript of Beethoven's violin concerto. It was fascinating to see in some places indications in colored inks of three different versions of the violin line. Evidently Beethoven had not determined which he preferred. I copied these variations and decided that in doubtful situations the printed version now used (edited by Joseph Joachim) was musically the best solution.

We enjoyed Vienna's Modern Art Museum and were very pleased they had acquired a handsome large Maryan painting. We attended Wolf-Ferrari's delightful opera *The Four Rustics,* based on Goldoni's amusing play, and were delighted to see Leo and Tomiko Mueller, old friends from Los Angeles, one row in front of us. We had first encountered Leo, a Czech refugee, in Hollywood, where he conducted operas at City College. On his return to Vienna he was offered the post of directing a training program for young opera singers similar to the Piccolo Scala in Milan, where young singers are trained for opera performance. Tomiko had a lovely voice and was an ideal Madama Butterfly. We had a joyous reunion and visited their flat the next day to share our mutual experiences.

We flew to Budapest and again visited its fascinating museum and the ancient Roman site and museum on the banks of the Danube. I obtained tickets for a Kodály program at the opera. To avoid being delayed in traffic caused by heavy rain, we decided to take the subway from our hotel directly to the Opera House. The oldest in Europe, the Budapest subway has granite steps leading down to the trains. As we were walking up the stairs single file, a very large woman descended on the wrong side. I stepped aside to let her pass, lost my balance on the slippery stone steps, and fell on my knees. Annette heard the sound and turned to help me up, asking, "Are you all right?" I replied, "No problem, I'm fine." We enjoyed the performance and returned safely to the hotel. Before falling asleep, I mentioned, "I've a scratch on one lens of my glasses." Annette said, "We've time to have a new lens made here." I answered, "I'll wait until we return home." We flew to Athens and were happy to be again in its sunny atmosphere, which always appears close to the sky, the heaven of Greek gods. We greatly appreciated the Archeological Museum on this second visit and the splendid Greek Byzantine painters that influenced Rublyov, the great Russian Byzantine artist, whose flowing forms precede Botticelli.

We walked through the inspiring Acropolis area and Acropolis Museum, which has several mysterious, beautiful, archaic female korai, which I still find compellingly attractive. The next day we walked up the Lycabettus Hill to visit an ancient church and view Athens from its height. The next morning we flew to Crete. We arrived during the Greek Easter celebration. We stayed at a charming small hotel in Iraklion, which faced the sea. We immediately walked on a long rocky path to the extraordinary Minoan museum. I was enchanted by the ingenuity and beauty of Cretan pottery and art forms. About 2 P.M., a dark film covered my right eye. I couldn't see! I called Annette to tell her what had happened. She led me to a chair and said, "Sit down—wait here—I'll see if I can find someone to help—you may have a detached retina." Her mind recalled in an instant my fall in Budapest and my thinking my glasses were scratched. She ran to the entrance and shouted, "*Est-ce-que quelqu'un ici parle français?*" (Does anyone here speak French?) An attractive lady responded, "*Oui, moi-même.*" Annette explained my predicament and requested the name and address of a local eye doctor. The kind lady wrote this information in Greek for a taxi driver and said this excellent doctor would not be at his office until 5 P.M. Annette thanked her profusely.

She returned with this encouraging news. I insisted on walking about the museum and photographing with my good left eye the art objects that especially interested us both, in spite of Annette's counsel to wait quietly in a chair. At 4:30 P.M. we left the museum, entered a waiting taxi, and handed the address to the driver. We spoke French and English in Greece—we only knew a few Greek phrases. The taxi driver quickly drove to the indicated address and, to our astonishment, he turned, saying in English, "The sign on the door says doctor is on holiday, it's Easter, will not return for two days. You want eye doctor? My good friend BEST eye doctor!" Annette protested, "Please take us immediately to a hospital." The driver ignored her and drove to his friend's office—which proved to be the right action! His friend had studied eye surgery in Boston and Chicago for five years and was a retina specialist!

The doctor very carefully examined my eye and bluntly stated, "You have a retinal tear in your eye, and you only have a brief margin of four or five days at most to save your right eye." He added, "I would like to operate immediately [the retinal tear was too large for correction with laser], but I cannot as I leave tomorrow for an international retinal conference in Japan." I said, "It's probably best for me to return immediately to Los Angeles." The doctor replied, "You must, as undoubtedly all of Athens's retinal doctors will be en route to Japan." He bandaged my right eye and cautioned, "Be very careful." He wrote a note (in Greek) to assure all concerned that I should have medical priority for travel. This was imperative, as there were almost 250,000 tourists visiting Greece in this holy season.

Annette was frantic to leave overcrowded Iraklion. We discovered at the dock that *all* boat space was taken. Then we walked to the Olympic Airlines office, where three harassed young ladies were attempting to cope with a huge crowd of French, German, Italian, and Swedish tourists—all clamoring for tickets to leave Crete. Our accompanying travel agent whispered, "Ask for tickets to London via Athens." That phrase plus the medical pass worked like a charm. We received booking on the first morning flight and slowly walked back to our rustic beachside hotel.

I telephoned Los Angeles and spoke with the nurse of our doctor, who was not in his office. I told her we would arrive in Los Angeles on Friday and I desperately needed the best eye surgeon for my retinal detachment. We enjoyed a late, delicious Greek supper in a small taverna near our hotel, before slowly ascending the stairs to our bedroom. We arose very early to be dazzled by a splendid rosy sunrise over the Aegean Sea. Our plane to Athens took off at 5 A.M., and our seats adjoined a tiny, white-haired, elderly Cretan lady who generously handed Annette and me two hard-boiled eggs from her large bag as an Easter gift. We both murmured, *"Efaristo poli"* (many thanks), one of the few Greek phrases we knew.

This kindness to two anxious travelers seemed a good omen for our hectic trip. We reached Athens in time to cancel all prearranged tours in Greece and Yugoslavia, picked up our luggage left at our Athens hotel, and arrived at the airport at noon. To our dismay, we learned that there was a strike of the air stewards, which ended after three hours, so although our flight to London was quiet and restful, we arrived three hours late! Annette had wanted to take the first afternoon flight from London to Los Angeles, but fortunately I had insisted that we should stay overnight in London in case of any unforeseen delays.

I learned that all airport hotels and all London hotels were full to capacity! We both looked so forlorn, a tourist aid lady offered, "You may sit on the floor here if you like." There were many tourists already sitting and lying on the floor nearby. However, the Heathrow porter carrying our valises said, "Come with me to another part of the airport—there's a direct line to bed and breakfast accommodations." Annette guarded the luggage and I followed him. Amazingly, one hotel had a cancellation and promised to save a bedroom and bath if we paid five pounds, which I gladly did. A taxi drove us to the small Hotel Richmond and we found it agreeable. The manager had honored my reservation even though he had received several calls for the same accommodations while we were en route. The next morning, Annette dashed off some twenty letters to hotels and friends in Europe and England explaining our cancellation of plans and mailed them at a nearby post office.

We left London via TWA early Friday morning as scheduled. My "karma" was protecting me for, by an amazing coincidence, our good friends mezzo-soprano Claudine Carlson and her contra-bassist husband, Mike Rubin, were traveling on the same flight! Seeing my bandaged eye, Claudine thoughtfully alerted the TWA staff to aid me on arrival in Los Angeles. What a blessing that turned out to be! I really should have followed Annette's insistent request that I use a wheelchair, but I foolishly walked unaided and carried hand luggage, which greatly worried her. When we arrived in Los Angeles's overcrowded airport a TWA agent took us in tow, retrieved our luggage out of a huge pile almost immediately, maneuvered us through customs without inspection, and in less than twenty minutes put us in a taxi! Later we learned Claudine and Mike spent more than two hours retrieving their bags and clearing customs!

On arrival home, a waiting telegram from Dr. Alan Kreiger of the nearby UCLA Jules Stein Eye Institute advised, "Call as soon as you arrive—I'll be waiting to hear from you." I opened the door and immediately telephoned Dr. Kreiger, who asked, "What makes you think you have a detached retina?" I replied, "The eye doctor in Crete told me that's the condition of my right eye. He couldn't operate as he was leaving for Japan the next morning." Dr. Kreiger answered, "Yes, the head of our department is also attending that conference. Come to my office tomorrow morning at nine and bring an overnight bag; we'll keep you in the hospital for a few days."

After a good night's rest, I entered the Jules Stein Eye Institute Saturday

morning for retinal examination and evaluation of my general health and
then was placed in bed with both eyes bandaged for complete rest. Annette remained with me throughout all examinations and only left when
I fell asleep. She returned to visit with me the entire Sunday and helped
me eat, for I could not see. Early Monday morning, Dr. Kreiger operated
for three-and-one-half hours, sewing up my retina! He then smilingly
told a very anxious Annette that I was in fine condition—the operation
had been very successful. Tuesday morning the bandage was removed. I
was delighted. I again had a full field of vision. I am still grateful to the
doctors, known and unknown friends, taxi drivers, porters, and many
people en route from Crete and London who offered aid in saving my
right eye. My vision improved steadily; it was of great help also that I had
never smoked, and I have good vision (with glasses) in both eyes. This
was an important victory, as both Annette and I are inveterate readers of
books and music and pursuers of visual arts in many directions as amateurs and collectors.

We again encountered Nicolas Slonimsky, who had written program
notes for the Kaufman Quartet some twenty years earlier. He was teaching at UCLA and writing program notes for the Los Angeles Philharmonic. We shared many provocative evenings at our home discussing
music and literature and listening to recordings of unfamiliar music.

Orion Records engaged him to record his inventive *Thesaurus of Scales
and Melodic Patterns*. This publication became a source book for classical
and jazz musicians. Giveon Cornfield asked if he might use our living
room for the project, which Annette and I witnessed. After one of Annette's excellent dinners, Giv and I rolled up the living room rug and Nicolas sat down at our Steinway piano. He recorded all of the scales and
patterns of the entire collection, playing each only once. His flexible fingers needed no warming up, and as the inventive patterns were solely concerned with form and rhythm, they did not need poetic interpretation. A
remarkable feat!

Slonimsky compiled the eighth edition of *Baker's Biographical Dictionary of Music and Musicians* and was a pioneer in appreciating the musical
avant-garde. We read and enjoyed his *Music of Latin America* and his
amusing *Lexicon of Musical Invective*. His autobiography, *Perfect Pitch*,
published by Oxford University Press in 1988 when he was ninety-two,
received unanimous acclaim. Nicolas had hoped to call it *Failed Wunder-
kind*, which hardly suited his impressive accomplishments and gargan-
tuan knowledge of musical lore.

Nicolas Slonimsky and Annette, 1988.

Over the years we kept in touch with Miklós Rózsa, who wrote from Salita, S. Agostino, Santa Margherita, Italy on 27 July 1982:

> Dear Annette and Louis,
> It was really heartwarming to read the wonderful review, *The Kaufman Legacy*. True enough, there were (and are) very few concert violinists who play and record the music of their contemporaries, instead of the thousand times heard and recorded well-known works. But it needed courage, guts, and faith in the new composers and Louis had them—bless him.
>
> A whole generation of his contemporaries owes a debt to him. Fortunately he chose sane composers and Schoenberg's miserable concerto remained a closed book for him. Louis Krasner had his fun with this one and now that Stravinsky and Bartók became classics; who plays Schoenberg, apart from a few fanatics—no one. I hope it will stay this way.

Stephen Minde, conductor of the Portland Opera, heard the recording of Bernard Herrmann's *Wuthering Heights* and mounted a world premiere in November 1982. The premiere coincided with a "Louis Kaufman Week" arranged by the Portland Community Music Center to honor me, for Annette and I have supported the center with funds, bows, and fiddles for over forty years. Judge Gus and Libby Solomon, who introduced us to the school, hosted a lovely diner party for us with many guests at a large hotel.

Craig Reardon, a young fan of Herrmann's who had traveled to London to interview Benny a few years before his "rediscovery," flew up to Portland for fourteen hours to dine with Annette and me before the performance and attend the opera. He caught an early morning flight back to Los Angeles. At my suggestion Craig gave his Herrmann interview notes to Steven Smith for his Herrmann biography, *A Heart at Fire's Center*.

Minde wrote a most appreciative and moving note for the opera program, stating it would be fine if it proved a success, but even if not, it would be historically significant. We considered it a smashing success! The capacity first-night audience was transfixed by the poetry and drama of the music. The cast included Victor Braun, a handsome, tall, fascinating stage presence who sang with passion and colored his voice wonderfully—from the young ardent Heathcliff to the embittered old man. We had heard him sing Jupiter in the Richard Strauss opera *Die Liebe der Danaë* at Santa Fe and also "Loki" in the Wagner *Ring* in Seattle.

Annette and Louis visiting an ill Miklós Rózsa at his home in Hollywood, 1991. Photograph by Diana Ayres.

The Cathy, Barrie Smith, was also ideal in appearance and sang well in spite of a cold. Chester Ludgin as the drunken Hindley sang a remarkable aria expressing his hatred of Heathcliff, which recalled the intensity of Moussorgsky in color and drama! I was deeply impressed by Herrmann's beautiful, tender, expressive orchestral interludes.

The stage director, Malcolm Fraser, scenic designer Carey Wong, and costume designer Saundra Kaufman were uniformly excellent. We were enchanted and moved by the opera.

Minde directed with most sympathetic understanding and precision. The opera came alive in the theater! The audience listened intently and at the conclusion gave the conductor and cast a tremendous ovation. Annette and I felt that the premiere justified all the anguish Bernard had lived through in composing it, although with the changes Minde introduced to the score Benny would not have approved of the performance!

We had a heartwarming reunion in Portland with our dear friend Lucille Fletcher Wallop, Benny's first wife, who had written a splendid libretto, Benny's daughter Dorothy (Taffy), who had become a successful author of biographical novels, and his brother, Louis, and sister, Rosie, whom we hadn't seen for many years. What a wonderful week!

Ernest Bean and his wife, Ellie, the manager of the Royal Festival Hall in London, replied to our account of Bernard's *Wuthering Heights* on 28 November 1982 from their Dorking home:

Dear Friends:
I can't tell you what a pleasure you gave us in sending your account of the world premiere of Benny's opera. A pleasure deepened, yet tinged with sadness that he was not here to see the realization of his dreams. We put on the records of Wuthering Heights after reading the booklet and your vivid account of the premiere and were more deeply moved than hitherto by the way the music brought to life the genius of Emily Brontë in another dimension. . . . How we wished he had been sitting in our home as the records were played as he was when we had that unforgettable day when we got lost in the Yorkshire mists. The next day we played records of the Torelli concerti grossi, which you sent to us after your visit to Sussex—which has put us further in debt as ever.
    Ernest and Ellie Bean


In 1989 I was interviewed by Dr. John Yoell for *Fanfare Magazine*. Dr. Yoell, a medical doctor and a passionate record collector, had written a book about Scandinavian composers, and I mentioned my 1954 performance for Swedish radio of Lars-Erik Larsson's violin concerto. He wrote to Radiojänst, asking if they had saved a tape of the performance and discovered that they had. I requested a copy of that tape and then leased it from them. Music and Arts of America released that historic performance on CD in 1990. As Schopenhauer wrote, "How fortunate one is at the end of one's life to see that your work has not aged with you."

# Postscript

### Annette Kaufman

*Louis Kaufman*
*born Portland, Oregon, 10 May 1905*
*died Los Angeles,*
*California, 9 February 1994*

TRUE SHARING
Art is just the best
To whoever will aspire to be its peer
Has to be earned
its givers own it
All who made it or heard if call obeyed relayed it—
who earn it own it
—Jonathan Griffin, *In Earthlight*

Louis had great courage, kindness, and consideration to everyone during our sixty-two happy years together. He had unending *joie de vivre* and bore every discomfort (he suffered from extremely sensitive skin) or pain unflinchingly without complaint. I greatly admired his infinite patience and endurance during his last two years; I always considered Louis "half-Athenian and half-Spartan."

I was immediately attracted by Louis's sincere desire to be helpful to musicians, artists, his friends, and me when we first met in New York. He was truly enthusiastic in admiring the achievements of his contemporaries, a rare quality in the professional world. Throughout our lives he always wanted me at his side for every activity—travel, concerts, operas, theater,

Louis in New York City at age 84, 1989. Photograph by Philip Cavanaugh.

bookshops, fiddle-repair shops, long walks, museums and art galleries, swims, and sharing in his true pleasure in international cuisine. Frankly, I was delighted with his company and loved being under his tutelage.

Louis observed carefully—he studied and knew about painting, great sculpture, prints, folk arts, cuisine, and human relationships. It was fascinating for me to learn from his wide experience and to share in his musical

life and researches in America and Europe. I never heard him say unkind
words to tradesmen or persons he encountered. After our marriage, when
I first met his friends in various cities, they would draw me aside to request, "Annette, be very kind to Louis—he's such a specially good man."

Louis liked to shop with me for my clothing, and when we shopped
in markets, he enjoyed selecting fruits, vegetables, fish, and meats, although he could not cook. He always knew how everything should
taste—which was of infinite help, for I had never even boiled water
when we met! He enjoyed buying me rings, brooches, and earrings, and
wanted me with him when he selected his clothing. He always surprised
me by his fresh and practical observations in every field of endeavor. We
had an ideal relationship.

Louis loved listening to music—opera, orchestral music, chamber
music, and solo works. When he was about seventy-five he told me, "It's
time for me to stop playing in public, I'm beginning to find it a strain to
perform. Passages that I always have played easily are now tiring. I want
to stop while I still play well, it's time to listen to young people!" We continued to attend concerts and operas. We attended the Santa Fe Opera for
many years and several *Ring* performances in Seattle. He took great delight in hearing talented young musicians and singers. Louis then devoted
more time to editing editions of violin music and writing his memoirs.

Louis was deeply concerned about the damage a poorly designed chin
rest can do to fiddlers' chins. He had found an old German flat chin rest
which was comfortable for most violinists, and he persuaded William
Lewis and Son in Chicago to manufacture this model. Since he did not
want any remuneration, they sold it as the "Kaufman Chin Rest."

After a heart attack in 1992, followed by surgery, he did not wish to
have visitors (except for me) or to speak unnecessarily. Doctors and
nurses asked foolish questions—"Do you know where you are?" "What
day is this?" Fortunately I was there to suggest, "He won't answer that
sort of question. Ask him something intelligent and he'll reply." One
young doctor tried asking, "Mr. Kaufman, who is your favorite composer?" Louis immediately answered, "Beethoven."

He made a remarkable recovery and with Lance Bowling supervised
the transferring of his earlier LP records to CD. He dined with friends at
home and in favorite restaurants and attended concerts. During the years
that my mother lived with us, Louis and I would take turns reading aloud
interesting books. After Louis's surgery, when his eyes were tired, I would
read aloud to him, which he greatly enjoyed. Mother found it very touch-
ing that he would often remark as we were going to our beds, "This was a
great day and tomorrow will be fine too."

A few weeks before he died, he said, "Annette, we can be happy we never harmed anyone in this world, at least not consciously. It is fortunate the future is veiled from us." His acute hearing and intelligence were never lost. The night before he died, he told me of his problem as a lad in New York with "icy fingers!"

I know he would be very pleased that his editions of eighteenth-, nineteenth-, and twentieth-century composers are being widely distributed by International Music Publishers, so performers and students may have access to music unfamiliar to the "many," and I hope that his memoirs may interest general readers. I know that Louis would have been thrilled to learn that his recording of Vivaldi's *Four Seasons,* which was awarded a Grand Prix du Disque in 1950, would again be honored some five decades later by being inducted into the Grammy Hall of Fame in 2002! I enjoy knowing that his poetic, musical performances are being heard and enjoyed via CDs and radio. I am most grateful for the many years I have shared the love, work, and pleasures of this modest, charming, gracious gentleman.

His memorial service at the Beverly Hills Synagogue was attended by many friends and colleagues; Lew Ayres, Norman Corwin, Fred Hyatt, and Henry Roth spoke movingly of their memories of Louis's enthusiasm for music, art, theater, and friendship. Lance Bowling arranged for Louis's recordings to be played.

Any errors or omissions in *A Fiddler's Tale* are solely my own, for which I beg the reader's indulgence, and as eighteenth-century writers ended postscripts, *Vive Felice* (live happily).

Los Angeles, May 2003

Appendixes
Discography
Bibliography
Index

# *Appendix 1*

# Reviews

### *New York Times*

Mr. Kaufman, fair-haired and alert showed himself a player of clear and vigorous tone . . . incisive rhythm. (30 October 1927)

### *New York Telegram*

[Kaufman] displayed attainments of more than average order as well as a high degree of promise. (30 October 1927)

### *New York Tribune*

Mr. Kaufman is a young man of sturdy type and the development of his art is along the lines commensurate with his physical attributes. He plays with confidence and tonal security, resorts to no tricks, and presents his interpretations in a forthright manner. . . . (30 October 1927)

### *Portland Journal*

##### KAUFMAN SCORES HIGH AS SOLOIST

Only a few years ago, Kaufman was Portland's violin prodigy. Many in Monday night's audience had heard him when a boy of ten or twelve do things with the fiddle that presaged just such an event as this homecoming under the most auspicious and encouraging circumstances . . . he more than made good. Seven or eight spontaneous curtain calls established that. ([J. L. Wallin] 22 November 1933)

### *Portland Oregonian*

##### KAUFMAN DELIGHTS IN VIOLIN CONCERT

Kaufman [as] violinist gave a splendid accounting of his talents and training last night. Mr. Kaufman had ample opportunity to make his audience familiar with the breadth of his tastes, his feeling for various styles and demonstrated his wealth of violinistic talents. Among these gifts the most notable last night were a brilliantly finished technique and a vibrant warmth of tone. ([Hilmar Grondahl] November 1933)

## *The Portland News*

Louis Kaufman again demonstrated that he is in the class of the world's greatest violinists. His tone is full, broad and authoritative and his technical interpretative ability is most amazing. Annette Kaufman proved to be an accompanist of great poise. Her technique is fluid and her tonal values well balanced. Her musicianship leaves no opening for criticism. (4 December 1933)

## *Daily Mail*

### THE COMPOSER WITH SOME NOUVEL IDEAS

Anthony Collins, who used to be principal viola with the London Symphony Orchestra, rejoined his former colleagues at the Royal Festival Hall last night to show his prowess in three capacities: conductor, arranger, and composer. His Violin Concerto was given its first performance with Louis Kaufman as soloist. Mr. Collins confesses to some nouvel ideas. First he thought of his concerto rather as a ballet, the solo violin likened to a prima ballerina at the head of her corps de ballet. Secondly he is tired of the modern composer's "hack-saw" treatment of the instrument. The result is a fluent piece of writing. There are striking passages for trombones, but it would have gained in character if there had been just a little more roughness. His orchestration of Schubert's Grand Duo did not solve the problem of what is to be done with this outsize in piano duets. (9 March 1953)

## *New York Times*

### VIVALDI FESTIVAL IS STARTED HERE

*First of Two Programs to Mark Composer's Birthday Anniversary Presented at Town Hall*—The first of two concerts, which make a Vivaldi Festival was given last night at Town Hall, having been instigated by Louis Kaufman, the violinist, who has been making a special study of Vivaldi's little known music, soloists and Winifred Cecil, soprano for the requirements of the occasion. The program stated this was in honor of the two hundred and seventy-fifth anniversary of Vivaldi's birth, assuming quite a bit, since the exact date has not yet been ascertained. But let that go, far more important than a musicological detail, the quality as well as the astounding quantity of Vivaldi's music. Modern research has thus far indicated seventy-five sonatas, four hundred and forty-five concertos, twenty-three symphonies, forty-nine operas, and un-numbered vocal and choral works in sacred and secular styles. He wrote for an immense number of instruments and combinations as the program of last night showed with great brilliancy, spirit and imagination. Vivaldi also had a Latin's instinct for clear and artistic form.

The brevity, conciseness and clarity of the works heard last night demonstrated this most significantly. As a violinist, Vivaldi was well ahead of his time, and some of Mr. Kaufman's bravura stunts last night in playing certain of his concertos proved that if Corelli was the first great violinist in the noble, simple classical style, Vivaldi was the first great virtuoso. We know Vivaldi principally because Bach transcribed many of his concertos. The Bach clavier concertos are mainly transcriptions of Vivaldi violin concertos. Vivaldi's organ concerto transcribed by Stradella, long attributed to Friedmann Bach, the great Maestro's son, was J. S. Bach's transcription of a Vivaldi concerto.

German and English historians, apparently determined to play down an early Italian master whose music had so much to do with the development of the orchestra and symphonic form, having shoved Vivaldi back in the shelves. How effectively this has been done was hinted last night when we heard at least four American performances. First experiences of delightful music. The Concerto for string orchestra in C minor, which opened the concert, is a beauty, very spirited and vigorous and sunny, significant in slow movements for Vivaldi made much more of the slow movements of the "concerto" of that day than many of his predecessors and again sparkling, clear and radiant in the finale. The piece is short; the composer says only what he has to say, very wittily with no padding, in the most admirable style. There followed a bassoon concerto.

Then Mr. Kaufman played for the first time in America concertos five, six, seven and eight of Vivaldi's opus eight. Concertos seven and eight are particularly inspired. The slow movement of number eight is one that haunts the memory. These concertos have not the greatest strength of underpinning as other Vivaldi concertos have when Bach has done with them. But it is wonderfully transparent and blessedly Italianate, with fine structure, all light and symmetry of form. . . . ([Olin Downes]16 April 1950)

### New York Herald Tribune

The works of Antonio Vivaldi, now in process of collection into a definitive edition under director Gian Francesco Malipiero, constituted the subject of last night's concert played in Town Hall. Winifred Cecil sang a Cantata, Louis Kaufman played four violin concertos; Bernard Garfield was soloist in a bassoon concerto. There was a concerto for two trumpeters. . . . Your reporter found the program full of high musical values. Surely Vivaldi is one of the great men of music with his handsomely laid out forms, his animated rhythms, and his bold and vigorous freedom of melodic invention. He merits indeed a proper festival. ([Virgil Thomson] 26 April 1950)

### New York Herald Tribune

A generally stimulating evening . . . Miss Lane and Miss Paris sang sympathetically in the Gloria and the choristers with good quality of tone and clarity. Instrumental works found Louis Kaufman and other soloists in good form, and the Orchestra was both spirited and conscious of dynamic values and proportions. ([Francis D. Perkins] 11 May 1950)

### *New York Post*

Noted among the most inspired works was the short but impressive concerto for violin and violoncello with Louis Kaufman, violin and Phyllis Kraueter, cellist as soloists. Throughout the evening Scherman and his ensemble did themselves proud by performing with spirit and devotion—a task that enriched the ears and hearts of many music-lovers. ([Harriet Johnson] 11 May 1950)

### *La Presse (Tunis)*

#### LOUIS KAUFMAN AND THE SYMPHONY ORCHESTRA

Louis Kaufman plays the violin with all the authority, which announces his high and massive stature. He is not one of those flamboyant artists and his facility is so great that he gives the impression of treating his violin with graceful ease. In other aspects, his technique is perfect.

He was an excellent interpreter of Beethoven's concerto in D major with its varied themes and its tender Largo to the diabolic Rondo, which offered so many possibilities to the soloist. The symphony orchestra directed by Marcel Mirouze accompanied him remarkably. ([translated] 11 November 1951)

### *Petit Matin*

This violinist of enormous talent gave us an interpretation of the magnificent concerto of Beethoven in D major, the only concerto written by this genius of music devoted to the violin. It is of a very great beauty but enormous difficulty. It needs an artist like Louis Kaufman to not only attempt it but to bring out all of its best effects. What a mastery of the bow! What exquisite sensibility! What a profound interpretation! What virtuosity Kaufman has and how he gave us infinite pleasure in this concerto. . . . A beautiful afternoon for music-lovers. ([translated] 11 November 1951)

### *London Sunday Times*

Dispensing with a conductor, Louis Kaufman led his players in perfect eighteenth century style throughout the twelve concertos of Vivaldi's Opus IX, *La cetra,* the audience demanded more! They were rewarded by the repeat of a slow movement. (8 September 1953)

### *London Times*

#### ANTONIO VIVALDI—TWELVE CONCERTOS

*La cetra,* which being interpreted as the Lyre, is a set of twelve violin concertos in various keys, published in Amsterdam in 1728 and reckoned as Opus IX in

Vivaldi's output. The whole set of twelve was played at the Festival Hall last night, with two short breaks, by Mr. Louis Kaufman and the Goldsborough Orchestra with Mr. George Malcolm playing harpsichord. . . . His astonishing ability to ring the changes on a fairly restricted medium speaks of something more than the executive virtuosity for which he was famed in his lifetime. Violinistic figuration, mixed rhythms, registration in the organist's sense as when he reduces his accompaniment to second violins and violas, even the limited use of *scordatura* (unconventional tunings of the strings) all are subservient to the flow of ideas which seems unlimited. . . . Twelve concertos on end are, of course, too many, but the concentration demonstrated as nothing else could have done Vivaldi's fertility and resource and they fell gratefully upon the ear. Mr. Kaufman, having immersed himself in Vivaldi as editor and soloist, played the whole lot with a strong purity of style, employing a tone, that was robust but not forced in the vigorous movements, and a cantilena that was suave but not unclassical in the lyric movements. Sometimes there was a suspicion that he hurried his rhythm in vigorous passages but the fact that the orchestra, which was seated around him without other conductor, never seemed to get out of step with him may be granted to him as absolution from the accusation. (26 September 1953)

### Observer

#### ITALIA REDENTA

Vivaldi, who the more one knows of him, is the more clearly seen to be in the neighborhood of Bach and Handel not only in date (c. 1675-1741) but also in stature. The Vivaldi program consisted of twelve concertos entitled *La cetra*— Opus IX. The work for one or two violins, ripieno strings and continuo throughout, gives no idea of the Composer's immense variety of scoring, but does show the splendid range of his invention, his vigor, his pouncing originality. Louis Kaufman and the Goldsborough Orchestra were wholeheartedly engrossed in the music. ([Erich Blom] 28 September 1953)

### Daily Telegraph

#### A CONDUCTOR'S CONCERTO—INTERESTING DESIGN

Anthony Collins took part in the London Symphony Orchestra Concert at the Royal Festival Hall as Conductor, Composer, and Transcriber. Sibelius's majestic Symphony was given a performance that confirmed Mr. Collins's high rank among present day conductors. His own Violin Concerto (1949) was new to London. The excellent soloist was Louis Kaufman, an American artist, to whom the work is dedicated. It is a composition of interesting design, and if not intensely personal, full of evidence of a practiced hand. To hear Mr. Collins's orchestral transcription of Schubert's "Grand Duo" was a charming experience.

Though this is not Schubert at his most romantic, it is something the world ignores to its loss. Mr. Collins's scoring is exemplary. (9 March 1953)

### *London Times*

ROYAL FESTIVAL HALL — MR. ANTHONY COLLINS

Though much of his excellent all around musicianship has been given to America in recent years, Mr. Anthony Collins remains a British subject and now and again finds time to return to this country. Last night he appeared at the Royal Festival Hall in the triple role of composer, transcriptor and conductor, the occasion being one of the London Symphony Orchestra's series of Sunday night concerts.

Mr. Collins dedicated his violin concerto (1949) to the American violinist Mr. Louis Kaufman and was fortunate in having this poised, brilliant and sweet toned artist to introduce this work to London. The relationship of soloist and orchestra in this three movements in one concerto is in his own words "the same as that of a ballerina and corps de ballet, and ballerinas need exceptional gifts." His delicate scoring always enabled the solo part to keep well in the foreground, but the music was far more interesting for its imaginative tone coloring than for its substance. Writing for films has made Mr. Collins a master of the atmospheric rather than of the symphonic manner. (9 March 1953)

### *Los Angeles Times*

MUSIC OF KORNGOLD HEARD IN CONCERT

As Dr. Walter's tribute pointed out, a concert program of this type can reveal only limited aspects of Korngold's work, for he was best known as an operatic and symphonic composer. But always apparent in all the music performed were his fluency, his adroit craftsmanship and a certain prevailing joyousness combined with a typical Viennese sentiment and idiom that is never suppressed for very long.

Possibly the most serious work on the program was the *Third String Quartet* composed in 1945 when Korngold was beginning to relinquish film writing which had occupied him for nearly ten years. It is a soundly constructed work with forthright ideas extensively developed and it has a particularly attractive slow movement in folk song manner. The writing is grateful for the instruments and the Kaufman String Quartet offered a robust and brilliant performance. The *Third Piano Sonata* composed in 1931 has its serious moments . . . but also has a *Tempo di Menuetto* in lilting Viennese rhythms that might well be excerpted to repertoire of pianists. At least Mr. Crown's playing made it sound exuberant and genuinely pianistic. The Songs covered a wide range of sentiment, ending in an expansive *Sonnet for Vienna,* the composer's last tribute to the city where he first enjoyed renown. Miss Gustavson made the most of the melodious opportunities of the songs, Mr. Albersheim's accompaniments were expertly sympathetic.

The suite from *Much Ado About Nothing* is probably Korngold's most popular composition and has long been a favorite of violinists. It is music, gay, witty and tuneful, and Mr. and Mrs. Kaufman played it charmingly. ([Albert Goldberg] 9 June 1959)

### *Los Angeles Examiner*

#### KORNGOLD MUSIC WILL OUTLAST FOES

A memorial concert to Erich Wolfgang Korngold in Schoenberg Hall last night brought to attention a musical voice which may be regarded when the smog of controversy rolls away, as one of the most civilized and gracious of the twentieth century. Thirty years ago Korngold's idiom seemed advanced. Then came schools of atonalism, polytonality and general chaos and Korngold was suddenly placed in the category of the reactionaries. Among those who discarded him, there are few survivors. Korngold spoke forth last night with a richness of melody and a luxuriance of harmony that marked him for survival.

There is no defeatism in Korngold's music. He loved life, accepted life and he gave back to music the wonder that he found in it. Last night's program represented him as a composer of chamber music and of songs. There was not scope for a reminder that in *The Dead City* he wrote one of the great operas of his era.

John Crown played the composer's Third Sonata eloquently, and with obvious dedication to the frank lushness of his harmonic and melodic idiom. Eva Gustavson sang seven songs, some in English and some in German, in a rich contralto voice that left only clarity of diction to be desired.

Louis Kaufman, violinist with Annette Kaufman at the piano, played a Suite arranged from Korngold's incidental music to Shakespeare's *Much Ado About Nothing*. Kaufman warmed the charming music with a tonal quality that he can command when conviction prompts him, and the Garden Scene emerged in beauty that was both radiant and tender. The Kaufman String Quartet played Korngold's *Third String Quartet* as the concluding number. After Intermission Robert Ryan read a tribute from Bruno Walter, who was a friend and champion of Korngold in his early days as a musical prodigy. ([Patterson Greene] 8 June 1959)

# Appendix 2

# Los Angeles Program Notes, 9 December 1956

The concertos that comprise this series of concerts are not presented in a chronological manner . . . composed during 40 years (1700–1740) in which the form of the concerto became established. Telemann's concerto in A Minor [was] first performed in Hamburg in 1728 as prologue to his opera *Emma und Eginhard* in [a] three movement pattern (fast, slow, fast) determined by Vivaldi. The vitality and grace of Telemann, whom his contemporaries called a "French" composer (due to his long residence and success in Paris) is exemplified in the finale, which is a bourrée. Bach's concertos in E major and A minor are the only two of his solo concertos that have come down in their original form. Debussy wrote of the E Major Adagio, "Very sincerely one does not know where to place oneself or how to hold oneself to be worthy of listening to it."

Bonporti, always an amateur musician, lived in Trento and constantly attempted to become Canon of the Cathedral, a post he never attained. His place in music is due to Bach's admiration for a series of violin and harpsichord works that Bonporti composed entitled "Inventions." Bach copied four of these works in his own hand as he did Vivaldi concertos and so both composers' works were printed in the Bachgesellschaft as Bach's compositions. Their identity was established in our time. The Vivaldi concertos for this series are compositions from his late mature period and the amazing beauty and inspiration of the adagios well demonstrate the melodic genius of this master, now recognized as one of the towering figures of early music. Vivaldi's use of scordatura (a special tuning of the solo violin) in concerto six of Opus IX *La Cetra* exemplifies his ingenuity in searching [for] new color and effects, as well as his own technical attainments.

# *Appendix 3*

## The Changing Recording World

Although our friendship with Armand Panigel endured over forty years, we had never discussed our experiences during World War II. In 1991 during a three-day sojourn with him and his wife, Michelle, at Saint-Remy-de-Provence, he recounted, "After the fall of France I was assigned to radio and film services from 1939 to 1944. At this time none of us believed that Germany could be defeated. Both English and German forces tried to assemble as much armament as possible. But Montgomery's successful battles against the 'Afrika Korp' and finally his great victory at Tobruk changed the course of the war. I received a call from Major Cecil Robson in Tobruk ordering me to fly there immediately. It was a one-hour flight. When I arrived, the air was still filled with fire and smoke and the dreadful odor of burning bodies, houses, and tanks. It was a Bosch vision of hell! Major Robson was in the German Officers' Club. He asked me to inspect a cache of tapes near a machine that appeared to be a movie projector with wheels on both sides with brown tape, which obviously was not film. Major Robson remarked, 'We don't know how to operate this machine. What is the purpose of the tape?' I suggested, 'Call a German prisoner, they will know.' When the German officer arrived, he was astonished to see me in a uniform bearing a French insignia, for he believed France to be completely out of the war. He activated the machine and we heard the ranting voice of Hitler. Evidently I. G. Farbin had invented this tape to send Hitler's speeches and orders to his officers throughout his far-flung armies. On hearing the Fuhrer's voice the prisoner gave the Nazi salute and stood at attention while it played."

No one dreamed at this time of using this brown tape commercially. It was only used for speech and was widely known throughout the French, American, and British armies. Bing Crosby on a USO Tour noticed this tape. Some years later in Hollywood, not wishing to travel to the broadcasting studio, Crosby suggested that this tape that he had seen in Germany might be useful to record programs at his home. This proved to be the beginning of the revolutionary process of recording speech and music of all kinds worldwide. This incredibly important discovery changed the whole course of duplicating every type of musical sound, which continues to evolve in great leaps.

# Appendix 4

# Violin Editions of Louis Kaufman

Anon. O Fairest Värmland (Swedish folksong). Arranged for violin and piano by Louis Kaufman. Bryn Mawr, Pa.: Theodore Presser Co., 1956. Out of print.

Goetz, Hermann. Violin Concerto in G Major, Opus 22. Arranged by Louis Kaufman. New York: International Music Co., 1989. Complete score and orchestral available on rental.

Kaufman, Louis. Warming-Up Scales and Arpeggios for Violin. Originally published by Theodore Presser Co., 1957. Out of print. A new and expanded edition is published by International Music Co., New York, 1969.

Pugnani, Gaetano. Six Duets for Two Violins, Opus 4, in Two Volumes. Edited by Louis Kaufman. New York: International Music Co., 2002.

Spohr, Louis. Sonata Concertante for Violin and Harp, Opus 113. Bryn Mawr, Pa.: Theodore Presser Co., 1966. New York: International Music Co., 1969.

Spohr, Louis. Sonata Concertante for Violin and Harp, Opus 114. Bryn Mawr, Pa.: Theodore Presser Co., 1969. New York: International Music Co., 1969.

Spohr, Louis. Sonata Concertante for Violin and Harp, Opus 115. Originally published by Theodore Presser Co. Out of print. A new edition is published by International Music Co., New York, 1969.

Telemann, Georg Philipp. Six Sonatinas for Violin and Harpsichord/Piano. Continuo realization by Louis Kaufman. London: Boosey-Hawks, 1954. A new edition is published by International Music Co., New York, 1985.

Telemann, Georg Philipp. Six Sonatas for Violin and Harpsichord/Piano. Originally published by Theodore Presser Co., 1957. Out of print. A new edition is published by International Music Co., New York, 1985.

Veracini, Francesco. Sonata in A Major, Opus 2, no. 6. Edited and realized by Louis Kaufman. New York: International Music Co., 1995.

Vivaldi, Antonio. Concerto for Two Violins (with original Vivaldi cadenzas). Edited by Louis Kaufman. New York: International Music Co., 2000. Complete parts and score available on rental.

Vivaldi, Antonio. Twelve Concertos from La Cetra, Opus 9. Violin parts edited by Louis Kaufman. Continuo realization by Louis Kaufman. Harpsichord/ piano reduction by Hans Brandt Buys. New York: International Music Co., 1997–2002.

# *Appendix 5*

## A Louis Kaufman's Filmography: Concertmaster in the Golden Years, a Partial List

### *For David Buttolph*

20th Century Fox — *The Adventures of Sherlock Holmes* — 1939
20th Century Fox — *Stanley and Livingstone* — 1939
20th Century Fox — *Chad Hanna* — 1940
20th Century Fox — *The House on 92nd Street* — 1945

### *For Charles Chaplin*

United Artists — *Modern Times* — 1936 (arranged by David Raksin)
United Artists — *The Great Dictator* — 1940 (arranged by Meredith Willson)
United Artists — *Monsieur Verdoux* — 1947 (arranged by Ray Rasch)

### *For Aaron Copland*

United Artists — *Our Town* — 1940
Paramount — *The Heiress* — 1949
Republic — *The Red Pony* — 1949

### *For Adolph Deutsch*

Warner Bros. — *High Sierra* — 1941
Warner Bros. — *The Maltese Falcon* — 1941

### *For Robert Emmett Dolan*

Paramount — *Holiday Inn* — 1942
Paramount — *Going My Way* — 1944
RKO — *The Bells of St. Mary's* — 1945
20th Century Fox — *The Three Faces of Eve* — 1957

### *For Hugo Friedhofer*

RKO — *The Best Years of Our Lives* — 1946
RKO — *A Song Is Born* — 1948

20th Century Fox — *Boy on a Dolphin* — 1957
20th Century Fox — *The Sun Also Rises* — 1957

### For Richard Hageman

United Artists — *The Long Voyage Home* — 1940
RKO — *She Wore a Yellow Ribbon* — 1949

### For Leigh Harline

Disney — *Snow White and the Seven Dwarfs* — 1937
Disney — *Pinocchio* — 1940
20th Century Fox — *Ten North Frederick* — 1958

### For Bernard Herrmann

RKO — *The Devil and Daniel Webster* — 1941
RKO — *The Magnificent Ambersons* — 1942
20th Century Fox — *Jane Eyre* — 1944
Paramount — *Vertigo* — 1958
Paramount — *Psycho* — 1960

### For Bronislaw Kaper

20th Century Fox — *A Flea in Her Ear* — 1958

### For Erich Wolfgang Korngold

Warner Bros. — *Anthony Adverse* — 1936
Warner Bros. — *The Prince and the Pauper* — 1937
Warner Bros. — *The Adventures of Robin Hood* — 1938
Warner Bros. — *Juarez* — 1939
Warner Bros. — *The Private Lives of Elizabeth and Essex* — 1939
Warner Bros. — *The Sea Hawk* — 1940
Warner Bros. — *The Sea Wolf* — 1941
Warner Bros. — *King's Row* — 1942
Warner Bros. — *The Constant Nymph* — 1943
Warner Bros. — *Between Two Worlds* — 1944
Warner Bros. — *Of Human Bondage* — 1946

### For Alfred Newman

United Artists — *Bulldog Drummond Strikes Back* — 1934
United Artists — *The Count of Monte Cristo* — 1934
United Artists — *The House of Rothschild* — 1934
United Artists — *We Live Again* — 1934
United Artists — *Cardinal Richelieu* — 1935

United Artists— *Clive of India*—1935
United Artists— *Beloved Enemy*—1936
United Artists— *Dodsworth*—1936
20th Century Fox— *Ramona*—1936
United Artists— *These Three*—1936
United Artists— *The Prisoner of Zenda*—1937
United Artists— *Stella Dallas*—1937
RKO— *The Hunchback of Notre Dame*—1939
20th Century Fox— *The Rains Came*—1939
United Artists— *They Shall Have Music*—1939
United Artists— *Wuthering Heights*—1939
20th Century Fox— *Young Mr. Lincoln*—1939
20th Century Fox— *The Grapes of Wrath*—1940
20th Century Fox— *Hudson's Bay*—1940
20th Century Fox— *The Mark of Zorro*—1940
20th Century Fox— *Blood and Sand*—1941
20th Century Fox— *How Green Was My Valley*—1941
20th Century Fox— *The Song of Bernadette*—1943
20th Century Fox— *The Razor's Edge*—1946
20th Century Fox— *Captain from Castille*—1947
20th Century Fox— *Gentleman's Agreement*—1947
20th Century Fox— *The Diary of Anne Frank*—1959
United Artists— *The Greatest Story Ever Told*—1965

*For Lionel Newman*

20th Century Fox— *Hello Dolly*—1969

*For Alex North*

Warner Bros.— *A Streetcar Named Desire*—1951
Universal— *Spartacus*—1960
20th Century Fox— *Cleopatra*—1963
20th Century Fox— *The Agony and the Ecstasy*—1965

*For David Raksin*

Columbia— *The Men in Her Life*—1941
20th Century Fox— *Laura*—1944
20th Century Fox— *Forever Amber*—1947

*For Miklós Rózsa*

Paramount— *Double Indemnity*—1944
Paramount— *The Lost Weekend*—1945

United Artists—*Spellbound*—1945
MGM—*Ben Hur*—1959
Allied Artists—*El Cid*—1961

*For Louis Silvers*

20th Century Fox—*Lloyd's of London*—1936
20th Century Fox—*Seventh Heaven*—1937
20th Century Fox—*Suez*—1939

*For Max Steiner*

RKO—*The Gay Divorcee*—1934
RKO—*The Life of Vergie Minters*—1934
RKO—*The Lost Patrol*—1934
RKO—*Of Human Bondage*—1934
RKO—*Anne of Green Gables*—1935
RKO—*I Dream Too Much*—1935
RKO—*The Informer*—1935
RKO—*Roberta*—1935
RKO—*She*—1935
RKO—*Top Hat*—1935
Warner Bros.—*The Charge of the Light Brigade*—1936
United Artists—*The Garden of Allah*—1936
Warner Bros.—*Little Lord Fauntleroy*—1936
Warner Bros.—*The Life of Emile Zola*—1937
United Artists—*A Star Is Born*—1937
Warner Bros.—*Adventures of Tom Sawyer*—1938
MGM—*Gone with the Wind*—1939
United Artists—*Intermezzo*—1939
Warner Bros.—*Dr. Ehrlich's Magic Bullet*—1940
Warner Bros.—*Sergeant York*—1941
Warner Bros.—*Now, Voyager*—1942
Warner Bros.—*Casablanca*—1943
Warner Bros.—*Watch on the Rhine*—1943
Warner Bros.—*The Adventures of Mark Twain*—1944
United Artists—*Since You Went Away*—1944
Warner Bros.—*The Corn Is Green*—1945
Warner Bros.—*Mildred Pierce*—1945
Warner Bros.—*Saratoga Trunk*—1945
Warner Bros.—*Life with Father*—1947
Warner Bros.—*Key Largo*—1948
Warner Bros.—*The Treasure of the Sierra Madre*—1948
Warner Bros.—*Adventures of Don Juan*—1949

*For Herbert Stothart*

MGM—*The Barretts of Wimpole Street*—1934
MGM—*The Merry Widow*—1934
MGM—*Mutiny on the Bounty*—1935
MGM—*Three Hearts for Julia*—1943

*For Franz Waxman*

Universal—*Magnificent Obsession*—1935
Universal—*Rebecca*—1940
RKO—*Suspicion*—1941
Warner Bros.—*To Have and Have Not*—1944
Universal—*The Bride of Frankenstein*—1945
Paramount—*Sunset Boulevard*—1950
Warner Bros.—*Sayonara*—1957

*For Roy Webb*

RKO—*Becky Sharp*—1935
RKO—*The Last Days of Pompeii*—1935
RKO—*Abe Lincoln in Illinois*—1940
RKO—*Kitty Foyle*—1940

*For John Williams*

20th Century Fox—*John Goldfarb, Please Come Home*—1965
United Artists—*Tom Sawyer*—1973

*For Victor Young*

Paramount—*China*—1943
Paramount—*For Whom the Bell Tolls*—1943
Paramount—*Frenchman's Creek*—1944
Paramount—*The Story of Dr. Wassell*—1944
Paramount—*Golden Earrings*—1947
Republic—*The Quiet Man*—1952
United Artists—*Around the World in 80 Days*—1956

# Louis Kaufman Discography

The late American violinist Louis Kaufman was undoubtedly among the most recorded violinists of the twentieth century. With a career that spanned nearly seven decades, Mr. Kaufman made over 175 major recordings of his classical repertoire, and was heard as the concertmaster in over 500 movie soundtracks between 1934 and 1965 including *Gone with the Wind* (1939), *Showboat* (1936), *Modern Times* (1936), *Dodsworth* (1936), *Wuthering Heights* (1939), *The Magnificent Ambersons* (1942), *Intermezzo* (1939), and *The Treasure of the Sierra Madre* (1948).

Mr. Kaufman's recording legacy goes back to the mid-1920s when he made his first recordings for the Gennett and Edison labels. This romance with the microphone would continue on an additional twenty-seven labels through the 1970s. During the mid-1980s, with the advent of the compact disc, Mr. Kaufman began to review his vast discography for the purpose of presenting potential historical CD projects to various record labels. He was quite successful, as Bay Cities, Music and Arts, Biddulph, and Cambria were receptive to his proposals.

The following discography contains all known commercial releases and reissues through the year 2000. Mr. Kaufman also left a considerable non-commercial recording legacy consisting of radio broadcasts, concert recordings, and interviews that are beyond the scope of this discography. That material will ultimately be deposited at the Library of Congress.

Determining the date of the original recording sessions has been problematic as many recording companies did not maintain complete data files or are now defunct. Where only a year is listed in the "Date Recorded" column, the information is approximate and was culled from information in the Kaufman archive now at the Library of Congress and from verifying issue dates from old record catalogs.

Lance Bowling
Director, Cambria Master Recordings
March 2001

| Composer | Title of Work | Artists | Label (*indicates CD) | Matrix # | Date Recorded | Misc. |
|---|---|---|---|---|---|---|
| | "The Yankee Fiddler" Radio documentary on Louis Kaufman | Radio Documentary—Station KUSC, Jim Svejda, commentator | Orion Custom Cassette | | 10/22/1988 | |
| Achron, Joseph | Stimmungen (1913), op. 32 | Louis Kaufman, violin Theodore Saidenberg, piano | CHC58 MB1041 ICM793 | | 1947 | Recorded in Los Angeles |
| Achron, Joseph | Stimmung | Louis Kaufman, violin Columbia Symphony Orchestra Bernard Herrmann, cond. | LAB079* CD1063* | | 1949 | |
| Albéniz, Isaac | Spanish Dance | Musical Art Quartet: Sascha Jacobsen, violin; Paul Bernard, violin; Louis Kaufman, viola; Marie Roemaet-Rosanoff, cello | Col2068D | 147800 | 1929 | |
| Anon. | Londonderry Air (traditional Irish ballad) Arranged by Kreisler | Louis Kaufman, violin Paul Ulanowsky, piano | Vox PL6530 CCL7513 L8165 ICM793 MB1041 CD1063* | | 4/16/1952 | Recorded in New York City |
| Anon. | "Deep River" Arranged by Held | Musical Art Quartet: Sascha Jacobsen, violin; Paul Bernard, violin; Louis Kaufman, viola; Marie Roemaet-Rosanoff, cello | Col1953D | 14757 | 1928 | |

| Composer | Title of Work | Artists | Label (*indicates CD) | Matrix # | Date Recorded | Misc. |
|---|---|---|---|---|---|---|
| Anon. | "Nobody Knows the Trouble I've Seen" Arranged by Held | Musical Art Quartet: Sascha Jacobsen, violin; Paul Bernard, violin; Louis Kaufman, viola; Marie Roemaet-Rosanoff, cello | Col1953D | 145996 | 1928 | |
| Anon. | "Drink to Me Only with Thine Eyes" | Musical Art Quartet: Sascha Jacobsen, violin; Paul Bernard, violin; Louis Kaufman, viola; Marie Roemaet-Rosanoff, cello | Col134-M | | 1929 | |
| Bach, J. S. | Concerto in E Major for Violin and Chamber Orchestra | Louis Kaufman, violin Bach Chamber Symphony Group Jacques Rachmilovich, cond. | TT4600 TT2044A | | 1945 | Recorded in Los Angeles |
| Bach, J. S. | Sarabande from Partita no. 1 in B minor—5th mvt. | Louis Kaufman, violin | TT TT2044A | | 1945 | Recorded in Los Angeles |
| Barber, Samuel | Concerto for Violin and Orchestra, op. 14 | Louis Kaufman, violin Lucerne Festival Orchestra Walter Goehr, cond. | OR79355 CHS1253, H1653 (set E-9) Record Hunter-1253 MMS105 OC772 LYS533–537* | CHEL-8 | 1949 | Also listed as the Concert Hall Symphony |
| Bennett, Robert Russell | Hexapoda—Five Studies in Jitteroptera (1941) | Louis Kaufman violin Robert Russell Bennett, piano | Col7727D OC80c | AM1376 AM1377 | 1942 | Recorded in Los Angeles |

| Composer | Title | Performers | Catalog | Date | Notes |
|---|---|---|---|---|---|
| Bennett, Robert Russell | Violin Concerto in A Major | Louis Kaufman, violin; Columbia Symphony; Bernard Herrmann, cond. | MB1032 BCD1019* CD1078* | 3/1945, 1946 | |
| Bennett, Robert Russell | Song Sonata for Violin and Piano | Louis Kaufman, violin; Theodore Saidenberg, piano | CHS1062 CD1078* | 10/1947 | |
| Bennett, Robert Russell | Hexapoda—Five Studies in Jitteroptera (1941) | Louis Kaufman, violin; Annette Kaufman, piano | CT6004, MHS3974 | 1978 | Recorded in Los Angeles |
| Bennett, Robert Russell | Song Sonata for Violin and Piano | Louis Kaufman, violin; Annette Kaufman, piano | CT6004, MHS3974 | 1978 | Recorded in Los Angeles |
| Bennett, Robert Russell | Violin Concerto in A Major | Louis Kaufman, violin; London Symphony Orchestra; Bernard Herrmann, cond. | CT6004, MHS3974 BCD1008* | 1978 | |
| Bishop, Sir Henry Rowley (arranger) | "Home, Sweet Home" | Musical Art Quartet: Sascha Jacobsen, violin; Paul Bernard, violin; Louis Kaufman, viola; Marie Roemaet-Rosanoff, cello | Col29-M 14371 | 1927 | Recorded in New York City |
| Bloch, Ernest | Sonata no. 1 for Violin and Piano (1920) | Louis Kaufman, violin; Pina Pozzi, piano | OR79355 CHS1253 CH H18 OC772 CD638* | 1954 | Recorded in Zurich |
| Brahms, Johannes | Sonata no. 1 in G for Violin and Piano, op. 78 | Louis Kaufman, violin; Hélène Pignari, piano | Classic Club X83B MMS109 CM9 | 1954 | Recorded in Zurich |

| Composer | Title of Work | Artists | Label (*indicates CD) | Matrix # | Date Recorded | Misc. |
|---|---|---|---|---|---|---|
| Bryan, Alfred and John Klenner | "Japansky" | Louis Kaufman, violin solo<br>Louis Spielman, piano | | | 6/1928 | "New Electrobeam process" |
| Chausson, Ernest | Concerto in D for Violin, Piano, and String Quartet, op. 21 | Louis Kaufman, violin<br>Arthur Balsam, piano<br>Pascal String Quartet | Gennett-6437B<br>OR73134<br>CL6217,<br>CHS1071<br>CHS<br>OC773<br>CLP1071 | | 1950 | Recorded in Paris |
| Copland, Aaron | "Hoe-Down" from Rodeo (1942)<br>Arranged by Copland | Louis Kaufman, violin<br>Annette Kaufman, piano | Vox668 (in set 627)<br>CHC58<br>CHS1140B<br>MB1032<br>OC800 | VX8100.5 | 5/3/1947 | Recorded in Los Angeles |
| Copland, Aaron | "Hoe-Down" from Rodeo (1942)<br>Arranged by Copland | Louis Kaufman, violin<br>Annette Kaufman, piano | BCD1019* | | 1947 | Recorded in Los Angeles |
| Copland, Aaron | Ukulele Serenade | Louis Kaufman, violin<br>Annette Kaufman, piano | CH set C10<br>CH96 (in set 10)<br>CH58<br>CHC57<br>CHS1140B<br>Vox668 (in set 627) | VX8102.3 | 5/3/1947 | Recorded in Los Angeles |

| Composer | Title | Performers | Catalog | No. | Date | Notes |
|---|---|---|---|---|---|---|
| Copland, Aaron | Nocturne no. 1 from 2 Pieces (1926) | Louis Kaufman, violin; Aaron Copland, piano | MB1032 BCD1019* CH96 (set C10) CH58 MB1032 Vox668 (in set 627) OC800 | CHS361.1 | 1948 | Recorded in New York City |
| Copland, Aaron | Sonata for Violin and Piano (1943) | Louis Kaufman, violin; Aaron Copland, piano | CH set C10 96/8 OC800 MB1032 BCD1019* | | 1948 | Recorded in New York City |
| Davis, Benny, and Jesse Greer | "Mike" | John Ryan, tenor, Louis Kaufman, violin obbligato | Gennett-3345A | 9962 | 4/1926 | |
| Davis, Benny, and Jesse Greer | "I Don't Want the World" | Sterling Trio — Accompanied by Tovian Trio | Gennett-3379B | X-33 | 5/1926 | Louis Kaufman was violinist for Tovian Trio |
| Delius, Frederick | Violin Sonata no. 1 (1892) | Louis Kaufman, violin Theodore Saidenberg, piano | CHS124/5 (set AO), CHS1062 CHS62 ICM784 | 12-428 | 11/1947 | Recorded in Los Angeles |
| Douglas Scott, Lady John | "Annie Laurie" | Musical Art Quartet: Sascha Jacobsen, violin; Paul Bernard, violin; Louis Kaufman, viola; Marie Roemaet-Rosanoff, cello | Col134-M | | 1929 | Recorded in New York City |

| Composer | Title of Work | Artists | Label (*indicates CD) | Matrix # | Date Recorded | Misc. |
|---|---|---|---|---|---|---|
| Dowling, Eddy | "Little Log Cabin of Dreams" | Louis Kaufman, violin<br>Louis Spielman, piano | Edison Diamond Disc52301 | 18462 | 4–5/1928 | |
| Drdla, Franz | "Souvenir" for Violin and Piano | Louis Kaufman, violin<br>Paul Ulanowsky, piano | CCL-7513<br>L8165 | | 4/16/1952 | Recorded in New York City |
| Dvořák, Antonín | Four Romantic Pieces, op. 75 | Louis Kaufman, violin<br>Arthur Balsam, piano | AD<br>CCL-7506<br>L8112<br>LCB8112<br>MB1041<br>ICM793 | | 1949 | Recorded in Paris |
| Dvořák, Antonín | Humoresque no. 7 in G-flat<br>Arranged by Kreisler "in G," op. 10 | Louis Kaufman, violin<br>Paul Ulanowsky, piano | CCL-7513<br>L8165<br>CEC004<br>FAP8208 | | 4/16/1952 | Recorded in New York City |
| Dvořák, Antonín | Trio no. 3 in F Minor, op. 65 | Louis Kaufman, violin<br>Marcel Cervera, cello<br>Arthur Balsam, piano | CHS1117<br>Classic<br>Club6248<br>Classic<br>Club X69 | | 1952 | Recorded in Winterthur, Switzerland |
| Foster, Stephen | "Old Folks at Home" | Musical Art Quartet:<br>Sascha Jacobsen, violin; Paul Bernard, violin; Louis Kaufman, viola; Marie Roemaet-Rosanoff, cello | Col129-M | 14335o | 1927 | Recorded in New York City |

| Composer | Title | Performers | Catalog | XPARTS | Date | Notes |
|---|---|---|---|---|---|---|
| Franck, César | Sonate en La Majeur pour Violon et Piano (1886) | Louis Kaufman, violin Hélène Pignari, piano | MMS2066 MMS103 Classic Club X83A MMS103 | 35-629 | 1954 | Recorded in Zurich |
| Glazunov, Alexander Konstantinovich | "Alla Spagnola" | Musical Art Quartet: Sascha Jacobsen, violin; Paul Bernard, violin; Louis Kaufman, viola; Marie Roemaet-Rosanoff, cello | Col5085M | | 1929 | Recorded in New York City |
| Glazunov, Alexander Konstantinovich | "Interludium in Modo Antico" | Musical Art Quartet: Sascha Jacobsen, violin; Paul Bernard, violin; Louis Kaufman, viola; Marie Roemaet-Rosanoff, cello | Col5085M | | 1929 | Recorded in New York City |
| Glinka, Mikhail | Quartet in F (1830) | Louis Kaufman, violin Joseph Stepansky, violin Louis Kievman, viola George Neikrug, cello | SFM1001 S7006 CSPR164 | | 1958 | Recorded in Los Angeles |
| Goetz, Hermann | Concerto in G Major, op. 22 | Louis Kaufman, violin BBC Scottish Orchestra Ian Whyte, cond. | MB1042 LYS533–537* | | 4/18/1956 | Taken from broadcast performance |
| Guarnieri, Carmargo | Canto I for Violin and Piano | Louis Kaufman, violin Theodore Saidenberg, piano | CH58 MB1041 | | 1947 | Recorded in Los Angeles |
| Guarnieri, Carmargo | Sonata no. 2 for Violin and Piano (1947) | Louis Kaufman, violin Arthur Balsam, piano | OR79359 album D16–17 CH DL17 (set D17) CD1078* | | 1949 | Recorded in Zurich |

| Composer | Title of Work | Artists | Label (*indicates CD) | Matrix # | Date Recorded | Misc. |
|---|---|---|---|---|---|---|
| Haydn, Franz Joseph | Quartet in C Major, op. 54, no. 2 | Musical Art Quartet: Sascha Jacobsen, violin; Paul Bernard, violin; Louis Kaufman, viola; Marie Roemaet-Rosanoff, cello | Col set 69 67320–22D | | 1929 | Recorded in New York City |
| Haydn, Franz Joseph | Quartet in D, op. 64, no. 5 Vivace | Musical Art Quartet: Sascha Jacobsen, violin; Paul Bernard, violin; Louis Kaufman, viola; Marie Roemaet-Rosanoff, cello | Col set 69 67322D | VX8103;3 | 1929 | Recorded in New York City |
| Helm, Everett Burton | Comment on Two Spirituals for Violin and Piano "No Hidin' Place" | Louis Kaufman, violin Annette Kaufman, piano | CH CHC58 Vox666 (in set 627) OC800 MB1032 CD1078* | 148374 | 5/3/1947 | Recorded in Los Angeles |
| Helm, Everett Burton | Comment on Two Spirituals for Violin and Piano "Sinners Don't Let this Harvest Pass" | Louis Kaufman, violin Annette Kaufman, piano | CH CHC58 Vox666 (in set 627) MB1032 CD1078* | VX8103;3 | 5/3/1947 | Recorded in Los Angeles |
| Herbert, Victor | Serenade | Musical Art Quartet: Sascha Jacobsen, violin; Paul Bernard, violin; Louis Kaufman, viola; Marie Roemaet-Rosanoff, cello | Col2068D | | 1929 | Recorded in New York City |

| | | | | | |
|---|---|---|---|---|---|
| Hindemith, Paul | Second Sonata (1920), op. 11, no. 2, in D | Louis Kaufman, violin Arthur Balsam, piano | Cap P8063 CTL7001 ICM784 | 1950 | |
| Kahn, Gus, and Ted Fiorito | "Someone to Love" | Sterling Trio Accompanied by Tovian Trio | Gennett-3379A | X-32 | 5/1926 | Louis Kaufman was violinist for Tovian Trio |
| Kern, Jerome | "Smoke Gets in Your Eyes" | Louis Kaufman violin Leonard Berman, piano | BCD1019* OC800 MB1032 | 11/1/1946 | Arranged by Kaufman and Berman |
| Kern, Jerome | "The Song Is You" | Louis Kaufman violin Leonard Berman, piano | BCD1019* OC800 MB1032 | 11/1/1946 | Arranged by Kaufman and Berman |
| Khachaturian, Aram | Violin Concerto in D Major (1940) | Louis Kaufman, violin Santa Monica Symphony Jacques Rachmilovich, cond. | CH126/9 set AN CH173/80 OC799 MB1050 CHC2 LAB079* LYS533–537* CD1063* | 1945 | Recorded in Los Angeles |
| Kodály, Zoltán | Adagio in C Major (1905) | Louis Kaufman, violin Theodore Saidenberg, piano | CHC58 MB1041 ICM793 | 1947 | |
| Korngold, Erich Wolfgang | Suite—Much Ado about Nothing, op. 11 (1919) | Louis Kaufman, violin Annette Kaufman, piano | K1001* | 6/7/1959 | Korngold Memorial Concert, UCLA, 1959 |

| Composer | Title of Work | Artists | Label (*indicates CD) | Matrix # | Date Recorded | Misc. |
|---|---|---|---|---|---|---|
| Larsson, Lars-Erik | Violin Concerto (1940), op. 42 | Louis Kaufman, violin Swedish Radio Symphony Sten Frykberg, cond. | OC799 | | 1/23/1955 | From broadcast performance |
| MacDowell, Edward | "To a Wild Rose" | Musical Art Quartet: Sascha Jacobsen, violin; Paul Bernard, violin; Louis Kaufman, viola; Marie Roemaet-Rosanoff, cello | Col794D | 147858 | 1929 | Recorded in New York City |
| Manfredini, Vincenzo | Concerto no. 12 in C, Pastorale 1st mvt. Christmas Concerto from 12 Concerti, op. 3 (1718) | Louis Kaufman, violin Anton Fietz, violin Concert Hall String Ensemble Clemens Dahinden, cond. | CH F7 | | 1951 | |
| Martinů, Bohuslav Jan | Five Pieces Breves — no. 2 Andante (1930) | Louis Kaufman, violin Pina Pozzi, piano | CH E12 MB1027 | | 1950 | |
| Martinů, Bohuslav Jan | Five Pieces Breves — no. 5 Allegro | Louis Kaufman, violin Pina Pozzi, piano | CH E12 MB1027 | | 1950 | |
| Martinů, Bohuslav Jan | Sonata for Two Violins and Piano (1932) | Louis Kaufman, violin Peter Rybar, violin Pina Pozzi, piano | CH E12 | | 1950 | |
| Martinů, Bohuslav Jan | Concerto no. 2 for Violin and Orchestra (1943) | Louis Kaufman, violin l'Orchestre National de la Radiodiffusion Française Eugène Bigot, cond. | MB1027 OC787 | | 1954 | Broadcast of French premiere |
| Martinů, Bohuslav Jan | Concerto no. 2 for Violin and Orchestra (1943) | Louis Kaufman, violin ORTF — France Jean-Michel Leconte, cond. | CD1063* | | 1955 | Taken from broadcast performance |

| Composer | Work | Performers | Catalog | | Date | Notes |
|---|---|---|---|---|---|---|
| Massenet, Jules | "Méditation" from Thaïs (1894) Arranged by Martin-Pierre Marsick | Louis Kaufman, violin Theodore Saidenberg, piano | Vox PL6530 MB1041 CCL7513 L8165 | | 1947 | Recorded in Los Angeles |
| Mattheson, Johann | Sonata no. 6 in E for Flute or Violin and Clav. From 12 Sonatas (1720) | Louis Kaufman, violin Antoine Geoffroy-Dechaume, harpsichord | Eurochord LPG627, Lyrichord LL8 | | 1955 | Recorded in Paris |
| McBride, Robert | Aria and Toccata in Swing (1946) Arranged by Louis Kaufman | Louis Kaufman, violin Annette Kaufman, piano | CHC58 CHS1140B Vox666 (in set 627) OC800 MB1032 BCD1019* | VX8105.2 | 5/3/1947 | Recorded in Los Angeles |
| McBride, Robert | Aria and Toccata in Swing for Violin and Orchestra (1946) | Louis Kaufman, violin Columbia Symphony Orchestra Bernard Herrmann, cond. | CD1078* | | 7/9/1947 | |
| Mendelssohn Felix | Concerto in E Minor, op. 64 | Louis Kaufman, violin Netherlands Philharmonic Orchestra Otto Ackermann, cond. | MMS7 Classic Club X71 MB1042 CL LP1001 CLP MLPY7 LYS533–537* | | 1952 | Recorded in Utrecht |

| Composer | Title of Work | Artists | Label (*indicates CD) | Matrix # | Date Recorded | Misc. |
|---|---|---|---|---|---|---|
| Mendelssohn, Felix | Quartet in E-flat, op. 12, no. 1 | Louis Kaufman, violin<br>Joseph Stepansky, violin<br>Louis Kievman, viola<br>George Neikrug, cello | SFM1001<br>S7006<br>CSPR164 | | 1958 | Recorded in Los Angeles |
| Milhaud, Darius | 12 Saudades Do Brasil (1920/1). no. 5, Ipanema<br>Arranged by Levy | Louis Kaufman, violin<br>Theodore Saidenberg, piano | CHC58<br>MB1041<br>OC800<br>OC772<br>CD1c78* | | 1947 | Recorded in Los Angeles |
| Milhaud, Darius | Concertino de Printemps (1934) | Louis Kaufman, violin<br>French National Orchestra<br>Darius Milhaud, cond. | OR7625o<br>Cap8-86013<br>CTL7005<br>P8071,<br>5337-1<br>5338-1<br>OC771<br>OC787<br>CD620* | | 1949 | Recorded in Paris<br>Rereleased on *Darius Milhaud Conducts Milhaud*, Dutton Laboratories CDBP9711*, 2001 |
| Milhaud, Darius | Danses de Jacaremirim (1945) | Louis Kaufman, violin<br>Arthur Balsam, piano | OR7625o<br>Cap<br>CTL7005<br>P8071<br>MB1c41<br>ICM793<br>CD620* | | 1949 | Recorded in Paris |

| Composer | Work | Performers | Catalog nos. | | Date | Notes |
|---|---|---|---|---|---|---|
| Milhaud, Darius | Second Violin Concerto (1946) | Louis Kaufman, violin / French National Orchestra / Darius Milhaud, cond. | OR7650 OC771 Cap6F8-7027/9 (set ECL8072) CTL7005 P8071 CD620* | | 10/1949 | Recorded in Paris / Rereleased on *Darius Milhaud Conducts Milhaud*, Dutton Laboratories CDBP9711*, 2001 |
| Mozart, Wolfgang Amadeus | Concerto in D—K. anH 294a "Princess Adelaide" (1766) | Louis Kaufman, violin / Netherlands Philharmonic Orchestra / Otto Ackerman, cond. | CH G10 OR7210I OC774 LYS533–537* | E2 KP 8268 | 1952 | Cadenzas by Paul Hindemith / Limited edition 3000 copies |
| Nevin, Ethelbert | "Mighty Lak' a Rose" | Musical Art Quartet: Sascha Jacobsen, violin; Paul Bernard, violin; Louis Kaufman, viola; Marie Roemaet-Rosanoff, cello | Col17794D | | 1929 | Recorded in New York City |
| Piston, Walter | Violin Concerto no. 1 (1939) | Louis Kaufman, violin / London Symphony Orchestra / Bernard Hermann, cond. | MB1050 BCD1019* LYS533–537* | | 4/14/1956 | Taken from broadcast |
| Porter, Quincy | Sonata no. 2 for Violin and Piano (1929) | Louis Kaufman, violin / Arthur Balsam, piano | OR79359 CH DL16 (set D16) album D16–17 OC772 CD638* | | 1949 | |

| Composer | Title of Work | Artists | Label (*indicates CD) | Matrix # | Date Recorded | Misc. |
|---|---|---|---|---|---|---|
| Poulenc, Francis | Sonata in D (1943) for Violin and Piano "In Memory of García Lorca" | Louis Kaufman, violin Arthur Balsam, piano | Cap P8063 CTL7001 | | 1949 | Recorded in Paris |
| Poulenc, Francis | Sonata in D (1943) for Violin and Piano "In Memory of García Lorca" | Louis Kaufman, violin Hélène Pignari, piano | OR7292 CD620* | | 1954 | Recorded in Zurich |
| Prokofiev, Sergey Sergeyevich | Gavotte no. 3 (1941) from Cinderella Ballet, op. 87 Arranged by Heifetz | Louis Kaufman, violin Theodore Saidenberg, piano | CHC58 MB1041 | | 1947 | Recorded in Los Angeles |
| Ravel, Maurice | Sonata for Violin and Piano (1917) | Louis Kaufman, violin Arthur Balsam, piano | CHS E-6 CH EL6 (side two only) | | 1949 | Recorded in Zurich |
| Respighi, Ottorino | Sonata in B (1927) | Louis Kaufman, violin Theodore Saidenberg, piano | MTT 2078 ICM784 | | 1947 | Recorded in Los Angeles |
| Rimsky-Korsakov, Nikolay Andreyevich | Hymn to the Sun (1910) from Le Coq d'or Arranged by Kreisler | Louis Kaufman, violin Paul Ulanowsky, piano | Cap CCL7513, L8165 MB1041 ICM793 CD1063* | | 4/16/1952 | Recorded in New York City |
| Saint-Saëns, Camille | Violin Concerto no. 3 in B Minor, op. 61 | Louis Kaufman, violin Santa Monica Symphony Jacques Rachmilovich, cond. | Disc Asch805 (4120/2) MTT2078 | CPM12-4 03/08 | 1945 | Recorded in Los Angeles |

| | | | | | | |
|---|---|---|---|---|---|---|
| Saint-Saëns, Camille | Concerto no. 3 in B Minor, op. 61 | Louis Kaufman, violin<br>Netherlands Philharmonic Orchestra<br>Mauritz van den Berg, cond. | LAB079*<br>LYS533–537*<br><br>OR75177<br>MMS62<br>MB1041<br>OC773<br>LYS533–537* | | 1952 | Recorded in Utrecht |
| Saint-Saëns, Camille | Havanaise, op. 83 | Louis Kaufman, violin<br>Netherlands Philharmonic Orchestra<br>Mauritz van den Berg, cond. | OR75177<br>MMS62<br>MB1041<br>OC773<br>LYS533–537* | | 1952 | Recorded in Utrecht |
| Sauguet, Henri | Concerto d'orphée | Louis Kaufman, violin<br>ORTF—France<br>Jean-Michel Leconte | CD620*<br>OC787 | | 1955 | Recorded in Paris |
| Schubert, Franz Peter | String Quartet in A Minor, op. 89 | Musical Art Quartet:<br>Sascha Jacobsen, violin; Paul Bernard, violin; Louis Kaufman, viola; Marie Roemaet-Rosanoff, cello | Col set<br>M-86<br>67413, 14,<br>15, 16 | | 1928 | Schubert Centennial Edition, electric |
| Schubert, Franz Peter | Menuetto from Quartet in E Major, op. 125, no. 1 | Musical Art Quartet:<br>Sascha Jacobsen, violin; Paul Bernard, violin; Louis Kaufman, viola; Marie Roemaet-Rosanoff, cello | Col set<br>M-86<br>67416D | 98487 | | Electric |

| Composer | Title of Work | Artists | Label (*indicates CD) | Matrix # | Date Recorded | Misc. |
|---|---|---|---|---|---|---|
| Schubert, Franz Peter | "Hark, Hark, the Lark" | Musical Art Quartet: Sascha Jacobsen, violin; Paul Bernard, violin; Louis Kaufman, viola; Marie Roemaet-Rosanoff, cello | Col set M-96 67456D | | 1928 | Electric |
| Schubert, Franz Peter | Quartet in E-flat, op. 125, no. 1 | Musical Art Quartet: Sascha Jacobsen, violin; Paul Bernard, violin; Louis Kaufman, viola; Marie Roemaet-Rosanoff, cello | Col set M-96 67454–56 | | 1928 | Electric |
| Schubert, Franz Peter | Ave Maria, op. 52, no. 6, D.839 Arranged by Wilhemj | Louis Kaufman, violin Paul Ulanowsky, piano | CCL7513, L8165 MB1041 ICM793 | | 4/16/1952 | Recorded in New York City |
| Schubert, Franz Peter | Sonata in A, op. 162, Duo for Violin and Piano (D574) | Louis Kaufman, violin Pina Pozzi, piano | CH H14 ICM793 | | 1954 | Recorded in Zurich |
| Schumann, Robert | Sonata no. 1 in A Minor, op. 105 | Louis Kaufman, violin Arthur Balsam, piano | CCL7506 L8112 NLSB8112 MB1042 | | 1950 | Recorded in Paris |
| Schumann, Robert | "Träumerei" from 13 Kinderszenen, op. 15 | Louis Kaufman, violin Paul Ulanowsky, piano | CCL7513, L8165 CEC004 FAP8208 (10 in) | | 4/16/1952 | Recorded in New York City |
| Sibelius, Jean | Two Pieces, op. 2, no. 2 Epilogue | Louis Kaufman, violin Theodore Saidenberg, piano | CHC58 MB1041 ICM793 | | 1947 | Recorded in Los Angeles |

| Composer | Work | Performers | Catalog | Date | Notes |
|---|---|---|---|---|---|
| Smetana, Bedrich | Trio in G, op. 15, for Piano, Violin, and Cello | Louis Kaufman, violin / Rudolf Firkusny, piano / Willem van den Berg, cello | Vox669/71 (set 628) / DC1009/11 | 1948 | Recorded in Los Angeles / Listed by New York Times as "Best Recording of 1949" |
| Spohr, Louis | Three Sonates Concertantes for Harp and Violin, ops. 113, 114, 115 | Louis Kaufman, violin / Susann McDonald, harp | OR7262 / OC744 / OC634 (op. 114/115) / CD905* | 1971/1972 | 11/20/71—Opus 115 / 11/28/71—Opus 114 / 12/4/71—Opus 113 |
| Still, William Grant | "Blues" from Lenox Avenue (1937) Arranged for Violin and Orchestra | Louis Kaufman, piano / Columbia Symphony Orchestra / Bernard Herrmann, cond. | CD1078* | 1946 | |
| Still, William Grant | "Blues" from Lenox Avenue (1937) Arranged by Louis Kaufman | Louis Kaufman, violin / Annette Kafuman, piano | Vox667 (in set 627) / CH / CHC57 / CH58 / CHS1140B / MB1032 / OC800 | 5/3/1947 | Recorded in Los Angeles |
| Still, William Grant | "Here's One" | Louis Kaufman, violin / Annette Kaufman, piano | Vox667 (in set 627) / CH / CHC57 / CH58 / CHS1140B / MB1032 / OC800 | 5/3/1947 | Recorded in Los Angeles |

| Composer | Title of Work | Artists | Label (*indicates CD) | Matrix # | Date Recorded | Misc. |
|---|---|---|---|---|---|---|
| Still, William Grant | Suite for Violin and Orchestra (1943) | Louis Kaufman, violin Standard Hour Symphony Henry Svedrofsky, cond. | BCD1033* CD1121* | | 1947 | |
| Still, William Grant | "Blues" from Lenox Avenue Arranged by Louis Kaufman | Louis Kaufman, violin Annette Kaufman, piano | OR752 WGSM-1001 OC63 BCD1019* | | 1972 | Recorded in Los Angeles |
| Still, William Grant | "Carmela" (arranged for violin and piano by Louis Kaufman) | Louis Kaufman, violin Annette Kaufman, piano | OR752 OC63 BCD1033* CD1121* | | 1972 | Recorded in Los Angeles |
| Still, William Grant | Danzas de Panama for String Quartet, nos. 1 and 3 | Kaufman String Quartet: Louis Kaufman, violin George Berres, violin Alan Newman, viola, Terry King, cello | OR7278 WGSM-1001 OC63 CD638* | | 1972 | Recorded in Los Angeles |
| Still, William Grant | Danzas de Panama for String Quartet, nos. 2 and 4 | Kaufman String Quartet: Louis Kaufman, violin George Berres, violin Alan Newman, viola, Terry King, cello | BCD1033* CD1121* WGSM-1001 OC63 | | 1972 | Recorded in Los Angeles |
| Still, William Grant | Ennanga for String Quartet, Harp, and Piano (1956) | Lois Adele Craft, harp Kaufman String Quartet: Louis Kaufman, violin George Berres, violin | OR7278, OR79359 WGSM-1001 | | 1972 | Recorded in Los Angeles |

| | | | | | |
|---|---|---|---|---|---|
| Still, William Grant | "Here's One" Arranged for violin and piano by Louis Kaufman | Alan Newman, viola, Terry King, cello, Annette Kaufman, piano | OC800 OC633 CD638* | 1972 | Recorded in Los Angeles |
| Still, William Grant | Pastorela (1946) Arranged by Louis Kaufman | Louis Kaufman, violin Annette Kaufman, piano | OR752 WGSM-1001 OC633 BCD1033* CD1121* | 1972 | Recorded in Los Angeles |
| Still, William Grant | Suite for Violin and Piano (1943) | Louis Kaufman, violin Annette Kaufman, piano | OR752 WGSM-1001 OC633 | 1972 | Recorded in Los Angeles |
| Still, William Grant | Summerland (no. 2 from Three Visions) (1936) | Louis Kaufman, violin Annette Kaufman, piano | OR752 WGSM-1001 OC633 BCD1033* CD1121* | 1972 | Recorded in Los Angeles |
| Strauss, Richard | Sonata in E-flat, op. 18 | Louis Kaufman, violin Arthur Balsam, piano | CHF15 ICM784 | 1951 | Recorded in Zurich |

| Composer | Title of Work | Artists | Label (*indicates CD) | Matrix # | Date Recorded | Misc. |
|---|---|---|---|---|---|---|
| Stravinsky, Igor | Duo Concertant for Violin and Piano (1932) | Louis Kaufman, violin Hélène Pignari, piano | OR7292 MMS107 MAR561I OC771 CMS | | 1954 | Recorded in Zurich |
| Tartini, Giuseppe | Sonata in B-flat | Louis Kaufman, violin Antoine Geoffroy-Dechaume, harpsichord | Eurochord LPG627 Lyrichord LL8 | | 1955 | Recorded in Paris |
| Tchaikovsky, Pyotr Ilich | Trio in A, "To the Memory of a Great Artist," op. 50 | Louis Kaufman, violin Kurt Reher, cello Theodore Saidenberg, piano | Vox VLP6530 | | 1947 | Recorded in Los Angeles |
| Tchaikovsky, Pyotr Ilich | Andante Cantabile—2nd mvt. from Quartet no. 1 in D, op. 11. | Louis Kaufman, violin Paul Ulanowsky, piano Arranged by Kreisler | Cap CCL7513 L8165 ICM793 MB1041 CD1053* | | 4/16/1952 | Recorded in New York City |
| Telemann, Georg Philipp | Concerto for Three Violins and Strings—Concerto in F, T.II, no. 3 | Louis Kaufman, violin Peter Rybar and Anton Fietz, violin Concert Hall String Orchestra Henry Swoboda, cond. | CHS DL-12 (in set D12) | | 1949 | Recorded in Zurich |
| Telemann, Georg Philipp | Concerto in F for Violin and Strings | Louis Kaufman, violin Concert Hall Chamber Orchestra Dennis Stevens, cond. | CH G17 | | 1951 | Limited edition 3000 Recorded in Zurich |

| Composer | Work | Performers | Catalog | Year | Notes |
|---|---|---|---|---|---|
| Telemann, Georg Philipp | Suite in D, T.II, no. 1 for oboe, trumpet, strings and harpsichord | Louis Kaufman, violin<br>Sam Zilverberg, oboe<br>Fred Hausdoerfer, trumpet<br>Concert Hall Chamber Orchestra<br>Dennis Stevens, cond. | CH G17 | 1951 | Recorded in Winterthur, Switzerland |
| Telemann, Georg Philipp | Sonata in A for Violin and Harpsichord | Louis Kaufman, violin<br>Antoine Geoffroy-Dechaume, harpsichord | Eurochord LPG627<br>Lyrichord LL8 | 1955 | Recorded in Paris |
| Telemann, Georg Philipp | Sonata in G for Violin and Harpsichord | Louis Kaufman, violin<br>Antoine Geoffroy-Dechaume, harpsichord | Eurochord LPG627<br>Lyrichord LL8 | 1955 | Recorded in Paris |
| Telemann, Georg Philipp | Six Sonatas for Violin and Harpsichord | Louis Kaufman, violin<br>Fredrick Hammond, harpsichord | OR7272<br>OC634<br>CD905* | 1972 | Recorded in Los Angeles |
| Toch, Ernst | Spitzweg Serenade | Louis Kaufman, violin<br>Grissha Monasevitch, violin<br>Raymond Menhennick, viola | Vox set t77 t6081–082<br>MB1051 | AM2004/5, M2008/9 | 1946 | Recorded in Los Angeles |
| Toch, Ernst | Quintet in C, op. 64 | Louis Kaufman, violin<br>Ernst Toch, piano<br>Grissha Monasevitch, violin<br>Ray Menhennick, viola<br>J. Kahn, cello | Col set M-460,<br>MB1051 | 1947 | Recorded in Los Angeles |
| Toch, Ernst | Sonata no. 2 (1927), op. 44 | Louis Kaufman, violin<br>Ernst Toch, piano | MB1051 | 1947 | Taken from broadcast |

| Composer | Title of Work | Artists | Label (*indicates CD) | Matrix # | Date Recorded | Misc. |
|---|---|---|---|---|---|---|
| Toch, Ernst | Serenade in G, op. 25 (1917) | Louis Kaufman, violin<br>J. Stepansky, violin<br>L. Kievman, viola | C6002<br>S7016<br>CD1126* | | 1958 | Recorded in Los Angeles |
| Toch, Ernst | String Quartet in D-flat, op. 18 (1909) | Louis Kaufman, violin<br>J. Stepansky, violin<br>L. Kievman, viola<br>George Neikrug, cello | C6002<br>CSPR165<br>S7016<br>CD1126* | | 1958 | Recorded in Los Angeles |
| Torelli, Giuseppe | Concerto Grosso no. 3 in E Major | L'Ensemble Orchestral de L'Oiseau-Lyre<br>Louis Kaufman, director | DO17039<br>CH F17 | LM85 | 1951 | Recorded in Paris |
| Torelli, Giuseppe | Concerto Grosso no. 6 in sol mineur | Ensemble Orchestral de L'Oiseau-Lyre<br>Louis Kaufman, director | DO17039<br>CH F17 | LM86 | 1951 | Recorded in Paris |
| Torelli, Giuseppe | 12 Concerti Grossi, op. 8, no. 8 (1709) | Louis Kaufman, violin<br>George Alès, violin<br>Roger Albin, cello<br>Ruggiero Gerlin, harpsichord<br>L'Ensemble Orchestral de L'Oiseau-Lyre<br>Louis Kaufman, cond. | OL-50089/90<br>box set<br>LL115/<br>LL116<br>ICM785 | | 1954 | Recorded in Paris |
| Triggs, Harold | Danza Brasiliana | Louis Kaufman, violin<br>Annette Kaufman, piano | Vox667 (in set 627)<br>CHC58<br>OC800<br>MB1032<br>CD1078* | VX81044 | 1947 | Recorded in Los Angeles |

| Composer / Work | Performers | Date | Records | Notes |
| --- | --- | --- | --- | --- |
| Vaughan Williams, Ralph<br>Concerto Accademico in D Minor (1925) | Louis Kaufman, violin<br>Winterthur String Orchestra<br>Clemens Dahinden, cond. | 1951 | CHS1253 F8<br>OR79359<br>OR72101<br>Record Hunter-1253<br>OC774<br>LYS533–537* | Also listed as Concert Hall Symphony, Zurich Radio Symphony; Rec1253 says Walter Goehr is conductor, which is incorrect |
| Vivaldi, Antonio<br>12 Concerti, op. 8 (1725)<br>Concerto no. 2, in B-flat, F.I, no. 23 "L'Estate" | Louis Kaufman, violin<br>Edith Weissmannn, harpsichord<br>Edouard Nies-Berger, organ<br>Concert Hall Orchestra<br>Henry Swoboda, cond. | 1947 | Amphion AD381/6 (set AR)<br>Classic Club X65<br>CH79/84 (set AR in 2 volumes)<br>CHC1<br>CHC1001<br>MMS56<br>LYS533–537* | Recorded in New York City |

| Composer | Title of Work | Artists | Label (*indicates CD) | Matrix # | Date Recorded | Misc. |
|---|---|---|---|---|---|---|
| Vivaldi, Antonio | 12 Concerti, op. 8 (1725) Concerto no. 3, in F, F.I, no. 24 "L'Autunno" | Louis Kaufman, violin Edith Weissmann, harpsichord Edouard Nies-Berger, organ Concert Hall Orchestra Henry Swoboda, cond. | Amphion AD381/6 (set AR) Classic Club X65, CH79/84 (set AR in 2 volumes) CHC1 CHC1001 MMS56 LYS533–537* | | 1947 | Recorded in New York City |
| Vivaldi, Antonio | 12 Concerti, op. 8 (1725) Concerto no. 4, in F, F.I, no. 25, "L'Inverno" | Louis Kaufman, violin Edith Weissmann, harpsichord Edouard Nies-Berger, organ Concert Hall Orchestra Henry Swoboda, cond. | Amphion AD381/6 (set AR) Classic Club X65, CH79/84 (set AR in 2 volumes) CHC1 CHC1001, MMS56 LYS533–537* | | 1947 | Recorded in New York City |
| Vivaldi, Antonio | 12 Concerti, op. 8 (1725) "Il Cimento dell' Armonia e dell' Invenzione" (nos. 1/4 Le Quattro Stagioni) Violin and Strings | Louis Kaufman, violin Edith Weissmann, harpsichord Edouard Nies-Berger, organ Concert Hall Orchestra | Amphion AD381/6 (set AR) Classic | | 12/1947 | Recorded in New York City, Dec. 1947 Winner—Grand Prix du Disque, 1950 |

| Composer | Title | Performers | Label/Catalog | Year | Notes |
|---|---|---|---|---|---|
| | Concerto no. 1, in E, FI, no. 22 "La Primavera" | Henry Swoboda, cond. | Club X65 CH79/84 (set AR in 2 volumes) CHC1 CHC1001 MMS56 CERG120 Rarities Collection-302 Record Hunter CHS1253 ICM700 LYS533–537* | | Listed by New York Times as "Best Recording of 1949" *Four Seasons* inducted into Grammy Hall of Fame 2002 |
| Vivaldi, Antonio | Concerto in A Minor, op. 3, no. 8 | Louis Kaufman, violin and cond. Thurston Dart, harpsichord Vivaldi Festival Orchestra | OR76252 | 1950 | Taken from Vivaldi Festival, 1950 |
| Vivaldi, Antonio | Concerto in D Major, op. 3, no. 9 | Louis Kaufman, violin and cond. Thurston Dart, harpsichord Vivaldi Festival Orchestra | OR76252 | 1950 | Taken from Vivaldi Festival, 1950 |
| Vivaldi, Antonio | Concerto in B Minor, op. 3, no. 10 | Louis Kaufman, violin and cond. Thurston Dart, harpsichord Vivaldi Festival Orchestra | OR76252 | 1950 | Taken from Vivaldi Festival, 1950 |

| Composer | Title of Work | Artists | Label (*indicates CD) | Matrix # | Date Recorded | Misc. |
|---|---|---|---|---|---|---|
| Vivaldi, Antonio | 12 Concerti, op. 3 "L'Estro Armonico" Concerto no. 10, in B Minor, P.148, F.IV, no. 10 | Louis Kaufman, violin<br>Peter Rybar, violin<br>Anton Fietz, violin<br>Giuseppe Piraccini, violin<br>Winterthur Symphony Orchestra<br>Clemens Dahinden, cond. | CH E2 | | 1950 | Recorded in Zurich |
| Vivaldi, Antonio | Concerto in D, P.159 for 2 Violins, Strings and Orchestra | Louis Kaufman, violin<br>P. Rybar, violin<br>Winterthur Chamber Orchestra<br>Clemens Dahinden, cond. | CH E2, MMS84 OR76252 | | 1950 | Recorded in Zurich |
| Vivaldi, Antonio | Concerto in D Major for 2 Violins, Strings and continuo | Louis Kaufman, violin<br>Winterthur String Orchestra<br>Clemens Dahinden, cond. | OR72101 | | 1972 | |
| Vivaldi, Antonio | La Primavera | Louis Kaufman, violin<br>Henry Swoboda, cond. | | | | 10 in side # 2. Sample record |
| Vivaldi, Antonio | Concerto op. 8 Il Cimento dell' Armonia e dell' Invenzione, op. 8, mvts. 9–12 | Louis Kaufman, violin<br>Clemens Dahinden, cond. | CHS (gold label sries) CHC-1064 Rarities bootleg | | | |
| Vivaldi, Antonio | Concerto for Two Violins in D | Louis Kaufman, violin<br>Peter Rybar, violin<br>Clemens Dahinden, cond. | MMS84 | E4KL0245 | | Recorded in Zurich |
| Vivaldi, Antonio | 12 Concerti, op. 4 "La Stravagnanza" Concerto no. 6 in C, F.I, no. 185 | Louis Kaufman, violin<br>Clemens Dahinden, cond. | MMS104 | | | Recorded in Paris |

| Vivaldi, Antonio | 12 Concerti, Concerto, op. 9, no. 7, in C, F.I, no. 186 | Louis Kaufman, violin Louis Kaufman, cond. | MMS104 | Recorded in Paris Record lists Clemens Dahinden as conductor, which is incorrect |
|---|---|---|---|---|
| Vivaldi, Antonio | 12 Concerti, Concerto, op. 9, no. 9, in F, F.I, no. 188 | Louis Kaufman, violin Louis Kaufman, cond. | MMS104 | Recorded in Paris |
| Vivaldi, Antonio | 12 Concerti, Concerto, op. 9, no. 11, in D, F.I, no. 190 | Louis Kaufman, violin Louis Kaufman, cond. | MMS104 | Recorded in Paris Record lists Clemens Dahinden as conductor, which is incorrect |
| Vivaldi, Antonio | 12 Concerti, op. 8 (1725) Concerto no. 5, in E-flat, F.I, no. 26 "La Tempesta di mare" | Louis Kaufman, violin Concert Hall Chamber Orchestra Clemens Dahinden, cond. | CHC104, Nixa CLP104 LYS533–537* | Recorded in Zurich |
| Vivaldi, Antonio | 12 Concerti, op. 8 (1725) Concerto no. 6, in C, F.I, no. 27 "Il Piacere" | Louis Kaufman, violin Concert Hall Chamber Orchestra Clemens Dahinden, cond. | CHC104 Nixa CLP104 ICM785 LYS533–537* | Recorded in Zurich |
| Vivaldi, Antonio | 12 Concerti, op. 8 (1725) Concerto no. 7, in D, F.I, no. 28 | Louis Kaufman, violin Concert Hall Chamber Orchestra Clemens Dahinden, cond. | CHC104 Nixa CLP104 ICM785 LYS533–537* | Recorded in Zurich |

| Composer | Title of Work | Artists | Label (*indicates CD) | Matrix # | Date Recorded | Misc. |
|---|---|---|---|---|---|---|
| Vivaldi, Antonio | 12 Concerti, op. 8 (1725) Concerto no. 8, in G, F.I, no. 16 | Louis Kaufman, violin Concert Hall Chamber Orchestra Clemens Dahinden, cond. | CHC1064 Nixa CLP1064 LYS533– 537* | | | Recorded in Zurich |
| Vivaldi, Antonio | 12 Concerti op. 8 (1725) Concerto no. 9, in D, F.VII, no. 1 | Louis Kaufman, violin Concert Hall Chamber Orchestra Clemens Dahinden, cond. | CHC1064 Nixa CLP1064 LYS533– 537* | | | Recorded in Zurich |
| Vivaldi, Antonio | 12 Concerti op. 8 (1725) Concerto no. 10, in B-flat, F.I, no. 29 "La Caccia" | Louis Kaufman, violin Concert Hall Chamber Orchestra Clemens Dahinden, cond. | CHC1064 Nixa CLP1064 LYS533– 537* | | | Recorded in Zurich |
| Vivaldi, Antonio | 12 Concerti op. 8 (1725) Concerto no. 11, in D, F.I, no. 30 | Louis Kaufman, violin Concert Hall Chamber Orchestra Clemens Dahinden, cond. | CHC1064, Nixa CLP1064 ICM785 LYS533– 537* | | | Recorded in Zurich |
| Vivaldi, Antonio | 12 Concerti op. 8 (1725) Concerto no. 12, in C, F.I, no. 31 | Louis Kaufman, violin Concert Hall Chamber Orchestra Clemens Dahinden, cond. | CHC1064, Nixa CLP1064 ICM785 LYS533– 537* | | | Recorded in Zurich |

| Vivaldi, Antonio | 12 Concerti op. 9 (1728) "La Cetra" Concerto no. 1, in C, P.9, F.I, no. 47 | Louis Kaufman, violin French National Radio String Orchestra | Concert Hall (set CHS1134) | Recorded in Paris |
|---|---|---|---|---|
| Vivaldi, Antonio | 12 Concerti op. 9 (1728) Concerto no. 2, in A, P.214, F.I, no. 47 | Louis Kaufman, violin French National Radio String Orchestra | Concert Hall (set CHS1134) | Recorded in Paris |
| Vivaldi, Antonio | 12 Concerti op. 9 (1728) Concerto no. 3, in G, P.339, F.I, no. 52 | Louis Kaufman, violin French National Radio String Orchestra | Concert Hall (set CHS1134) | Recorded in Paris |
| Vivaldi, Antonio | 12 Concerti op. 9 (1728) Concerto no. 4, in E, P.242, F.I, no. 48 | Louis Kaufman, violin French National Radio String Orchestra | Concert Hall (set CHS1134) | Recorded in Paris |
| Vivaldi, Antonio | 12 Concerti op. 9 (1728) Concerto no. 5, in A, P.10, F.I, no. 53 | Louis Kaufman, violin French National Radio String Orchestra | Concert Hall (set CHS1134) | Recorded in Paris |
| Vivaldi, Antonio | 12 Concerti op. 9 (1728) Concerto no. 6, in A, P.215, F.I, no. 54 | Louis Kaufman, violin French National Radio String Orchestra | Concert Hall (set CHS1134) | Recorded in Paris |
| Vivaldi, Antonio | 12 Concerti op. 9 (1728) Concerto no. 7, in B-flat, P.340, F.I, no. 55 | Louis Kaufman, violin French National Radio String Orchestra | Concert Hall (set CHS1134) | Recorded in Paris |
| Vivaldi, Antonio | 12 Concerti op. 9 (1728) Concerto no. 8, in D, P.260, F.I, no. 56 | Louis Kaufman, violin French National Radio String Orchestra | Concert Hall (set CHS1134) | Recorded in Paris |

| Composer | Title of Work | Artists | Label (*indicates CD) | Matrix # | Date Recorded | Misc. |
|---|---|---|---|---|---|---|
| Vivaldi, Antonio | 12 Concerti op. 9 (1728) Concerto no. 9, in B-flat, P.344, F.I, no. 57 | Louis Kaufman, violin French National Radio String Orchestra | Concert Hall (set CHS1134) | | | Recorded in Paris |
| Vivaldi, Antonio | 12 Concerti op. 9 (1728) Concerto no. 10, in G, P.103, F.I., no. 49 | Louis Kaufman, violin French National Radio String Orchestra | Concert Hall (set CHS1134) | | | Recorded in Paris |
| Vivaldi, Antonio | 12 Concerti op. 9 (1728) Concerto no. 11, in C, P.416, F.I, no. 58 | Louis Kaufman, violin French National Radio String Orchestra | Concert Hall (set CHS1134) | | | Recorded in Paris |
| Vivaldi, Antonio | 12 Concerti op. 9 (1728) Concerto no. 12, in B, P.154, F.I, no. 50 | Louis Kaufman, violin French National Radio String Orchestra | Concert Hall (set CHS1134) | | | Recorded in Paris |
| Vivaldi, Antonio | Double concerto in B-flat, F.IV, no. 2 | Louis Kaufman, violin Jacques Neilz, cello French National Radio Orchestra Roger Désormière, cond. | CAP (in set KCM8091) (45 rpm) OC744 | | | Recorded in Paris |
| Vivaldi, Antonio | Concerto in D, P.310, F.I, no. 11 "Senza cantin" | Louis Kaufman, violin French National Radio Orchestra, Roger Désormière, cond. | Cap6F8-7036/8 (in set KCM8076) | | | Recorded in Paris |
| Vivaldi, Antonio | Concerto in G, P.383, F.XII, no. 3 "Per l'orch. di Dresda" | Louis Kaufman, violin French National Radio Orchestra Roger Désormière, cond. | Cap6F8-7036/8 (in set KCM8076) | | | Recorded in Paris |

| Composer | Work | Performers | Record no. | Date | Notes |
|---|---|---|---|---|---|
| Vivaldi, Antonio | Concerto in E-flat, P.429, op. 33, no. 1 | Louis Kaufman, violin<br>French National Radio Orchestra<br>Roger Désormière, cond. | Cap (in set KCM8091)<br>NLSB<br>E3801/2 | | Recorded in Paris |
| Wayne, Mabel | "Ramona" (1927) | Louis Kaufman, violin<br>Louis Spielman, piano | Edison–52301<br>Edison cylinder–5537<br>(dubbed)<br>MB1032 | 18463B<br>4/1928 | |
| Wirén, Dag | Concerto for Violin and Orchestra, op. 23 | Louis Kaufman, violin<br>Swedish Radio Orchestra<br>Sten Fryberg, cond. | MB1027<br>LYS533–537 | 10/25/1953 | From the broadcast of the world premiere |
| Yellen, Jerome | "Dream Kisses" | Louis Kaufman, violin solo<br>Louis Spielman, piano | Gennett–6437A | 6/1928 | "New Electrobeam process"<br>Recorded in New York City |

# Label Information

| Code | Label |
| --- | --- |
| AD | Amphion |
| BCD | Bay Cities |
| C | Contemporary |
| Cap | Capitol |
| CCL | Capitol |
| CDXXX | Music and Arts |
| CDXXXX | Cambria |
| CEC | Capitol |
| CERG | Crowell-Collier Radio Guild |
| CH | Concert Hall |
| CHC | Concert Hall |
| CHS | Concert Hall Society |
| CL | Classic |
| CLP | Nixa |
| CMS | Chamber Music Society |
| Col | Columbia |
| CSPR | Protone Cassette |
| CT | Citadel |
| CTL | Capitol |
| DC | Celson |
| DO | Disques de L'Oiselet |
| E | Telefunken |
| FAP | Capitol |
| H | Concert Hall |
| ICM | Immortal Classical Masterpiece (Orion) |
| K | Korngold 1001 — (Private CD recording produced by Cambria) |
| KCM | Capitol — 45 RPM |
| L | Capitol |
| LAB | Biddulph |
| LCB | Capitol |
| LL | Lyrichord |
| LPG | Eurochord |
| LYS | Dante Records — L'Art de Louis Kaufman — 5 CD Set |
| MAR | Book of the Month Club |
| MB | Masters of the Bow |
| MHS | Music Heritage Society |
| MM | International Guilde du Disque |
| MMS | Musical Masterpiece Society |
| MTT | Tempo |
| NLSB | Telefunken |
| OC | Orion Cassette |
| OL | L'Oiseau-Lyre |

| Code | Label |
|------|-------|
| OR | Orion |
| Rarities | Rarities label (bootleg) |
| Record Hunter | Record Hunter (bootleg) |
| S | Society for Forgotten Music |
| SFM | Society for Forgotten Music |
| TT | Tempo Classics |
| Vox | Vox |
| WGSM | William Grant Still Music |

# Bibliography

Applebaum, Samuel, and Sada Applebaum. *With the Artists: World Famed String Players Discuss their Art.* New York: John Markert, 1995.

Baker, Theodore. *Baker's Biographical Dictionary of Musicians.* 8th ed. Revised by Nicolas Slonimsky. New York: Schirmer Books, 1992.

Bennett, Robert Russell. *The Broadway Sound: The Autobiography and Selected Essays of Robert Russell Bennett.* Edited by George Joseph Ferencz. Rochester, N.Y.: University of Rochester Press, 1999.

Bihalji-Merin, Oto. *World Encyclopedia of Naive Art.* 1984. Reprint, Scranton: Harper & Row, 1985.

Breslin, James E. B. *Mark Rothko: A Biography.* Chicago: University of Chicago Press, 1993.

Bureau of Musical Research. *Music and Dance in California and The West.* Edited by Richard Drake Saunders. Hollywood: n.p. 1948.

Carroll, Brendan G. *Erich Wolfgang Korngold, 1897-1957: His Life and Works.* Edited by Konrad Hopkins and Ronald van Roekel. Paisley, Scotland: Wilfion Books, 1989.

Carroll, Brendan G. *The Last Prodigy—a Biography of Erich Wolfgang Korngold.* Portland, Oreg.: Amadeus Press, 1997.

Copland, Aaron, and Vivian Perlis. *Copland 1900 through 1942.* New York: St. Martin's Press, 1989.

———. *Copland: Since 1943.* New York: St. Martin's Press, 1989.

Cornfield, Giveon. *Note Perfect: Thirty Years in Classical Music Recordings.* Honolulu: Chaminade University Press, 1993.

Creighton, James Lesley. *Discopedia of the Violin, 1889-1971.* Toronto: University of Toronto Press, 1974.

*Disques Guide Francais.* Paris, France: 1952.

Doring, Ernest N. *The Guadagnini Family of Violin Makers.* Chicago: William Lewis Co., 1949.

Ferencz, George Joseph. *Robert Russell Bennett: A Bio-Bibliography.* New York: Greenwood Press, 1990.

Gill, Dominic, ed. *The Book of the Violin.* Oxford: Phaidon Press, 1984.

Goodkind, Herbert K. *Violin Iconography of Antonio Stradivari.* Larchmont, N.Y.: published by author, 1972.

Gramophone Shop, Inc., New York. *The Gramophone Shop Encyclopedia of Recorded Music.* 3d ed. Edited by Robert H. Reid. New York: Crown Publishers, 1948.

*Gramophone Shop Encyclopedia of Recorded Music.* New York: Simon & Schuster, 1942.

*Guide français du disque.* Paris: n.p., 1952.

Haas, Robert Bartlett. *William Grant Still and the Fusion of Cultures in American Music.* Los Angeles: Black Sparrow Press, 1972. 2d ed. Flagstaff, Ariz.: Master-Player Library, 1995.

Hall, David. *The Record Book Supplement.* New York: Smith Durrell, 1941.

Harvey, Steven. *Louis M. Eilshemius (1864–1942): An Independent Spirit.* New York: National Academy of Design, 2001.

Harvith, John, and Susan Edwards Harvith, eds. *Edison, Musicians, and the Phonograph.* New York: Greenwood Press, 1987.

Hemphill, Herbert Wade, and Julia Weissman. *Twentieth Century American Folk Art and Artists.* New York: E. P. Dutton, 1974.

Hill, William Henry, Arthur F. Hill, and Alfred Ebsworth Hill. *Violin Makers of the Guarnerius Family, 1626–1762.* Rev. ed. New York: Dover, 1989.

Hobbs, Robert Carleton. *Milton Avery.* Introduction by Hilton Kramer. New York: Hudson Hills Press, 1990.

Holmes, John L. *Conductors on Record.* Westport, Conn.: Greenwood Press, 1982.

Karlin, Fred. *Listening to Movies: The Film Lovers Guide to Film Music.* New York: Schirmer Books, 1994.

Karlstrom, Paul J. *Louis Michel Eilshemius.* New York: H. N. Abrams, 1978.

Kaufman, Louis. "Violinist for Sound and Concert Stage" (oral history). Interviewed by Sybil Hast. 1991. UCLA, Oral History Program.

Kinnick, B. Jo, and Jesse Perry, comps. *I Have a Dream.* Menlo Park, Calif.: Addison-Wesley Publishing Co., 1969.

Kolodin, Irving. *The New Guide to Recorded Music.* New York: Doubleday Co., 1950.

Myers, Kurtz. *Record Ratings: Music Library Association's Index of Record Reviews.* Edited by Richard S. Hill. New York: Crown Publishers, 1956.

Ray, Man. *Man Ray: Paris, LA.* Santa Monica: Smart Art Press, 1996.

Roth, Henry. *Great Violinists in Performance.* Los Angeles: Panjandrum Books, 1986.

———. *Violin Virtuosos From Paganini to the 21st Century.* Los Angeles: California Classic Books, 1997.

Rudolf, Anthony, ed. *Sage Eye: The Aesthetic Passion of Jonathan Griffin: A Celebration in Poetry and Prose.* London: Menard Press, 1992.

Saint-Front, Yves. *Peintures de Polynésie.* Papeete, Tahiti: Édition Avant & Après, 2002.

Saleski, Gdal. *Famous Musicians of Jewish Origin.* New York: Block Publishing Co., 1949.

Shaffer, Karen A., and Neva Garner Greenwood. *Maud Powell, Pioneer American Violinist.* Ames, Iowa: Iowa State University Press, 1988.

Skirball Museum. *New Beginnings: The Skirball Museum Collections and Inaugural Exhibition.* Berkeley, n.p., 1996.

Smith, Julia. *Aaron Copland: His Work and Contribution to American Music.* New York: E. P. Dutton, 1955.

Smith, Steven C. *A Heart at Fire's Center: The Life and Music of Bernard Herrmann.* Berkeley: University of California Press, 1991.

Still, William Grant. *Fusion of Cultures in American Music.* 2d edition. Flagstaff, Ariz.: Master Players Library, 1993.

Svejda, Jim. *The Record Shelf Guide to the Classical Repertoire.* 3d ed. Rocklin, Calif: Prima Publishers, 1992.

Wantt, Sylvan. *Violin Virtuosi* (in Chinese). Jiulong: Zhen zhu chu ban she, 1954.

With, Karl. *Autobiography of Ideas.* Edited by Roland Jaeger. Berlin: Mann Verlag, 1977.

# Index

*Page numbers in italics indicate illustrations*

# Louis Kaufman CD Playlist

1. Antonio Vivaldi. Concerto no. 2, Opus 9. Louis Kaufman, violin and conductor; French National Radio String Orchestra. 1951.—[9:10]
2. Camille Saint-Saëns. *Havanaise*, Opus 83. Louis Kaufman, violin; Netherlands Philharmonic Orchestra, Mauritz van den Berg, conductor. 1952.— [8:29]
3. William Grant Still. *Pastorella*. Louis Kaufman, violin; Columbia Symphony Orchestra, Bernard Herrmann, conductor. 1946.—[8:58]
4. William Grant Still. "Blues" from *Lenox Avenue*. Louis Kaufman, violin; Columbia Symphony Orchestra, Bernard Herrmann, conductor. 1946—[2:40]
5. Darius Milhaud. *Concerto de Printemps*. Louis Kaufman, violin; French National Orchestra, Darius Milhaud, conductor. 1949.—[8:23]
6. Erich Wolfgang Korngold. *Much Ado about Nothing Suite for Violin and Piano* ("The Maiden in the Bridal Chamber," "March of the Night Watchmen," "Garden Scene," "Hornpipe"). Louis Kaufman, violin; Annette Kaufman, piano (taken from the Korngold Memorial Concert, Los Angeles). 1959.— [11:21]
7. Aaron Copland. Nocturne for Violin and Piano. Louis Kaufman, violin; Aaron Copland, piano. 1948.—[4:26]
8. Aaron Copland. *Ukulele Serenade*. Louis Kaufman, violin; Annette Kaufman, piano. 1947.—[3:43]
9. Aaron Copland. "Hoe-Down" from *Rodeo*. Louis Kaufman, violin; Annette Kaufman, piano. 1947.—[2:42]
10. Robert Russell Bennett. *Hexapoda—Five Studies in Jitteroptera for Violin and Piano*. Louis Kaufman, violin; Robert Russell Bennett, piano. 1942.—[6:54]
11. Jerome Kern. "The Song Is You." Louis Kaufman, violin; Leonard Berman, piano; arranged by Kaufman/Berman. 1946.—[3:14]
12. Jerome Kern. "Smoke Gets in Your Eyes." Louis Kaufman, violin; Leonard Berman, piano; arranged by Kaufman/Berman. 1946.—[3:01]
13. Fritz Kreisler (arranger). *Londonderry Air* (traditional Irish ballad). Louis Kaufman, violin; Paul Ulanowsky, piano. 1952.—[3:38]